The Ends of the Earth

First published as *Die Enden der Welt*
by Roger Willemsen
© S.Fischer Verlag GmbH, Frankfurt am Main, 2010

Published in Great Britain in 2015 by
The Armchair Traveller at the bookHaus Ltd
70 Cadogan Place
London SW1X 9AH
www.hauspublishing.com

English translation copyright © Peter Lewis

ISBN 978-1-909961-02-9
eISBN 978-1-909961-03-6

Typeset in Minion by MacGuru Ltd
Printed and bound by Liberduplex in Spain

The Ends of the Earth

Roger Willemsen

Translated by
Peter Lewis

Armchair Traveller
at the bookHaus

Contents

Eifel – *Departure* // 1

Gibraltar – *The Ne Plus Ultra* // 11

The Himalayas – *In the fog of the Prithvi Highway* // 38

Isafjördur – *The blind spot* // 62

God's Window – *The final curtain* // 71

Minsk – *The stranger in the bed* // 87

Patagonia – *The forbidden place* // 101

Timbuktu – *The Boy Indigo* // 141

Bombay – *The oracle* // 161

Tangkiling – *The road to nowhere* // 175

Kamchatka – *Ashes and magma* // 197

Mandalay – *A dream of the sea* // 234

Lake Fucino – *Wasting away* // 255

Gorée – *The door of no return* // 276

Hong Kong – *Poste restante* // 301

The Amu-Darya – *On the frontiers of Transoxania* // 324

Toraja – *Among the dead* // 344

Tonga – *Taboo and fate* // 359

Kinshasa – *Scenes from a war* // 393

Chiang Mai – *Opium* // 412

Orvieto – *The fixation* // 425

The North Pole – *Contemplation* // 453

Acknowledgements

This book describes journeys that I made over a period of thirty years. In four of the chapters, I have drawn upon material that was previously published elsewhere.

I would like to thank all those who accompanied me, or who facilitated my travelling or returning home, among them Lilian Henriquez Cruz and Manuel Antonio Berrocal, Anastasia Owchinnikowa and Sergei Markov, Monika Knapp and Rajiv Nepali, Nadia Nashir Karim and Mirwais Nashir, Hanni and Viktor Alder, Jasmin Pienaar, Jan Willemsen, Joseph Vogl and Insa Wilke.

My thanks are also due to Christina Ihle, whose help in researching material was invaluable, and to Wolfgang Jamann for his friendly companionship. I am most grateful, too, to the first readers of this book, Frauke Abraham and Werner Köhler for their perceptive comments on the manuscript. My especial thanks must go to my editor Jürgen Hosemann, the ideal reader, and Michael Horbach, whose generous support for this project was like that of some latter-day Maecenas.

Roger Willemsen

Eifel

Departure

I came to town looking for the lucky ones, those who yearn to get away. They have no fixed abode, I thought, or rather they have no real point of fixity on the earth, at least. They are never simply in the place where their physical being resides; distant shores are already weighing upon their shoulders even before they depart, and they are called 'restless' by those who are not. As such they live in a permanent state of departure. At the time I was living in a village, and I came to the city in search of both homesickness and wanderlust.

Those were the years of rapture. They couldn't last. Linked by the stars, the meridians, by railway tracks, migrating birds, shortwave radio, waterways and by the distant roar of the world, remote parts of the globe thrust themselves upon me precisely because they were so far removed, and just as one's conscious mind often crystallizes what is missing, so I only became aware of that remote world as a kind of phantom-limb pain one New Year's Day around noon.

Twelve hours before, under crisp and frosty skies and warmed by anticipation, we had slipped from one embrace to the next and then stood stock still, gazing at each other with the kind of ironic yearning that locks on to those present as though they were absent and saying:

'Happy New Year!'

'And a happy life to you, too!'

With the impression of fleeting kisses still on our cheeks, we stepped out into the night of New Year's Eve; we'd raised our glasses to the heavens for the umpteenth time and refilled them, formulated a few resolutions, and the lovers who'd just split up a couple of weeks ago vowed that they would always remain good friends. Next to them, the eternally-cheerful-one, popular with everyone, got upset because her boyfriend had kissed the wrong girl on the stroke of midnight, upon which he rushed into the bushes to throw up. And so yet another New Year's Eve had faded away in a minor key. A few hours later everybody had found a bed, a mat in some corner, or drifted off into the first sleep of the year in a landscape of sofas.

The next morning I groped my way outdoors in my pyjamas – it had snowed during the night – to find my friend with a pickaxe, hacking at the frozen vomit, which was flying off in all directions in colourful shards. The others joined us, some already clutching coffee mugs, and inspected his work, the first of the year.

Soon after the whole group can be found traipsing through the landscape of the Voreifel, down some snowy country path towards wide-open fields and distant woods. We were walking in several little groups and not saying much. Some amble along aimlessly, while others plod purposefully like they did when they were children, fired up by the languid euphoria induced by the craving for fresh air. We strayed from the path. The crusted snow is lying so deep on the field that it's like walking on a meringue. The landscape is tautly stretched and uniform: on our right hills covered with scrub, and on the left hills with mixed woodland against the backdrop of an open horizon. We walk on.

A random point is reached. We all stop, and nobody takes another step. The wind skims over the featureless plain we're standing on, huddled together like we've been swept into a pile. One of us says:

'There's nothing here. Let's turn back.'

And none of us dares take another step further across the imaginary line. As though catching the echo of the border, everybody raises their head, listening and slumping into motion: Everyone nods. Everyone turns on their heels. And trudges homewards.

'See how worn my skin is already,' says the girl with the pageboy cut to her boyfriend, waggling her chin between two fingers.

The wind carries her words across the untouched field. Nobody looks back, and I'm left standing there with a woman friend, looking at the virginal snow, which is not going to be trodden on after all. What was it about this landscape that said: No further, go away, turn around, clear off?

'There it is, then, the landscape that says no. There's nothing for us here,' I remark, drawn by this human-repelling, lacklustre zone untouched by any emotions.

'It's almost like we've gone round to the back of the landscape,' says the friend. 'Why do we even imagine we'll discover something pristine here, of all places?'

'Maybe because people think of themselves as somehow pristine? Because inside they, too, don't have anything on show, either?'

'That at least would explain the terror such landscapes conjure up, the terror of the sublime. People see in these landscapes what they don't want to see in themselves: the deserted, uninhabited and uninhabitable?'

Then we pondered whether landscapes could be seen as anything but symbolic, given that every range of hills, every sparkling lake, every mood of the light over a valley reflected an inner situation, be it sweet or sick or raw. Every landscape is experienced like music, as a manifestation of the soul.

'And that's where the traveller gets his favourite cliché from, the one which says that the real reason for travelling is to journey into yourself?' I concluded.

'But what if you reach an inner landscape like this? One that denies you?' asked the friend.

'Then that's no landscape to procreate in.'

'Precisely!' she said. 'Let's go. I'm famished!'

Back then I thought that if you travelled far enough, to be sure that at some point you'd touched the end of the world, then maybe you'd also attain a new, totally different state of arriving. A state where you couldn't help but believe that all journeys must have an end even though they're actually inconclusive. These places would radiate a power just like those in fairytales, where the giant likewise gains his strength from touching the earth.

Might it be the case that it's not the travellers who move, but rather it's the world beneath their feet picking up speed whilst they remain static? In truth, all one ever does is reach another destination which is hurrying one along, only to set off again, perhaps ultimately to reach that inconstant place I only call 'home' because it accumulates more rituals than others; the home of repetition. I can't even claim that I know home better than any other place – on the contrary, tourists abroad dutifully visit all the notable landmarks while completely neglecting those at home. It's perfectly possible for me to feel more at home with the music in an airport lounge in Timbuktu, with a photo in an ad, or a television image that I might see anywhere in the world showing the Berlin bear dancing in a tutu, than I do in a German railway station. At least I probably know the plausibility of the music or the image better than the local Tuareg do, who are being forced to inhabit the media history of the West.

A freezing cold New Year's Day in the Voreifel had given way to a clear and frosty night by the time I left for my first engagement of the year. Brigitta hadn't been free to celebrate New Year's Eve with us. She was a nurse and had agreed to do the holiday shift on the children's ward because of the special atmosphere, and, as she put it, because she liked to be there when the children looked forward to their new year.

When I entered the nurses' room, she was still wearing her white coat, cap and name tag on her lapel. When I was a student in my first semester I'd called Brigitta my 'romance'. Her kindheartedness was intimidating, and so were her round eyes in her freckled face with its slightly pouty lips. Only when she took off her coat and cap to reveal the brown woollen pullover over her ample breasts did she suddenly seem to have a body.

And then, when I held her in my arms a moment too long or our greeting kiss became too intense, she began to breath more heavily, and again I was no match for her. The body as an object of medicine and as an object of desire were on a par for her. For me, the two did not even coexist in the same space. Sometimes Brigitta gave me drawings of big plump girls, holding sunflowers, with their hair done up in a bun. In their innocence and their corporeality, I saw these drawings as the epitome of a beautiful world that was inaccessible to me.

That evening she was alone when I entered the nurses' room. She glanced up briefly from sticking labels on small plastic boxes, even let me kiss her on the cheek, but was remote, her sensuality suspended. But then we hugged each other for a brief moment and, downcast by the present, vaguely wished one another something good for the future. She said 'our future'.

We were going to have a quiet evening. I sat down at the square Formica table, where she was now busy filling a syringe, and put my hand on hers. All of a sudden, she burst into tears.

It turned out it was about a boy called Tom, an eight-year-old kid, with the same brooding disposition she had. She'd taken him on as her special charge since they'd transferred him to the ward shortly before with a brain tumour. At first, and in rather vague terms, it had been explained to him that he was ill, very ill in fact. This had left him confused, as he wasn't feeling any pain or impaired in any way. But in no time he came to see his illness as some inward sign of nobility, and started moping about the corridors demanding his immediate release.

On the day of my visit Brigitta had been landed with the task of telling the boy the truth about his illness. She'd closed the door, sat down on the edge of his bed and uttered the word 'cancer'. When Tom kept staring at her, unmoved, she added 'incurable', and when he still kept looking at her like he was searching for a roadmap in her face, she realised her emotions were as useless to him as all her words, and she divulged the final bit of information the doctors had told her: he had three months more to live – no one was prepared to give him any longer than that.

Tom had walked over to the window and named the makes of two cars that had recently appeared in the car park, and

Brigitta left the room. When she reached this point in her story and was wiping the tears from her eyes with her knuckles, the door suddenly opened and in walked the boy in his pyjamas. In stubborn and reproachful tones, he announced:

'I'm bored!'

No sentence could have been more poignant at that juncture, and I immediately felt responsible for the boy. I recalled the virgin snowfield we'd turned back from that very midday, and took Tom by the shoulders, led him back to his room and lay next to him on his bed. In a spirit of solidarity, we stared at the ceiling. How much reality there was going spare – landscapes, swimming pools, clothes, funfair rides, theatre – how much stuff there was for him still to do, and yet it would remain there, unused, for the rest of his life, without him ever being able to experience it. We lay on his deathbed, and I was in a quandary: was it better to leave him in the narrow confines of his reality, or should I try to push open windows and show him the big, wide world out there? Should I tell him he wouldn't be missing much, or should I try and make up for what he'd never have?

His life – you could hardly call it a life's journey – was drawing to a close and I asked myself: Where would he have travelled to? Where would he have fetched up? What would have driven him? What unique experiences might he have had? Where might he have encountered that thing people call 'self-discovery'? Maybe in a room full of hot and humid air with a backdrop of honking car horns, the cold blast of the air-conditioner and slightly tipsy on rum? What pictures would have accumulated in his memory: long, colourful fingernails, the tilt of a head nestling on an arm? Perhaps he would have left behind all the waiting and the silence and ventured out to find some freedom of movement, some received sense of self-loss and a different experience of time.

And so we lay there on the hospital bed, side by side, and stared at the chalky-white ceiling, the monotonous and probably final image that would impinge on his consciousness.

'Come on, let's go on a journey,' I said.

'Where to?'

'Wherever you want.'

'Really?'

'As real as we can make it.'

This qualification was necessary, because I suddenly found myself in the same position as all those stay-at-homes who are beset by phobias, idiosyncrasies, obsessions and neuroses, and asked myself their fundamental question: How can one travel somewhere while actually remaining at home the whole time? So I told Tom about a Dane named Søren Kierkegaard, who together with his father re-enacted Sunday strolls in their living room, though they could easily have taken these walks through town for real. They greeted fellow citizens left and right, dreamt up little conversations and admired a newly erected building.

I told Tom about Xavier de Maistre, a French general who in 1790 had been placed under house arrest after fighting a duel and so hadn't been able to escape in a Montgolfière like he'd done once before.

'What's a Montgolfière?'

'If he'd been free, he'd have climbed into a balloon and floated up and away. Instead, he journeyed through his room and wrote about all the adventures he had on the way, about how he'd crossed the carpet and ascended the sofa. And after him more and more people started travelling through their rooms, their handbags, their houses or their tents.'

'That's good,' said Tom. 'I want to travel as well.'

'And that would be to where, exactly?'

'To the end of the world!'

'The end of the world's an invention,' I replied. 'The world has no end.'

'I don't want that.'

'You can always decide for yourself where your world ends, where it actually seems to you to end.'

So I painted pictures of landscapes for him that had no showy façade, landscapes where nothing begins and which turn their backs on the onlooker just like the reverse side of an embroidery, where all the threads hang out. I conjured up situations for him where you can actually penetrate deeper into landscapes like this, and venture deeper into foreign parts without them becoming more foreign, just further away. I actually meant landscapes like the ceiling, Tom's end of the world. But I didn't say as much. Instead I told him about the tracks in the snow, and the place where all steps stop and you see the untouched, untrodden earth, rejected by … But by then he'd fallen asleep.

When Brigitta came by to look in on us, I put my finger to my lips. In the same way that Tom seemed unmoved by his dying, so I was rendered helpless by the unconscious presence of death in this obstinate, reserved boy. Thinking about the world he'd never see for himself, I now imagined places where death had intervened; empty, deserted tracts of land, places of dying, of departure; all places where the earth is not round, but finite. There are regions you go to where you are certain that something has come to a full stop, and that this end does not harbour a new beginning. Not you, not here, not now, these landscapes seem to say, and: You're the one who's out of place here. You daren't look me in the eye.

At some point I returned to the nurses' room to take Brigitta out into the first night of the year. She was still wearing her nurse's coat and was staring intently at a game of patience she hadn't yet started.

Gibraltar

The Ne Plus Ultra

The hotel on whose twentieth floor I'm lurking, peeking out at the city of Tokyo from behind the curtain, is called the Century. Everything here's epoch-making, it seems; the breakfast is called the Century Breakfast, the pool the Century Pool, and there's even a Century Souvenir Shop as well, in case I should ever forget this Century in the years to come.

The skyscrapers opposite are rooted in the ground like the chitin carapaces of extinct insects, lit from within. In the lifts that race up and down, there are cut flowers and Julio Iglesias endlessly crooning 'Amor, Amor, Amor'. Yes, he's here, too. You can't get away from love.

It's beautiful and awful at the same time, for while the tear-jerking song maunders on about love, the couples themselves seem loveless, and the masseuses, who are all booked up long past midnight, could sing you another, quite different song about love. I run into one of them in the lift. She's snorting dismissively, rubbing her arms and shaking her head. Something to do with one of her clients.

After midnight on the vast, empty square in front of the new City Hall, in the middle of the mussel-shaped piazza with its atmosphere of Mussolini-esque Roman bombast, a girl is standing, all alone, taking pictures of the full moon with her mobile. Who for? Is there anyone among the thirty million inhabitants of Greater Tokyo who's incapable of looking up at the night sky this evening? Someone who's ill, maybe? Or in prison? Or working underground? Maybe a subway conductor or a bar hostess or a bridegroom in a subterranean banqueting hall in one of the large hotels? Or perhaps the moon is being e-mailed direct from the display of her mobile beyond the country's borders, maybe even across the ocean to Europe, where the moon hasn't actually risen yet, but where it will now appear, eight hours too early, on the screen of somebody else's mobile?

This young woman could send the picture to her lover and text him: *There you go, my darling, once more I'm sending you the moon that you'll be sleeping under yourself in a couple of hours' time. Amor, Amor, Amor* ... The girl lets out a little giggle that bubbles back off the marble walls. As I draw closer, she quickly moves off, the moon safely tucked away in her pocket. The place couldn't be more deserted.

I can't think of another city where the daylight dawns so greyly as it does over Tokyo, the only city that starts out as anthracite and whose concrete surfaces then gradually – ever so slowly – brighten and grow lighter, becoming mouse-grey, then dust-grey, then flannel-grey, then pale and then bright. Grey walls reflect back the grey light, with the early morning mist lathering in even more subtle gradations; even the steam from the air-conditioning units mingles in. The first things you can make out are the news tickers on the outsides of buildings, then the characters chiselled into the façades, and finally billboards and banners.

Three days later I can say: the sky was always beautiful. Not a cloud remained, and all cares were confined to my dreams. At four o'clock in the afternoon, the employees could be seen through the windows of their offices preparing to do their physical exercises. At three in the morning, the only lights still burning in the large hotels were those of the jet lag patients. Up to 4 a.m., they are the only ones awake. At six I went downstairs to have breakfast, where I had a plate of spaghetti followed by some French Toast with my cup of Century Instant Coffee.

Meanwhile, what's happening out on the streets? All the alleyways, bridges, trains, shops, pavements, entranceways and transport arteries of all kinds are crammed with sixteen-year-old girls, all the same height, all with the same pallor, and all the same age. It's as if there'd been some cosmic pollination, some Golden Shower raining down on the city one day that impregnated millions of women simultaneously, who then all gave birth in the same instant to little girls who grew into identical little skirts, shoes, and blouses.

These novices' voices all ring out when they encounter their peers, their millions of friends, down in the courtyard. One of them is wearing a beret, another a baseball cap made from sandpaper. Little ladies in sailor suits are also there, along with ones sporting the uniforms of the major department stores. Together, they disappear into a café with a Western-style façade, the Bread Restaurant, where you serve yourself at the counter from baskets containing fifteen different types of bread: sesame bread, pumpkin bread, onion bread, seaweed bread, algal bread, bread bread.

Other girls are still busy out on the street, distributing paper napkins printed with adverts or hanging around between tiled walls, dressed in Black Forest costumes with starched aprons and neat white bows tied round their backs, handing out free samples of Indian curry to passers-by.

There's something cult-like about the orderliness out on the street. Even those unfortunates with the social function of 'beggar' are all lying in a neatly-arranged line of cardboard boxes. Some of the boxes have 'Made in the Philippines' printed on them, while others just say 'Enjoy' or 'Bananas'. Inside, you can see the beggars lying on their backs, staring at the roof of the box. There's no writing there. Even good order can make you sad, and leave you feeling isolated.

Four days have passed and I've barely spoken four sentences. It's considered impolite to look a stranger in the eye. You could be invisible and hardly notice. Julio Iglesias is still singing away in the lift; little by little, he's singing me to my knees. As darkness falls, the girls and boys – the lovers, the piners and yearners – start to assemble at the Hachiko, the monument to the faithful imperial dog. Faithful? Fewer than 5 per cent of all animals are monogamous. But come what may I'm sitting pretty here, with a grandstand view of the fulfilled and the frustrated lovers alike, and wishing I was one of them.

So, it's back to the twentieth floor of the hotel, where I stick myself to the plate glass window of the room like an autumn leaf. Night falls with all its promises, but at the moment all I can call to mind are those that have not been fulfilled, and never could be. The people, the moods, the atmospheres, and all the fleeting and incidental things simply aren't there. The coat tail caught in the car door is missing, and the spoon that misses the mouth.

The following evening, my fear of loneliness takes on a physical dimension. It feels like agoraphobia. You start issuing orders to your head, but they only succeed in making it do the exact opposite. You say to yourself: look, you're among other people here. But the only mental image you can conjure up is of yourself as a stranger who's becoming odder by the moment, yet who only appears that odd from *one* person's point of view, namely your own.

On the third evening, I picked up the receiver and called Hamburg.

'Christa,' said the voice at the other end, though it sounded like 'basta'.

'Christa, it's me,' I said, as nonchalantly as I could.

Her voice took on the same cadence as mine: 'Oh, it's you!'

Evidently she'd been expecting someone far more interesting. All the same, it had only been a couple of weeks since I'd been sitting on the floor of her tiny flat in Altona listening to her and her Terry Callier records, and as the music rhapsodized about love, she held forth about all the unforeseen pitfalls of producing a documentary film. Her story was so long-winded that I had plenty of time to study her face as she spoke, that generous, freckled face with the broad forehead, the too-wide mouth and the I-could-tell-you-a-thing-or-two expression. Due to my silence, at the end of the evening she called me a good listener, which I hadn't been at all.

Her documentary was about the 'Doomsters', people who predict the end of the world and who respond in a number of different ways: sometimes with panic, sometimes esoterically, sometimes conspiratorially, and sometimes even competently and rationally. That evening, Christa had been wearing a sleeveless bodice, so that for the first time I'd been able to see her broad shoulders. Her skirt was stretched three hands' width over each of her muscly thighs, and her feet had clearly not seen the insides of shoes for that whole summer.

She talked and talked, and her subsidiary self, the professional Christa, kept slipping the whole time into the jargon of her line of work. Time and again, the talk was of 'you try your level best ...', 'and so on, and so forth ...', 'so I said, you look like it', and 'no way, that was a complete non-starter!'

She wasn't always like this, just when she was around her world of work. I asked her:

'Do you still believe in your film?'

'No, not one hundred and ten per cent.'

She went over to the window and gazed out silently at the night, which in that instant was not illuminated by any nearby source of light.

I reached for the next bottle of Soave and asked 'Shall we be sinners and crack this open?'

She turned to me, her face registering lukewarm interest. Then, looking at the bottle, she said:

'Why should alcohol be a sin, anyhow? Are grapes sinful?'

'Sure, lay them down for a few years and then drink them, and they are right enough, aren't they?'

I managed to get away before midnight, disentangling myself from the web of images she was spinning for herself, images that simultaneously over- and underestimated her self-worth, professional and sentimental images, bourgeois stereotypes and loose ends, such as the imaginings that came fluttering after the word 'sin'. Even so, the loose ends remained just that. Besides, her voice had something so calm, so nocturnal about it, and her gaze occasionally lingered so long, unthinkingly, on my own that she suddenly gave a start and snapped out of the spell.

And that was just how her voice sounded now.

'Why are you calling? Any special reason?'

'No, nothing special,' I replied. 'I was just thinking of you.'

'Is that all?'

'I found a quotation for you. Listen: "Anyone who still has their own world must be prepared to have it perish alongside them."'

There was a pause.

'And that made you think of me, did it?'

'Yes, it did.'

'Because of the film?'

'Amongst other things.'

'I don't get it at all.'

We chatted more freely and calmly than that time in her flat. There were more loose ends, free evaluations, spontaneous conjunctions, while with many sentences we almost seemed to physically touch one another. In fact, we were truly conversing for the first time.

After we'd been speaking for twenty minutes, Christa had to leave the house.

'What a shame,' I said.

'Same here. Where are you?'

'In Tokyo.'

She didn't hesitate for a moment:

'Would you like to ring me again tomorrow?'

I promised I would. The next morning, I started clearing away the working day that lay between me and her voice. If only because of how much I was looking forward to it, by all rights the phone call should have gone badly, but in fact she picked up and said:

'I'm all yours.'

'Christa!'

'Are you still in Tokyo?'

'The very place. And it's strange.'

'As in nicely strange?'

'No, strangely strange.'

She didn't need any run-in or warm-up. She was right into the thick of things straight away.

'What can you see from your window?'

I went and stared down at the city. Cars were moving off in batches from the green traffic lights and there was someone sleeping on a footbridge, and over there a businessman carrying a briefcase and a helium balloon. Some office windows weren't just lit, you could also see people behind them, hunched over their work or doing physical jerks.

'Go on, let's go out onto the street!'

So I led her to Shinjuku; we had something to eat there, walked through a park full of red terracotta busts, and visited a *Pachinko* arcade.

'Now show me somewhere special!'

I took her to the Hachiko monument.

'What kind of people come here?' she wanted to know.

'Lovers,' I said, 'It's a meeting place for lovers.'

'Happy lovers?'

'Happy and unhappy.'

'I think I've got to know most about Japan from its pornography,' she remarked.

'And you a woman, too!'

'Well, I did make a documentary about it.'

'Why, though?'

'I'm fascinated by secret worlds, things behind closed doors. The USA and Japan are the most perverted countries. Americans are so prudish that things can't be too filthy for them in private, while the Japanese are so degenerate that they like things as childish as possible in the privacy of their own homes. You don't think so? What about their fascination for women in glasses, nurses, schoolgirls and innocent lambs, then? The Japanese are obsessed with innocence, aren't they?'

'That's true, but they're also hung up on ritual, on staged set-ups: they love role-playing, mock rapes, the danger of being caught. They do it in public places and in limousines, but the key thing is that it all has to look like some great act of passion.'

'Shamefully shameless.'

'What are you wearing?' I asked her.

The windows of my room went right down to the floor; I stood there in the darkness above the ravine of the street. But in actual fact we were listening, from our opposite ends of the earth, to the space between us – our cocoon. I pictured her in front of me, her kind face, broad shoulders, her dark blonde mane of hair and her large hands, absentmindedly fiddling with something or other.

'It's nice talking to you on the phone,' I said.

'Yes, it does me good,' she replied, and we just let the ensuing silence hang there.

'It feels like we're two strangers who've fetched up in the same train compartment and struck up a conversation.'

'Precisely.'

'Maybe that's what we should do sometime, then: go on a railway journey lasting days, and never leave the train, just sit there opposite one another in our compartment,' I suggested.

By the time we'd finished, we'd been on the line for an hour and a half, and had made a firm arrangement to meet up. One evening ten days from now, I'd be waiting at Dammtor station in Hamburg, ready to set off into the wild blue yonder on a train journey – with Christa if she turned up, and without Christa if she'd thought better of it in the meantime. But the one thing we'd agreed on was that if we did end up travelling together, it wouldn't be about getting to any particular place, but about experiencing the train journey in each other's company.

'But you ought to let me know what I should pack,' she said.

Then we left one another to silently contemplate our options and agreed not to call one another again before our departure.

From this moment on, I got on just fine with Tokyo. On Sunday afternoon, I strolled through Roppongi and found what I was looking for: the cold leftovers of the night, women who'd stayed overnight in the arms of disinterested men. Recent American swing was in the air, interspersed with snatches of lounge music, while now and then came a twanging of strings from the doorways of Chinese Dim-Sum restaurants, ascending and descending the pentatonic scale. Brasseries exhaled the smell of mopped floors.

Standing alone at a crossroads between the nut sellers and the newspaper vendors was a twenty-year-old girl with dyed chestnut brown and bobbed hair. In front of her stomach she held a sign inscribed with Japanese characters, with an English translation underneath: 'Slave'. Was she some kind of artist? Or a prostitute? She was carrying a book of photographs of Audrey Hepburn under her arm. Shamefully shameless. It was summer, and my cheerful anticipation at meeting Christa was casting a glow of goodwill over everything I saw.

So, one evening a week or so later found me standing, armed with tickets, a small travel bag and a bottle of champagne in a plastic bag, on the long-distance platform of Dammtor station in Hamburg. A quarter of an hour before the train was due to leave there was no sign of Christa; ten minutes to go and she still wasn't there. But five minutes before the train arrived, she appeared at the top of the escalator with a large suitcase and rushed to meet my embrace.

We drank the champagne in our sleeping car berth to Paris. We kissed a bit to make it clear what the deal was, and then once more after Christa had slipped on her pale blue pyjamas in the wet room and chosen the top bunk; this meant that I could kiss her while I was still standing up, and make her head sink down into the pillow. Later, lying on my back and staring into the blue glow cast by the night light, in my mind's eye I could picture her lying on her back too and staring into the blueness of the night, as we were lulled to sleep by the rocking and rattling of the train. In the morning, the conductor rapped on the door with his square socket key, and moments later, Christa's brown feet were dangling in front of my eyes. Looking at her, I felt an immense holiday mood wash over me.

In Paris, we left the Gare du Nord to go and have breakfast on the Place Napoléon III, where we ordered pastries from the cabinet, coffee and *citron pressé* and sat blinking at the sunlight and the traffic. Christa dragged her pullover over her head, rubbed sun cream onto her bare arms, donated her croissant to a beggar, called Paris the 'City of Lovers' and shot me a challenging look.

The next train left the station heading south. Once again, we sat opposite one another at the window seats and settled in for our journey, which would take us right across France.

'It's all about the journey, not the destination,' she said sententiously.

'But we don't know where we're going anyhow.'

We gazed into each other's eyes or out at the landscape, or looked through our eyes reflected in the compartment window at the landscape, or conversely through the landscape at our eyes. We didn't need to say much. It was enough that we were undertaking this journey together for the same good reasons.

So why were we doing it? In order to dive into that gap that corresponded to the air space in which we'd met during our telephone conversation. It wasn't about places, or trading places. It was about the journey itself in all its unfathomable fleetingness. The scenery flitted past: old mail depots, a station buffet, a forecourt, a monument, a drinking fountain for those waiting for connecting trains. Behind the stations, settlements fanned out, and behind the settlements intermediate landscapes, which we only ever sped past, but which were always full of people in transit, comers and goers and people still *en route* to somewhere or other.

'What is it about these places?' asked Christa, unable to tear her eyes away from the landscape. 'Why are people so drawn to empty, passionless things? To bland architecture and blind convention?'

'Oh, let them be. Vacuity can be really restorative.'

'You mean not always taking things so seriously, seeing things as so significant and intentional? Well, maybe.'

'I mean just let them lead more pointillistic lives.'

Her gaze took stock of the landscape. All through the morning and into the afternoon, her constant refrains were: What am I seeing, what am I hearing, what was that moving here? But by the time dusk fell, she was asking: 'What moves me, what am I missing, what is distant and irretrievable?'

She was a farsighted person; anything that was still distant, or far in the past, she could see pin-sharp. But anything that was close at hand, in her immediate vicinity, she was unable to make out with any clarity, and so she wrapped it up in stereotypes. Her rhetoric was passionate where anticipation or parting were concerned, in other words, for things that weren't yet an actuality and those that were no longer present. What were we to do? Initially, we travelled toward one another in order to animate the closeness that we'd felt at a distance with our physical presence, but gradually the suspicion grew that all we'd ultimately find was an empty space. Sure, we travelled full of longing, but in the end we were embarrassed, because now there was a body sitting where once there'd only been a spectre.

The first night, we chose a room in a guesthouse already in the foothills of the Pyrenees; it had the tiled floor of a monk's cell and was cold and clean, with no running water, sagging mattresses and felt-like synthetic blankets on the bed, covered in cigarette-burn holes and the residue of moth powder.

In the evening, we entered the lounge through a curtain made of brightly coloured plastic strips. Behind it, as if to order, the men were already sitting playing cards: frozen images in which time refused to move on, and even the strangers who came into this space all assumed the same expression.

The next morning we bought tickets for Tangier, Morocco. In our train seats, face to face, we were always far more engrossed in the passing countryside than we were in each other. Quite right, too; rather than expecting too much of one another, it was better that our gazes should lose themselves silently among mixed woodland, abandoned signal boxes, rusty carriages, and blooming agaves and spiraeas. Second-class waiting rooms flashed by, along with grain silos, garages and nurseries, and occasionally I'd glance across into Christa's face, as she sat lost in thought, and found it diaphanous and attractive.

The creeping ghettoization of the provinces was also clearly on show in these parts. There they were, all corralled together: the council houses and the guest-worker estates, where people dreamt of the shop windows of far-off pedestrian zones; and alongside these housing developments, all the usual Import–Export businesses, wholesale vegetable warehouses and builders merchants' yards. Between them, like the figures on a revolving mobile, the faces of desperate people kept popping up – the barely employable, the burger-flippers. Their faces looked like empty prams; every now and then, a face would appear that had tried to give itself some individuality by latching on to international sunglasses fashion.

On one occasion, Christa lifted her head up from reading Bruce Chatwin's *The Songlines* and I caught my breath:

'I'd really like to say something tender to you now.'

Her gaze, still immersed in what she was reading, flitted over the landscape: 'Tell me later.'

Later, that is fifty kilometres further south, she took off her Walkman for a moment, shook her head, looked at me with deep vertical creases puckering together above the bridge of her nose and said disapprovingly: 'Sometimes I find Mozart a bit too ornamental!'

Then her eyes were glued to the page once more.

'A bit like *The Songlines*, then?' I asked.

Not looking up from her book, she replied:

'You're talking rubbish!'

The next night, we slept in a Spanish dive just outside a village in the middle of nowhere. The windows gave on to the railway embankment, and you could look out at the vault of heaven, coloured blue and midnight blue, with shades of blue-black and dusky blue, with the contours of a line of hills visible on the horizon. Rummaging around between her legs under her nightdress, Christa used a towelling glove to wash her pubes in the small hand basin in our room.

Outside, the streetlights were starting to come on, as swallows kept surfing between the houses right up to nightfall, and a single mosquito drifted through the open window. In the distance, car headlights came snaking down a mountain track, as if returning home from a world far beyond that only knew metalled roads. Opposite, a woman was sweeping her balcony and beating a doormat, while in a nearby flat a girl who'd just taken a bath was stepping into her trousers and shaking her hair dry in front of the mirror. Then someone shouted sharply at a dog barking outside. The noise of the far-off car was now just a faint hum.

We turned the sign on the door to 'Do Not Disturb', and instantly felt more snug and intimate. And so we were, as we climbed into our beds, into the aroma of fresh country laundry washed in unfamiliar detergent. I groped for Christa's right hand and found it, and planted my lips on her shoulder; she let it happen. Outwardly we were a couple, inwardly we were a convenient arrangement. The following day, I called the situation a 'dalliance'.

'Loving you must be wonderful,' I said senselessly.

'You're very fond of love, aren't you?' she replied. 'I really believe you. But you'd like it even better if it didn't have to consist of emotions.'

This was original, but too complicated for the present situation.

'Why can't we at least love one another more pointillistically?' I repeated. But she punished me for this with a glowering look. It was the wrong moment for such debates, especially as we were on our way to the station at the time where we would learn that the next train wasn't due to leave until the afternoon. So we strolled round the neighbourhood. I remember a large market and a small black-bronze monument to a local hero. Now and then, Spanish peasant women would lure us over to their pyramids of honey jars and we duly showed theatrical awe like small children in a department store. The women market traders told us that Don Quixote had once passed through this region.

Finally, we ended up playing pinball for a couple of hours in a frowsty dump behind the station. Next to us, a man was standing in front of his own personal gaming machine and gazing intently at the flashing box like he was awaiting some token of love. The expression on his face suggested he expected the machine to declare that it had his best interests at heart, and that he didn't want to believe that, in rejecting him, all it was doing was flirting with him and teasing him. He evidently thought that it would ultimately give itself to him and cough up everything, finally yielding to the one it had been waiting for all along. Meantime, our pinball machine responded:

'See the clown perform his amazing tricks,' and we shot the ball through the 'Spinning Wheel' and waited to hear the little fanfare announcing that we'd got a free ball.

Still at a loss how to kill time, we left the little town and wandered out into the fields beyond, a landscape not unlike that of the place where I'd grown up in the Voreifel. When you travel, you don't just journey to another place, but also under another sky. Images of home fade only gradually. You can travel for years, yet they still never fade away entirely. Travelling only proves the indestructibility of home, albeit of the home you've lost.

Two tractors were parked on the side of the road, the brickworks chimney was smoking, and a pair of chickens flew past with extended necks; I craned my own neck towards Christa, but she said:

'I'm not kissing you in countryside like this.'

In the afternoon, once we'd found a compartment to ourselves, she immediately clamped her headphones over her ears once more and buried herself in her book. After an hour, she looked up, stared out the window for a spell, and then announced dreamily:

'There must be an incredible number of walnut trees in this country!'

I doubled up with laughter at this, and she snapped:

'You get more intolerable by the day!'

Sometimes, in my thoughts, I returned to the starting point of this journey, in Tokyo, when everything had still been just a promise and the railway noises, the summer air rushing in pregnant with the scent of blossom, and the fading of the lights in the evening had all just been a faint aromatic eddy. Now I felt more like a traveller who doesn't want to travel anymore but who instead just wants to turn to stone. For him, the main thing is feeling his feet on the ground, just in order to feel some connection to this foreign place. He wants to turn around on his own axis and feel what's surrounding him: something specifically alien, distant, the impossibility of instantly being on familiar territory. This, then, would be the traveller who moves in order to come to rest. He constantly touches upon circumstances that make life difficult for him. In low-grade hotels, he stares at the ceiling, hemmed in by the street noise and by the music from the next-door room. His travelling shifts the demarcation line to what is unbearable.

I looked at Christa, with her pretty legs in a light blue summer skirt and her matching light blue, stern eyes, which avoided looking at mine, and in which I could, with increasing clarity, detect disappointment, and not just with me.

She loves telling me what she dreamt last night or some other night earlier in her life. She gives me a blow-by-blow account, with a pedantic love of detail; indeed, she even corrects herself. Yet most of her dreams show a distinct lack of fantasy, except for one, in which a cobra ('no, my mistake, it was a python!') had squeezed her to death and Helmut Blüm ('yes, he really was called that!') just let it happen:

'What do you think of that?'

In the middle of the Iberian Peninsula we interrupted our journey, because a little red-brick town that our train pulled into looked just so alluring. But its streets were silent, and the inhabitants plodded along cobbled alleyways, dragging long shadows behind them. So, we visited the local church and gazed in awe at the blossoming orchid-like stigmata of Christ the Lord, which drew the faithful into their meditation. The wound had a deep glow, and the agate strata of the blood-red paint grew darker the deeper they went into the gash, like in a horror film.

On the town's squares, we witnessed popular recreation spread itself out evenly over playgrounds, a football pitch and a small patch of land with fairground rides. Christa viewed this spreading jollity indulgently and formulated one of those sentences that begin with 'Spain is …'

Later, we wilfully chose the best restaurant in the town and ordered sparkling wine, to boot.

'I assume the date's been added to the price here,' she whispered and picked her way, her eyes on tiptoes, through the menu. She'll order cautiously. She doesn't like this feeling, this uncomfortable feeling, that she might have been able to eat more cheaply. That's why she likes to call expensive indulgences 'unnecessary'. But that's the point: if they weren't precisely that, they wouldn't be indulgences, would they?

Scanning the menu, from dish to dish, Christa considers whether food with this or that name is worthy of her attention. Yes, she decides, she does feel like that kind of food after all, if only to have had the experience of eating it. But the waiter regretfully informs her:

'Sorry, that's off today.'

Her facial features betray a sudden slump in enthusiasm. Suddenly, the dish that she wanted is precious to her. She doesn't even look up, she gets a grip on her expression, but takes a long time to make up her mind.

'How about this?'

She points at the menu.

'Ah, I'm so sorry, madam …'

'So, what have you got, then?'

'Everything else is on, except for the duck …'

The laugh she emits is meant to indicate amused tolerance, intended to convey an aura of 'We're not too bothered,' but ends up sounding contemptuous. The waiter doesn't just voice his deep regret, he looks inconsolable too.

'No matter,' she says, 'no problem.'

The customer service part of her is wounded. She's a good consumer and knows what she's entitled to. She accepts the suggested dish as though it were an unwanted child.

When the dessert arrives, for decorative purposes, the half pineapple next to the pile of sorbets has been left unpeeled.

'There are enough waiters standing around here twiddling their thumbs,' Christa says in German, her eyebrows raised as far as they will go, 'you'd have thought one of them could have peeled the pineapple.'

Back in our room, the first thing she does is pull the curtains. Sometimes churlishness and the desire for privacy go hand in hand. From her Walkman, which she's now taken to wearing even in bed, her music blares out at me, delightfully sad.

Sometimes, we get off the train just for a few hours and saunter through one of those transitional regions, a threshold town. The squares in these places are full of the insane and the eccentric, selling lottery tickets or discussing politics. These are the real hubs of genuine local life, but here too they are peopled only by the malcontents, the garrulous, the disturbed and the dogmatists.

Way up high above the houses, drying washing flaps on a wire line, directing the shadows it casts on the ground below. The wind gusts around the silver birches, and blue, green and red window-frames swagger; the scent of winter wafts through the high summer as if snow was already dormant in the summer clouds. The grass in the old-fashioned meadows smells like it's been cut, without having been so. The wood stands there gawping stiffly. The clouds have left a smear like a semen stain on the sky, and the paint flutters down in swirling flakes from the veranda. It's beautiful.

One time, I stopped in front of a statue of the Madonna, which was standing in a niche on a house façade like someone waiting at a bus stop. Her breasts were those of a young mother, and the prominent set of her pelvis under her dress seemed somehow suggestive. I called this rustic saint on her pedestal 'womanly'. Christa called me 'sexist' for saying that, and I said I hadn't heard that in a long time, and she said the label still fitted me all the same, and I said it didn't fit remotely, and she said it did too, and that was just her personal opinion. I replied: Oh yes, her oh-so-personal opinion, and that from a member of a family where the mother dragged Bob Dylan into her marriage? She lapsed into an embarrassed silence.

The engine of the passing lorry blared out like a chorus of trumpets. The sky was wearing jumble sale clothes, and the air now had the coolness of groundwater. Our next train pulled in, and once again we had the compartment to ourselves.

'The more I get to know you, the more difficult you become,' said Christa.

I countered with a phrase from the playground: 'Thanks for the compliment; coming right back at you unused ...'

That enraged her even more. In protest, I read aloud a newspaper article from start to finish about 1,130 women in the USA who'd just gained the world record in mass breast-feeding.

'It's a mystery to me how you can stand your own company even for a whole day ...' she remarked.

The first substitute for individuality is arrogance. If you're exposed to it for a long period, you quickly get claustrophobic among all those stereotypical associations and trains of thought and unshakeable judgements in matters of taste. You then react in the heat of the moment.

'... and you can't manage to go a hundred metres without secretly competing with every sight we come across.' I said.

Sometimes when I'm on my own or when I'm longing to be in the arms of a woman who's no longer young but who's familiar, I suddenly catch sight of a married couple like that, who have been together for, say, ten or twenty years, and their expressions aren't just cold or sober, but devoid of any interest whatsoever. But I'm not repelled by that; on the contrary, I want to have a wife like that, too, who'd look at me in that bossy, incorrigible way; I long for that air-conditioned hell of marriage, that spring-gun mechanism painstakingly constructed over years – anything but my solitary confinement.

'If you must know, this is my reality – a man who listens to my dreams in the morning, who I can share a house with, build a garden with, and enjoy a prospect with. And you haven't got a clue about that.'

'I know so few people's reality,' I said lamely.

To punish me, she read out the entire menu for the buffet car. I picked up an old French newspaper, read the headline: 'Fine Weather Over the Sahara' and under the heading 'A Shallow Grave,' an article about a dictator who'd refused to have an entry in 'Who's Who?'

That evening, we made love silently in a Spanish family guesthouse, in a spirit of tolerance and reconciliation, with each of us thinking something else. During our lovemaking her face changed from a countenance into a mug, and back again, and her thrashing legs couldn't keep still for excitement. I found this remarkable. We both entered into the strangeness of her life, in order to remain just that: estranged, and everything that we might do together would only foster that strangeness, and not any affection for one another.

At breakfast, Christa said:

'Tangier, the *ne plus ultra!*'

Ne plus ultra. 'Nothing beyond this' ran the inscription supposedly carved on the Pillars of Hercules by the hero himself. According to legend, one of the two pillars was located on the Rock of Gibraltar and the other on the mountain of Jebel Musa in Morocco. Other sources cite Monte Hacho in the Spanish exclave of Ceuta on the North African coast as the site of the second pillar. But that's not important. The key thing is that the Ancient Greeks believed that Hercules had placed his two pillars at these straits to mark one of the ends of the earth.

The two pillars were reputed to hold up the sky. But what did that mean? As Grillparzer once said, 'If anyone believed that trees were there to support the sky, then they'd all strike him as being too short.'

The Pillars of Hercules are also mentioned in one of Pindar's Odes, and in the Book of Job; the verse where God is setting the limits of the oceans run:

'Hitherto shalt thou come, but no further/ And here shall thy proud waves be stayed.'

After all her research into prophesies about the end of the world, Christa was well acquainted with the myths surrounding the limits of the earth.

'Plato places his Atlantis on the far side of the pillars,' she said, 'maybe in order to underline their mythical character.'

'But there were also some authors who thought the pillars were situated in Frisia, or even on Heligoland. They're pictured on the Spanish coat of arms, and even the two vertical bars in the dollar sign – which was originally a symbol for a Spanish gold weight – are thought to derive from the Pillars of Hercules.'

'But if you say 'Thus far and no further',' Christa objected, 'then you've set a limit, for sure, but at the same time, you've drawn everyone's attention to what might lie beyond that limit. So all you've succeeded in doing is making its transgression conceivable, right?'

'More than that, you've actually compelled people's fantasies to focus on the magical act of transgressing the border. In succession, Socrates, Tertullian and Epicures all had the following maxim ascribed to them: *Quae supra nos, nihil ad nos*: "What lies above us does not concern us".'

'So, that effectively made the geographical boundary of the perceptible world also the boundary of our perception.'

'A frontier for all curiosity,' I say.

We were drawing near to Gibraltar and to our crossing to Tangier, to that multilingual, multifaceted, multi-ethnic city. But dusk settled so pinkly over the southernmost province of Spain that we couldn't help getting off the train once more. This was our fifth day on the move. The hotel, an old half-timbered postal guesthouse with heavy dark beams in the bedrooms, was located at the head of the marketplace. I leant out of the window. My eye was drawn to a woman down on the square. At first I couldn't work out why, then it suddenly struck me: she was the only one sauntering along.

The following midday saw us standing on the Rock of Gibraltar, in sight of the African continent. The small site on the peak, which was once the haunt of fishermen, hermits and cloven-hoofed animals, was now fated to belong on the itinerary of international day trippers, and consists of a monument with a sea view. The monument itself is a cheap bit of ground cover and has spread to take over the peak of the hill so completely that you can only catch occasional glimpses of the original limestone bedrock among the gaudy plastic, the painted corrugated iron and the woven folk art souvenirs. Pity, it would be a sight to behold. But even the sea breaking against the base of the monument has once more taken on the dingy colour of an embroidered sofa cushion.

Travellers from all four corners of the earth come to Gibraltar and pay an entrance fee to visit the nature reserve on the eastern slope of the rock, or go to the western side to scoop up souvenirs. Finally, they like to abandon themselves to the universal human satiety with material goods that can set in when you sit yourself down in a chair facing the sea. And as the Apocalyptic Horseman of Boredom ascends the cloudless sky, in the mass catering establishments stomach and bowel upsets begin to stir into life thousands of times over; the tourist sneaks out to acquire himself a souvenir that will remind him of nothing except the purchase of said souvenir, a little ship, say, emblazoned with the buyer's name; or a doll in national costume; or a stuffed Barbary ape; or a wind-up matador, who moves across the ground like creeping constipation. Yes, Gibraltar is a place where the souvenirs either remind you of themselves or of failed attempts to disappear.

In the glaring midday light, then, we really are standing on the legendary rock itself and looking at the coast of Africa, just a couple of kilometres away, at the far side of the *Ne plus ultra*, and experiencing our freedom. Ancient man did not dare venture any further here. A borderline had been drawn, a ban imposed on the almost sinful yearning to set foot on virgin territory. More than this, a warning had been issued against the bold ambition of seeking to shoulder the attendant risk. After all, beyond this frontier, all manner of unforeseen categories of danger might be lurking.

In this moment it felt as though my journey, which had begun in Tokyo, had reached its end. But this destination had shifted, not unlike that change that also overtook journeys in the past: formerly, a traveller's inquisitiveness was characterized by an unfocussed desire for knowledge, the urge to follow a scent without really knowing what was leading him on. This, then, was the confident motion of the questioner; confident in that it permitted the questioner to go off on a wild goose chase. Precisely at this borderline to the forbidden, unknown world his thirst for knowledge must have been piqued. Alongside all other dangers, the traveller also has to overcome his scepticism when faced with a welter of pointlessness. Curiosity keeps running up against this. It's vital that it should turn away from its own self and face the world, even without knowing what it will find. Even so, it can happen that it ultimately broadens the horizon, an achievement pioneered by navigation and astronomy.

I remembered seeing an image on the title page of a work by Francis Bacon of Odysseus's ship on the far side of the Pillars of Hercules. Odysseus, whom Dante places on the lowest circle of his Inferno, and who is the only person not to recant his past, appears thereafter as an emblematic figure symbolizing curiosity and exploring beyond the bounds of the known world.

'Fascinating, isn't it?'

'But that means that the demarcation line of the *Ne plus ultra* has already been crossed,' Christa objected.

'Precisely, and that's why Emperor Charles V's motto was '*Plus ultra!*'. He did that once it became clear that the *Ne plus ultra* did not signify the end of the geographical world. So: *Plus Ultra!*' I cried once more and clicked my tongue.

'So, this would be the right moment to tell you that I'm going to turn back now,' she replied, looking at my astonished face like some museum exhibit.

'Run out of curiosity, then?'

'No, you exhausted it for me. But don't take it personally.'

A few hours later, she was on the train back to Madrid, where she could stay the night with friends. I walked her to the platform, where we gallantly kissed each other goodbye on the mouth, so as not to bring it all to too tame an end. The next day I left the Pillars of Hercules behind, crossed to Tangier and set foot in the world beyond all on my own. But it was only when I heard Julio Iglesias singing in the lift of the hotel there that sadness overtook me. There's no *Ne plus ultra*. It's impossible to leave the known world behind.

The Himalayas

In the Fog of the Prithvi Highway

Today the clouds were no less of an imposing sight than the mountains. Staring at them, I chilled out in my hotel room until I got hungry. But by that time it was four in the morning, the whole place was asleep, and I had to grope my way down the corridors. At half past six, a woman staggered out of the lift into my path, giddy from the fumes of insect spray. I held her in my arms for a moment. It was clear we only felt so euphoric in that instant because the smell of the insect repellent was so overwhelming.

Then came that brief early morning flurry of activity: the sound of splashing water, the rasp of twig brooms on the pavement, the cawing of crows and the shuffle of flip-flops on stone floors. An old man rambling away to himself, and the exuberant twitter of birds in the hedgerows. The hotel owner comes out into the garden and surveys his domain. Suddenly, he spots the guest sitting in the courtyard sipping his coffee. Faced with the choice of saying nothing or initiating a pointless little morning conversation, he opts for initiating a pointless little morning conversation.

'How are you today?'

Fact is, the air-conditioning unit exhaled a damp, muggy stream of air over the bed, all the while emitting a loud rattle that sounded like its housing was about to fall off. The light bulb cast a dim glow. The mattress was resting on a slat that had been broken twice already, while the duvet seemed to be filled with an assortment of rags. The unwashed synthetic bedsheet alone attracted swarms of mosquitoes. Sleep was out of the question.

'Thank you, fine.'

Kathmandu waits behind the Himalayas' back. This city derives its aura not from its own interior, but primarily from the presence of the mountains that surround it. It's a city in the shadows, a collection of dwellings tolerated by nature, as provisional as it is cultic, and all the while gazing at the presence of a higher being. Provisional because what is its architecture when measured against that of a rocky massif? And cultic because the power of nature is ever present as both a sensual and spiritual dimension. The clay brick buildings are surrounded by bamboo scaffolding, with steps running up the external façades. Everything is multilayered, ambiguous, with rooms behind other rooms, shading off into the hidden and the secret. And in stolen glances from behind barred windows, questions brood over the dust-shrouded street.

The façades sweat out this dust like the perspiration of the overheated planet. People flood from the villages into these walls. Representatives of fifty ethnicities, some of them already dying out, come here to eke out a living. They bring monkeys with them and bales of cloth on their handcarts. Leaning against the rusty iron stanchions supporting the bamboo scaffolds, the women – with their olive-skinned complexions, black mothers' mouths, and colour-saturated saris – peddle deep-fried snacks and mouldy fermented drinks, specialities of their native regions. A beggar woman supporting herself on crutches, haggles up the price. Behind the bars of the windows, faces appear and disappear; there are silent witnesses all around.

The heart of the city is a temple complex that sprawls over the entire centre. The frowsty odour given off when doves flap their wings fills the air; it smells of dusty fur. Now and again there's the sound of a bell, a tinkling noise piercing the haze like some *memento mori*. Then comes the shuffle of the women in their flip-flops, and chanting and murmuring.

The roof supports, the carved skeletons of the houses, rear up palely above the street. This could be a model village, a film set or an open-air museum, but in actual fact it's a living environment: people dwell in the temples and fill the spaces between them with markets. They're the haunts of the soothsayers and beggars. From a chain of buckets hanging from a swaying bamboo scaffold, workers lob up onto the roofs clods made from a mixture of clay and elephant dung, where they are used to hold the tiles in place. At the foot of the scaffold sits a man blowing a flute, while another's staring fixedly out from behind a barred window, the lover in the crickets' cage. All around, houses are being put up, top-heavy and labyrinthine, like someone's trying to recreate Schloß Neuschwanstein, with all these pointed roofs groaning with gables, pillars, oriels, friezes, grilles, lunettes and curlicues.

A country's character can also be represented through its relationship to what's secret and hidden, be it in its pomp and circumstance, its rituals, its architecture or in relations between people. Here, I can only ever penetrate just a few centimetres into the dark looks of the women with their golden jewellery. Beyond this, everything grows black. No, I can't even understand what keeps these people rooted to the earth or why they keep their eyes fixed on the heavens. The beautiful old ladies in their shawls gob out the red juice of the betel nuts onto the ground – just one more colour – and the beggars keep rattling their empty tin bowls as though trying to prove that hunger really exists.

Already, hundreds of bright plastic containers had been placed right outside the temple to the white rain god: that was how soon they were expecting him, in the form of the long-awaited monsoon. The rainy season had begun once already, a few weeks ago. The farmers rushed to buy their seed in at inflated prices, so great was the demand, and prepared their fields – only then to look on helplessly as everything shrivelled and died when the monsoon suddenly and capriciously stopped. Now lots of farmers don't have the wherewithal for a second sowing.

The mugginess gets trapped between the walls. The women sway like lanterns at an open window, a man goes by carrying three flower-pattern pillows on his shoulders, and rouged children clutch with painted hands at the milk-white complexions of the women. Where everything is bizarre, it's perfectly possible for the bizarre to seem unremarkable.

With its temple complexes, flights of steps, bridges, canals, hearths, and stepped pagodas, the Hindu shrine at Pashupatinath is a sacred site of solemn ritual. The smoke that rises up from the cremation of the dead drifts over the site, colouring and impregnating the air. That taste on your tongue is the sweet, smoky tang of cadaver.

There are six of us, a mixed party of aid organization workers and their local guides, and when we realize what we're breathing in and suddenly clasp handkerchiefs to our mouths, the *sadhus* smirk at us from the pagodas, conscious of their photogenic attractiveness, but at the same time as decadent and spoilt as the little monkeys that run through the maze of alleys in the temple area, constantly preening themselves.

Hanuman Baba is also sitting there, dressed in glowing orange. He's now 103, the oldest of the local ascetics. But the money that tourists give him in return for taking a photo is usually snatched away by the younger, more worldly *sadhus*.

'No matter, I have no need of it,' he'll say, and as the only truly selfless person among profiteers, he really does mean it.

As we're talking, plumes of smoke, sometimes light blue, sometimes darker, billow up from the cremations taking place in the background as the flames lick around some body fat or gnaw on a bone. Hanuman Baba's been sitting here long enough that he can read every different wisp of smoke as it wafts its way up to heaven. He's been living like this for the past fifty-five years, the last sixteen of them in the four square metres of his tabernacle, smoking hash and praying, for nowhere, he claims, can he find such inner peace as here.

'What good do your prayers do?'

'I see everything when I'm praying. Some things are hard to make out and sometimes I see things that have long since passed. The best things I've ever experienced have been in my dreams.'

'Were you always like this?'

'No, I was quite different once. But when I was fifteen, I saw a dead boy. That's when it dawned on me: children are something man-made and material, too. The soul's a different matter, though. So I wanted to get away from this life of corporeal things.'

The eccentric seer: looking at the dead boy, he realizes that he's man-made, born from flesh into flesh. In his former life, everywhere he looks all he can see are material things. And what about beauty, grace and harmony? But where the eye can see nothing, namely in the soul, there he recognizes something divine, and now he can see it in a breath, a mere exhalation; the man's a positive Neoplatonist.

'So did you have an epiphany?'

'A conversation. In the Indian town of Assam I had a conversation with God.'

'What did he say?'

'People warned me not to go to that place. They said a spirit lived there. But there are good and evil spirits, so I told them: Why shouldn't I go there, maybe it's a good spirit? So I did just that, and settled down to pray. Suddenly there was this noise, and a voice said: You can stop praying now, your prayers have been heard. I opened my eyes, but there was nothing there, nothing in the undergrowth. I could only see God with my eyes closed. That's when I realized: I have to be there for God. That's the most important thing of all. And ever since I've been living like this.'

And saying this, he screws up his eyes like they've seen something disgraceful, beyond the realm of appearances. You can't tell on what plane of phenomena this old man's gaze is resting.

'Do you see evil things, too?'

'When I'm at prayer, I'm in a kind of force field. Evil things can't penetrate it, but I can see them. I see demons who bring death and pain. They frighten me. But I cling to the truth. It stops me from being intimidated.'

All religions recognize this state of higher truth, of grace, of 'vision', yet it appears as some egocentric phenomenon, and is celebrated within the confines of the self; it seems the stairway to heaven is peopled with nothing but soloists.

'Does the state of the world concern you?'

'Yes, it really does. I pray for its happiness. I've dedicated my life and my soul to that end. But the soul is not just resident here in my body. It moves around, it can even fly – and it sees everything.'

'Is your soul younger or older than your body?'

'You can't call a soul "younger" or "older". It just is. That's all there is to it.'

'Have you foreseen the end of the world?'

'I'm afraid that the end is drawing nigh. But if people would only listen to their souls, things would be different. After all, the demons find it hard destroying us, because we have the power of prayer.'

'So you're at war with the demons?'

'Yes, I'm trying to multiply our defences against the demons.'

Looking at him, at those impassive eyes, at his economy of expressions and gestures, at his diffident smile that seeps off into his face and trickles away somewhere, I'm thinking: all our questions to him have just as far to travel to get an answer.

'You're a wise man, so tell me: how should I lead my life from now on?'

'We are nothing, mere bodies. The rest belongs to God. If we plant something in this field, we have no way of knowing what we'll reap. Which plant will wither, or which will yield more than we expected. That's why we should just focus on the here and now.'

'Okay, then, so how should I live right now?'

'Cling to the truth. It's not just you who'll benefit from this, but everyone. Our bodies are just material, some beautiful, some not, some fat, some thin. But the soul is eternal. Our inner eyes see well. Open them, take a good look, and then decide for yourself, do it from your innermost being.'

'But then all I'll be doing is focusing on myself the whole time!'

'If you do it as I've told you, it'll work out fine for you and for others. Not everyone should lead the kind of life I do, but if you're not close to God, then the soul is blind, and you won't be able to come to the right decision.'

Where should I direct my gaze? Up over the grey stelae of the temple complex, the sight of which was echoed yet simultaneously curtailed by the anthracite colour of the sheer wall of the Himalayas rising up in the distance? At the grotesque facial expression of the inspired, jolly old man opposite? Or at the smoke billowing over towards us from the cremations in clouds tinted as delicately as mallows?

'Your hair's over two metres long – do you wear it like that for religious reasons?'

'No, it's more like a hobby of mine, letting it grow.'

Saying this, he takes hold of the long, felt-like tress that looks as though it's being held together internally by microorganisms and yet slowly decomposing from the inside, and throws it round my shoulders. I find myself in the embrace, in the clutches, of some perfumed constrictor snake, and perhaps already infected by the plague of the teeming inhabitants of his pigtail.

'Are you healthy?'

'Fit as a flea,' he crows, 'I've never been ill my entire life. If ever I feel weak, I just go out and find the right herbs.'

'Have you any idea where the soul goes when the body no longer exists?'

'It goes nowhere. It stays here. The body gets cremated. But the soul doesn't burn. The soul remains the soul, whatever creature it happens to inhabit.'

Away from the centre of Kathmandu, on the canal, a dead boy is lying under a red hand towel. Three women are standing beside him, crying. As they clutch at the hand towel in their grief, it slips, revealing the face of a sleeping youth, as elegiac as a Pre-Raphaelite poster boy.

Prayer doesn't call the shots here, death does. There are stories of people who have woken up on the way to their cremation. Their relatives refused to take these seemingly dead people back, and so they had to remain up at the temple complex. As revenants, they are obliged to live the rest of their lives in the caves above the river. They even marry one another. We look up at their dwellings, which are little more than starlings' nesting boxes in the rock wall, with their little tilled allotments by the side, and their tools under tarpaulins, and sheds made of wooden planking and crates. Today, they'd withdrawn inside their burrows, but there was clear evidence that people lived there, on the margins of the temple district, but still within its precincts.

Here, it's not uncommon for old people who are approaching death to say: I'll take my leave of you now and go and die. They take one last meal in the company of their family. At these occasions, custom demands that their daughters or their daughters-in-law pour water for them as they eat. If this isn't observed, guilt will take on tangible form and come back to haunt them in the shape of demons or other visitations – or traumata, as we might put it. One old woman who was possessed by spirits kept wandering around the temple grounds, incessantly screaming: 'You didn't pass me any water while I was dying!'

Passers-by lower their eyes at the sight of this apparition, which is both woman and spirit, person and demon. Can she be helped? According to prevailing beliefs hereabouts, through its cremation on the banks of the river, the abandoned body ascends to a higher plane of existence. Everything is good. In a lovely, peaceful ceremony the bereaved then prepare a final meal. What reason is there to despair? Even people who die on the street, but who are then given a decent burial, have a good chance of being reborn under favourable circumstances.

Monika, the German founder of 'Shanti Griha', an aid organization for young Nepalese, has also seen the flipside of this detached attitude to death, for instance with regard to the kind of problems that can arise at the scene of an accident. Here, the question of who was to blame is often the quickest to be resolved: basically, the stronger party is always the guilty one. If the person who caused the accident tries to do a runner, the residents of a neighbourhood block the highway until the person responsible is apprehended. The guilty party then pays for the fatality according to a scale of charges that can be haggled over, but which are broadly fixed.

The more tricky cases are when people have been run over and maimed. Because they have a claim to lifelong support, they tend to theatrically dress up their injuries to improve their negotiating position. In these circumstances, then, you've got to prepare yourself for a good deal of play-acting and tiresome argy-bargy. Even then, survivors still often barely receive enough to live on.

One time, Monika was driving along the highway and stopped at the scene of a crash, where a child was lying in a pool of its own blood. Already, the street was thronged with residents all rushing around trying to identify the culprit, but Monika insisted that the child be taken to hospital without delay. That was quite impossible, she was told in no uncertain terms, until it was clear who would stump up for the damage – and, what's more, it still hadn't been resolved who would pay in the awkward instance of the child dying while it was being transported to the clinic.

'Who's responsible in that case, then?' they berated her, 'Bet you haven't thought about that, have you?'

It sometimes happens that the kid is lying there dying while those involved in the accident haggle with the parents over compensation, and it's not unheard of for a lorry to deliberately reverse and run a person over for a second time just in order to make the question of who's liable to pay damages crystal clear.

'Look, if we invite you to dinner,' a bystander explained to her, 'you come. Same applies here: if God invites you to die, you've got no option but to obey.'

Monika still finds herself having to battle against these sorts of convictions, but at the same time, she's also well aware of the fact that in this part of the world the whole reason why children are born in the first place often has to do with the parents' wish for financial security and care in old age.

The next day, we set off in Monika's small, beaten-up car and as we ascend we get a panorama down over the sea of clouds and a view of the outline of the Himalayas – the steeply soaring Machapuchare with its pyramidal profile, an almost perfectly regular isosceles triangle, and to the side of it Annapurna, and then the highest peak of all in the group, Dhaulagiri. But my favourite mountain – here, everyone's instantly required to name their favourite mountain – is Ama Dablam, because it has a face. When God was standing in the shower, he modelled this crag out of soap.

We follow the riverine landscape through the more densely wooded mountains. The current here is ochre-yellow, and fishermen using bow nets line the banks, lethargically scanning the swollen river, while boys wash themselves in the water. All faces have their national characteristics: the Nepalese face, it appears, emerges from darkness and quickly prepares to sink back into it.

So here it is, then, the fearsome Prithvi Highway, a narrow strip of tarmac that snakes its way westwards, in the shadow of the Himalayan mountain chain, threatened on one side by rockfalls and on the other by the yawning abyss just beyond the soft verge of the metalled road. The massive lorries that drive it have names like Road King, Road Hero, Road Tiger, Night Sleeper, Broken Heart, or Slum Star, and their bumpers sport stickers with slogans such as 'Follow Me', 'My Life is Journey', 'Slow Drive, Long Life', and 'Hey God – Save Me'. Perched high up in their cabs, the drivers gaze down stony-faced on the traffic; they're the mightiest presences on the road, for sure, but also by common assent invariably the ones at fault, too. But ever since the Maoist rebels summarily started blocking the highway some years ago – just because they could, and also to demonstrate the Delhi government's impotence – the lorry drivers have become everyone's last hope in the interminable traffic jams. At least you can shelter safely under their trucks at night, and if you tip a driver twenty rupees, he'll even cook for you and take you under his wing.

Only when it's jammed like this does the stream of traffic bring to light all the organisms that teem within it. There are men in uniforms, shabby-looking types, people wearing kaftans or union suits and weathered veterans; lively-looking youths clamber down from their vehicles, mingling, trading, haggling, arguing, tugging on ropes to test how secure their loads are, sizing up their own or their neighbour's cargoes, and swapping news on impending strikes.

But in the end the road itself is really just an allegory, and certain elements stand out from the general flow of traffic. It's an introduction to deprivation and to the opulence of observation: A child crosses the road, carefully balancing a blue mug; in a dried-up river bed, a woman chops a lump of wood into faggots; in front of a billboard bearing the legend 'Playboy-Whiskey', a girl sits combing her long, dark hair; a boy tweaks another's ear in passing; an old man carries a goat kid slung over his shoulder; a child shows his mother the only fruit on a tree; a girl shoves a trickling water hose into her mouth; a young woman in a red dress squats down and chips away at a stone, her knees banging together with every blow; women carrying their loads in panniers on their backs, with all the weight supported by a band around their foreheads – to relieve the strain this places on their neck muscles – walk for kilometres with their arms folded above their heads; cattle trucks trundle past, a dull mooing emerging from their interior, and gravel lorries with water streaming out of their tipper trailers; a woman washes her child's feet in the river; tarmac-layers with blackened faces sit huddled round an open fire, boiling pitch; children lug panniers full of rocks, transporting them from one side of the river to the other across a bascule bridge; every roadside kiosk is a shrine full of bright, shiny bags, colourful bottles, and gaudy packaging; the bossy old man sitting in a rickshaw hits the runner with a stick; young men play cards on the roof of a minibus; a group of pilgrims have fixed a red flag on the bonnet of their car to placate the Maoists; calves are fitted with muzzles to stop them suckling their mothers' milk; a man weighs down the roof of his hut with bricks; an old man pushes an old woman along in a wheelbarrow; an unconscious boy is carried to hospital in a basket; an elderly man rubs ointment into the stump of his severed leg; another has one arm in plaster; a stunted little guy pisses great lasso-loops of urine into a ditch; a man carries stacks of grey-looking laundry.

Above, there are vultures and paragliders; a loudspeaker van speeds by, making a public announcement, the man's voice sounding threatening and a woman's ingratiating. A large-eared old woman racked by a coughing fit. Five girls all wearing their hair in a bun. The buses have barred windows like prison vehicles; a lorry graveyard; a large family sitting amid aluminium canisters; farm labourers with plough harnesses slung over their shoulders; an old woman picking her way through the puddles and holding up the hem of her skirt; the goddess at the tomato seller's stall; an overturned hay lorry; women in red lying on wet straw; the inhabitants of an unfinished house; the old ladies bent under panniers full of dry leaves; men in pink pyjamas on the street; the van with 'Finest Butter Caramel' written on the side; the dribble of water in the riverbed.

The road is a route, and the route is an end in itself. Everything flows along, carrying goods and stories alike. Every image is only briefly captured in one's gaze and then swallowed up by the stream once more. This road is a bloodstream, an aorta. And yet, at the same time, it is a stretch of road on which people pay daily with their lives for joining the traffic flow. A

Japanese researcher, it's said, once counted all the accidents in one day here. He arrived at the figure of twenty-seven for this bit of road alone, and when he told all his friends in the hotel about it, they promptly decided to take a plane from Pokhara to Kathmandu. The aircraft crashed.

You can't skirt the Prithvi Highway, all byways eventually lead you back onto it, and in the same way so do the symbols of life's journey coalesce here as well. The road-killed animals on the tarmac are as flattened as dried flowers pressed between the pages of a book. In some areas, as a reminder of a serious smash that took place, you can find lakes of shattered green glass, overshadowed by the roadside hibiscus bushes. Gawpers are everywhere, and nowhere do they go unrewarded – vultures swoop down from on high where a crashed car has come to rest, hyenas forage round accident sites for any trophies left behind and spirits drift among the mementoes of all the accidents – the splintered tree, the black skid mark on the tarmac, the innards of a bus, pieces of wreckage hanging from branches, and keeled-over minibuses. The trails of collisions, disasters and ascents to heaven. The survival of the majority of those who drive in Nepal, and also those whom we see living alongside the roads, hangs by a silken thread – or rather by several such threads. Why else would the Nepalese have a pantheon of three million gods?

Now the rainclouds are puffing up like dust balls over the ridge of the mountains. The trees there are only saplings, of varying sizes. A cloud of dense, sultry air seems trapped in a curve of the road. There a group is sitting, crouched in front of a cube-shaped building that is their home; they squat there on a plot measuring just twelve square metres, yet they're full of grace. They're constantly making movements that have been filtered through their unconscious; weightless, routine gestures that have always been there, which arise from their preconscious state and are called up as though from their cellular memory: the absent-minded action of stirring a pot, say, or straightening clothes that have slipped out of place, or cutting up a piece of fruit, combing a child's hair, or sweeping up ash. All mute reflex actions that are performed automatically, while the person's eyes scan the section of road in their purview.

Nor do these people build their houses, shops, sheds, or offices into large edifices all in one go, either. They start by building small, and then add on until they've created a whole complex of boxes. All these dwellings have a little loggia outside, with one or more tables under it. That's the way we do things, they say, and sit there and receive guests. And every stranger who pitches up in these refuges is handed sweet tea and a bowl of sugar with ants ploughing through it.

The mountain we're approaching generates its own climate. In photos, it always appears bare. But in reality it keeps itself almost constantly shrouded. However clear the day might be, the summit remains hidden in cloud, which only heightens its mystery. One of the drivers says:

'I've been living here for ages now, and I've never seen it without its cloud cover.'

If you ever do see an image of the mountain when it's bare, it's like looking at some piece of topographical erotica, with its bulky body and its snowy peak appearing grey-blue and white. Compared with the clouds, a mountain peak such as this is pent-up energy in another kind of material. And when we look at these mountain ranges, we also think of the people who live up there and struggle to survive: the Thakali, Gurung, Sherpa, Raute, Chepand, Kirat, Dolpo, Magar, Rai, Dhanuwar, Tharu, Satar, Limbu, Gine, Mugal, and Lhomi. The names of these peoples resonate like chords played on an unfamiliar instrument.

These mountain peoples share their environment with the Mikado pheasant and the Formosa macaque, species which when displayed in a museum look like they've only just died in the glass cabinet, while the plants in these parts boast names of Linnean elegance: *Anemone vitifolia, Bergenia eiliata, Lagotis kunawurensis, Inula, Selinum* and *Taraxacum.* And finally, the habitat at this altitude is also home to the mysterious *Cordyceps sinensis,* a creature that is an insect for six months of the year and a plant for the rest, and which is only found at heights of 4,500 metres above sea level or more. It is prized for its supposed aphrodisiac qualities and commands high prices.

But why should human morphology be any less complex? There was one occasion when I was sitting up there at a refuge, well above 2,000 metres. The careworn proprietress, who usually lived at an altitude of 5,000 metres, but who came down here for two months each year to cook soup and sell her woven fabrics, anxiously watched every mouthful that I swallowed; she was wearing gold jewellery in her dirty earlobes and, as the owner of three plastic tables on the Sarankot Ridge, was a poor, rich woman.

If she hoped for anything for the future, then it would surely be for the past to return, at least that's what the demeanour of a woman who hadn't really got to grips with the present was telling me. She immediately put me in mind of the Chepang headman who, before he was driven from the mountains, told me the bees were dying up there, and the native languages, too, and that a semi-nomadic lifestyle just wasn't possible any longer in a place which the young were already leaving to try their luck down on the plains, where their sort really didn't want to live for cultural reasons, and really shouldn't have to. When the Nepalese king once asked the Chepang headman what he wanted – a car or a house, maybe – the latter replied that all he really wanted was his forest back.

We pull over at a bend in the Prithvi Highway under a lowering sky, amid a cacophony of bleating goats and scowling faces. One young girl, wilfully modern, is sporting a T-shirt with the slogan 'Stars and Straps'. Does she know what it says? In this area, several young girls have recently been abducted by their teachers. Their parents then generally received a ransom note. But though they met the kidnappers' terms and paid up, the children were long since dead. The police reported that when the bodies were recovered, they were found to be dissected into ten parts, stripped out for the illegal trade in organs. The old man who told me about this ended his story by saying:

'And so they unwittingly helped solve the problem.'

'What problem?' I asked him, as he propped himself upright in the slush with his stick.

'The problem of what to do with unwanted kids.'

And as he continued to whisper into the roaring of the passing lorries as they came round the bend, he slowly began to cough up all the facts: in many cases, girls are simply packed off into the cities to work in kitchens. Often, they're raped there. And the children that are born as a result only make the problem worse.

I turn around. Those barns there, these three tables under the porch, the towering cliff behind and the view of the Prithvi

Highway; this, too, could well be somebody's home, the vanishing point of a yearning born in a kitchen in the big city. It's an evil déjà-vu: we regard hardship so reproachfully because it's so unoriginal. Everywhere the same relationship between poverty and hygiene, everywhere the same squalid housing, the same burden-carriers without a voice, the children longing for a future, the old women in faded clothes that were once gaudy, and the victims trying to wash the misery out of their faces. The neglected members of the masses: you're like everyone else.

Here, too, there's housekeeping in the absence of any men. The grandmother is preparing soup for the evening on the fireplace, while the mother pulls a beret made of orange felt onto the head of a young boy with two cataract-blind eyes and gets him ready for his journey. His eyes look like someone has clumsily inserted them into the sockets, the way they squint in different directions. Yet the facial features of this boy, despite being jarringly disturbed, are really quite exquisite. He gazes out at the world through eyes that are like irregular pearls, and the smile he gives as he mounts the pillion seat of a motorbike, squashed between his father and mother, dissipates absently into space. Then he's gone, as the motorbike threads its way into the stream of traffic.

We eat *Dhal-bat* from a tin plate, and even this white pilau rice dish can't escape its liberal sprinkling of ants. That's all right and proper. After all, this is a poor person's dish, made from millet, rice or potatoes mixed with curry sauce or any vegetables that happen to be to hand. To accompany it, there's always a soup made of lentils (*dhal*), and so the name *Dhal-bat* even gets applied here to what elsewhere would be called a water soup with three lentils floating in it. To finish, the old lady brings some honey that she has detached from the honeycomb using lemon juice. She mimes to us how we should suck up this sticky preparation and spit out the bits of wax. Her Nepalese English sounds like someone chewing puffed rice at the same time as they're trying to speak. Then comes the tea, which tastes of joss-sticks, with some sugar stirred in that has lots of yellow blotches in its large crystals. Even so, it still looks grey, and the ants continue to burrow through its spoil heaps.

'Look out,' the old lady warns us as we silently drink our tea. She looks anxiously at the trickle of pebbles falling off the crag above us: 'there might be a rockfall!'

But the only thing that's been hit by a rockfall for miles around is the sign warning people about the danger of rockfalls.

Beneath the heavy cloud layer, on the other side of the road, lies the rubbish-strewn riverbed, with dogs foraging around it, and all the while the jungle drums of the passing traffic never let up. The residue of street life has washed up in our bend in the road. It's like the bend in a river polluted by industrial waste, full of filth and flotsam. A hundred metres further on, the road curves round an outcrop and then descends to the valley.

Our hunger's sated now, so we're curious to learn what awaits us on the far side of that far bend, behind the rocky outcrop. The old woman who prepared the meal for us and who's been living here since she was a girl, looks at me inscrutably.

'Tell me: what's on the other side?'

'No idea.'

'But you live here!'

'I've never gone round there, though.'

'Why not?'

Many years ago, she tells me, she had a dream that warned her never to go round that bend in the road, 'because of the misfortune that could befall me,' she explains in her broken English. But didn't she want to know … wasn't she at least curious?

'Not at all,' she replies. 'After I'm dead I can always go and check it out.'

But because there's life before death, and seeing as we'd already chatted to one another for a while undisturbed and quite intimately, I'm finally allowed to hold her hand and so, taking her feather-light old lady's hand in both of mine, we teeter out of the hut to the edge of the road, and walk across the gravel lay-by covered in puddles, gradually approaching the far bend. But what if something should happen to her, what if the prophecy were to come true after all?

'You see, we're really doing it,' I say.

She nods, her face beaming with self-confidence, and now her hand is gripping mine really tightly. We're walking along in step; limping slightly, but still basically in step. But just as we reach the brow of the road when the bend begins, the old woman suddenly stops dead in her tracks. She laughs, like she can only do so standing still, disengages her hand from mine, slaps me heartily on the back and cackles:

'You didn't really think I'd spent my whole life on this side of the bend only to have you come and lead me round it now, did you?'

So we turn round and she can't stop laughing, even while she's walking along now, safe in the knowledge that her superstition is far stronger than the arrogant rationality of some transient European, a now shamefaced passer-through, who can keep the far side of the bend as far as she's concerned, the side with the unknown dangers, those things that threaten the life of an old woman.

And so when we do finally leave, with the old woman's hand shooing us away more than waving us goodbye, when we actually do round that bend, the first thing we come across is a white buffalo heaving its enormous bulk from one side of the road to the other.

'Buffaloes are every bit as stubborn and single-minded as camels,' says Monika, who founded aid organizations in Africa before coming to Nepal.

We've barely been underway twenty minutes when our car is brought to a grinding halt. There's a crowd of people blocking the road; a social conflagration: in the centre of this hubbub is a bridegroom sporting a thin moustache and a skullcap, and with his eyebrows and lashes blackened with kohl. Behind him, swaying on her mother's arm, comes the bride, her young head bowed deep into the shade of a pink umbrella to stop her from seeing her husband. But this isn't the real reason why we've all come to a standstill. Further on, up the road, 'something' must have happened.

Immediately, the first rains start to fall: at first, droplets that scarcely brush the twigs of the trees and merge into the earth as soon as they hit the ground; you almost expect to see a time-lapse sequence, where the seed becomes a panicle, which becomes a twig and which once more reaches out to drink up the rain. The line of vehicles hasn't just stopped, everyone's turned off their engines as well. In little melodic phrases the birdsong in the lessening rain begins to assert itself. The road winds into the distance; no one knows beyond how many curves they'll encounter a roadblock or a serious accident. Someone is dispatched to scout out the situation. Those who are left behind climb up to the rise overlooking the valley and exchange awkward platitudes about the view.

We go and sit on the crossbar of a gate overlooking the plain, which looks like a landscape painted by a Flemish old master. Someone starts telling a story about a man and his love for cheese sticks. But I can't stop thinking about the family of the old woman back on the other side of this range. If this traffic jam continues to build, it'll stretch back to the bend where we stopped, and the old lady will say: You see, no good comes to people up on that road. But our driver Rajiv is worried that it's not the Maoists this time, but rather yet another accident that's caused the road to be closed.

'I had four dead people in the car one time,' says Monika. 'Rajiv was holding a woman in his lap and stroking her head, but she was long since dead. I told him to worry about the ones who were still alive, as there was this one young woman who was still breathing.'

But even she hadn't made it, as it turned out.

The densest of the fogs down in the valley begin to lift, and clouds and rivers appear. Monika's colleague from the aid agency is still recounting his story:

'… anyway, we just gave him a glass of wine and some cheese sticks, and he was as happy as Larry.'

The mist wafts up, and the chit-chat abates. There's a major accident somewhere at the head of this queue. A short while later, and a towering bank of fog has settled over the road. We can look down and see the people on the national highway disappearing into this wall, and all the while, cloud after cloud of fog keeps billowing up from the valley. At first, the mist takes away the contrast between things, then it softens the contours, then it dulls the whole image, and finally it makes everything look opaque, as if seen through frosted glass or creates an atmosphere that is as dense as soup. Grimacing, the people who ventured into the fog emerge out of the uniform grey of the precipice, carrying pieces of luggage, canisters, or rolls of cloth in their hands. One man keeps shaking his head, with the thumb and forefinger of his right hand pressed into the inner corners of his eyes like he's trying to concentrate, while in his left he's clutching an orange beret.

The people emerging from the fog gesture to others to keep away.

'Don't go in there!'

'Oh God, no, the motorbike …'

The people who run into the fog grow colourless, and then become two-dimensional, turning into mere silhouettes, disappearing into the wall of fog like some flat template. And now people are even beginning to look like they'd been formed out of fog themselves, losing all their three-dimensionality, and sinking back into the realm of shadows. The relief of their bodies is flattened out, the colours all fade, and the silhouettes find their entranceway into the wall of fog and pass through. Ultimately, they are nothing but a dark recess in the breath of the night, and step through this into oblivion. Ahead of us lies the afterlife, and behind us the forbidden bend, and at our backs are the intimidating Himalayas. We who have been spared cower between these steep rock faces. The only spot of colour to be seen far and wide, so luminous that it seems to be the only thing to have resisted the effect of the fog, is the boy's bright orange beret, still dangling from the messenger's hand.

Isafjördur

The Blind Spot

The only sound still audible at night is the slapping of the halyards against the flagpoles. That's how it all began: a noise in my head, and a mood to match. Inspired by the urge to hear it, I set off. The landmark I longed to experience, then, was a noise, dispersed in a wind that carried the taste of snow. Add to this my predilection for unlovely things, and for the clammy feeling you get when gusty squalls buffet your body. Even the summer on Iceland is still overshadowed by the long winter, and by the demands of having to doggedly fill the time somehow in a general state of torpor. People's temperaments seem in the process of thawing, but outside of Reykjavik no one's going around freaking out just because the sun's getting stronger by the day.

Beyond the capital, the solitude of life forms is maintained in the desolate landscape. These are contemplative places that invite you to disappear, places that have also been shaped by the concessions that we grant to nature, to its spirit and spirits, as compared to civilization. Icelandic villages squat in this landscape like so many micro-organisms which blossom only briefly after a long period of dormancy.

Living on the outskirts of Reykjavik as I was, I couldn't hear the halyards smacking on the flagpoles. But among the people around me, I could hear how words fluttered away into the gaps between associations. Among their vocabulary, I found as few imports as I did among the goods on the island, though the antique shops had portraits of National Socialist bigwigs hanging on their walls and their shelves full of the Nazi book collections of former Party members. Many of them had once fled here, to the land of the old Icelandic epic, the *Edda*. Occasionally, I'd run across eccentric forms of amusement, for instance, really obscure board games I'd never seen or silent children's charades. Here, then, I was confronted with a country of barely a million inhabitants, but which had its own trade journal for national show requisites, a country that preserved its own individuality by venturing into the realms of the whimsical, and which had once been governed by a woman president who began her term of office with the words: 'The hand that rocks the cradle can rock the system.'

Here I encountered people who were still unpolished by any basic social conventions: relationships began with them staring fixedly, literally gazing at you without batting their eyelids even once; this was accompanied by a bare minimum of gesticulation or facial animation. Only on meeting someone for a second time did you begin to establish connections, born of recognition and a recollection of the dumb-show that had gone before. Only the children tended to remain stand-offish.

Before the world ends, it will heave a sigh and emit a blue burp. Tourists call the first of these 'seismic activity' and the second a 'geyser'. They stare in awe at the spectacle, wallowing in sulphurous pools and expecting the water to act like some fount of eternal youth.

The best thing you can do is leave them lying there and get away from the central massif of Iceland; dispense with your travel guidebooks, too, where there's no mention of the end of the world. In the rear-view mirror of the 4×4, you can still see how the land soars up to a high mountain range in the south-east or bunches itself up into little towns, before the road goes snaking off across the narrow orchid-neck of the isthmus that lies in the northwest of the island, heading for Westfjords, that desolate region that has been blighted by rural depopulation but which was once supposedly viable farming land. Nowadays, nowhere else on Iceland do you see so many abandoned farm-houses as in these hills. The first port of call for those migrating from the countryside was the provincial capital Isafjördur, but before long most of them preferred to head off to Reykjavik or out into the wide world beyond.

The formations in the skies are echoed on the ground, behind the humps of the female or the male mountains, as they are des-ignated here, in the igneous rocks and the beds of moss. Now a stiff wind is blowing the spray back up the waterfall, and people are peering out of their windows with faces as white as snow, or bleached by the long nights. Here, too, the drowsiness of a hard winter lies heavily across the summer landscape.

If you walk into an inn round here, a few of these ice-bound faces will be raised from strange games to look at you, and everyone falls silent for a moment. Then a waitress swings by, her legs clad in thick woollen socks, and thumps down an album with four hundred Polaroids in front of you:

'So, here you can see how a building site became the guest-house you're in today.'

I really must see this. At least, that's what she solemnly tells me, quite unaware of how grating such forced chumminess is. So there's nothing for it but to knuckle down to earnestly studying the photographic record of the build, like you're reading the small print on the leaflet that comes with a medicine. You dutifully express surprise at the right junctures while you eat your hard-boiled egg and leave those present to their fond memories. No sooner have you disappeared than you become one such memory yourself.

The road obeys the wilfulness of the fjords, which have eaten impractically deep into the coastline. It's a long drive to get anywhere. Sometimes, a sheep appears round a corner, sometimes there's not a soul in sight. Nature lays claim to older rights than civilization, which as a result still strikes a defensive posture. Unhurriedly, you move back down the evolutionary scale, to a state where everything still consisted of ice, fire, ash, sand and magma. Harbour installations stand rusting in the inlets, with plaster flaking off the walls and children staring out at empty streets.

Isafjördur is situated at the end of all the roads, and all the fjords. This isn't a town; it's a deposition of things that the icy sea has washed up. This settlement even has the fjord in its name, which means 'ice fjord'. It's been built in the form of a semicircle on a sandbank, which has constantly had to be raised and now juts far out into the fjord. In the ninth century, the town's founder, a man called Helgi, supposedly found a harpoon here, which he named 'Skutull'. Apart from that, he hadn't done much, it seems. He was followed by traders from other regions of Iceland, as well as Norway and Denmark, and, later still, merchants from Germany and England also established commercial settlements in this area.

What was life like here back then? The town records for the year 1656 note that one Jón Jónsson Jr. was burned at the stake in Isafjördur, alongside his father, for possessing books of witchcraft and also because the younger man had allegedly used magic symbols in order to make a girl break wind.

There's no doubt that a state of isolation makes you susceptible to messages from the 'other side'. For two whole months in winter, the sun skulks dejectedly below the level of the mountain ridge that surrounds the town, which lies in a basin, on three sides. The town's streets are often covered in snowdrifts and are impassable, while even journeys across country, along the numerous gravel tracks that meander along the shores of the fjords, become extremely arduous. There are guardian spirits who help ward off the challenges of cosmic and human nature, and who hover above the hospital, the school, playgrounds and the old people's home, and you can also follow footpaths leading to the realms of the fairies and the elves on maps specially produced for the purpose.

Today, this centre of the Westfjorde has fewer than 4,000 inhabitants. From the eighteenth century on, this region, which was rich in cod stocks, grew relatively prosperous on the profits of drying and curing the fish. Isafjördur was also formerly the site of Iceland's largest shrimp processing plant. But over time this factory switched to producing deep-frozen sushi, and because fishing became subject to restrictive quotas from the 1980s on, people started leaving the town and life here isn't like it used to be. As a rule, Icelanders aren't keen on working in local industries anymore, so their place has been filled by immigrants from around forty different countries, who eke out a living hereabouts. Here you can find workers from the Balkans and Poland, but also from Asia and Africa, and the first of April even witnesses celebrations for the Thai New Year.

Hardly anyone notices that this is where the world comes to an end, for the simple reason that hardly anyone ventures here, except for a few travelling salesman, who wolf down their 'continental breakfast' in the town's only hotel and don't know where to go from there. It's even said that a blonde woman tourist stayed here for weeks without any complaint. After her departure, a local crank rented the room she'd stayed in for one night and was discovered rubbing himself against the shower curtain that must have been clinging, just the day before, to her blonde body. The town's sole policeman was notified, but he couldn't find any law relating to this particular misdemeanour.

The town has a post office staffed by women who earn a living from putting the gum on the back of postage stamps. They are very straight-faced and reluctant to connect phone calls through to Europe. 'Telephone' in Icelandic is *Sími*, which literally means 'wire', in the same way that 'television' is *Sjónvarp*, literally 'picture transmitter'. It's as though modern technology has been translated into the vocabulary of the early days of tool use, though if truth be told, television is less about transmitting pictures than tranches of information. Isafjördur also boasts a small airport. From here you can fly down to Reykjavik, sure, but most of the traffic goes north, to a place that was once romantically and wholly inappropriately 'the endless realm of ice', that is, to Greenland, to nothingness.

During the day, Isafjördur is a remarkable little place full of shy individuals who think nothing of walking for miles carrying a garden fork or a plastic bag, who are always on the move, and who take a kindly view of village idiots. In the café, people fortify themselves with slices of layer cake, while the local youths drive their cars up and down the couple of hundred metres of main drag at their disposal, wind the windows down, crank up their car stereos and strut their stuff – but to impress who? If only it was the first week in August, when the annual swamp football tournament takes place!

As evening draws in, the town's only cinema is showing some film or other from some far-flung country abroad. The sound wafts out onto the street. People living next door even open their windows and lean out, staring at the outside of the building and listening to the movie soundtrack. In summer, by the time the picture's finished, the sky's still light, but the streets are deserted.

Even at the weekend, by ten o'clock in the evening a deathly hush reigns over the town. Your gaze is drawn heavenwards; today, it's an ochre-grey colour. In the cemetery, the children's graves stand in rows like cots made from wood or stone, neatly enclosed like the little ones were being tucked back into the security of their sleep.

But if you step out onto the street just an hour later, it's jam-packed and there's a deafening roar of motorbikes. A fairground ride has even been installed on the square, a Loop-o-plane to be precise, which shakes up the drinks in the stomachs of those riding it into cocktails. Drinking yourself into a state of complete stupefaction is now the order of the day, and it's only in the cold light of dawn – but when is that, given that it's half-light here the whole time? – that everyone finally rolls home. Then the place reverts to playing dead once more.

The following day, it's early afternoon before people open their curtains again, and look out once more into nothingness, to where the snowfields are waiting somewhere on Greenland's east coast. A picket fence and a flowerbed, and beyond them the jetty and rusty boats exuding a stench that's a blend of algal bloom and rotting fish. The entire town consists of maybe three rows of houses. Some of them have been clad against the weather with corrugated iron, while others are painted defiantly brightly. But the sea air eats away at everything. Beneath the peeling façades, a few flower borders still brave the elements, but then the place capitulates, and your eye roams out across a natural hollow unbroken by any vegetation or roads, and you catch sight of a crystal-cold strip of water, and beyond it, in silhouette, a range of hills. Hidden in its snowy valleys are animals with white coats, while in the blue waters of the sea lurk blue fish.

The world comes to a definitive end in Isafjördur. Every day here, it draws its last breath and suggests to the visitor that he should make himself scarce. On a permanent basis, mind.

When the dance music in the inn faded away, and a window casement yielded to the wind and flew open, then at last I was able to hear the flag halyard slapping against the pole. The face of the policeman, who was sitting beside me, took on a deeply reflective air. The last murder around these parts had taken place over twenty years ago. But for the boisterous drunks, he'd have nothing to do. And if it hadn't been for the fact that, a while ago, a polar bear had drifted into the sound on a stray iceberg from Greenland, or for the arrest of the man in the shower curtain, he wouldn't have had a great deal to talk about. As it was, he spent most of his time just looking out of the window.

'So, you're a lonely person,' I said, feeling it was the right moment to get personal.

'Why should I be lonely?'

'Because you're too smart not to be.'

He looked at me without really seeing me. His eyes filled with tears, which was a shame because it instantly made him withdraw inside his hard shell.

'Alone,' he answered, 'did you know it comes from "all one"?' And saying this, he swigged down the dregs of his beer, tottered in a quite un-policeman-like way onto the stage and began belting out a rumbustious version of 'C'est la vie, c'est la vie'. I closed the window so the sound of the halyards wouldn't put him off his singing.

God's Window

The Final Curtain

How should things conclude? What kind of landscape should this continent come to an end in? When you've traversed it, from North to South, undaunted by the continent's brooding, its unstable serenity and its inertia, and its susceptibility to emergencies – where do you then fetch up? It's perfectly possible to cross this continent from top to bottom in such a way that all you've ultimately done is endure it. But it can't just end. You cannot conceive of any chord on which it might finish, or of any crescendo or finale it might rise to. So all it can do is come to a diminuendo and just fade away.

At some indefinable point before you get to Cape Town, Africa recedes and turns into some cosmopolitan region, a neat and toothsome place full of street sweepers and wine growers, leisure activities and golf courses. And out of this decidedly Swiss ambience, Cape Town arises, with its 'served apartments' and 'guarded communities', its beachfront strip with bistros and cappuccino bars, surfers crossing the road carrying their boards, and white widows sipping colourful cocktails. Viewed from Cape Town, Africa is as far away as India.

'Keep the Cape in Shape', posters urge. Women doing Pilates exercises bend and stretch on the lawns, watched by groups of workmen in high-vis vests holed up in their trench in the road or sitting on two garbage dumpsters they've pushed together to create a makeshift seat. Their attention is split between this spectacle and the beach, which is like one big shop window, with all its tempting goods on show.

The tourists strike poses like the goddess Aurora with the sun star, reaching up and arching their backs into a hollow and stretching both arms up to the sun, as naked as the sun worshipper Fidus doing his nudist physical jerks in the open air. Look, the female tourist's psyche whispers to her, I'm free to go native here too, while the almost totally naked athlete next to her stretches himself in the heavenly, all-embracing light.

Nowadays, the whites are well-versed in carefully regulated and well-covered-up bouts of defensive sunbathing. The sun has become more hostile and people have become more pragmatic. Now the sole purpose for the sun shining is so that designers can come up with sunglasses to protect against it, chemists can develop a sun cream with a high anti-UV factor, and sunbathers can slap on an ointment to guard against allergens.

By contrast, in old photos sunbathers can be seen sprawled-out invitingly, soaking up the sunlight; indeed, their utter devotion to it has something almost obscene about it, like they were positively urging the sun to 'take' them. It was all such a lustful business back in the old days of sunbathing. All that leg-spreading, stretching out, all that complete self-abandonment! And even now young people show their willingness and are spendthrift with their nakedness, while the old people spend their time cowering and shying away from the light. They lie there like flotsam; sometimes even a brief spell in the sun is too much for them, and they go all limp at first before getting irritable.

The black workmen on the dumpsters sit and stare at the beach like anthropologists. The white man is inherently comic, and even more so when he's a sun worshipper. A human spatula, a gourmet sublimating himself into a delicacy by lying, turning and grilling himself in the sun, all the while promising himself beneficial effects from it.

The 'Miner's Convention' is meeting in the city.

'Is that good for business, then?' I ask the taxi driver.

'The Diabetes Symposium was better,' he replies.

The local paper, the *Weekend Argus*, concurs with him. '12,000 diabetics in one place' runs the headline, '– that's a real gold-mine!' Likewise, a former Miss South Africa, who now spends her time organizing charity dinners with Nelson Mandela as the star guest, rhapsodizes about the diabetics in terms that are normally reserved for political party donors in the USA. We are sitting in a large circle at a waterfront restaurant. Africa is nowhere to be seen; our field of vision is restricted to a coastal road, and we're drinking, by turns, *latte macchiato* and white wines from all over the world, as well as some pretty run-of-the-mill plonk.

But if you stroll along the shore a piece, you come across a row of brightly painted bathing huts lining the beach for 'Blacks' or 'Coloureds', who are all just lumped together as 'Africans' here-abouts. Here they keep themselves to themselves in a kind of beach reservation, standing around for ages in the surf before decamping to little family groups huddled around a towel, where they spend their time chucking balls to one another.

I'm walking through the receding tide when a square scrap of grey paper washes up at my feet. Unfolding it, I see it's the bleached-out passbook of a South African man born in 1981, whose stamped photo makes him look like someone who's just been caught red-handed. Who might he be – someone who fell overboard from a ship? Perhaps it was stolen from him. Or maybe he drowned. Someone who has departed this life, either voluntarily or forcibly. Your imagination can't help but be stimulated when the Atlantic washes up an identity card as jetsam. Later, I sit down in an internet café and try to trace the man on the highways and byways of the web. But no one of this name appears; his life remains an unsolved puzzle, a mere anecdote whose only remarkable feature is that there should be anyone in this day and age who has left behind no trace of himself and, what's more, someone who has lost his identity in the ocean.

At the end of the street there's an antiques shop. Among the revue photos, stuffed animals and the autobiography of a professional bird photographer entitled *I Walked Into the Woods*, I come across the handwritten diary of a mountaineer. Tucked inside the book is the photo of a woman, hugging the two men standing either side of her energetically, like she's effecting a reconciliation – a kind of mountaineering *Jules et Jim*. I purchase the diary and start to decipher it that evening under the glare of the bedside lamp. Wouldn't it be nice, sixty years after their climbing exploits, to pick up the trail of this trio once more? But I'm thwarted by the fact that the diary entries name not a single person; instead, the climber expended all his energy on describing his exertions, the climbs themselves, and the flora he saw *en route*. In these gruelling conditions, though, all individuals obey the same diktat: they become ciphers and speak in platitudes, even if those platitudes are extreme ones. But the three people in the snapshot hail from a quite different life that lies invisibly beyond the realm of exertion. So I put their photo with the passbook of the unknown South African.

The thought subsequently occurs to me that these photographic testimonials do indeed attest to something: despite leaving no footprints beyond the confines of the picture, they are still snapshots from the lives of people, and at the same time contain both life and nothingness. Strictly speaking, the first thing that strikes the observer in these frozen instants is generally a feeling of nothingness and how all-embracing it is: I glance up, for example, into the face of the South African television newsreader, and instantly what she's talking about becomes empty and meaningless; no, rather, it's she herself who is hollowed out and, for the duration of her appearance on the screen, is filled with non-existence, a total absence of meaning even. The same thing can recur in any given context, no matter where: a waitress balances a tray on her hand, but she's asleep on the job; a building signifies no particular style, no expression, it may well not bespeak any great passion behind it; the voice of the pilot, the train manager, the guy sitting next to you, all of them are of such a consummate unintentionality, as if they wanted to say: Please disregard me. I've no desire to importune you with my presence.

Later that evening, I return to the restaurant. My friends are still sitting there, perched above a rock in the sea on which two sea lions are flapping their flippers and giving themselves over to the business of procreation. On the next table, the waxen-faced old squire with the complexion of a miso soup and a patrician mien has finally made up his mind; today, he is full of the joys of life. By contrast, his gay friend beside him is struggling to maintain a youthful front. Inevitable really, because you can see from around his eyes how old age has penetrated through them into his very being, and is making him wilt from the inside. Soon, he'll give up bleaching his hair blond, stop tinting his long sideburns, and take off the native-chic bracelets he's wearing. The old man bends down to his friend's hairy ear and whispers:

'Cheer up, Prince Grumpychops!'

At our table, Pierre, the South African golf pro, is busy recounting the remarkable spectacle of two elephants mating, which he'd witnessed on a visit to Kruger National Park.

'It looked like one cathedral mounting another.'

'Oh, you saw elephants,' chips in the charity beauty queen, 'elephants for me are like Wow!'

Suddenly there's a shriek, high-pitched and affected like someone ostentatiously hooting at a joke. But on the table next to us, a spirit lamp has tipped over and sent a tongue of flame shooting across the table straight onto the polyester shirt of the mutton-dressed-as-lamb homosexual, and he's screaming like someone who's put on an exaggerated falsetto to mimic a gay man. By now, his shirt's completely ablaze and he's struggling to tear it off, and no sooner has he succeeded in plunging his hands into the flames and dragging it over his head than his chest hair catches fire too. The blaze licks inexorably upwards. At first it smells foul, then acrid, and his neck's thrashing around in a ruff of flames.

Then someone appears and rips the remaining tatters of burning polyester off his chest. A lesbian giantess at a neighbouring table had been planning to use this evening to introduce her girlfriend to her parents, but hadn't yet summoned up the courage to kiss her in the full public gaze. Now, showing great presence of mind, she rushes up and smothers the burning man in a tablecloth. For a moment he's enveloped in the linen, a pall of smoke, and the arms of his helpers, whilst still emitting a piercing wail, but then all of a sudden he rears up, erect and pallid-skinned, from his tablecloth swaddling and stands there in his gaudy underpants, slightly askew and looking for all the world like Edvard Munch's painting *Scream*. A strong smell of burning pervades the restaurant, mingled with artificial perfumes wafting in from the entranceway. A man sitting nearby leans forward to get a better view, as the victim is led away and the ashen-faced head waiter starts dashing round from table to table, desperately explaining how the accident could have happened. Meanwhile, some diners fall to speculating that this could see the place closed down for good, as the ensuing court case would be unwinnable.

From the toilets, we can still hear the burned man whimpering as he kneels on the floor having his neck doused with cold water and dusted with flour, which someone has recommended as a remedy for burns, while someone else offers the opinion that 'it's the worst thing, I repeat absolutely the worst thing, that you could do in this case.' Stunned, the manageress appears at our table as she goes round collecting up all the spirit lamps; as she does so, she formulates the following statement in the little-used future perfect tense:

'This will have been a black day for us.'

Soon after, we hear the wailing of the ambulance siren, and as everyone's gaze is drawn to the door, the lesbian giantess takes the opportunity to kiss her nonplussed girlfriend, like she's ambushing her, and a man at the next-door table attempts a witticism: 'Seems they even flambé the guests here.'

Some people start talking, like dogs lifting their legs.

The following day, we set off finally for the Cape, a self-evident – too self-evident – endpoint of the world. The terrain leading up to it is like Heligoland, sparse and shrouded in mist, and finally we run up against a locked gate, which according to the information on an adjacent notice board, should have been open from early morning. So is it going to be open today at all? We hang around for a while, but there's nothing doing, so we give up.

Later that evening, returning from our excursion to the wine-growing regions, we pitch up at the farthest extremity of the Cape once more. The landscape is still timelessly covered in fog, but this time the gate's open. A board in front of it informs us that this is the entrance to the southernmost tip of the continent. A bus full of Japanese tourists pulls up and does its utmost to fulfil every cliché in the book. Fully kitted out with umbrellas and hats, its occupants stream out, take snaps of the sign and then board the bus again straight away without going in. We, on the other hand, are keen to push on to the farthest point of the Cape. But the warden in the hut next to the barrier points at his watch.

'It's six o'clock. We're closing.'

In actual fact, it isn't yet six, but the point is it could get to six and we might fail to make it back here in time. We try to negotiate the non-negotiable. Our rights are forfeited. The man has the tip of an entire continent under his control.

'But you opened too late this morning. Can't we simply recoup the time lost then at this end of the day?'

'No.'

Ultimately, then, this end of the world remains closed off to us. Nevertheless, from a favourable vantage point, at a curve on the road heading west, we caught sight of the fateful promontory. It didn't appear to have anything in common with the continent; rather, it just seemed to be some kind of knoll on some chance hill, a one-off disclaimer, a belvedere or bella vista, Land's End and Finisterre. We'd saved ourselves the embarrassment tourists must feel when faced with this vista.

So we pulled over at the curve and experienced the drama of the traveller, who is forced to conclude that nothing really moves him and that he can find no point to his trip and consequently none to his day-to-day working existence either, which he only put up with so he could afford to come on the trip. When speaking about his future, he refers to 'great expectations'; regarding the weather or the stock market, it's 'a fine outlook'; and when describing his illusions, it's 'rosy prospects'. But if all these should fail to transpire, he will lapse into black pessimism.

But in one particular context, these 'prospects' occur in the singular form: the lovely view, the bella vista. That kind of outlook is genuinely thrilling, which is why guesthouses are often called this, places with fine views of a coastline, or a mountain range, or a tower. The visitor slows down, pauses a while, and feasts his eyes on the view. It tells him that he's reached the right altitude, precisely the appropriate angle of incidence, and that 'The Great Whatever' has only just finished dabbling in nature, his breath still wafting over it. A view, then, is always beautiful when, confronted by it, the viewer feels small; then it becomes sublime, and the viewer is reduced to the status of an insignificant nothing.

Yet the true magic of the moment occurs when an individual's personal prospects converge with a grandiose view: in such cases, you enjoy the beautiful view over the landscape in a symbolic way. Only by forgetting yourself in the contemplation of such a view can space and time commingle. All of a sudden, the future appears in this panoramic view into the far distance, putting the observer in a peaceful and pious frame of mind. Then he snaps a photo; it captures the view, but never the future.

As a result, there are plenty of travellers who never get further than the first step. They follow their impulse to disappear. But in this façade, they penetrate neither to a state of joy nor to a fulfilment of their own needs, but merely get caught up in photographs, in their own country, in their origins, or in analogies to things they find familiar. And consequently never get away from themselves.

The opposite case is that of the happy person who only truly comes to his senses on the summit, like that man who had climbed all the highest elevations in Europe and responded to my question as to whether he'd also reached high-points of experience in doing so as follows:

> Yes, absolutely, with every peak I ascend, however small. I find I'm instilled with a feeling of elitism because I know I'm the only person doing this kind of thing. Mixed with gratitude that I'm able to do so. As I'm approaching a peak, I tell myself that no one can take it away from me, and soon enough, I'm up there on the summit. Then I need at least an hour to celebrate what I can only call a kind of personal act of devotion. Sometimes, I'm overcome by fits of sobbing on peaks that hardly warrant such a reaction, because they're really nothing special. Then again, I'm nothing special either.

The Cape of Good Hope may be a stubby little promontory, an unimpressive hill, but in truth foreign places everywhere reveal something familiar to the traveller – the sweep of a twig broom over the floor of the railway station, the broken hook on the toilet door, a beam of light with motes of dust dancing in it, or the sight of a person yawning as they read the paper. At the obvious ends of the earth there are often no man's lands, occupied by shacks. They turn their back on the sight of nothingness and towards the people who wash up here – all those people, all those expectations. Tourists are always looking for a route into the moment that can be authenticated with a souvenir.

'I'll take you somewhere where the world really does come to an end,' Pierre says. 'It's called God's Window, and it's over in Mpumalanga province in the east, not far from the Kruger National Park.'

So, we set off. Sometimes, the rainforest closes in over the track, while at other times the villages lining the roads sit there like they're in the savanna. Then again, sometimes the cattle farmers have protected their compounds and huts with palisades against free-roaming big cats, while in other places a steppeland opens up, a landscape of barren, sandy plains dotted with adobe-brick huts exhaling the heat and glare of the sun. The ground is blotchy, like some pigmentation disorder marking the earth's skin.

We eat on a veranda at a bend in the road. Along with our food, the waiter serves up the following story: a woman gets mauled by a lion while she's on safari. Her grieving husband sprinkles the corpse with rat poison, so that if the lions return, their hunger will be the death of them.

The roads start climbing again. High above the 'lowveld', as the land stretched out one thousand metres below the Panorama Route is known, the ancient primary forests lie stunned and dense. The newly forested islands of trees curl next to the woods like florets of broccoli. At the places where the water plunges into the ravines, the crags with their shattered anatomy soar into the sky like hollowed out vertebrae. But no sooner have you passed such a river bed than the wood is free to stretch out once more and finally make way for fields, and presently nothing is as astonishing as the fact that nature in these idyllic circumstances is really quite nondescript.

The place we have travelled all this way to see ultimately turns out to be a balcony measuring six metres squared, floored with natural stone flagstones and marked off by a balustrade coated with peeling, rusty-orange coloured paint. The balustrade has been put here to prevent the trippers in their brightly patterned leisurewear from plunging into the abyss along with their handbags and binoculars. The fact is that summer visitors, after making the long trek up here, are so entranced by the sight of the abyss that they have to be physically restrained from plummeting to their deaths by wooden posts and crossbeams. Indeed, their behaviour up here in general clearly has less to do with the landscape than with these dark temptations – the only sinister dimension to many a tripper's life.

So the traveller likes nothing better than to have himself photographed at this dizzying altitude, captured not just in an instant of imperious sovereignty over the panoramic landscape but also striking a self-possessed pose. As if teasing the vertiginous drop, he likes to stand with just one hand resting on the balustrade. At the same time, this lends the pose a studied insouciance, which only serves to heighten the sublime nature of the moment. The man leaning on the balustrade becomes a monument, while his horizons open out into the infinite distance.

'God's Window' is a balcony perched over a steeply plunging ravine, which is around 1,000 metres deep, formed from shining rock walls overgrown in places with vegetation; the ravine is washed with falling spring water and echoes to the sound of chirping crickets and twittering birds. It's a chasm whose walls seem to be straining towards one another, as though a rock curtain were about to close over the view into the depths, across the woods and streams, and over the distant prospect of Mozambique.

The deciduous trees wear their crowns like umbels and sway gently in the odour of mint. Sprouting directly out of the cliffs, long-stemmed saplings grow askew, teetering precariously as swallows wheel around them. An endless succession of rocky outcrops, covered with climbing plants, stretches into the distance. Lilies dazzle ostentatiously in white and orange. The branches point, gesticulating into the landscape in which, at least from this elevation, there is not the slightest sign of a human presence. The wind creates a parting in the forest canopy. You could easily imagine you're standing at the back entrance to the Garden of Eden or some equally inaccessible tract of land where everything is just as it always has been, since time immemorial.

The wood here isn't just any old ground cover, but rather a living entity, and full of surprises. Right now, the sap-oozing vegetation is filling the air with an aroma of curry and jasmine, followed by the scents of carrion and wet stone. What appeared to us to be a mountain when we were down below, now turns out to be just a hillock, domed like a hand grasping a doorknob, while the arteries of the wood, the streams and rivulets, run off into the distance, growing ever more tiny as they do so. A landscape drama is being played out here, to which humans are just chance observers.

The evening mist descends in swathes on the valley. Then the wind suddenly picks up amid the twitter and shriek of flocks of birds as they pass through a late rust-red shaft of sunlight; briefly illuminated by its glow, they soon vanish above the network of meandering lakes. And the landscape, left to its own devices with its armpit hair, its furrows, warts, clefts and scars, scabby and overgrown as it is, slowly disappears in the darkness.

But then comes the entrance of Fuji dot.com, huge, with its red and green livery, climate control and roaring engine. Its doors hiss open to disgorge its contents: the women chattering like mockingbirds and the men, with their shaved necks and open mouths, already pulling out their cameras.

With my back to this hubbub, I sit on a crag, a thousand metres above the forest, above the ravine where the waters meet and the rock of the cliffs pile up in their different strata. Immense ferns push out into the haze of spray created by the waterfalls. In the gloaming, the great columns of rock facing one another look like sketched, deeply indented bodies. The water gushes down into the valley and washes up and down at the foot of the cliff, as the cries of bats begin to assert themselves over the roar and chirp of the waterfall.

The night nests in the hollows of the rock clefts, where total darkness already reigns, and into which the first animals are withdrawing to sleep. Tinged with yellow and red, the receding hill brows line up in front of their rocky amphitheatre like so many puffballs. Clouds hang over the arena, and shadows play across the rock faces, which are flecked with tenacious sulphur-yellow lichens. Anyone who spends time here, inhabitants and visitors alike, wear this landscape like a poncho. Everyone feels folded in, enclosed, even by the magnetic pull of the abyss. Indeed, the chasm seems to have its own gravitational field, which draws you in inexorably, and which has a single goal: 'The Void'. Emptiness.

'Buses Only,' shouts one of the tour guides, no one knows why, and is answered by staccato bursts of Morse code from the ravens overhead. Down below is a forest that's still permitted to remain a mystery, where unconquered nature may still spread, and beyond it broods Mozambique.

'Oh my Lord, this is awesome!'

The first of the coach party set foot on the platform.

'Oh man, Oh Lord, Oh wow, isn't this beautiful?'

One of these endomorphs is content just to stand there breathing in the atmosphere. The rest stand around and feel the urge to name the landscape they're looking at: What's the name of that mountain, what's that river called … There then follows a kind of rising chorus of adulation, almost a litany:

'Oh shit, isn't this beautiful?'

'Oh look at this, for Christ's sake, this is fuckin' beautiful!'

And they get it all down on film, while clenching the temple arms of their sunglasses in their teeth. Then they have pictures of themselves taken in front of God's Window.

'Beautiful background!'

Plumes of smoke drift through the evening air.

'God's burning incense,' says a Swiss woman in German, pausing for a moment to savour the poetry of her metaphor. 'But why's this place called God's Widow?'

Small, shameful settlements lie down in the valley. They have gathered their huts together as though they knew full well that it wasn't right for them to be there. A washed-out light stagnates in the young plantations. Some tree trunks stand naked on the hillsides or are perched over the abyss. The birds don't fly up as high as this, but they do rise some way from the valley floor, and we can look down from above on their outer plumage, stretched out perfectly to catch the wind … Seeing here is inhaling, and as the mood takes hold of her, the tour guide with the booming voice steps onto the platform, turns to her group and intones in a *fortissimo* of pure zeal:

'Now! Let's have a silent conversation with God here!'

I slip the washed out passbook from the sea under a rock and leave God to his interlocutors.

Minsk

The Stranger in the Bed

The airport at Minsk looks as if it's been welded together from a pile of air-conditioning cowls. Beyond its gates lies the monumental architecture of Belarus in all its bombastic grandeur and, as in the old Soviet empire, there are still those endless sets of railings, just as I'd imagined. You need to be led and guided, orders must be anticipated and followed, and proscriptions have to be imposed. And yet, in amongst all these restrictions there arises a desire to transgress the boundaries, accompanied by sheer craziness and subversive thoughts. You feel you've just got to break out, scream and shout, commit some outrage.

But instead people bow their heads and keep their eyes firmly fixed on the green and red lines on the airport floor, which mark the prescribed pathways you're expected to follow. Shuffling along these, in line, are a woman with peroxide-blonde hair done up in a bun, an elderly man with a reptilian face, and an office wag dressed in a wrestler's singlet. They don't even dare to strut their stuff. Their compliance is provocative. No sooner have they passed by, as introverted as female Pietists, than the soldiers on guard duty checking their documents resume their sullen expressions. But a foreigner approaches them and enquires:

'Might you have a toilet for me?'

This clumsy formulation rebounds firstly off the uniforms and then the demeanour of the soldiers. Only their walkie-talkies keep on twittering.

Once outside, waiting is the order of the day. There's no avoiding it. People wait in large throngs for buses, drivers, wives. Some of them even manage to stay happy in this perpetual state of waiting. They're the lucky ones. It's like they're saying: as long as we live, we'll be grateful for everything that's also alive. It's the elderly who feel the rigours of the arduous journey more deeply, yet it's they who still wait more patiently, more self-sufficiently than others, just trembling in their exhaustion. Business travellers, on the other hand, are always a step ahead of the current situation. One of these White Russian bundles of energy has started to make conversation with me:

'Have you seen your Paris Hilton on the poster there?'

We both turn to look at the woman on the advertisement, lounging there drinking canned prosecco. Seen from Minsk, it would appear she belongs to my world.

'Stunning woman,' the businessman tells me appreciatively, like I was responsible for creating her. For my part, I search in vain for anything stunning in that entirely vacuous face.

'And you know what's really stunning about her?'

'The prosecco, maybe?'

'Her composure.'

So, this guy's lust is of a more refined type. Even so, I'd rather retreat into my own sense of composure by gazing at the blank walls between the posters. The soldiers continue to cast a beady eye over the new arrivals as they stagger helplessly out of the airport terminal.

A white-faced Goth wearing a miniskirt and woollen tights is led aside by a policeman. She looks flattered by the attention. On her thigh, there's a badge with the number 23 on it; from where she's pinned it, a ladder has started to run up her tights, which soon bends purposefully inwards towards her inner thigh. Suddenly, the heel of her left shoe gives way, sending her sprawling onto the tarmac, a monstrous apparition composed of black and white clothing and face powder. As the policeman tries to drag her to her feet again, she makes like she's disabled, theatrically spreading her legs, showing everything to passers-by. That's how she wants it. Evidently her shame isn't at a premium.

Hours later, and I'm already on the streets of the capital. Where is the city centre? I'd enquired, and the taxi driver replied with a gesture like he was trying to mock me: Up there, down there, it runs for kilometres all the way to the horizon, it's all the city centre. So now I'm standing bang in the middle of it. A man with neurodermatitis is leafing through a rotating stand holding reproduction posters from the Soviet era, groaning with pleasure like it's a sexual experience.

Certain places like Amman, Kabul or Bombay are cities at high tide. But Minsk is a city decidedly on the ebb. Only survivors emerge from it, grimacing as they do so like people who've escaped by the skin of their teeth, and blinking in the bright light.

In truth I'm enjoying the possibility of being in a city and yet being unable to truly locate it. The streets are so wide it seems they're trying to burst their banks. The settlement must lie at their confluence, the city sea churning in the swell of the high-rise buildings. The façades are smooth and impermeable.

Somewhere out back, in their courtyards, urban life must be going on. The park is almost deserted, with just a few dull-looking types sitting under the trees, chatting. Between the trunks, uniformed men stand around like peeping Toms or exhibitionists. The palaces impose themselves as colossal monuments of a feudal age. They render people superfluous, and people duly walk around as if they feel themselves to be so.

Just one little *Inconnue de la Seine* has the ghost of a smile on her face. But she's so drunk that her face can't help but wear a smile. She's clutching a wilting bunch of black tulips. At her side is a smiling man blowing on a yellow pinwheel to make it go round. Evidently, he's beyond the phase of having to 'play the man', at least in her company. You can see it clearly in the looks he casts, and in hers too.

There are girls on the street, too, girls walking along with an exaggeratedly upright posture, because it's only a fortnight since their breasts developed. Beneath loose-knit woollen sweaters, they're balancing the visible achievements of a womanliness that their faces have already been rehearsing for a long time. Give it a few more months, when they've got completely used to being looked at, and they'll already be past masters at adopting that fixed expression that focuses on a point in the far distance. You really do want to gaze at them, and so you glance in their direction, but it's like you don't exist, such is the immature coldness of these girls.

'The most beautiful thing bar none,' said Vassili, who accompanied me on my strolls round the city for a couple of days, 'is Belarussian women.'

But all the ones I saw were wearing beige tights and had expressions as hard as those of transvestites. I'd see them on the main boulevard and in the park outside the Linguistics Department. Sometimes, they'd have flashy golden chains round their ankles and be wearing gold-coloured sandals. Those girls always had long legs and short skirts. Finally, as I was sitting there in the park as inconspicuously as I could, they all ended up congregating around me and smoking, all those bottle-blondes and bottle-redheads, and the girls clad in fake leopard skin, all those girls who for some reason or another were standing and waiting there, letting their lives pass them by.

There hasn't been such a hot summer here for ages. Bank employees are wearing their shirts outside their trousers, and as a group of nuns shuffle past, they leave a distinctly frowsty odour in their wake. It's far too steamy for any contact. Anyone who goes around in these conditions holding hands must really be deeply in love. At the market, they're busy putting up sunshades, even over the lilies planted in troughs, but even so they're still beginning to wilt from midday onwards. A Roma father and his son play 'Petite Fleur' on an accordion and clarinet, three times in succession until they run out of steam, and I struggle somewhat to suppress a wave of emotion that swept over me as I remembered the sound of Sidney Bechet playing this same song in my nursery, and I yearned one day to have something as elegant and sophisticated in my life as the things his clarinet spoke of.

Flies dozed off on the tourists' salads, two women pulled their bras off through the hole at their armpits, and the pigeons failed to make it up onto the head of the statue, and settled for just loafing around the plinth instead. And then a trumpeter hove into view and, straining every muscle, gave a rendition of 'Il Silencio'. But the passers-by angrily shooed him away:

'Give it a rest! You're getting on our nerves!'

So the trumpeter moved off and took up a pitch further on.

But the people there reacted the same: 'Don't play here either! You're annoying us!'

In fact, the only 'Welcome' I encountered that day was the one woven into the mat in the lift.

Sunday afternoon. The city's full of brides. You can tell from their faces that the wedding night is going to be an ordeal for them. And for the bridegrooms too. Everyone keeps crossing themselves the whole time. It's only when you follow their line of sight that you notice they're looking at a church or a tabernacle. The old chess player's been sitting in the park since seven that morning, but it's only now that he gets out his board and plays a few games against himself. Then he gets up and goes from bench to bench, asking whether anyone would like a game with him. Mostly he returns empty-handed, and goes back to winning against himself.

Meanwhile, I'm busy looking at two women and a man who are crouched over a camera discussing the photo they're about to take. I approach them and ask:

'Here, give me the camera, I'll take it for you, then you can all be in it.'

They protest weakly, but I tell them:

'No problem at all, afterwards you'll be glad I offered. I'll take a landscape format, then a portrait. Just to be on the safe side.'

In the photos, they stand there awkwardly like they're not with one another. Finally, the three of them gently explain that they're actually not a group – the second woman was just a passer-by whom the couple had stopped in order to get her to take a photo of them. That same evening, I'm playing 'Petite Fleur' to her on my laptop.

'Not bad,' Elzbieta says. 'But have you got Utyosov singing "Lilies of the Valley"?'

The next morning finds me sitting on the Cathedral Square among the tourists; some of them are gazing, others observing, still others examining, a fourth group researching, a fifth travelling in the capacity of experts, and others as people who have simply been marooned here.

'I really don't want to be here,' says the perplexed man sitting next to me.

I'm thinking I'd like to get far away from this place, too, to a country where aspirins are called 'Aspjelena', where the souvenir booths have signs proclaiming 'Memories' and the women have deep belly buttons, with wisps of downy dark hair growing out of them, pointing the way downwards. But then it struck me that I *was* far away already; I am precisely in that country already, and am still searching for the reality of this city.

Minsk lies on a river, a busy commercial river whose eight lines divide the city in two over a length of sixteen kilometres. From time to time you're forced to veer off into side streets to get away from the noise, but it's impossible to escape it. And no sooner do you enter the parks than you're surrounded by exhausted citizens – old women in tracksuit bottoms, and middle aged ones who seem to grow more jaded before your very eyes. They either look all out of focus and puffy like Boris Yeltsin, or rapt with concentration like Marika Kilius.

The city was flattened by German bombardment in the Second World War. Afterwards, because there were so many unexploded aerial mines and bombs under the rubble, it was decided to rebuild Minsk at a site forty kilometres away. But when a referendum was held among the inhabitants it turned out that they wanted everything to be rebuilt exactly the same and in precisely the same location as before. And so, from 1958 onwards, the entire inner city was reconstructed in its original style. The upshot was that socialist labourers were engaged to recreate iconic examples of imperial architecture from the late eighteenth and nineteenth centuries. They were painstaking and pedantic in adhering to the plans in order to achieve complete accuracy, but somehow the spirit of the original buildings eluded them; the honest truth of it being that socialist workers found themselves incapable of erecting plausibly imperial and imperious buildings. Instead, what they created were Potemkin villages, mere mock-ups.

These historical buildings are situated far apart from one another, like on a Monopoly board. They maintain a safe distance, keeping a watchful eye on each other. Only the churches are teeming with people. Beneath the soaring vault of the central nave, the multitude of the faithful undulate like dough that's still proving, all the while murmuring and mumbling. So huge is the crowd that some people are even standing outside the main porch, listening to the service relayed on loudspeakers that blare tinnily across the square.

Everything is spick and span in this city, progressive in other words, with the housing estates laid out in straight lines and all the monuments free-standing in plenty of space. Across the board, the city planning laws have prevented any agglomeration of new developments, only the residential silos on the outskirts cluster together. The banks of the river are devoid of all life too. It might just as well be the bed of a watercourse that's made its way underground and isn't flowing visibly anymore. As I sit there on the fringes of the green space, still nonplussed by everything around me, beggars approach my bench with faces full of yearning but no language with which to express it. Lush meadows are sprouting all around me, with over-manured wild herbs, dandelions and marsh marigolds in full bloom. And suddenly I really couldn't care less where I am. The main thing is that I remain enveloped in the sheer foreignness of it all.

Travellers are people who become what they are while underway. Their movement transforms places into settings. They arrive, look around, and observe how people in unfamiliar places go about their business and interact with others, and this very act of observation alienates the alien. Everyone living here is history, and hauls their history with them through the space. Only the traveller is pure immediacy, only he sees the city in its here-and-nowness.

On a leaflet in the drawer of the bedside table in my room, I find a German translation of the hotel's safety procedures, which informs me that 'If the hotel is on fire, place a couple of wet hand towels against the base of the door, open the window and give the fire brigade a wave.' For the rest of the day, I wander through the city looking for anything that might resemble such 'a wave'.

The following morning Minsk wears rainy weather like a dress. It is a city that wants to be seen like this. On Belarussian TV, a housewife in a miniskirt can be seen cleaning her apartment to the strains of the Brandenburg Concertos. She's very pretty, and when she gestures with the pan she's holding, she does it ironically, like she knows full well that she's too pretty to be a housewife, but just pretty enough to play a Belarussian housewife accompanied by a bit of Bach.

I call up Vassili, and we cruise the streets in his big car. He eyes the streets warily. In his anecdotes, certain stretches of road loom up as the site of wars, crises, accidents, or arrests. You get the impression that the city's an environment he feels compromised by. By contrast, the thing that doesn't embarrass him is his son, a boy whose head is full of his future prospects rather than girls. I ask him:

'Doesn't he see himself settling down with a girl sometime?'

'No, he's really mature. One time, he told me: "Father, I don't go out with girls, they have only two things in their head: Pizza and fucking."'

'Pizza?'

'He reckons all girls are prostitutes.'

'All of them?'

'Well, he distinguishes between two types of prostitution: lazy prostitution and dirty prostitution.'

'So he has no need of a girlfriend, then?'

'He did have one. Her name was Pralinka. But they'd only been going out for a couple of weeks before he came to me and said: "Dad, I've got her pegged. She's an airhead."'

'At least he's still got pizza.'

'Now he's got a carp in a pool instead. I dunno – I guess it's better than some unfaithful girl. But honestly, you tell me: what kind of person keeps a fish as a pet? Do they give you any warmth? Or follow you? Or let you stroke them? I'll tell you what my best mate said: only a man without a dick would keep a carp as a pet. That's what he said.'

On the scraped-up earth in the front garden of the building behind my hotel there are a pile of wooden fence slats and a few posts covered in peeling paint. Women in burgundy-red pinafores are sitting in a line on one of the remaining fence cross-bars and chewing gum. They're in the same position they were yesterday. Yes, they're nurses, pale Belarussian ward angels. I wander through the entrance to the hospital – looking for what? Perhaps for some place where I can finally become real, or for a state, a situation, that I might cling on to, just so as to be able to experience something resembling a situation in this city and then to leave it behind. The patients let me pass; they've got other worries. And passers-by cast indifferent glances at me.

I'm treating this whole thing as a dare, and have entered the hospital in the hope of finding someone who'll stop me. But the only people sitting in the vestibule are two old hags in mini-skirts who are smoking and who don't notice me. So I go on, down the stairs. In the cellar, there is a glass screen; you pass through a door in it and find yourself in a neon-lit grocer's shop like in a children's book, with jams with old-fashioned photographed labels on the shelves. In a display cabinet, there are warty gherkins in glass bowls, which an assistant fishes out with wooden tongs and puts in wax paper for you. Likewise for the silverskin onions, cooked beetroot and fillets of buckling.

The shop assistant is tinkering away absentmindedly on the floor behind the counter, which she does for a full ten minutes without noticing me. Her bib has slipped out of the waistband of her skirt, revealing a large expanse of her pelvis, on which the broken veins in her skin have left a distinct delta pattern. When she finally gets up, her face is red and square, and she's got a dramatic case of nasal herpes which looks like a piece of bark on her face. She's finished stacking a cube of soya milk cartons and now stands with her chin jutting forward at me, her only customer. I buy two large gherkins in greaseproof paper and make myself scarce, because she's giving me a look like I really ought to clear off.

On the first floor, the glass doors are opaque and closed. On the second floor, they are also frosted, but at least one opens onto a corridor, whose sole occupant is an old man shuffling along while hooked up to a drip stand. I find the door of the second ward along ajar. Looking in, I see that the nearest bed is unmade but empty, while in the far bed a lonely, pale profile is propped up against the pillows. I pull up a chair, put my gherkins down on the edge of the bed and stare at the face of the sleeping old man. This is where I was meant to end up.

The man's breathing sounds thin and watery. He inhales air with a noise like sucking through a straw, and it is gradually swallowed by his narrow chest. Then he goes on snoring, barely audibly, until he suddenly comes to a stop. You can hear the clock ticking. Then, with a long sigh, he's in the clear once more, as though the breather has to take individual leave of every breath.

The old man's flannelette pyjamas are made of a well worn, washed out, blue-grey fabric, as threadbare and transparent as the man himself. They're stained, but still clean, as the dirty patches have been bleached out by being put through so many wash cycles. The faded fabric exhibits the same kind of sophisticated decay as aged Roquefort. Of an outmoded design, it is faintly reminiscent of something that was formerly known as 'deathly chic'. These pyjamas are like a dog that has grown old and grouchy at the side of its master, but still manages to be a source of comfort to him.

One of the old man's hands is lying on the bedspread; brown and raw, chapped and hard from all the work he had to do; it lies there like a hand that has never caressed anything, like a piece of farmland. Perhaps the frail man had become so familiar with the soil that he didn't want to let it go, and likewise the earth seemed to have grown so accustomed to him that now it was only allowing him to depart with great difficulty.

I look long and hard at his face: the sparse eyebrows, the liver spots that have themselves been bleached out on his pale skin, the irregular patches of pigmentation on his lips, the wrinkled mallow leaves that are his eyelids, the bitterness of the lines that have formed around his mouth, and the flat moles that seem inlaid all around his eye sockets.

Where might all his relatives be? Anyone who hovered around expectantly at his birth and enthused about his future life must be long dead, while all the new people who only came into his life later on were presumably simply indisposed today, had to go to the cinema, or had just forgotten about him altogether. But it might just be the case that he was someone without any particular charisma, lacking the urge or the knack of attracting people. Yes, perhaps he clung to life in its deserted form. How else to explain it?

I'd loved to have known how life came to him and unfolded within him, and at what stage he'd grasped it with both hands and shaken it. I'd loved to have known when he'd been at the pinnacle of his *joie de vivre*, and when and how it had then ebbed away from him, and when he'd started to lose his grip on life. The sweetest smile he'd ever received may have been just a fleeting one, and the most moving music he'd ever heard may have been 'Lilies of the Valley' by Leonid Utyosov. Perhaps he'd never yearned to move or to be what he wasn't. People with different, less peasant-like hands would have talked of the 'art of the moment'.

And still I longed to know more about him: on his path through life – the only feasible path he could have taken, the one that he was predestined to travel – at what point had he become a boy or a teenager, or a man and a grown-up, a worker and a citizen, a sickly old man, or a frail dotard on his death-bed? And as one phase morphed and developed so seamlessly and unconsciously into the next, what did his conscious mind hanker after then, once these things had come to pass? Did he long to transcend the perceived world? To what end?

By the time I got up to go, the man's breathing was no stronger than the merest exhalation wafting over the downy hair on the face of a baby. I stood up when his breathing came to a halt once more, not daring to wait and find out whether it might ever become audible again. In the doorway, I turned around; all I could see was his motionless profile, standing out from the pillows like it was a wooden cut-out, and his carp-mouth gaping in anticipation. These were the final moments in a failed struggle for life, which now appeared devoid of any impact or pathos. It was only when I was out on the main boulevard once more that I remembered the two gherkins I'd left behind on the edge of this deathbed.

Patagonia

The Forbidden Place

I travel from a season that is just drawing in and arrive in one that is just on its way out. Even so, autumn in Patagonia has more of May about it than our March. I set off and muse on the general state of exhaustion into which I'll be venturing, on the signs of departure, decline, fatigue and capitulation that I'll encounter in nature. A journey almost always takes you to somewhere on the friable demarcation line between the familiar and the unfamiliar, whose past and whose continued existence you have no knowledge of. Back home, you step straight back into the narrative, yet initially even this jerks and stops, regardless of how short a time you've not been an eyewitness to it.

This mood pervades every journey, a mood dominated by a sense of escape. You still haven't arrived anywhere, nor do you have any desire to do so. Your sole impulsion is to be underway, enucleated, and you're happy to be homeless. This departure from the familiar corresponds to all the transitional spaces and waiting rooms where foreigners are already present, letting their parts of the world flow in, and banding together into a society of international faces; but behind this façade, all that's really there are tired and unpainted faces that seem to have no ambition.

They're just like that in the waiting area at Lima Airport, for instance; next to me, an Asian man with dyed blond hair is looking at pictures of rhinoceroses on his laptop and sighing. Right in front of where I'm sitting, the metal shutter covering the shop window of H. Stern the jeweller rolls up at 6.45 a.m. Behind it, a television set has already been switched on, showing an old game involving the reigning World Cup holders Brazil.

Places like this keep spreading inexorably. Even shopping malls barely have any regional distinctiveness anymore, but instead have taken on the status of landmarks. They've reduced what little architectural features they ever had in favour of expanding their display areas. The most appropriate people to fill these spaces are those who also make a public show of everything internal. They stand around in these shops, and their bling is their camouflage.

On arrival in Santiago de Chile, at first the foreign scene that confronts me is nothing more than a road, a strip of grass and a row of houses. Primulas are wilting next to a container. A man who is the spitting image of Pinochet, somehow exalted by the nobility of cruelty, emerges from one of the houses and dumps waste paper in a wheelie bin. On a terrace above the newest shopping mall, I sit and drink two Pisco Sours, and suddenly feel all fired up and find everything fantastic. Back in the hotel, I doze away the first part of the afternoon and then wake myself up under the effect of a shower gel which goes by the name of 'Magellan Breeze'.

As evening falls I find myself out on Santiago's main *corso*. The Colo-Colo football team has just beaten the local favourites, and the streets are thronged with jubilant crowds. The cripples without arms or legs lie alongside one another by the hats they've laid out and snap eagerly with their mouths at the brims, but hardly anyone has dropped a coin in. Nearby there's a man holding the misshapen stump of his leg out into the flow of traffic like a marzipan log. A dance troupe is busy practising some new routines, and as she sails through the air, the prettiest dancer opens her eyes and arms wide and arcs towards the pavement, but never comes into contact with it.

A karaoke singer in hot pants enthralls the gawpers, a conjurer has just humiliated a mortified lad in glasses for the third time in front of a hundred onlookers, and an accordion player descends into a wild cacophony. But where the two main arteries of the pedestrian zone cross, several teenagers are parading back and forth, holding up colourful placards with the hand-painted legend *Abrazzos gratis*: 'Hugs for free!' For fear of having their pockets picked, hardly anyone stops, so the kids take to hugging each other over and over again to show that they mean no harm.

By this time, I've been wandering round for some time on my own, and the cheerful sight of the kids embracing one another only makes me feel all the lonelier. As I head straight towards their group, a corpulent girl in her twenties with a peasant's face suddenly blocks my path. I spread my arms, she does likewise, and we walk towards one another over the final couple of metres smiling like people who just don't belong together but who nonetheless have got betrothed, and passionately embrace one another for a few seconds. She's got a strong grip, and locks me in it before pushing me away with both arms; in unison, we both say '*Gracias*' and break into laughter.

Later, when I delve into my pocket for my pen, I don't find it missing – to the contrary, there's another, newer pen there as well, a small black metallic ballpoint pen. I use it to write down this account.

The name of the province I move on to – the southernmost in Chile – is Aísen. The name goes back to Darwin, who supposedly said that the 'Ice ends' here; this remark was corrupted by those who heard it into its present form. At the small airfield at Coyhaique, I descend the aircraft steps directly into the wind, a wind that has every kind of nuance: it can be either full or wan, or it dabs or sweeps like a paintbrush, it breathes, it propels, it blows, it buffets, it comes panting round corners, it's a dimension all of its own and is truly the breath of nature. It can even flatten flowers in their beds.

Lili is standing in this wind in bright clothes that she's sewn and knitted herself. She wastes no time. Her brief gestures hop over the mountains, while her large eyes take stock of the landscape. This is the old empire of the Tehuelche, the local aboriginal inhabitants, who shared the same fate as the Indians of North America. Drawn into conflict by the colonists and almost entirely wiped out, the survivors were packed into reservations and exposed to the ravages of alcoholism; at best, their memory continues to exist on a folkloristic plane. They left handprints behind on rocks in either red or blue pigment. Sometimes, they would press down with the flat of the hand, and sometimes use their palm as a template and draw around it to leave an outline. In this way, they marked places that they used as lookouts. We latecomers lack their clarity of vision. Night falls, and we retire early.

A Tehuelche doll has also made it onto the mantelpiece of our guesthouse. Peoples die out, and then they get resurrected as souvenirs. The other ornaments above the flickering hearth on which maté tea is brewed each morning, are: two carved drakes, a pair of wooden cut-out fish with drooping mouths swimming above a varnished board, and, beneath these, collections of miniature bottles of spirits, coffee mills, two carved boats containing mineral geodes, a stuffed cockerel and a ram's horn. The house is still shrouded in night and wind, but when Lili comes in from outdoors in her rubber boots, a sliver of morning light also shines in momentarily through the open door, and the howling wind makes the lid of the enamelled teapot rattle as it heats up on the fire.

Today's plan is to take a trip through the town; a small, insubstantial settlement with utilitarian housing, distribution depots, a single main shopping street and a few monuments, all of them several centuries younger than the events they commemorate. There are settlements that are self-sufficient and then there are others that can only be understood by looking at the countryside surrounding them. Coyhaique belongs to the second group.

At lunchtime, we repair to the 'Casino de Bomberos', the fire station canteen, because here, so the rumour goes, they do the best food in the neighbourhood. The place has a wooden floor and wood panelling, from which copper bas-relief panels and landscape paintings look down on tables laid with green and white tablecloths. Everyone who comes into this room seems either to have come straight from the wilderness or to be getting ready to disappear into it once more. The homecomers greet one another, going from table to table dispensing information on the levels of various rivers and the weather conditions in other parts of Patagonia, giving people the latest updates on the state of certain roads, and also imparting news: two people have been killed, one of them drowned because he fell into a whirlpool dressed in clothing that was too heavy, while the other fell over a cliff. Today's menu consists of ugly-looking fish with a mouldy smell served with avocado, and for dessert *conserva* – tinned peaches.

There are three of us at our table. Lili has invited Manuel, a father of three children who's barely thirty years old and who has a perpetually mobile face. As our driver, he starts telling us about the condition of the car and of the 1,500-kilometre route that lies ahead, 1,400 of which will be on dirt tracks; this is his professional persona talking. But in actual fact he's a true romantic, who dreams of love, the sanctity of the natural environment, and humanity, and who expends all his curiosity and intelligence on thinking about these concerns.

Later, I'll get to hear about the great love story that was his marriage, and learn how he and his wife became estranged. Manuel himself fell in love with a mountain guide. But she never came back from a course of study in the USA involving park rangers from several countries. Her body was found washed up on the banks of a river and no one could or would explain exactly what had happened to her.

Meanwhile, though, his wife had also fallen for one of the local rangers. But before the affair really came to anything, he drowned in a river during one of his tours of duty. He had underestimated the strength of the current. So now the husband and wife find themselves forcibly cooped up with one another again, and when they look in each others' eyes all they can see are the remnants of a story that they have no wish to revisit, and both of them make strenuous efforts to shield the children from the knock-on effects of their shattered dreams.

'Stories here are always like that,' Lili says. 'It's the country. Things have a way of panning out dramatically here.'

Her own life bears this out just as forcibly. She was living in Santiago and was nine years old when the military coup was staged in 1973. It was several days, however, before she began to recount what had happened during her childhood:

'There was a curfew then that started at eight in the evening. My little brother and I, we were supposed to pick over lentils and beans until it was time for us to go to sleep. But one day my mother wasn't there at our bedtime, so I took my brother out onto the street to look for her. There were soldiers posted on the top of every high-rise building and they had orders to shoot at anything that moved after curfew, and that included us. But that night we managed to find Mum and get her and ourselves home unscathed. My stepfather had been interned in the football stadium, like so many others. They tortured people there. Every day, we'd ask my mother where he was. Outside the stadium, people would call out the names of their relatives, and you could hear the screams of those who were being inter-rogated. You could smell the blood, too. I was skinny enough to slip through the bars of the pens. So I shimmied through and started calling out my stepfather's name. You had to shout out the name so that everyone knew that there was someone mourning a loss, that at least someone was awake and cared. The torturers couldn't have cared less, but it meant a lot to the victims when their names were called out. I saw all these hopeless wretches, who had resigned themselves to their fate and were wracked with pain. They'd given up. The screams of people being tortured rang unceasingly through the air. I can still picture the mother whose son was torn from her arms; later, she had to listen to his piercing screams from behind a screen. Then the torturer emerged with bloody hands, and the mother kept shouting: "You pigs, you pigs!" And all the time I was going from cell to cell calling out: "Is there an Antonio Cavallos here?" I'll always remember the blank, fearful eyes of the detainees; the looks they gave will be seared on my mind forever. As a child I was so disillusioned with humanity. All that hatred! Those looks horrified me, both those of the torturers and of the tortured.'

'And yet you've still come back to this country, where many of the torturers are still living?'

'I wanted to make my peace with the place. I wanted to change myself so I could change other things around me. Plus I also wanted to start the process right at the source, with animals, with nature. You become more and more part of this earth; I must preserve that and pass it on. I won't even leave so much as an avocado stone behind in nature, so that a tree doesn't grow where it shouldn't. And I make things from Alpaca wool and sell them at the market.'

Her face was constantly etched with worry. Just think how much the Chilean government is spending on reafforestation – but what's it doing? Undertaking all the ecological programmes with non-native trees! These push out the local varieties; for instance, the wild brier has already displaced the Magellan barberry, and even the unassuming little thorny, round-berried Neneo plant is becoming a less common sight.

'That's right: all you see now are rose hips everywhere.'

'We're altering the whole balance of nature. We must protect the eagle, the flamingo, the condor and the ibis. Red deer, rabbits, wild boar, pheasants – they were all imported in the first place, so we could export them again as game meat. Trouble is, these species don't have any natural predators, so they're threatening the survival of indigenous species, and one day the outcome will be completely devastating. I can see the balance changing daily.'

'Maybe the country's too caught up in dealing with the polit- ical Chile of the past, and considers such concerns a luxury?'

'But it's a different Chile nowadays.'

'And is your son part of this new Chile?'

'He's about to become a detective. At first, that was a dreadful thought for me, but then he must do what makes him happy. He's helped me open my eyes to the changes that have taken place. In fact, I now see him as part of the new start. Given that we need a police force, then better that it's made up of people like him.'

Lili lives on a farm. At least, that's what she calls it. But when we arrive there the following day, it turns out to be an adobe house with a corrugated iron roof, just thirty square metres in size and with no electricity. The fridge consists of a small wooden crate outside with fresh air blowing through it. She and her husband are self-sufficient; they slaughter their own animals, make jam, produce goods from felt, and only buy things that they can't possibly make or barter for themselves. Occasionally, they travel for many kilometres just to get hold of a few bottles of beer or some second-hand books from a guesthouse. And even the beer they're planning to brew themselves in future.

Lili's got a pretty face, which her black lashes, eyebrows and hair somehow make look like a bit of graphic design. For a moment, she has an impish expression, but it soon gives way once more to her habitual careworn look, a deep-seated anxiety that focuses in turn on the environment, nature, our route, the weather, food, and sometimes just on life in general.

We set off the next morning, heading away from Chaitén into the depths of the wilderness whose expanses lie north of the much visited southernmost tip of the continent: largely unknown tracts of land in the shadow of that tourist honeypot. We soon get off the beaten track, and I learn to read landscapes.

The topsoil is sparse hereabouts, and the bedrock below roughly volcanic. The towering pyramid-shaped peaks, rock needles, steep table mountains, elegant hills, concretions of blocks and isolated cones succeed one another as though in a steady rhythm, in that dynamism of a landscape which commutes everything into pressure and movement, compression, swerve, momentum and fluidity. The weather, meanwhile, supplies the soundtrack: the Castillo mountain chain has just shrouded its sublime peaks in cloud, as if to protect the dignity of its anonymity.

Makeshift wooden bridges sway above watercourses, and wherever there are poplars, you're sure to find a settlement in their lee, since poplars are grown round these parts primarily as windbreaks. In their shadow, huts and tin shacks defy the great breath of nature, standing there cowed by the land, like they don't want to be any bother. Before the broad horizon, nature left to its own devices stretches into a distance that only desires to be distant, putting up rows of silhouettes just made for distance vision. Everything moves away from the viewer and in an ever-changing way, the landscapes stretch out so as to become backcloths. By contrast, the human being, made small by the sheer superabundance of nature, loses himself in this panorama of the uncommon, of unexploited nature and of a landscape that seems to want to continue on into the sky.

Sometimes, by the side of the track there are little shrines with water bottles in the middle of the wilderness.

'Those,' Lili says sentimentally, 'are votive offerings to Difunta Correa: in the war, she set off across the pampas from Argentina to Chile to show her newborn baby to her husband. The child survived by suckling at her breast, but the mother died of dehydration *en route*.'

And so she is commemorated in a totally secular cult, with people placing water bottles at wayside chapels and bends in the road so that her spirit shall not die of thirst.

Yes, it's still a country where such stories and such heroes abound: They come over the mountains and through the rivers, the gauchos with their neckerchiefs, berets and canvas shoes, their baggy pants and their red sashes. They always carry a knife tucked into their belt, either for the constant animal slaughtering they have to do or to clear stones out of their horses' hooves. Lots of modern gauchos also carry chainsaws. Time was that they would spend weeks driving their cattle to market. Nowadays, though, all they do is ride for a day at most to the nearest store. They are always shrouded in an air of solitude, for whatever it is that they do, they do it alone.

A person can't really conceive of a landscape that is remote even from the dirt tracks hereabouts, the landscape of their homeland on the far side of the mountains. The kind of characters that can bear such solitude, without any distractions such as books or films, are unsociable and immersed in their own world. Sometimes, they'll appear from over the hills with their wives in tow, who like them are of small stature; on such occasions, they'll come striding along in the midst of a gaggle of kids and dogs.

We've been driving for hours when we finally come across the next store, a dismal shed with shelving all round the walls and fruit in woven baskets on the floor. The store owner is perfectly happy for all the farmers from the surrounding region to offer their produce for sale here – provided, that is, that they bring their own price labels with them. As we pull up, a man in a cowboy hat is busy splitting a pumpkin on the floor, while another is unwrapping eggs from a cloth. The shopkeeper tells us that jam, vegetables and cigarettes always fly off the shelves, and the man with the pumpkin says people snap up whatever happens to be in stock at the time, be it mixed pickles in a plastic tub, children's aspirin, spirits or even a mouldy lemon.

Leaving the shop behind, we make our way back to the scrubland on barely visible tracks, crossing a ravine, teetering along trails cut into sheer cliff faces and over rickety bridges, until, in the lunar landscape of a rocky hilltop, a gate suddenly appears, the first man-made object we've seen for many hours. Beyond it, a footpath runs between some rather sparse-looking vegetable plots to a corrugated iron shack with a view over a pond.

You could easily have taken the woman standing in the middle of her garden with her back to us for a sculpture. But in actual fact this embittered forty-year-old woman was the widow María, who had lost her husband to stomach cancer two years before. Ever since, her face has been haunted by an autumnal look.

'Why don't you leave that shack of yours in the back of beyond?' her children and friends had urged her, 'and come and live with us in the village. We'll look after you.'

But the time has long gone when this weather-tanned woman was still capable of living in a flat, in a permanent settlement among other people. No, she has to remain here now, come hell or high water, with her animals, her horse, her vegetable plot and her pond.

Her hooded eyes range about gloomily, unsettled and worried. Nothing is worth resting her gaze on for any length of time. So now she just hangs on, lurking in the wings of her lost love story, living without any company or any electricity. Now and then, a gamekeeper will drop by, or a farm labourer, and tell her what's going on down in the valley or even in the city of Coyhaique.

Sometimes she takes her horse and rides bareback for four hours to go and fetch cigarettes – only to discover that they haven't got any in that day. The stage on which her life is played out is the bleakest setting imaginable, a rocky wasteland constantly embattled by the wind.

María is busy drying onion skins, which she will use to dye her home-knitted woollen clothes. Clutching just a single candle, she wanders through the rooms in her house; the flickering light falls on finished garments, coarse-knit items in green, purple and orange, which she tips out of a plastic bag onto the table. There's a strong smell of soup in the room. Hanging on the washing line in front of the door, secured with two pegs, is a little transistor radio whose aerial is sticking out into the wide blue yonder. Apparently you get the best reception that way, and it needs to be good for local people to send all their important messages: 'Miguel, come home, you're dinner's ready', 'Pick up some beer, would you, Pablo?', 'Carlos, the cow's run off again.' In a place like this where there's no mobile phone reception, CB radio is often the best way for locals to communicate with each other.

Suddenly, though, a blast of Mexican accordion music accompanied by the wail of a maudlin Mariachi singer issues from the transistor radio dangling from the washing line. Presently, the wind will swing round and carry his voice away. The draught inside the shack sets a mobile made from mussel shells jingling. I grope my way through the darkness once more out into the open, where I take a stroll round the foundation wall of the building. It feels like the home of a person who has simply stuck a stick in the ground in the wilderness and erected a property around it.

For instance, within the boundary fence a plot with a kitchen, tiny rooms and turquoise-painted walls has been put up, a living unit that stands pretty much unprotected up on the knoll that rises by the side of the pond. Up there, the wind constantly catches hold of anything that's hanging on the outside wall or is trapped between the roof shingles and makes it rattle, hum, bang, hammer or thunder. It's impossible to try and make sense of the ensuing cacophony, or to try and read each individual sound separately. All you can do is sit round the oven and listen to the wind and its percussion section.

The inhabitants of this area live such an isolated existence that the local authorities had community centres built so that people could meet up and compare notes and create some sort of local network. But the people round here never used them. Since the Pinochet period, when neighbours turned out to be traitors, informants and even torturers, they have become untrusting, shunning all community activities and keeping themselves to themselves.

The widow's got toothache, so she's stuffing her cheeks full of cloves and mentally adding this suffering to all her other woes.

She reckons that someone who's lost her husband shouldn't have to put up with toothache as well. But on the other hand, we've got white wine, we're all together and safe and we're enjoying each other's company. If we have to nip out to use the loo that's behind the vegetable plot, we strap on little head torches to find our way. María's child-sized bathtub, which can just about hold a little puddle of cold water, is matched by her tiny bed, which smells of wet wool, like the inside of the mattress and the bed-spreads have been steeped in it.

We eat all the things that she grows here: beetroot, pota-toes, red cabbage and the leftovers of a home-butchered lamb. Manuel picks up the leg bone and gnaws the last scraps of meat off it.

'My grandfather taught me that you always eat women and lambs with your hands.'

Lila tells María the fairytale of the princess and the pea.

'Hang on, though,' the widow says when she's finished, 'why did she need so many mattresses, was it that cold?'

'No, they wanted to find out whether she was really a princess.'
María doesn't get it.

'So she could still feel the pea?'

'Yes.'

María is happy, and we're all happy. Even on a barren, storm-lashed hill in the middle of nowhere in Patagonia, it seems, a European tale taking the mickey out of the decadence of the rich is still quite intelligible.

María gets by on very little indeed, and there's nothing here to take her out of herself – no TV, no company and no alcohol. If we didn't happen to be there today, she'd just be sitting in the middle of her room in the dark, listening to the wind and watching the wisps of smoke and steam rising up from her cooker and her pot of maté tea.

'Have you got any friends?'

'Oh, everyone wants to have a good friend, but nobody's prepared to be one,' she replies, sidestepping an answer.

On the wall, I discover a page from an old calendar with a picture of Berchtesgaden. From thousands of kilometres away, I find myself looking at the small format landscape of Europe. It makes us, our landscapes, and our mountain panoramas look dinky. By contrast, in Patagonia, individuals are crushed, their hovels are buckled and they are forced to take shelter in the shadow of the mountains, condemned to utter insignificance. Even the roads prefer to follow the rivers; paths that nature has willingly granted to humans, so that they can loiter on the margins of insignificance.

Here, the normal state of affairs is turned on its head, and you learn not to interpret nature in human terms. Anyone who settles here lives under sufferance, protected in their allotted little corner, and spends their time staring into candlelight or a fire. This power that humans have of keeping themselves to themselves, and cultivating an inner life which never leaves them in the lurch and never threatens them, is positively monumental.

'Where are you heading to?' María asks.

'To Chaitén,' I tell her.

'You'll be lucky. Chaitén's off-limits.'

Lili doesn't react, but just keeps staring straight ahead.

'But I've heard that there are still eight people living there.'

'Troublemakers. After the volcano erupted on 2 May last year, the police evacuated the town. They won't let you in. It's dangerous, anyhow. The mountain could blow up again at any moment.'

It's true that after the unexpected volcanic eruption there have been sixty smaller explosions. Ash rained down on the surrounding region and contaminated the water. And then when, a year later, the lava dome inside the crater also collapsed and a new river of fire poured into the sea, the authorities evacuated the last of the inhabitants and warned them not to return.

We talk about killing. Lili mimics the ways fish gasp for air when they've been landed, then the heart-rending cries of young goats, and the ways cows bellow in mourning, sometimes for as long as twenty hours, when they've lost one of their calves.

'It's real torment,' says Manuel, 'but it's got to be done.'

The sadness in the widow's eyes has given way to a look of ferocity. It's a harshness that she unpityingly transposes from her own life to that of the animals.

She tells Lili: when you've castrated an animal, you've got to keep its tail tied back so the wound won't get dirty and infected. Sometimes, the kids will even block the other goats' ears when we're doing slaughtering. But we usually do the castrating with our teeth, it's a kind of quick scraping action that you've got to do out in the open. In the barn, the animals would smash everything to pieces in no time with all their kicking and struggling.

Even though they're generally kind to the animals, the children like cutting off their cocks. When they're roasted in the oven the bristles drop out and you can easily suck out the rest of the flesh. Yes, Lili admits, the first time she'd had to slaughter an animal herself, her hands couldn't stop shaking, whereas now ... Now it's another image entirely that haunts her:

'After you've slaughtered a cow, the others form a circle round the pool of blood and cry. It's awful, it's terrible.'

For sweet, there's jelly that tastes of Gummi-bears. Heaven only knows how that chemical product managed to find its way to this barren hill. Suddenly, everyone starts talking about their childhood, and when that particular reverie is over, María turns the conversation to the childhood of civilizations, and shows us the ancient spearheads that she found buried in the sand. These came from the civilization of the Patagones, she tells us, the 'big-foot' people who once lived and hunted here; they were tall aboriginals who were eventually displaced to Argentina.

'It's a crying shame,' Manuel chips in, 'all you find right across the world are the last remnants of extinct peoples and the descendants of their conquerors ...'

'... and they spend their time manipulating their guilty conscience into folklore.'

We turn in early and feel the poverty like a gift.

As we're leaving at the crack of dawn, the widow stands there at the barred window, transformed into a shadow. She gets ever darker, losing all her colour. If there's such a thing as incarnation, then why not 'inumbration' too? The death of her husband has made her life the way it is: now she's sure it's nothing but an illusion, held together by illusions.

As we journey on that day, scrubby landscapes begin to close in around our route, criss-crossed by milky rivers. At the bottom of pools, the stones arrange themselves into the shape of pumpkin seeds. From the swaps rise the dead trunks of the *Bosque Muerto*, which was left behind as a kind of ghostly wood after an earlier volcanic eruption in 1991. Yellow pancakes of lichen hang down from their naked branches, swaying in the wind. By the side of the track, the next roadside shrine is waiting, this time dedicated to the family of a doctor from Santiago who came to grief here.

It seems that his car careered through the crash barrier; he and his wife were thrown clear of the wreck and died instantly. Their eldest daughter was found further along the road, after wandering for several kilometres in a daze, completely unharmed but with her clothes all torn to shreds. When asked about her younger sister, who was nowhere to be found, all she could say, in a flat emotionless voice, was that angels had abducted her and taken her up to heaven. And indeed, she did seem to have vanished without a trace. Even so, they spent weeks searching for her. The first miraculous stories began to grow about around her – the germ of a cult that was just waiting to blossom forth – when she was finally found forty metres away high up in the crown of a tree.

Later, fire burned the mythical wood to the ground, which – with its charred tree stumps, and the white buds of the first new plants starting to poke through and the fiery-red colour of fuchsias on its fringes – still looks as though the embers of the conflagration are only just dying down.

We follow the marshy path through the Patagonian rain, passing large tracts of remote terrain. The colour of the lakes is tinged with grey, with their shores covered in dense drifts of wild roses laden with rose hips, so large they shine from the branches like plump little tomatoes. Beneath the shadowy walls of the mountain ridges, the banks of cloud glisten like greasy waxed paper. Even the massive looming bulk of the mountains appears to rush down with the speed of river rapids.

The women in this region wear thick woollen pullovers, which reveal no bodily contours. Hunched over, as though they've been bent double by the wind, they stand in the fields, with their skin tanned by all the fresh air and their hair clinging to their skulls like wavy, dark caps. The townspeople occasionally venture out into the more remote parts of this landscape to turn their dogs loose before the long summer holidays begin. Several times, these wretched creatures cross our path, with drooping chops and bloody paws.

We are accompanied on our travels by a pair of plump rainbows, which arc over the northern ice fields against a base of shimmering violet. We gaze up from the shadows at their magnificence. The cold breath of the Sierra Contreras with its dirty glaciers wafts over us and skims the deep turquoise of the mountain lakes, and the waves that its gusty blasts stir up slap against the rock faces like a peal of chuckling. The snowfields are coated with a layer of anthracite-coloured dust.

This is a landscape for people who turn away, away from community and towards solitude, away from settlements and the zone of pleasant pastimes, and games for grown-up children. When all's said and done, there's little to be learned from what these recluses get up to in their isolation, but the breath with which they turned away continues to enliven this distant vista. And yet in this place even the old farmers fear solitude. Their children up sticks and leave, and slowly but surely all the farmsteads around Puerto Bertrand are being sold up, and even the settlers admit:

'We're trying to live here in the face of our homesickness. Most people succumb to it after ten years. But we don't hold with this urge to go home, in fact we don't feel like turning around ever.'

And saying this they strike a defiant pose, fully prepared to take preventative measures to disenfranchise themselves if they should ever feel tempted to think otherwise. So what they're all hoping for is a tourist boom. But the trickle of visitors who do make it as far as here hardly bring in any money, so in the meantime, the locals spend their time building up the infrastructure in anticipation of the great influx. But every cinder track you set off on hereabouts, you find yourself simply turning round on and driving all the way back. Roads just stop in the middle of nowhere, and where they end they just dwindle to a path that runs behind a hut and then fizzles out in the undergrowth at the foot of the Andes.

The little settlements here are places of refuge and retreat, where communities grow up, and in whose midst one day the urge to find new places of refuge will be born. Also, because the air is so clear, all colours appear vibrant. The wind tugs on Tibetan prayer flags on the line, while, in front, smoke streams horizontally from the chimney pots. Each of the oval wooden signs conveys a painted promise: a lovely view, a soft bed, a warm oven. In one of these living rooms, I sat and wolfed down so many of those fried eggs done in oil with their marsh-marigold-yellow yolks that even several days later I could still feel the nausea well up in me in great waves and then abate again. Suddenly, the silence is abruptly shattered by the roar of chainsaws. The clearings are eating ever further into the wilderness – all for the future of a country that only blossoms for a few months a year.

At the end of the long process of subjugating nature, it was inevitable that such a phenomenon would arise: a love of dominant landscapes on the part of travellers. Nowadays, they like seeing nature in a state where it is not yet lost. All they do is visit it, and gaze upon its rebelliousness with respect, but also with indulgence. People still settle here humbly, defensively, and dissemble about their own hazardousness – like the wild rose, or the fox or the hare. These all bring with them into this piece of the natural world the principle of infiltration and of hostile takeover.

But the traveller enjoys the landscape so long as it doesn't look subdued. He marvels at it, as though marvelling at his own pre-civilized past in it. But in that very moment, it has already capitulated. The talk has long since been of these 'lost paradises', and this is said in an elegiac tone, from a posthumous perspective.

The rain spatters in the trees, making a humming and sighing sound. Now and then, the sun sends a fleeting ray through the leaves, turning the tropical shower first glassy, then invisible. Yet its drops still speckle the blades of grass, and because it is so still, all they do is yield to this incessant dripping. As life reawakens outside, all of a sudden you can hear dogs barking, a chainsaw howling, the chugging of a tractor being started, the owner of the neighbouring plot chopping wood, and the shingles creaking as they dry. Nothing but the sounds that are constant here.

Further on, the sometimes barely passable track, interrupted by large fallen boulders and streams, leads us into a riverine landscape such as you find on the Malay Archipelago, with swarms of parrots, catalpa trees, the red calyxes of hibiscus flowers, and livid green mosses – the landscape of Tortel. The rain spatters millions of tiny craters into the sluggish broth of the river. The steps are stairways hewn directly into the cliff face.

Thickset melancholics with the faces of heavy drinkers wait, with their chainsaws resting on their shoulders, under a shelter. Shy women with lady-sized chainsaws creep past on the board-walks. With their trousers rolled up at half-mast, they deftly saw the firewood up into manageable chunks. The whole area here seems to pine for a bygone era when the loggers did not climb down from the rocky plateau, but arrived here by travel-ling upstream on the river in ships and boats, and then had to disembark at the point where the gorges became narrow and impassable.

Here, at the end of one such gorge, where the row upon row of wooden huts climb up the slope, one on top of the other, here is where the stranded loggers of old fetched up, and the axe was king. The world was far away, and travellers only rarely found their way to this remote corner. Now, though, there's a road which runs from up on the plateau down to the outskirts of the settlement, and the village is busy getting itself ready to receive the world. Soon, it will become too expensive, too loud, and too squalid, and the sense that when you arrive here you could be at the ends of the earth will only have a very limited shelf life.

Yet while this process is still in train, this little tropical spot will briefly have dreamed the same dream that Las Vegas once did. After all, isn't the river a marvellous grey-green colour and almost motionless? And don't the colours on the slope radiate with the intensity of Bengal fire, with the different fuchsia-reds, brick-reds, hibiscus-reds, and redwood-reds of the freshly felled and rain-drenched tree trunks, and the blue of the bonfire smoke? You can't move an inch here without being accompa-nied by soggy, grubby dogs, who needily and dozily dog peo-ple's every footstep. The rain will grow more intense over the next few days, boulders will be washed down onto the dirt roads and make them finally impassable, and even the armadillos will cower down deep in the roadside ditches, when they can no longer find the entrance to their burrows in trenches that have filled with mud.

Now the only perceptible movement is the veil of rain falling through the still air. It scarifies the atmosphere like etched cross-hatching in a piece of glass. Everything pauses and endures. The bulrushes stand tall and wait, the dead trees rise up from the ashy ground, which now takes on a deeper black hue as the smooth trunks look even more glistening. Many people lift their eyes to the heavens to study a patch of sky. If it keeps on raining for a long while, the sheep will be bound to die. Their wool will become saturated and heavy and they won't be able to find shelter or warmth anywhere. They'll either freeze to death or waste away from infections brought on by the cold.

The thinnest clouds billow up between the precipices. Higher still, the snowfields merge like pieces of a jigsaw puzzle into the clouds that shroud the mountain tops.

By the end of the third night, the rain finally gives out. Throughout the entire day, the sun evaporates moisture up from the road. A mist hangs over the asphalt, and a haze covers the dirt track. 'We're selling the tranquillity of the South,' proclaims a hand-painted banner.

We read this notice on the road in the mood that comes over us after the rain. That same evening, we run across it again when we have reached the steppe, the dry steppe, which is exhaling even though no rain has fallen here for a long time. The ground here is comprised of a slightly springy layer of steppeland grass, and yields under our footfall. We're walking here on the surface of a dried-out lakebed, and its craquelured mud trembles like cork, and is covered with the impressions of countless foot-prints. In a few places, muddy pools have formed, while others have piles of bones that have been dragged here and left.

Sometimes the air is filled with the bleating of a guanaco, and sometimes with the twittering of some small songbird. But occasionally, we come across a guanaco that's been torn to shreds by a puma. Mountain lions love hunting down these llama-like creatures; for them, the chase is the real thrill, as after just a couple of mouthfuls, the puma will often leave the rest of its prey to the vultures. And indeed, as a flock of vultures feeds on one of these carcasses, a single beam of sunlight shines down from beneath a dark wall of cloud, brightly illuminating this dead sea. It's the light of God, flipping open its fan, and it also briefly lights up the grassy slopes of the steep natural amphitheatre all around, before the cold evening descends, filled with the hollow whistle of the wind.

Overnight, winter has arrived. Snow has dusted even the lower cliffs, and now there's a thin layer of hoar-frost on the rounded, wooded hilltops, too. Even so, the power of the sun is still irrepressible, and where the fat, green flowing glacier squeezes itself between the massifs, you can hear the melt water steadily dripping. Where it falls from the glacier's icy fringes to collect in a black stone basin, the pool it forms is large enough for you to paddle a canoe in. You can get right up close to the glacier by venturing out on the lake produced by the melt water. Rivulets of bottle-green and milky water run-off it into the fjord.

When, after travelling for a long while, we finally reach the elbow of the fjord, we find ourselves once more in a settlement of former Sudeten Germans. The first house we come to on the square is the Hotel Ludwig, while the *Avenida* leading off the square is called Otto-Uebel-Straße. Hawks are perched on the town rubbish dumps, all around are small wooden huts that look like they were put up by Quakers, and porpoises leap from the water in the fjord. The water gives off a smell of seaweed and reeds, and the surrounding meadows are an aggressive green colour. From every chimney stack, a small plume of blue smoke drifts up into a cold sky. Bits of rotten wood are lying around all over the place, and out of the briars peeks a fantastic doll's house petrol station, with four pumps of 1950s design.

In the evening, a fire is lit in the lounge of the Hotel Ludwig. It's an imposing, solid German wooden house, full of features that are familiar from the Alps. The hotel library is full of German books by Freud, Jung and Kafka, and Mozart's clarinet concerto is playing. The spirit of exile here is tinged with a gentle melancholy, as the proprietress sits in this faraway land and thinks back on the happy times she spent in German meadows. Only the kitchen help has laid her head on her crossed arms, and dozed off, there and then.

The following day, we enter a gigantic *arroyo*, an area that is strewn with driftwood and boulder fields. The crystals of the volcanic soil here glisten in the sand; all around us are uprooted and dead bushes, and stumps of vegetation from whose hearts bamboo canes are shooting. The tracks of pumas and red deer are evident in the sand between the wrinkled rocks that look as though they are pockmarked.

A couple of hours further on by car, we catch our first glimpse in the distance of the metalled road once more, and as we turn a corner, the landscape unfolds before us like a woman throwing back the bedclothes. But the anticipated beauty turns out to be an illusion, as this region is reputed to be haunted, and at the bridge that arches over the river ahead of us the ghost of a dead woman is said to appear regularly in her wedding dress.

A chapel has been hewn out of the rock face beside the bridge, forming a moss-covered cave. Lanterns are set into its rear wall of bare rock, and people have deposited little prayer slips, along with photos of cars that have been involved in accidents and snaps of smiling spouses who have been snatched from these happy moments by death. The tears of wax dripping from the lanterns have spattered down over everything, including a pair of pink woollen baby bootees, a plastic sword and a dummy. The smell of sheep pervades the air, as the animals take refuge in here at night.

'Thank you for protecting me,' says a note in felt-tip pen affixed to the Madonna. 'I have to find out where my wife is,' begs another. 'I forgive her. Please help me find her. I want you to grant us a life together.' And: 'I have been lost for days. For several days now, I have been longing to be the person I once was: happy, contented and so on.' The writer of this last note has added a bunch of artificial flowers, wrapped in cellophane. Manuel tells us that the supplicants even come here from across the border, in neighbouring Argentina, in order to make votive offerings to the 'Madonna of the Cascade', and to pray to her. One note simply reads: 'Virgin Mary, I don't know you, but I've heard that you are a good person. Please take care of my son, who has to go away.'

As if it wasn't dark enough already, this gloomy cave has recently been made even darker by a mysterious, still unexplained, story: in the space of a single month, no fewer than eleven teenagers have been found dead under the bridge here, one after the other. All eleven were good-looking, and all of them allegedly mixed up in drugs or the sex trade, and all of them supposedly committed suicide. What's more, several local mayors were said to be implicated in the whole business. And all of this right under the nose of the Madonna of the Cascade!

The mayors put the teenagers' suicides down to depression, which is not uncommon round these parts because of the appalling weather. But who would believe them? Who'd be inclined to solve the mystery, and ultimately who round here wouldn't find the intrigue surrounding the affair much more fertile and poetic?

'What did I tell you?' repeated Lili, 'stories tend to take a dramatic turn here in Patagonia.'

Dramas like this are sleepers. For any given situation that arises, tension can mount and come to a head. Where everything happens in the midst of such solitude, events are few and far between but extraordinary. You can see them in the distance, and then rumours take hold of them and carry them off, and in the twinkling of an eye, they have entered into the popular history of this barren region.

We are travelling across the fault lines of this history, shaken by the seismic shocks emerging from the inner life of the past. Not far from the dark pilgrimage bridge, we come across the last genuine supermarket at the end of the world. It's frequented by gauchos, and they really can find everything they need here: telescopic sights, guns, alcohol, kids' tricycles, nappies, pills, fertilizer, rotting fruit, American muesli, sweaty cheese, and fresh cream horns. The women here stand around the aisles looking stunned. They've got oval faces and no chins, and they have the muscular shoulders of female wrestlers and a clear-sighted, straight-shooting expression on their faces.

Behind the supermarket, the toilet at the end of the world smells of the End of Days, too.

'And the toilet roll,' I tell Lili, 'only had a single sheet of paper left on it.'

'That's laying it on a bit thick for the end of the world, isn't it?'

'Fair enough. In actual fact, there wasn't any paper at all left on the roll.'

We're in Cochrane, a substantial settlement, on whose streets people arriving out of the surrounding wilderness wander around like strays, homeless characters, leading their horses behind them. Round a beige-coloured house laid out like a compound, there's a high wall topped with barbed wire – this is the regional, correction, the provincial gaol. We're intrigued to find out how the authorities make offenders feel the loss of their liberty in a completely dead-end place like this.

The guard at the gate treats us like some unexpected task, but spotting in us an opportunity for advancement, the man solemnly promises to put in a good word for Lili and me with his superior. We wait, and in due course we're granted an audience.

The brawny commandant in his stiff, padded uniform that accentuates his stockiness is only twenty-four years old, but already sports a star on his epaulettes. The recent wedding photo of him and his wife has pride of place on his desk, and he sits enthroned on his chair. In the photo, his wife is blond and smiling. But on the wall behind the desk, the female chief of police watches over the room from a larger frame. Austere and thin-lipped, she gazes down from her photo onto the wedding photo. In a glass case, there are also several cups, won for fly-fishing and six-a-side football. We engage in a conversation, the most remarkable aspect of which is that it is such a free and easy chat, a genuine dialogue including little snapshots from our family and professional lives. Just three people playing variations on a single theme entitled: Look, I'm just a regular guy when all's said and done.

The commandant leads us through the double security doors, showing us first the cells housing the trustee prisoners, with three bunks, a television constantly on, and a bath towel with a pin-up girl printed on it. The corridor outside houses the windowless solitary confinement cell, with just a single bed in it. For serious misconduct, a prisoner can be kept in here for a maximum of ten days; during that time, he's permitted just one hour's recreation a day out in the courtyard. The prisoner in the next-door cell is leaning out of the window with his top off; he listens in on our conversation and then calls out:

'And when our women come here, a cell's prepared specially for conjugal visits.'

The tiny courtyard is scarcely more than a gap between the cell blocks. Out there, a prisoner with the dull, fixated look of a simpleton is doing clean-and-jerk weightlifting with a dumbbell made from an iron bar with two buckets of concrete set on the ends, back and forth, from the ground to his chest and back down again. All the bodybuilding equipment out in the yard is home-made kit like this, created from tin cans, metal poles and cement castings.

Most of the thirteen prisoners housed in the gaol are in here for crimes like rape, GBH, criminal damage, drunkenness or even just public disorder – in any event, nothing with fatal consequences. They all have either evil, dull, neutral or disillusioned

expressions, indeed, sometimes their faces appear more criminal than the crimes they've been convicted of, or they look like
they've only taken on the appropriate physiognomy after being
banged up. One little crook clearly wants to come across like Al
Capone. There are eighteen warders employed to guard them
and minister to their needs.

The prisoners also run a little joinery workshop, where they
do repairs for local people, fixing up broken chairs or gluing
cabinets. Right now, though, it's a rocking horse that's propped
up on the workbench; once it's been restored, it'll find its way
into some nursery room. It has a similarly poetic feel to it as the
other work they're doing at the moment – little plaques with
verses carved into them. Laughing, the commandant points out
a prisoner who's in for GBH and now spends his time engrav-
ing simple aphorisms, metaphors or moral maxims, painted up
in naïve, sentimental colours; all imparting homilies that he
transgressed against.

Next door, there's a workshop for processing animal hides.
There, a piece of tanned goatskin is in the process of being
transformed into a cushion cover, while the finishing touches
are being put to riding tack and harnesses, and a sheepskin
bedside carpet has just been completed. Off to one side of the
workshop, a prisoner is engrossed in plaiting a leather bullwhip.
After I've spent some time observing him, he suddenly holds
it up surprisingly high above his head and says, laughing, 'the
symbol of the state's power'.

The inmates are permitted to have their wares sold at the
local market and keep the small profits that accrue. It's cool in
this room, but the prisoners clearly don't notice this, especially
because they're also well aware that nothing concerning them

can be expensive. Accordingly, everything's very low-key, and the heating is only allowed to come on after five o'clock in the afternoon.

There's a French film about criminals where one gangster offers the opinion: 'In life, there are doers and spectators. The problems are always caused by the spectators.' Where the convicts are concerned, this apportioning of roles hasn't changed even though they're in prison. They continue to be the movers and shakers, whereas the guards are the spectators. So the warders stand around, with their cudgels and their sabres on their belts, but at least they don't have revolvers. They drink maté tea with the prisoners, chat with them about the football results, and occasionally it will even be the case that one of the prisoners will interrupt the warders or even the commandant while they're talking.

They all rub along with the conditions here: the cold, the confined spaces, the workshops and the communal rooms, and the warders even eat food that's been prepared by the prisoners. One time, the commandant tells us, the prisoners came to him and asked him whether they could grow salad leaves and lettuces and some other vegetable on the narrow external fire escapes.

'I told them I'd turn a blind eye if they did.'

For all his youth, the commandant knows the appropriate junctures at which to break the rules, and so now he spends his time looking approvingly at the lush salad crop that he can't officially see.

He also shows us the prison's sick bay, with its two beds, and the room where prisoners' lawyers can meet them, with its concealed panic button on the wall, and the booth where he holds his regular Friday meetings with prisoners, taking down their complaints in writing:

'That means that I can't then go and do the dirty on them.'

Outside, the warders are liaising on walkie-talkies. The prisoners listen in with sad faces. The chain of communication between the prison staff is one of the chains binding them.

When we're out on the street once more, Lili stretches out her hand in front of her. She makes no attempt to disguise the fact that she's trembling, and now she turns to me and says, half tearfully:

'It really does still exist then, the good Chile! Now I'm sure it does. I'm so happy. My son's due to join the police force. It was always so hard for me to accept that. But I know that it doesn't have to be like how I remember the country in the past, it can be different now. Take this young commandant, for instance. He was so friendly. He's got a difficult job, too. Just think about the young wife he's just married. She's given up everything to come and live with him here.'

She's talking and looking down as she walks along, her eyes fixed on the pavement.

'Did you hear? They interrupt him. They're even free to contradict him. That's a good man.'

He could be her son, the way she's talking.

I wonder if the young commandant knows that he's just changed a person's life? A solitary visit, a single encounter, and suddenly Lili's perspective on her country has altered; for the first time, she's started to refer to it as 'my country'.

A small rodeo show has set up shop by the side of the street, and a bit further on sits Carancho, the vulture, while on the fence close by a black eagle is watching him. They've killed a small rabbit, first plucking out its eyes and then dragging out its entrails, which are shimmering red with fresh blood, and spreading them out. Up in the trees, the other carrion birds hold a chattering conference. The ghost of a smile still plays on Lili's face.

'Come on then,' she says, and the tone of her voice is suffused with euphoria, 'let's try and get into Chaitén after all! Maybe we'll have some more good luck with the authorities.'

When the volcano erupted in 2008, the coastal settlement of Chaitén, the gateway to Patagonia, had to be evacuated for the most part. Half a metre of ash rained down on the town and the sea rose in a high tide of filth, sweeping away all the possessions of the people who lived along the shoreline, and all the while the volcano kept smoking so violently that even now nobody wants to live anywhere in the vicinity.

Before the eruption, this was where the large cruise liners bringing tourists to Patagonia called. A small holiday industry had grown up, with guest houses and hotels along the promenade, a school, a hospital, and parks, through which pumas would roam at night. The few people who still live in the dead town now have simply refused to leave their homes, believing neither the authorities nor the geologists, who are predicting an even larger eruption anytime soon, which will completely obliterate the surrounding region.

The thick drifts of dust on both sides of the road are the first indication that we are approaching the site of the catastrophe. The guards have set up their post in an abandoned school four kilometres from the mountain. Uniformed men in high-vis jackets are hanging around a barrier across the road; their caps are emblazoned with an emblem showing two crossed rifles.

At the checkpoint just outside the exclusion zone, there are two policemen on duty, who demand to see our passports and ask the reason for our visit. They're negotiating. The fact that we've come from a long way away, that we don't plan on taking any photographs, that two natives of this region are in the car, and that nobody's requested access in ages – all this seems to improve our chances of being allowed to visit the ghost town.

While they're deliberating, our eyes are fixed on the one cloud in the sky that's not drifting by; the heavy cloud which steadily ascends into the heavens, pushing upwards into the bank of normal cloud. This has a quite different source, in the magma, in the earth's core. It keeps billowing over the snow-capped ridge of the Andes as though it's feeding on itself, like an autonomous, solitary creature that has no natural predators and is beyond any correction, and which no weather can extinguish or blow away. Perhaps it's just out of a sense of respect in the presence of the volcano, but in any event the officers wave us through the barrier with their faces averted.

We enter the exclusion zone by driving over the Puente Amarillo. A plane crash-landed here forty-five years ago. The wreckage was never cleared away, and for the last fifteen years a hippy has been living in the fuselage. But now there's no sign of him, only the smell of eucalyptus and sulphur and the sight of fruit trees left unharvested. The traffic signs point to nowhere and washing is still hanging on lines; it's taken on the colour of the dust that's settled all around.

We carry straight on up to the ridge of the Andes, heading towards the rock face through the grey veil of the abandoned fields. It looks for all the world like a great gust of bad breath has passed over the orchards here. The ground is covered with large, floppy, scorched leaves, and a thick layer of ash covers even the tables outside the abandoned houses. The only thing that has cheerfully revived is the robust green of the meadows.

The settlement is lying beneath a powdery shroud, but one which has solidified. The piles of ash that have been shovelled up have hardened, and the buildings have been left to their fate. Even recently-built houses are ageing fast under the grey veil. Fallen apples are rolling round the street, yellow water collects in the puddles, and the school, the monuments and the playground have all become spaces without a function, which mean nothing anymore but merely signify something. On the playground, the memorial with the frozen images of life carved into its stone surface now comes across as a mockery of the current situation: fishermen are shown fishing, while farmers till the fields. But the pathos of the religious figures of salvation flanking the monument pales when set against the sublime misery of the actual scene here. 'Chaitén ne morirá' – 'Chaitén will not die', someone has scrawled on this monument in a dead town, and they've written the same message with their finger in the dust on the windowpanes of the abandoned houses.

Sometimes, there are deep drifts of ash even inside the houses. In one home, it has covered the cups and filled the plates left on the breakfast table. By the side of the road, some cars that have been dug out of the ash stand waiting to be cannibalized for spare parts. A Mercedes with an invitingly open bonnet has already lost some components from its engine, despite the fact that a police car patrols the area regularly specifically to prevent looting. Two men heave a fridge onto the bed of a pickup truck, but, as far as we can see, they are the only human beings for miles around. One of them comes up to us and complains about the volcano, the government, the vandals and God, and all the while he's talking, the mountain rumbles threateningly beyond the foothills. It's omnipresent and unchanging, and yet in the sky, nothing changes so fast as the column of smoke rising over this running sore that reaches down into the bowels of the earth.

An empty billy-can rattles across the road, a pile of crockery lies smashed on the asphalt, and paw prints lead up to it through the dust. The walls are painted with garish graffiti from the post-eruption period, and yet the war memorial nearby, with its crossed guns, continues to admonish: 'Siempre viven los por la patria mueren' – 'Those who die for their country shall live forever' – a permanent homage to all those who laid down their lives for the fatherland. But it comes across as fey, now that the volcanic ash has also blanketed the history of conflict.

There's an unhealthy smell coming from the sewers, and the signs reading 'The State is Watching!' are everywhere – which evidently wasn't the case, as quite a few former inhabitants of the region have, in the interim, grown rich on the compensation they've claimed.

The traffic signs showing a woman leading a child by the hand and children crossing the road are still in place, too. Now empty warnings, devoid of meaning. A few of the houses have only been half-destroyed by the tide of volcanic ash; they stand there with their skeleton on show, revealing small bookshelves with piles of cheap novels that have tumbled to the ground. Even the sea has receded into the zone behind the embankment, where a solitary house has been picked up and carried almost to the fringe of the surf. It lies there, keeled over on its side, beyond a broad strip of some sulphurous sludge, which is seeping out onto the dirty beach and collecting in pools, and on whose periphery a cooker and a fridge have been washed up. Mattresses are piled up on the bank leading down to the foreshore, and household items are strewn all around like after an explosion. It's only on the horizon that a narrow green strip of open, clear and unpolluted water appears.

The bridge has collapsed as well. The charming façade of the Cabañas Brisa del Mar with a view of the promenade puts you in mind of a self-indulgent life of bathing, of tea with cream and sun hats. Yet the surrounding area is so completely smothered with ash that it's much harder to envisage it restored to good order than to imagine nature simply reclaiming all this.

The small restaurants still have their special dishes chalked up on their frontages, the Hospedaje Astoria is empty, the dusty shop window of the Farmacia Austral gapes at you, a board promotes 'Turismo Rural', and the church proudly announces its name: La Iglesia de Jesuschristo de los Santos de los Ultimos Dios. Hortensia bushes are growing unnaturally profusely, and in between the twitter of birdsong, the silence is complete.

This is where the road begins, which up until the eruption marked the northern gateway to Patagonia. Previously, it linked the harbour with the interior, and as a result was well maintained. Now, three horses and a foal are the only *flâneurs* strolling elegantly along the empty promenade where the road meets the sea. Now and then they stop, look out over the sea, bend down to crop a few tufts of poisonous-green grass from the verge before moving off again. Horses have even taken over the dwellings here and, however surreal it may seem, make themselves comfortable in sitting rooms. They can still find things to eat all over the place, and the police leave them be. Animal rights campaigners have left behind protest messages on some of the house walls: 'You've scarpered, leaving your dogs and cats behind. Shame on you!' The evacuation programme didn't include animals.

Finally, on the harbour breakwater, we run across two hitch-hikers who've managed to make it here, and who are waiting for the large cruise liner that used to bring tourists. But it'll never come.

The hiss of the distant surf forms a steady background to the crunch of our feet on the pebbly beach. Set amid grey-tinged lawns is the hospital with its lime-green barrack blocks and its doors all flung wide open. The volcanic ash has also perme-ated here, covering the corridors and the beds and even the two operating tables, but in the courtyard a few Israeli hitchhikers have pitched their tents and are singing hiking songs. As they do so, high above them the vultures are circling.

That's right, even months after the catastrophe, there are still vultures over the town. They swoop down in wide arcs and strip animal carcasses of their flesh in the drainage ditches, or burst open the bloated stomach of a dog that's lying dead outside a latrine. By and by, though, even a handful of stubborn locals have put in an appearance. Two of them are digging in the cemetery with shovels. When an old man comes by, trun-dling along a wheelbarrow containing something covered with a sheet that we're not meant to see, they nod conspiratorially at him. Another keeps intoning the same phrase:

'*Una tortura, una tortura!*'

Yes, it really is a torment to be uprooted and displaced, and a catastrophe to see your own home swallowed by the natural disaster. But an elderly man whom we find sitting, leaning on his stick, above the eroded bay tells us that all nature's doing here is settling a score, because it was the only way it could respond to what humanity had been doing.

In the midst of this destruction, he'd found his niche as a prophet of the town's downfall, and he's determined to remain so even now it's weathered the disaster. For who can say with any certainty, while life hits the 'Pause' button, that somewhere out there evil isn't simply regaining its strength and the next disaster just waiting to strike? The sun is shining, the larks are singing, and the sea air is just a gentle breeze. Let other places at the ends of the earth stretch out helplessly towards oblivion, that's not the case here. Here the landscape is basking in an idyll of decline.

Timbuktu

The Boy Indigo

There it lies, the land of the Sahara with its layers of scurf in yellow, light pink, blood-red; its settlements penned in, surrounded by some kind of nature which could at any moment dispatch dangers out of sparse woodlands, low-lying mountains or arid plains, while the Niger flows broad and dour, populated in one of its luxuriously wide basins by little islands with postage-stamp fields on them. Then come the marshes, and after them the broad flat expanses containing nothing, and then the hut of a recluse – but what has he withdrawn from, and to where? Has he gone into quarantine, say? Then you encounter small oases with clay buildings made from adobe-bricks grouped around a yellow pool. Yes, that's how it keeps growing stronger, this overwhelming superiority of landscape, which isn't exactly beautiful, but rather comes across like weather-beaten skin, like a person's well lived-in face.

You won't find any modern physiognomy hereabouts. People here have the facial features of ancient prophets or idols, with their light grey eyes surrounded by a watery corona, and even the river isn't blue or green, but rather flows in a greenish-yellow stream between banks that look like chapped and calloused skin. The fields are dusty, and the huts the colour of dust, while the ground appears scuffed and eroded because here the elements – the sun, the heavily pattering tropical rain, the heat, the desert wind and the sandstorms that arise in the summer months – degrade everything. Sometimes the water in the pools stagnates, and sometimes it's evaporated by the sun so that only caked, baked mudflats remain.

The life cycle here is a swift affair; an abrupt blossoming, a speedy wilting sweep over the depressions of the desert floor: everything is in a state of meander – the ridges of the sand dunes, the overflow channels by the river, the margins of the fields, the bright sandbanks and the roads, all on a colour scale that has dirt as its basic shade.

Time and again, the Niger, a delta comprising countless rivulets, individual watercourses, streams, channels and outlet bays, becomes a line of demarcation between wetlands and the red desert. And then its influence suddenly wanes again, and it carries the green of its banks just a few metres inland at best. Places like desert cemeteries line its route. They appear like an irritation of the proper order of things, a wrinkle, or like fossil imprints in the sand. The airport at Timbuktu is guarded by five soldiers holding their guns at the ready. We're meant to crouch down and make a dash, flanked on both sides by the military, for the terminal building.

Timbuktu is surrounded by a ring of woes, a ring of heat, of deprivation, of thirst, and of war, and if all that weren't enough, there are also signs that the city's dying from within, degenerating, wasting away. Its symptoms are in evidence everywhere: all-but-extinct nomadic peoples encamped in their rags in the shade of adobe-brick walls, lines of peasant women at poor markets, each of them offering for sale three fruits, three tubers and a small bundle of vegetables. On the fringes of the markets are scavengers, and ill and mentally disturbed people roaming free, and the war wounded hobbling about on homemade crutches or wheeling themselves along on little trollies.

But here, in this legendary location, in the midst of all this desolation, indigo is traded. It's as if this blue is the colour of this city's lifeblood, and even its inhabitants seem blue-skinned. Why don't they get away from this place? Elsewhere they'd find water, healthcare, support, security. But to get there means crossing the desert, running the gauntlet of heat, massacres and ambush – in effect, making your way through an inferno with yourself as the live quarry.

Dog-tired, we stumble into a hotel room flooded with the grubby light of dawn. We're too exhausted even to think straight. Just dumb observers, we take in the whitewashed walls, the rugs and the room decoration. On the wall there's a picture of a bamboo hut, with a couple of half-naked natives squatting in front of it like in one of those casually racist old travel documentaries. It's an instant snapshot, whose subjects weren't seeking to attract the world's attention. Look, the image seems to proclaim, here are a few Blacks we've caught on film. Apart from this, there's no other decoration in the room.

Timbuktu, this city in the Southern Sahara that's steeped in myth and which lies at the point where the Niger Delta and the Sahara meet, was once a politically important centre of learning, inhabited by scholars. Founded in the twelfth century, the town, as the seat of Qur'anic scholars and philosophers, played a key role in spreading Islam across Africa. It was also a vital trading post, with the continent's gold being ferried here across the Niger, as well as a transport hub. Even nowadays, the caravan routes still fan out from here to the oases in the North;

latterly they have been joined by the routes taken by migrants fleeing their homelands and heading for Europe.

Anna shucks off her blue and red African batik-pattern dress and, wearing just her pants, flakes out on the hard bed, which is covered with a stiff, coarse-weave throw. Her entire body – her stomach, legs, shoulders, and arms – is glistening with beads of sweat. She doesn't move a muscle and yet still her skin keeps on perspiring frantically.

I take a look inside the bedside table, which has been occupied by a colony of ants, before stepping out onto the balcony and gazing down at the lazy pool. Two figures are moving around in it, a woman in a black bathing suit and a little girl who's holding the woman's hand as she wades through the murky water. Then the mother starts swimming on her back, watching her own splashing feet as she moves along. Her thrashing, trampling and trembling motions look like nothing so much as some kind of clumsy yet erotic choreography. Idly, I imagine a man grasping hold of her and making love to her. Meanwhile, Anna's dozed off; in temperatures like this, sex seems a far-off prospect.

Timbuktu is sand, sand first and foremost, everything sinks into the sand, is made of sand, or takes on the colour of sand, and even its smell. The sand reflects back the sun's heat, and the sand reclaims the city like it's destined to return to sand. The only object that's clearly exempted from this general decay is the bronze plaque on the façade of a building reading: 'Former home of the African explorer Heinrich Barth. German president Heinrich Lübke visited this house in 1956.'

This will endure.

Deep in contemplation, holy men wander through the streets with the *muthala* root clenched between their teeth, the chewing stick which, with its natural antibacterial plant extracts, still plays a major role in dental hygiene in Africa. In a rear courtyard we watch men breaking rocks. The dust this produces is mixed into food for pregnant women as a nutritional supplement. Pissing men stand, their legs akimbo, on the riverbank or the hillsides. On griddles, bananas are transformed into something that tastes like chestnuts. The town's cinema is nothing but a chilly garage with a few loose wooden benches and a U-matic projector. When a crudely animated trick snake appears on the screen, a woman in front of me leaps up screaming and jumps back two rows.

The bald, gold-chained, short-trousered, gay French hotelier is standing with his arms folded across his chest and is berating his simple-minded bellboy, a lad with a dull-witted, prematurely aged face. The owner is telling the boy to make sure the shutters on the hotel's windows are closed before ten in the morning, to shut out the heat, and to get a new mosquito net and hang it without delay. The lad just stands there defiantly; the boss is getting nowhere with his orders. The next thing the bellboy's supposed to do is to go and get some provisions in. The owner stands there, pleading and wheedling with his employee in a high-pitched whine like a woman mourner, but the boy just stares at him with undisguised contempt. Realizing that he can't penetrate through to the boy's consciousness, the boss suddenly grabs him by the collar, forcing him to make a slight bow. The lad looks up at him angrily, and makes out like the owner's hurting him, squealing like a rat in a pile of garbage. Finally, the owner offers him his bicycle to go and run the errand, telling him 'it's better than the minister's!' The bellboy just scoffs at this. Their argument tails off.

Two gold merchants come into the hotel, VIPs in slippers, simply but well clothed, and with an air of great gravitas. They disappear behind a door into a room. The air-conditioning drowns out the low murmur of voices as they conduct their transactions.

News travels fast round these parts. That evening, a succession of men turn up in the hotel courtyard to try and do business with us as they've supposedly heard that we were asking about this or that item, or how far away something was, or some hotel or other, or some mode of transport. So it is that a whole string of them appear and sit at our table: a man selling silver crosses from various clans (he's heard that I purchased a neck chain for Anna); a lad with cassette tapes, who I bought a couple from the day before, and who's now replenished his stock; a guy who's quit the local taxi syndicate and set up on his own, and who calls our attempt to get to Bobo Dioulasso under our own steam 'cheating'. He starts haggling, offering us prices the like of which we'd never get from the syndicate, but undermines his own negotiating position by drinking like a fish the whole time. Before long, he's completely drunk and is becoming quite abusive.

No sooner have we got rid of him than an oriental carpet salesman finishes his prayers and comes over to warn us about the crazy taxi driver.

'You'd be better off investing your fare in a rug.'

Okay, the carpet he has with him isn't a flying one but, the man tells us, it can be unrolled. And so it is duly unrolled. The next one, a disc jockey, assures us that he doesn't want to sell us anything, but he still has 'sales representative' on his card. And by and by his entourage turn up in the courtyard, variously offering us Tuareg jewellery, postcards and dried fruit. They're all dismayed to find so few foreigners in the hotel.

'*Monsieur, moins cher!*'; 'Monsieur, half price!'

The Western separation of work and leisure, of earning money and recreation, doesn't apply here. You just spread out a cloth on the pavement and start selling your wares. Everyone's a family member, it's all family business. Talking about games, laughing, exchanging money, hounding tourists: it's all one, along with buttonholing someone and recounting stories while stringing pearls. These are all just formulaic ways of attaining a state, so to speak, which constitutes work but at the same time transcends work – and in reaching this state, you've arrived at a different way of spending your time.

Africa also demands that you shift your perspective on space; it organizes life on the plain and requires – whether you're on a low hill, or in a depression, or in sparse scrubland, or a village – that you orient yourself toward the horizontal. Canaries are chattering in the bushes. A group of boys are crouching by a ditch and using a dead fish as bait to try and lure something larger. The stream flows into a muddy pond, where a brawny man in his mid-thirties is teaching a tiny white girl to swim and dive. Her father is sitting on the bank and painting the creek and pond in lurid acrylic colours. Two car mechanics in overalls, rubbing their oily hands with rags, step round the side of the artist's easel and start criticizing the daub on the canvas. Orange-blossomed trees line the bank, alternating with hibiscus. Two women are hitting coconuts with sticks so violently that it looks like they're trying to punish them.

The way to appropriate this reality is to steep yourself in its monotony. Everything seems both isolated and nullified in the harmony of ponderous, synchronous events, into which only the children suddenly irrupt, emerging from the water with their eyes frantically struggling for survival with that mixture of terror and delight.

I went down to the Niger, knelt down and dipped both hands in the water, just so I could say I'd done it. I noticed an old man sitting on his haunches nearby. He seemed to understand what I was about and nodded and smiled, while the women, who were sitting on the ground roasting corn cobs on an open fire, beckoned me over and gave me a cob to celebrate the occasion. They cover the roofs of their huts with trash to hold them down and stop them flying off in high winds.

In front of a cactus a pelican was settling down in the detritus, preening its breast with its beak. Next to it, a young goat had found something to eat in a cardboard box, but was soon forced to share it with four other kids. A child picked up a goat's skull by the horn and hurled it into the river, while a man in a deep violet-coloured *bubu* appeared and, with a tiny silver pipe clenched between his cracked lips, started telling me about his lover, who he referred to as 'my ninth'.

Now I'm sitting in the hotel courtyard again, and the lad with his box full of cassette tapes sidles up to my table once more. The hotel owner with the women's spectacles observes me from a distance, but doesn't want to come over and disturb me when I'm busy writing. The kids on the street corner wave at me, but they don't pester me anymore.

I walk over an embankment down to a pond where three oxen are being watered. There are also three naked giantesses striding down to the pond, but they're naked for social rather than ethnic reasons. As a child, whenever I came across those specious documentary pieces about, say, the 'Mating Rites of the Mursi' in magazines, these natives never struck me as naked; after all, they were still wearing their skin colour.

Time and again when I'm underway, I catch sight of the vast plain, where goats are gazing between huts and sheds. A boy is keeping pace alongside me, knocking a holed bucket along the road with a stick. He stays with me until we reach a branch of the river, where another lad calls me over to his dugout canoe, and he takes me over to a sandbank in the middle of the stream. No sooner have I made land than I'm approached by the people who have set up home there:

'Where's our medication?'

At the sight of my empty hands, they just grow more agitated:

'My head's splitting,' says one of them, putting his hand to his head. 'I've got a stomach ache', says another, clutching his midriff.

'Did you bring any iodine? I'm itching all over.'

As Tuareg, they never leave their island, and never cross to the far side of the river. Even so, the sound of children shrieking drifts up from the other bank.

'Don't worry, that's just kids who are swimming over here for the first time, they're still a bit frightened.'

A corpulent woman with a glass eye that's set slightly skew-whiff fixes me with an intent gaze. There's a kind of madness in her face, like when an illness turns the body into the object of a great lassitude, chooses its own design, adds its own ornaments, shuts down certain functions, robs a person of one particular expression while magnifying another. That's how she looks at me – unstable, yet unwavering.

I evade her grasping spider fingers and eventually find myself at the end of a spit of land. A man blocks my path:

'Right out on the point here, just a few metres away, we're growing salad leaves. If you want to come and see it … I can do you a special price.'

Where there's no formal market, everything becomes a market, even inspecting greens. I tell the man that I've seen salad leaves before. He acts amazed, then turns his back on me disdainfully.

The kids are playing by the riverbank, the women are sitting on the steps of their huts and sorting through vegetables, and the men are ensconced like kings high up on roofs and walls. The rubbish tip here teems with life stories. For instance, over there is a kid who's poking around in a pile of mussel shells with an aluminium crutch, while above him, with their tattered and frayed wings, the vultures circle. The young girls, on the other hand, have withdrawn to the bluff above the lagoon to perform their ablutions, washing their feet and plaiting their hair, while the boys attempt a game of football with two balls. All the smells waft above a base note of fish guts and excrement. To the mournful cry of the vultures in the trees, shorn-headed children look on, wearing the expression of old people, as a shadow of indigo lengthens over the grove.

In the crown of the palm tree above us, a bird is busy building its fourth nest in a row. It takes it a day, and by the end of a week a new chick's heart could already be beating in the nest. When dusk falls, the waiter from Mali serves us Senegalese wine from a bulbous amphora of clouded glass. The wine is as heavy as apricot juice and a golden-yellow colour, but it's as astringent as resin, and Anna looks at me like the *chakra* on the crown of her head is just opening up to the desert sky.

The next day the road takes us out into the Sahel zone. The Sahara lies there like one of the earth's body parts, pulsating, blushing and blanching. The desert rises and stretches, some-times sending a shower of scrub bushes across the plain, and the dead trees by the side of the road are full of screeching irides-cent blue and yellowy-black birds. Squirrels and geckos encoun-ter one another on the tree trunks, and vultures hop across the collapsed skeletons of goats that they have picked clean. Occa-sionally you see a scrap of fibrous tendon dangling from the birds' beaks. But at least they have it easier than the goats and the long-eared cattle, which stand panting in the shade of some breadfruit trees. Nearby, other trees project their crowns into the sky like clenched fists, and on the road people pass by car-rying the greyish-brown half-carcasses of slaughtered animals.

The sky, the desert and the dusty air have all taken on the same colour, a sort of grey rubbed in beige, with reddish, yellow-ish and milky hues. Standing out against this overwhelmingly monochrome picture are the garish colours of people's clothes, like the deep indigo kaftans, as though nature was nothing more than a contrasting backcloth for humans, the medium that brings people to the fore in the first place. There will come a time when all you'll see here will be sand and haze, and over the foundation walls and adobe-bricks, over the bast-fibre roofs of the huts, there will stand a lowering sky that sucks up all the colour. Then the huts will blend into the landscape, and when everything's been reduced to desert, suddenly a single child will appear, just a silhouette approaching through a sandstorm, until it is swallowed up like a wraith.

That'll be the fate of Mohammed, for instance, the little Tuareg boy with the worldly wise eyes of a veteran, a lad maybe ten years old who also goes by the name of Indigo, and who suddenly disappears in the wall of desert sand whipped up by the wind. Then there's the old man carrying a couple of baguettes wrapped in a cloth, who raises his hand in a conciliatory gesture as he gets into our car and gives off a powerful smell of plant dye. He rides with us for a bit until we drop him off again somewhere or other. Or the young woman, who we pull up to give a lift to, but who refuses to get in because she's suspicious of our strangely accented French; she looks at us like we're slave traders. Or the little girl with the feather-light handshake and the basket full of warm food, who gets out and disappears into the dunes, where there's nothing. Or those men who are waiting in the roadside ditch when we stop. The first indication of their social class are their flip-flops: the upmarket ones are hand-painted, and the leather punched or appliquéd, or even plaited, whereas the ones that poor people wear are glued together and are frayed; they look like calloused skin and almost seem to become part of the wearer's body.

Outside all the villages here are extensive plots full of rubbish, and then heaps of scrapped cars looking like skulls, and, looming over these plots, there's always the same advertising hoarding, set way up high, showing two Marlboro cowboys on horseback in their desert, a different desert far away. But their desert is paler and more orderly and less theatrical. Even so, can you really advertise on a desert road with the image of a desert? What do the people living here make of the poster? The ambience it exudes isn't one of remoteness or purity; what it shows isn't some exotic backdrop, but their everyday reality. What's so desirable about that?

The plinths of the gravestones in the town's main cemetery have enamelled photos of the deceased attached to them. Ancient wild men with sexless features stare out of the matt glaze of the enamel, faces from which either age or work has washed every last sexual characteristic. Underneath are legends like 'Fourth King' or 'Subject of such-and-such a king'. Gnarled, knobbly faces with so many scars it almost looks like they've been crossed out, and so that there should be no doubt in times of tribal conflict, their faces are tattooed as clearly as if they were the picture of a flag.

The kids take me by the hand and lead me to a spot where they've killed a rat with a catapult. There's blood on its head, but apart from that it looks clean and appetizing – cleaner in any event than the little stream they've laid it out in. In fact, it looks for all the world like it's gone out in a fur coat and is a cut above their station in life. But the children are merciless and load up their slingshots again to try and galvanize the tenacious rat into one last act of defiance. The boy Indigo is among them, too, but he shakes his head disapprovingly, because he senses I'm not impressed.

In the shadow of the mosque, a Swiss woman puffs and blows and says to her own personal Tuareg:

'Would you like a Ricola Orange and Mint sweet?'

'No thank you,' he replies, rubbing his stomach like he's anticipating dyspepsia.

Put out, the woman remains rooted to the spot like a mummified king, and photographs a poster with the slogan: '*Enfants du Monde. Venez nous voir.*'

The roadside verge is strewn with the outline shapes of snakes and lizards and geckos that have been squashed flat by cars. The reptiles' bodies have dried out until they appear like watermarks in the sand. There's a dead goat there as well, with a neck so long that it seems the head was trying to stretch away from the animal's body to reach safety. Now I'm feeling more at home.

From the sand of the desert we return to the colour of the desert: the air is cankerous, the walls sunburned and hardened, dusted with desert sand. The people here are clean, in the same way that sand is clean. No trace of refuse anywhere. Accustomed to decay, everyone here lives by consigning their waste products to the wind, which carries them all off into the Sahara. But social life here concentrates around a few institutions: the market, the mosque, the police station, the school and the university.

Everything is built of sand, of history, of resistance against the distant government, and everything exists as an embodiment of one great name: Timbuktu, home of the Indigo-men, the Tuareg. But those who go around with their faces covered, the armed men, cripples, beggars, flying merchants, priests, indeed everyone who lives here, does so because they can still survive here, not least because they've found a way of making a living from the traveller. The traveller is all too familiar with the faces of policemen, officials and civil servants, but he instantly finds everything to do with the Tuareg noble.

The Tuareg is a mysterious nomad. For just a single paltry coin, he'll don his traditional garb, strike just the pose and pull just the expression you're after. Even the sons of the desert have to be brought into line, after all, even they can't just be left as they are. We all know what that would lead to. No, far better to provide them with a bit of direction, for when all's said and done every glance leads to an outstretched arm, and at the end of every arm there's a begging hand performing a grasping motion, and sometimes, quite rarely, your own gaze unexpectedly meets that of a person who's just sitting there and displaying a kind of sympathy for you, which you're exposed to.

And then you withdraw through the transfixed gazes of veiled Muslim women, who passively greet you, as if they wanted to press you deeper into the hordes of children, the throngs of crutch-carriers with their waving leg stumps, and it occurs to you that you can't conceive of a history for a single one of these faces. Your only option is to give yourself over to incomprehension, and any sympathy, fellow feeling or commiseration you might show can only be translated into the mimicking idiom of your own cultural milieu, which isn't always understood here.

You walk through the gaze of beggars. They no longer need to lower their eyes to look at their palms to know what sort of coin has been placed there. The tourists dimly sense that these creatures are somehow ennobled through contact with them, these visitors from far-off lands; one woman, who has done the Tuareg the great honour of donating her sweet wrapper, tells her friends:

'What's the matter? For them, a wrapper's something really wonderful and unusual.'

It's evidently enough that the gesture of giving should be authenticated by the presence of the foreigner, but ultimately the flash in the pan of euphoria about being in this desert location quickly burns itself out, and things become troublesome, annoying and onerous instead. Or you catch the eye of one of these squatting people, a glance that wasn't meant for you personally and which even conveys some measure of condolence, condolence for the life that you've dragged here with you and will take away with you again when you leave.

The omnipresent boy Indigo also looks at me from out of a life that I can't begin to marvel at, because I simply know nothing about it. In the languid beam of this gaze, poverty is certainly evident once more, but it's purged of all the neediness and begging, it's more like a state of renunciation, of dignity in abstinence, which your own lifestyle is light years removed from. In places where all sense of entitlement is already extinguished, poverty is even more hopeless than elsewhere and is without any means of expression, and even if it does begin to speak, there is no true, proper and genuine way of responding.

The flotsam around the airport: Europeans never emerge from a state of permanent waiting here, whereas natives have never entered such a state. For instance, there's Fatima with the sensual mouth, the yearning eyes and a white, half see-through blouse, which is gathered around a great swelling belly. Now and then, enthroned, she glances down to check on her breasts, and if a foreigner walks by, she motions with them.

In a corner, someone has set up a television showing videos. Boys hang around it in clusters and can't decide what's more fascinating, the film – Bertrand Blier's *Tenue de soirée* – or the white couple, namely Anna and me.

But when the film suddenly shows two naked men lying in bed, it gets the boys' full attention, whereupon an old man wades into them waving his umbrella and shouting:

'*Ce n'est pas pour vous!*'

The boys smirk, scatter and regroup some distance away. There's one older lad with arrogantly curved eyebrows, a small one in a sleeveless girl's top, a rabid gum-chewer clad completely in sports gear, and the diminutive clown of the group, who keeps sliding up and down a metal pole and pulling faces: the gang on standby.

A magnificently dressed old man comes up and puts his hand on my shoulder:

'Good day to you, young man!'

'Young?'

'Well, I was born in 1926.'

Saying this, he takes a biro and writes the date three times, one under the other, on the palm of his hand and holds it right under my nose.

'Look how hale and hearty I am. I've already lived three times longer than expected!'

The boy Indigo's drifting around the airport concourse as well, very shyly, a silent companion. He keeps looking in from outside, wrapped in his cloak, a sand-coloured piece of linen. Sometimes, he gets shooed away, but he just circles around the periphery of his group before slowly making his way back to me. If anyone speaks to him, he answers them in halting French. His charm is subtle but irresistible. He has no self-awareness, and knows nothing of his own grace, which is only accentuated when he opens his mouth to laugh and shows his higgledy-piggledy teeth. But the next minute, he's sitting there like that famous Ancient Greek bronze sculpture of a boy pulling a thorn from his foot, with his flayed legs and his wrist with the barely healed puncture wound, sometimes lost in his own world and sometimes looking to establish a rapport like that of a pupil to his mentor, a secret bond, a discreet relationship based on submission and respect.

His eyes are always one step ahead. Whenever I glance over, he's already looking at me. Sometimes he'll arrange his boy's face into the wrinkled countenance of a grown man and rub his bare soles as he sits. Unlike all the rest, he doesn't offer his services to anyone, doesn't ask us where we're from, doesn't try and court 'Madame' and doesn't want to know anything about our country or our sports teams. Just once, he shrugs his shoulders apologetically: Yes, the gesture seems to say, these begging children are a nuisance, aren't they? But he doesn't mean it in any disparaging way to them, but rather in sympathy with me, because I might be finding them a pain.

It's our last day here. Just before we got to the airport, we drank tea on the sand with a Tuareg. His two camels were already saddled up.

'So where are you off to?' we ask.

'Back to my oasis.'

'How long will that take you?'

'Three weeks.'

'And what will you find there?'

'My four wives.'

'And what do you do there of an evening?'

'We tell each other stories.'

In my mind's eye, I picture the *Horror vacui* of a German husband forced to spend every evening regaling his wife with stories.

We take our leave of him by taking his withered hand and letting it lie there limply in ours for a moment. Then, just with Mohammed, the boy Indigo, I amble off to get our plane, taking a circuitous route. Now he's simply put his hand in mine, like Muslim men do in alleyways. We walk towards the turboprop aircraft: Anna surrounded by a pack of yelling children, and me with the boy serious and silent by my side. He's used to walking barefoot on the sand, though I can feel its intense heat even through the soles of my shoes, and keeps a firm hold of my hand. In my left hand, I've already got a banknote ready to give him, a note that to him will be big, very big indeed, the sole opportunity in this moment to alter the course of his life, to effect some lasting change. I hold out my hand to him to say goodbye and then press the note into his palm.

Calmly, he looks me straight in the eye with that creamy look which appears so unwavering that it looks like it's going to linger forever. But then his eyes break out of their reverie for the length of a blink, and he glances quickly down at his hand and then back up at me: Do I really mean it? Have I made a mistake and am I about to recant on my generosity?

Then he lets go of my hand, the note clutched tight in his fist, and runs – not back to where the other passengers are still milling around with their companions and their families, but out over the tarmac, past the aircraft steps, underneath the plane, across the runway, and up to the embankment on the far side and then down again into the sand dunes. He runs and runs, and never once looks back. The soles of his feet dig lightly into the desert sand; every time he lifts them up, he kicks up bright little clouds. And now his two minions are hard on his heels, but he doesn't turn around, he just keeps on running and running.

I let Anna and the other passengers go ahead of me up the steps, and stay looking at him until he's just a distant speck in the landscape, receding ever more slowly now, across the dunes and into the depressions. It's only when I'm seated at my window, and the plane's taken off and gained some height that I notice that he's running off into a wilderness, with no house, no hut, no settlement in sight. In this entire zone of the Sahara, there's nothing but his movement, the movement of a flight without a vanishing point, which is driven by nothing except the sheer possibility of fleeing.

Bombay

The Oracle

From the treetops high above the crossroads, parrots flew up in a green swarm; monkeys were balancing above the washing lines strung from the balconies; transistor radios were contradicting one another; and the cantankerous blaring of the car horns in traffic jams had an arrhythmic sound, like an Indonesian gamelan orchestra. The boy running alongside our car, so long as it kept crawling along at a walking pace, delivered his patter through the car window in several languages. He wasn't trying to beg or demand anything from us, nor did he want to sell us anything. No, this city warrior wanted nothing except to have a conversation with us, to chat and have us respond, and to get to know strangers. We stopped, and I got out and went over to sit with the lad in a small park by the roadside. He had tattooed ear lobes and asked me:

'So how much milk does your family's cow produce?'

On this particular matter, I couldn't really enlighten him, so the boy sat there hunched over, digesting what little I could tell him, while not grasping everything. Motionless, we looked at one another, two landscapes in conversation.

'I'm a street kid,' he announced, like it was his title.

'Right,' I replied. What else would you be? I thought.

'I've seen things that a kid my age shouldn't see.'

'Right,' I said.

'So when you're with your family, do you speak German English or English English?'

German German, I told him.

'What do you say when you're impressed by something, then?'

'We say: *Nicht schlecht, Herr Specht.*'

He repeated it, and then asked me to teach him some more phrases, but I told him I had to go into the house opposite, where I was due to interview two eunuchs.

'I know a transsexual, too,' he piped up. 'He was born a woman, but forced his ovaries to burst through sheer force of will. I'll wait.'

'What for?'

'For you.'

'How do you know what ovaries are?'

He gestured toward the street and said: 'University of Life.'

I'd only got halfway across the street when it was suddenly filled with the cacophony of whores soliciting my custom. Their calls sounded curt and challenging, like they were trying to draw my attention to something:

'Hey! Come here! Hey! Look here!'

They made it sound like I'd dropped something.

'Sir! Watch out!'

I found myself gazing up the steep slope of a large, brown upper thigh, which had been thrust forward out of a sarong and was now being waggled to and fro on a bench like a kilo of liver.

'Thank you,' I shouted, and tried to arrange my face into an expression of frustrated desire. The woman responded by covering her naked wares with a theatrical sweep of her hand, as her face took on a look of wounded pride. She went all coy, making like she had been stripped naked against her will. I dived into the dark entrance behind where she was sitting.

I find myself climbing the stairs of a tenement block. Inside, the building's core has been shot through with corridors, stairways, fire escapes, catacombs – a whole labyrinthine system of passageways opens up, in which I quickly lose my bearings. You dive deeper and deeper into it without getting anywhere; you take a turn and find yourself back where you started. The only light that penetrates the interior is the dim blue haze that filters through the tracery of the aerated concrete blocks that have been used to divide the external corridors from the courtyard and render the catacombs invisible from the outside. There's a glow of a small lamp from inside, while far-off in the depths of the building, a coloured light bulb dangles on a cord; an eternal flame lighting the way for all the pilgrims to this place.

I latch onto a man carrying a plastic bag; its light colour acts as a beacon for me in the gloom. When he turns round, he turns out to be a woman, who isn't exactly delighted at being followed. She quickly ducks under the washing hanging on the lines and disappears into a side passage. I keep following her, crouching low, but all of a sudden there's a matronly woman blocking my path, holding a shovel, and a man with the eyes of a drug addict, who stares sullenly at me. At first he just stands there in his white shirt, leaning back as though propping himself against a wall, and then he lifts his hand – not to strike me, but to show me the way.

I turn off into the next corridor. It leads through a tiled, sanitary environment that's long since ceased to be sanitary: the grouting between the tiles is covered in mould, and organisms have taken root in the cracks, bursting out from the stonework beneath. At a table to one side, two eunuchs sit eating a watery lentil soup; a couple of plastic chairs are pushed out of the way. An empty bed has shrugged off its pillows, but, as I draw closer, I see that it's not empty at all; instead, a monstrous, naked woman is stretching her feet out towards me, the joints of her toes covered with black hairs. A fan installed in the top third of a window pane is running, stirring up the air but not cooling it. Another woman keeps tossing her thick mane of hair this way and that.

I sit myself down beside the eunuchs with their lentil soup. One of them has got his hair in a mud-pack, but the heat and humidity in the room is making the dye trickle down his face in long runnels; I'm reminded of the dying Gustav von Aschenbach at the Lido in Thomas Mann's *Death in Venice*. One of the eunuchs is a sly ferret of a man, with the complexion of a pastrami roll and darting eyes. The other is a fair-skinned diva with the fleshy physiognomy of a boy in a Caravaggio painting and a broad, high forehead; he's a whole assemblage of round shapes, and would be quite beautiful but for the mud-pack oozing its contents down his face.

As village lads from the south of India, he explains, he and his boyfriend of the time castrated themselves to make it easier for them to find clients in the big city. But his friend died of his self-mutilation. He, though, the glamorous one, earns a reasonable living because he looks after himself, only uses the best beauty products, and always wears perfume ... he shifts closer to me. And it's true, all the fragrances of the Orient waft up from him. Plus, he's often invited to weddings as a good-luck talisman, and then, of course, there's all the love.

Surely he means the great lovelessness, otherwise called prostitution. He can't really mean love, can he?

'I'm not useful for much anymore,' he says. 'But I do still know how to host a gentleman.'

He gives a smutty chuckle at this, then starts talking about how, in love, giving is more important than … I've heard all this before, but in a context where the next part of the sentence was about an inner beauty. And as he goes on about the giving aspect of love, the teardrop, which has for some time been welling up in the inner corner of his eye, yields to gravity and, swollen with mascara, trembles down his pale cheek. The queen lets its run, even though it leaves a dirty trail behind it.

As I step out into the hallway again, the shadows on both sides disappear. I grope my way down the dingy corridor, towards some glimmer of light or other. Blue plaster crumbles, or rather sloughs off in great scales, to the ground. Now the wall looks like a map of the ocean floor, with continents made of mortar, concrete, and exposed bits of stonework and tile. As I feel my way along, the wall opens up into cavities beneath my fingertips, through which I can see images of deities, snake-armed beings with calves' heads, illuminated and charged with energy.

After a few steps down, a well-trodden staircase opens out – scarcely identifiably, like in a faded photo – into an open-plan suite of rooms. Its separate compartments all lead off this single passageway, and each little niche is fitted out with a bed. People sit around in the darkness, staring like they're customers, whores, children, fathers, relatives. In one booth, a wooden ladder leads up to a bunk bed, and even up there, all wrapped in ruffed fabric, sin waits, a great sin to judge by the ruffs, which tremble of their own accord, while from the abyss of darkness, punctuated by snatches of laughter, an old lady, who they call 'the mother', starts to cry.

The damp smell in these rooms seems to say: everything here is alive. Sheets, rags, clumps of dust, cats, bugs, pigeons, rats, even cockroaches gradually appear out of the gloom, and the faces of the people here are like those of ancient sibyls, dark like they've clambered out of a pit of history, with saturnine features, oppressed by a burden that's invisible and which sometimes seems to have nested above their beetle brows. There's a child with a swollen head sitting on the floor mat, too, groping about and forever clutching at something in front of it which isn't there.

'There's something there,' its mother says, sobbing. 'My child can see something, I'm sure.'

Extravagance in misery: here, there's a superfluity of the superfluous; the sheer extravagance of the *malas* – the garlands of flowers, the tattoos, the black kohl-lined eyes and twirled women's beards, the red nail polish, the painted balloons, the checked throws, the scents that waft up from the dark fluff on the women's cheeks and the devotional pictures of gods in their glass frames. Even the lush, flouncy fabrics of their garments, and the way their flesh billows in soft folds around their waists, are a kind of exuberant opulence. A couple of violet-coloured onions are lying on the ground, but my gaze drifts over them through the torn curtain. These tenement houses with their external corridors full of fans, washtubs, household appliances, rotary clothes lines, bowls and cloths are like a series of crickets' cages, one inside the other. And the falsetto beeping of moped horns is incessant.

I shy away, heading for the depths of this warren. I still haven't penetrated to the end of the corridor; I still don't know what final promises it holds. A strong, hairless arm lies across the passage. It belongs to the barefoot, sleeping pimp, who lies there prone like he was suddenly poleaxed by sleep on the way to see the object of his desire, and because he's not worth getting up for, the exhausted whore also fell asleep herself, on one of those sagging mattresses stained with the brown sweat rings of past orgies, which left behind their watermark on the sheets.

The fans are still humming away. Everywhere, clothes are moving and billowing in the wind, and everywhere there's the sound of breathing or snoring. The hollow people are exhaling in the scum wreath of their sweaty deposits. Sandals, mops, plastic cutlery and toys. New, hitherto unseen clefts open up in the walls, out of which more and more people emerge, lurching towards me. Rooms that were ostensibly unoccupied suddenly come alive, with the cockroaches, dogs and rats running out first, followed by people. The pimps drag a curtain aside, rabidly when they arrive and casually when they leave. They've all got the same thin moustache and mouths with fleshy lips, and they all seem hung-over, uptight, jaded and listless. Between the bars hang photos of food, naked and shining like grocery pornography. Wet washing drips from the ceiling; all it can do in this humid heat is grow mildew, never actually dry.

And so deeper into Purgatory I go! This is a serious business. None of my greetings are answered, no smile returned, we're not playing around here, we're living. Only a Japanese man, amazingly misdirected, comes towards me, wishing everyone 'Good Day!'

The whores live like troglodytic creatures, like naked mole rats in the smell of moist earth, in the exhalations of the many sleepers, in cubicles that are like coffins. In a puddle, some spilt blood is forming a rainbow; mangy dogs lap at it with their tongues. Even while they're sleeping on the ground, the women still sport their full whores' finery. The pimps tread carefully as they step over them, but noticing them the women wake up and rise briefly with a clink of gold jewellery, before slumping straight back down again.

A seventeen-year-old girl with a face that already betrays deep disillusionment lies draped over a bed like the *Grande Odalisque* by Ingres. She's not for sale, she announces unbidden. But a year ago, someone whispers in my ear, her mother took her to a rich client, who paid handsomely to have such an innocent girl. Hereabouts, the popular belief is that anyone who can afford it should take a girl's virginity once a year; it is thought to increase male potency.

On the floor, rice is being cooked on a camping gas stove, while fizzy drinks in unhealthily lurid colours are being thinned down from the tap. The little girls have been made up especially lavishly, draped with lots of gold chains and their faces heavy with make-up. The children who are a bit older already look at this world through knowing, possibly even corrupted, eyes. They are old before their time. The hardening evident in their faces is just the next stage on from cunning, cynicism and greed, and finally even this emotion is no longer fresh in eyes whose gaze encounters the person they're looking at with a dead stare.

In the penultimate cubicle off the passageway sits the mother/procuress on a dirty mattress. She's like a queen on her throne there; after all, she's offering something which in its own way is quite unique: her daughter. This mother, dressed in black, with black eyeliner and dripping with gold jewellery, still has the face of a girl. But something shifty has crept in too, and only when this face needs to exert its charm by making the smile linger just a bit too long, and the long earrings jingle coquettishly as she inclines her head, then, just for a fleeting moment, she's a hard, enterprising woman who's keen to get down to business. But her thickset eighteen-year-old with the greasy blue complexion is waiting all alone on her mattress in the last booth at the head of the corridor, where everything comes to an end. She sits there alone, playing with the ends of her hair and with a fixed, simple-minded stare. No, her daughter is among the youngest girls on this corridor, but not among the most attractive.

But what about desire? Where does it enter the scene here, and what are its outlets? Where does it fling itself into the arms of extravagance, of excess? Yes, where is the superfluous, the circumlocutory? Where does desire open up the space here for its boundless promise? The world-weariness of whores is an invention of the cultural superstructure. In these catacombs, too, there is no gesture that is not professional, not tactical. And indeed, why should the woman want to be anything other than 'the juice extractor', that mocking term men use, a machine simply designed to generate secretions.

Yet on the other hand, love in the West has evolved into its own unique sanitary realm. Suddenly, it's all got to do with hygiene, and health puts Eros in the shade. But what if the true relief provided by sex consisted precisely in surmounting all these health-preserving caveats? In the moment of climax, at least. The scourge of AIDS has made the act of love more narrow-minded.

The mother accompanies me to the end of the corridor and presents her daughter: Mumtaz, the stocky attraction under a tall room fan. She eyes me briefly, but it's clear she'd rather stare

THE ENDS OF THE EARTH

at the fan. Mumtaz is not just HIV-positive, she's got full-blown AIDS. You can tell that just by looking at her.

With her hair tied back, and looking pale and a little hamster-cheeked, the girl keeps on masticating and staring blankly; it could be a piece of chewing gum that she's chewing on, or perhaps she's just sucking her own tongue. Then, abruptly, her mouth is still; there's no further impulse reaching it. Now Mumtaz is just gawping. From a basic position of defiance, her facial expression transforms into one of annoyance. Mumtaz scratches her face, then the inside of her ears, and finally her hairline. Suddenly, she starts talking in a high-pitched voice, but her mother hushes her up.

'Pay no attention,' she says, 'what she's saying is all nonsense.'

Mumtaz opens her mouth to reveal a forest of teeth, so higgledy-piggledy that she looks really quite crazed when she laughs. Then her eyes fix on something on the blue rug across her lap, and she puts her head to one side, stops her mindless chewing and furrows her brow, holding this gesture for effect: a woman running through her repertoire of facial expressions, but then things start to swim before her eyes. She inadvertently bites her bottom lip and instantly starts sobbing, and does this a couple of times, long enough until she's evidently forgotten how to proceed. No, she won't cry after all, no, she's lost the thread and is already somewhere else entirely.

While we're still gazing at the girl's face with interest, the mother takes the opportunity to begin her sales pitch again: of course, she says, anyone who's already HIV-positive could have sex with Mumtaz without using any protection. If you stop to think about it, there's no reason why not, and how wonderful it would be for those poor unfortunates to acquaint themselves once more with the joys of unprotected sex. Others, though, would be well advised to use protection, but then again, it might prove a fascinating experience – she actually uses the word 'spellbinding' – to sleep with someone who, as you can see for yourselves, is mentally disturbed.

'Disturbed?'

Well, she continues, disturbed in the sense that she can sometimes pounce on a man and give him a right good seeing-to. She's got amazing stamina, so when she's like that you can take her long and hard. But at other times, it can happen that she'll just push a man away and won't let him lay a finger on her under any circumstances.

'I can't fathom it,' she says, 'but that's just the way she is. Spellbinding!'

Saying this, the mother looks at her own daughter with disgust. Mumtaz is sweating. Her movements now appear to have no causation whatsoever. She'll grab a face cloth without glancing at it first. When she rubs her face, it's like she didn't even know she had one. Her fingers, short and fat as they are, keep flying up and landing somewhere on her body and immediately start scratching, kneading, pinching or rubbing. Mumtaz isn't wearing any make-up except for the thick deposits of *kajal* lining her eyes. Her skin is covered with a patina of grease, her earrings are tiny and in all likelihood the only pieces of jewellery she possesses. They dangle down on either side of her yokelish face, with its look of blank incomprehension, like a malicious gag by someone who was deliberately trying to draw attention to this face, of all faces.

'Look,' says her mother, 'she's well put together'. She proceeds to demonstrate on her own body. 'Here, her heart's below her head, so her feelings can never be stronger than her brain. Right, Mumtaz?'

The girl just scratches her belly through her black blouse.

'But the least important thing for her is sex. It's in the lowest position. Even eating's more important than that. Right, Mumtaz?'

The question reaches her fine, but takes a long time to sink in:

'Nah,' says Mumtaz after a while, baring her collection of teeth, 'nah,' and actually manages to shrug her shoulders like a girl, smiling coyly, but grotesquely. Her mother responds by snatching everything from her – the words from her mouth, the cloth from her hand.

'You're being a real pain in the neck again!' she shouts.

In the background, there's the high tremolo sound of a song from a Bollywood movie, the raucous cry of a querulous old woman, a telephone ringing, the clatter of pots and pans, and cars honking. Now a tug of war's begun between the mother and daughter over the cloth. They take turns pushing the grubby red flannel into each other's faces, wiping off the sweat and the spittle round their mouths, and a faint smile plays across Mumtaz's face all the while, a look of superiority, like she's recalling some incredibly abstruse thought.

Then she yawns, without actually yawning; it looks more like an attempt to take the weight off her jaw. When the mother decides it's time she made light of this all and attempts a joke Mumtaz doesn't laugh, but instead takes the rag and uses it to wipe the dirt from the curve of her neck and the crook of her arm. She rubs and rubs until finally her mother slaps the back of her hand, whereupon Mumtaz starts using the flannel as a fan, but clumsily hits herself in the face several times.

Mumtaz: the serenely self-contained. Her face was surely never that of a woman, in any event it's become mannish and puffy, picking up dirt and sweat and exuding it again like a man's. It has a narrow range of expressions, and Mumtaz is even reluctant to utter her own name. She's not happy being herself; rather she's content at least to have the capacity to express what she doesn't want to be. Nor does her tongue sit easily in her mouth, lolling about sullenly from one corner to the other; whenever she pokes the tip out, she wipes it away with the cloth.

So there she sits ensconced, at the end of a long corridor called the Descent into Hell, behind her the wall, and in front of her the pimps, the procurers, the sick people and the animals, surrounded by an empty existence and accompanied by the soundtrack of the twenty-first century. All wrapped up in herself along with her impulses, her emotions, her reflexes – ill but still just about useful, the princess of the lowest class of humanity.

And all that she's capable of doing on her mattress-throne is to be that oracle which occasionally holds audiences with men, yielding to them with squeals of joy or driving them away and rejecting them. Who knows whether the men come to her for her bizarre desires or just out of curiosity, or whether they're making fun of her or wanting to submit themselves to an oracle?

But as for this visitor, this fine young man in his beige-coloured union suit, he's clearly visiting her with the best of intentions, and as he stretches his slim hand out to touch her cheek, she responds straight away by trustingly resting this plump cheek in his palm.

With a groan, the mother stands up and gestures to me to do likewise. The curtain is closed again. There is no reason to distrust the look of contentment on Mumtaz's face, no reason at all except for that moment when, as I'm making my way out of the building and have almost reached the start of the corridor again, I hear a human voice begin to drone, then rise to a bellow as if from the lowest registers, the deepest bass notes, of an organ – it's unlike any noise I've ever heard before. When it reaches the high notes, the voice twitters hysterically, flapping down the dingy passage; no one can say whether lust, pain or death is at the root of a howl like this. But then it dissipates into the wail of a child, a desperate screech like a baby kicking and screaming. The oracle has spoken: the gentleness of a man, his cajoling and his courting, was all in vain and his attempt to be affectionate towards Mumtaz was all to no avail.

No sooner have I made it out onto the street once more and taken a few steps than someone seizes my right hand from behind. But as I try to pull it away impulsively, the street kid who's been sitting on the low wall opposite waiting, shouts out:

'Leave him be!'

It was one of the eunuchs; he draws my hand up to his lips and then disappears.

'Congratulations,' says the boy, 'there's nothing luckier than having a eunuch kiss your hand.'

Involuntarily, I glance down at my hand.

'So,' the boys asks me, 'how was it?'

I can still hear Mumtaz's scream reverberating in my head. But the kid shoots me a reproachful look.

'*Nicht schlecht, Herr Specht?*'

Tangkiling

The Road to Nowhere

When you're swimming through the clouds at such altitude and so steadily over the desert, you lose the elemental feeling for movement. Down at ground level, all increases in velocity are accompanied by a visual sensation of speed. But this swooping through the air, this gliding over distant chequerboards and cross-hatchings, vaultings and distensions, planes and hollows deprives the eye of its capacity to perceive the normal speed indicators of the external world, the change in proportions and the dwindling and formation of its colourfulness.

During the stopover in Bahrain, I walked the length of the terminal building, just once up and back down again, through all the lavish mascarpone marble, passing pillars and columns, feeling dwarfed by the towering, blind caryatids of aviation, colossi supporting the great arches, past the lifeless counters and the line of sleepers, who lay slumped on polished benches with their heads buried in black cloths beneath the pictures of palm trees and presidents. In front of the airport mosque, there was a pile of fifty pairs of plastic sandals, though no sounds emerged from inside. But when the plane was airborne over the desert again, even the images of the marble, the pillars and the caryatids paled against its radiance.

'Did you see the mosque?' I asked the Swiss German in the seat next to me.

He kept staring straight ahead and answered:

'Yesyesyes.'

He seemed to reflect for a moment, then glanced in quick succession down the gangway, at his other neighbour's mouth, out of the window, at the title page of a magazine in the seat pouch in front of him, out of the window once more, and finally at my right leg.

'Yesyesyes. Interesting, interesting.'

By the time another hour had passed he'd drunk himself into a state of good-natured tipsiness, clearly in order to take the edge off his anxiety. He also amused himself by harassing the flight attendant, who came from Singapore and who was wearing a red uniform. She was just about to spend three days' leave with her boyfriend. The Swiss guy kept winking at her, which she ignored. For the summer, she planned to go on a cycling tour in Brittany for three weeks with her 'darling', as she now made a point of calling him. Did I know if you could hire bikes in Brittany? My neighbour chimed in to say that yes, you could. She left.

Next, he tried to engage her in a discussion about politics, but his English wasn't up to it. I found myself becoming more and more repelled by the faint smile that played over his face as he persisted in trying to chat up and touch up the stewardess, and when he finally started to tell me all about the Love of Jesus, I really began to feel hemmed in at my window seat, and stared ever more fixedly out of it.

Behind us already lay the industries of Balikpapan, the quaysides of the great oil-producing city on the east coast of Borneo, with its chimneys belching smoke and the refinery installations rapidly rusting in the tropical humidity.

The streets end at rivers, and the rivers end at other rivers. They determine the irregular pattern that has been created from the remains of a six-million-year-old primeval rainforest and the clear-felled areas in which the new settlers have erected their brightly painted barracks. Some way off in the jungle you can still make out the old scattered villages and even the odd longhouse; but everything is shrouded in dense smoke from smouldering open fires.

In former times, Dutch colonial officials, Filipino corsairs and missionaries and Chinese and Malaysian merchants all ventured from the river estuaries into this wilderness, the second largest jungle in the world. Nowadays, only very few white people travel to central Kalimantan or Borneo, but every month thousands of Javanese, Balinese and Madurans, in smaller or larger family groups, land at the harbour of the southern metropolis of Banjarmasin or at the airport at the capital Palangkaraya.

For several centuries now, Indonesia's population has been clustering on Java, the island with the most fertile soil; it's now the most densely populated area in the entire world. Two-thirds of all Indonesians live either here, on the offshore island of Madura, or on neighbouring Bali. Even on the largest of these three islands, the population density is still twice that of Germany.

As early as the beginning of the twentieth century, the region's Dutch colonial masters began relocating the Javanese to the wilder island of Sumatra. By the outbreak of the Second World War, some two hundred thousand people had left Java. According to the Indonesian regime, by the end of this century, that figure will have increased to around seven million people, who will have decamped from Java in the course of the world's greatest relocation programme, the so-called 'Transmigration'. They have been assured that a secure future awaits them, above all on Kalimantan and in the jungles of Borneo.

The people who arrive at the airports on those islands still sport their traditional garb: the prosperous Javanese – administrators, medics, or lawyers – in their garments with embroidered hems, the Balinese in their sarongs, or shorts, with batik shirts or T-shirts, and some of the women veiled. Those hanging around the airport here, stressed out and brimming with exhausted expectation, can barely understand one another. Indonesian is a recently-developed, synthetic official language that has been designed to replace 250 or more regional tongues, plus as many dialects again.

The only thing that the new arrivals have in common is anticipation, nothing else, and instead of receiving any proper preparation for their migration, they are given a promise. They will all be supplied with: a roof over their head, farmland, seeds and a photo of the president. In addition, they will receive some rudimentary training in farming and hygiene. But one fact they're already well aware of: after all, on Java too, any settlement of any size has its own monument to family planning, the symbol of a happy, small-sized family, and in the villages as well there is at least a traffic sign to the same effect: a hand with two outstretched fingers and the legend '*dua anak cukup*' – 'two children is enough!'

The washrooms in the airport at Banjamarsin have a pictorial sign in them, explaining how to use a Western-style toilet: 'Don't squat with your feet on the rim of the bowl, don't scoop any water from the pan, and don't put your head in it either!'

And next to the mirror is a list of rules for personal hygiene: 'Don't forget to clean your ears, your nose, and even your elbows!' The walls of the main departure lounge are covered with fading pictures showing rainforest animals and plants, alongside the beaming faces of people on 'Lifebuoy' posters, and black and white advertisements for ABC Drinks and Ultra Milk. No other pictures are in evidence.

At the washbasins, I once again found myself in the company of my Swiss neighbour from the plane. He was scooping up water with both hands from the basin and splashing it on his face, over and over again. As he did so, he kept talking to his own image in the mirror:

'Wake up, will you? Wake up!'

'Is someone collecting you?' I asked.

He rotated the whole of his upper body towards me and looked at me for a moment like I'd said something obscene.

'I really hadn't thought about that,' he replied. 'I put my trust in the Lord. I'd advise you to do the same. Who are you here for?'

'For my nearest and dearest,' I said as unironically as I could. 'And you?'

'For my brother,' he answered, evidently in all seriousness.

The villages, in which the arrivals from Java will be swallowed up, sometimes have a communal television set on a wooden podium, which people congregate round in the evenings to watch the only channel, showing news, pictures of military parades, medal-giving ceremonies and ritual dancing. As they do so, there'll be someone clearing vegetation, or running a flag up a flagpole or getting a boat ready, and in the meantime explaining who Lorne Greene is – who's still wearing his white padded ranching jacket and playing 'Pa' in *Bonanza* – or other big beasts of old television who they don't know about in Borneo, despite the fact that so many non-native species have become widespread or even endemic. Then again, even Lorne Greene has gone extinct in the meantime.

Television advertising was banned here by the authorities several years ago, in order to prevent it from stirring up 'false needs'. In the shops in their new villages, the settlers still came across all the shiny images of product marketing, but alongside were primarily basic commodities, natural products and non-designer foodstuffs like fruit, tubers, hens' eggs and green goose eggs, dried fish, packets of spices and in the display cabinets the lavish red-gold of the *Kretek*, clove cigarettes. On the walls were stuck a few pages torn from calendars, showing scenes of Tenerife or Garmisch-Partenkirchen.

Outside the airport, I'd shared a taxi with a young man who spoke a little English. Though he was only twenty-two years old, he proudly confided in me, he was no less than the leading leech researcher in Indonesia. That evening , he invited me over to the house of his father, who as a Shari'a court judge wielded considerable authority locally and yet, when evening fell, was also so friendly and forthcoming as to have some food taken out to the fifty or so children who'd turned up to see 'the white man'. Whenever we peered out over the window ledge, we could see them sitting there patiently in the twilight, waiting for us to make an appearance.

When I explained to the family over dinner that I really wanted to take a boat trip to Palangkaraya, they spread out a map, and we traced the route with our fingers, down all the many rivers, the branches where they divided, and estuaries, along the whole network of arteries through the tropical rain-forest until, at the end of all these capillaries, we finally found the node called 'Palangkaraya'.

The following day, they hire a helmsman and an engineer, and I find myself stepping aboard a boat. A number of times during our journey, we see snakes and crocodiles several metres long push themselves off the banks into the water. Even so, whenever a water plant fouls the propeller, the boatman doesn't hesitate to jump into the murky stew of the river armed with his machete and plunge down several times in order to cut us free, while the engineer keeps watch on deck to check for any predators approaching. Formerly the enemies of the jungle primates, the snakes and crocodiles are now themselves endangered. Their major enemy is also that of the orang-utan: man.

Back on the river, snakes slither though the roots of trees left exposed by the low water. On some trees, you can make out markings left by tribes living somewhere in the bush to demar-cate their territory. Some of these peoples even inhabit the tree canopy, while others have set up home in clearings or nearby tributaries. They follow animistic religions. Up to the 1950s, there were also supposed to have been cannibalistic tribes on Borneo, who had a penchant for hanging human scalps outside their huts to ward off demons. And there are persistent stories claiming that similar things have occurred even in the most recent past.

But in Palangkaraya, the capital of central Kalimantan, which was only founded in 1957, you can make photocopies and buy all sorts of technology. There are no fewer than four cinemas here, though the street lights have long since ceased to function. The town has a large hospital, but just one surgeon for all those who spend days travelling here in dugout canoes to have an appendix operation or to get a serious wound treated. There are banks, but none that will accept cheques or dollars. And there are computer specialists and corresponding members of scientific journals, but it's not uncommon to find that they're the same people whose faith observance includes ritual sacrifices and trance dances.

The last governor of the region, who to all intents and purposes had the rank of prime minister, stipulated in his will that his coffin should be made from the wood of a 'heart-tree', that is a tree which had had a human heart inserted into its roots when it was planted. Local people memorize the location of such trees in the jungle, and when I first visited Palangkaraya in the late 1980s, barely a year had passed since the great statesman's wish had been fulfilled.

After the government declared that the lifestyle of the Dayak people was 'outmoded', the headhunters have vanished into thin air too. While it's true that even as late as the 1970s, many indigenous people would not divulge where cemeteries were for fear that the headhunters might dig up the dead and steal their skulls, it's also the case that on many occasions in more recent times, animal skulls were substituted for the real thing in the hope that the sleeping spirits would not notice the deception. In any event, skulls buried beneath the four main posts of a house are believed to help a person choose a bride, and are supposed to represent the spirits who will serve the deceased in the underworld.

A woman anthropologist who had come to the rainforest with the sole intention of picking up the trail of these 'maneaters' was discovered one night in a native's hut in an extremely distraught and confused state; she had wrapped herself in a curtain and was naked and terrified. She had nothing to say on the subject of cannibals.

I stayed in Palangkaraya for a couple of days. Every evening in the village square, not far from the cinema, a storyteller plies his trade. He arrived in the afternoon by boat, and is wearing tattered clothes, animal skins and several amulets, one on top of the other. When he spreads out his blanket and starts describing the animals that will now emerge straight out of the ground and start walking about among the crowd, the crowd shrieks in terror, like it's living the experience at first hand. Given that the cinema is only a stone's throw from here, the soundtrack of whatever film it's showing forms a constant backdrop to the storyteller's tales. Above the entrance to the cinema hangs a sign with the legend: 'polite, orderly, quiet'. But this doesn't stop the 'Rambos' and 'Rockys' from muscling their way into our little world here.

Here, where several hundred languages and dialects are spoken, but not a word of English and only rarely even the sterile official language of Indonesian, where counting was concerned I at least managed to get by with a smattering of the latter. But when I asked a guy who worked on the quayside what time the boat was due to leave, and he stretched out the five fingers of his hand and told me '*Empat.*' I was confused – *Empat* means 'four'. So, I replied by saying '*Lima*' and holding my five outstretched fingers to him to indicate 'five'. No, '*Empat*,' insisted my interlocutor, holding up five fingers as before. And I countered with my five again, shouting '*Lima.*' Two hands, two sets of five fingers held up to each other but with two different results. Ultimately I found out what was going on: the inhabitants of

Borneo don't count the thumb as a complete finger. So you hold up two full hands to signal the number eight; in my attempts to translate, I'd gained an entirely new insight into the human body.

The next day, the storyteller from the village square appeared again, with his blanket and, after setting candles all round the perimeter, started to tell us all about the animals once more, the animals under the blanket. If he so much as lifted a corner or wafted the edge of the blanket a little, a huge scream went up from his audience. But when I stood up to leave, most of the children latched on to me and even hung around outside when I disappeared into my guest house and waited until I reappeared on the street. I whiled away some time reading the Bible in the dark with my torch; but I felt disillusioned when I realized quite how many of its moral tales hinged on rates of exchange.

I switched off my torch and asked myself: would I have got on better with my reading of the Bible if I'd done a bit of preparation beforehand? Maybe I should have listened to my neighbour on the plane and allowed him to tell me about the Love of Christ? But on the other hand, when was it ever the case that communication could be sustained indefinitely? Nothing – not my Swiss neighbour, not alcohol, not the Bible nor a dictionary – can save the traveller from his ultimate isolation, I thought, and slumped into a sleep filled with bad dreams.

The next day I went to visit three missionary nuns, who were sitting at a table underneath a strip of flypaper and eating a very spartan meal. They told me how their Indonesian housemaid, when she first arrived, would always genuflect with her hands clasped in prayer before the flypaper, because she thought it was some Christian relic that she was expected to venerate.

The sisters knew a great deal. Geologists, they report, have devised a scale for the quality of soil which ranges from one for infertile sandy beaches to ten for the soil on Java. On this scale, the soil of Central Kalimantan was only ranked as a two – an incomprehensible result for anyone who knew about the cornucopia of fruit on sale in the markets here or who had travelled for days by boat through vegetation whose biodiversity was only matched by a few coral reefs. Some 1.7 million species of animals and plants are thought to inhabit the tropical rainforest. Less than half of these are known to science, leaving aside all the research that still remains to be done into the enzymes, drugs and medicines that could be derived from them, all of which will be irrevocably lost if this habitat is destroyed.

Borneo's rainforest does not owe its fertility primarily to the soil. Rather, it has far more to do with what's up in the air, namely the green forest leaf canopy, and in the countless symbiotic relationships between plants and animals. In dead trees forty metres above the ground, grasses and flowers grow out of the abandoned nests of orang-utans. Seeds, rotting fruit, excrement and decaying vegetation all mulch down into a compost, which produces new microcosmoses with a highly vulnerable internal balance.

The nuns also told me about the Palangkaraya Road. In the wild heart of Borneo, there are paths and dream paths, but no roads. The settlements in the dense wilderness of maquis scrubland and tropical rainforest, and the scattered villages on the broad green rivers are only connected to one another either by waterways or the precarious flights provided by local airlines. So when, in the middle of the jungle, in the immediate hinterland of Palangkaraya, thirty kilometres of asphalt suddenly appear, this becomes a great object of interest and curiosity for former headhunters and other forest dwellers who paddle around the periphery of civilization in their dugouts. Indeed, just such a stretch of road was built many years ago by 'the Russians', for what reason no one here can remember anymore, given that Tangkiliang, its ultimate destination, had always been an utterly insignificant place.

The Palangkaraya Road, they explain, leads right through the area of tropical rainforest that has been scarred by slash-and-burn deforestation and which is still smouldering even now. The road allows people to get really up close and personal with the forest.

And it's true: at any given moment the primeval forest of Borneo is on fire in several places. The plumes of smoke hang like scraps of clouds between the mountain peaks or drift yellow-grey over Joseph Conrad's melancholy rivers. Sometimes smaller planes are prevented from flying for weeks on end by the smoke. But anyone who's already taken four weeks travelling by boat to the airstrip isn't about to turn round and go back, so they simply set up camp there and wait.

At the quayside it smells of oil and sawdust. From the outskirts of the town, Palangkaraya is smouldering in the humid heat from the smoke of the fires all around. On the one road out of the settlement, there are supposedly only six cars. They're never locked. After all, if one was taken, where else would it go?

So, I set off on foot, in the heat, with nothing in my pack except the confidence that there will be some provisions for sale on the roadside, someone selling water for instance, or a banana, or maybe at the end of the road a ride back into town.

Plumes of smoke drifted over the cracked asphalt; some flowers had even started pushing their heads through the road surface.

The settlers burn the bushes next to their huts with the same abandon that they set light to parcels of land measuring several hectares alongside their fields. Everything that the inhabitants have cleared themselves belongs to them, and anyone who has observed how many days it takes to fell a hundred-year-old woodland giant with just a stone axe understands the feeling of gratitude experienced by new inexperienced settlers when they move into areas cleared by logging companies to lay claim to a piece of farmland using slash-and-burn methods. The high level of humidity in the atmosphere and the marshy terrain underfoot gives them a sense of security from flying sparks accidentally spreading the fire.

However, in 1982, when the rainy season took an unusually long time to come, the marshes dried out and the forest fires destroyed an area of rainforest the size of Taiwan. This, the largest fire ever recorded in history, was only finally extinguished with the onset of the rains in 1983.

It was a year before the Indonesian newspapers began reporting this catastrophe. They had been alerted to the fire by foreign news agencies. Nowadays the government has charged pilots of small commercial aircraft with the responsibility for looking out for forest fires. Some people maintained that the great fire of 1982–83 was never properly put out, and soon afterward the next great conflagration, this time shortly before the turn of the millennium, duly broke out.

Even so, the diversity of the plant life here is intoxicating, and the variations and peculiarities in colour and form beyond all measure, even just on the verge of the road here; they bear witness to the richness of a natural world that basically thrives on parasitic conditions.

For instance, the orang-utan is the only animal that is at the same time both strong and inquisitive enough not only to harvest the heavy durian – a fruit that is a delicacy both for the native people and the great apes here – but also to carry it several metres back to their own nest, where the kernel, excreted into the droppings that remain in the nest, or thrown down from the treetops, has a good chance of surviving and germinating a new plant. If *Pongo pygmaeus* – the orang-utan – dies out, the kernels of the durian will just drop beneath the same trees every time, and so this legendary tree of Southeast Asia will also be threatened with extinction in this region.

A similarly symbiotic relationship has grown up between the resettlers and the lumber industry. No sooner have they descended upon the forest clearings than the settlers burn and scythe down all the low brushwood and scrub, so completing the clear-felling process that will also degrade their own living environment in the not-too-distant future.

The settlers in Central Kalimantan know that before their very eyes a type of forest is being destroyed which can never regenerate, and which in the long term cannot really be replaced by replanted monocultures or even by the establishment of a national park, but they are least best placed to afford any ecological scruples. On their laboriously cleared and tilled fields, they cultivate the most undemanding of all plants: pineapples and dry rice. The pineapples are often planted directly into the ashes. The fruit only grow to the size of a fist, and they flood the market; as a result, the price they fetch is low. The soil doesn't yield more than one harvest in a year.

The government supplies the seeds for rice growing. If a rainy season is delayed for too long – and climate change has made the seasons less predictable here, as well – people consume the seed stock and hope for a new handout. But, after two harvests all the nutrients in the soil have been exhausted anyway, and the ground is left fallow; nothing will grow here now except for the coarse Alang-Alang grass, which eventually covers the ground with such a dense mat that nothing else can penetrate through for ages. Only after about fifteen to twenty years will bracken and trees start to take root here again, and if the area is left undisturbed for over a century, a kind of secondary forest might develop, which would at least bear some resemblance to the original rainforest.

But the farmers simply move on. As I travel the road, I can see them walking along carrying all their worldly possessions. A pickup truck rattles past, too, overloaded with the belongings of these eternally disappointed, eternally mobile settlers. They find new parcels of land, join together once more to form 'Transmigration' settlements, and after two years dissipate to the four winds again. The occasional model village comes into existence, like Bukitrawi on the Kahayan River, for instance, a settlement that the government is eager to hold up as an example of the programme's success; after all, it has a primary school, a health clinic with six rooms, and a couple of shops. The women there beat out their wet laundry on the jetty, while below kids in rubber car tyres play in the river near the sewage outfall.

Anyone who can't make enough of a living from farming comes down to the river during the dry season, when the water level is low, to pan for gold. Even the most successful of them only manage to get barely one-third of a gram a day, for which they're paid the equivalent of half a cinema ticket.

I've already been underway on the road to Tangkiling for hours when a girl on a large black Dutch bicycle draws up alongside and keeps pace with me. She stares at me with undisguised curiosity, as if she's waiting for me to collapse at any moment. She's called Gugah and is fourteen years old, and every morning she cycles for three hours to get to her school in the town. She has to set off from her *Transmigrasi* village at the crack of dawn when the paths across the fields are still shrouded in darkness. The smoke from the slash-and-burn farming swallows the pale sunlight and is often so dense that you can only see a few metres ahead. From three o'clock in the afternoon onward, the sun is only visible as a faint disk behind a wall of haze. So, for six hours a day, Gugah rides through a ragged, almost desolate landscape. But because the teachers at the only school for miles around are paid very badly, and frequently months late, it's not uncommon for the pupils to have made the journey all for nothing, since it's more lucrative for the teachers to till their land or pan for gold.

Around a year ago, Gugah was admitted to one of the rooms in the health clinic with a respiratory disease. The town doctor recommended that she tie a handkerchief over her nose and mouth when she rode to and from school in future. She followed his advice. Whenever she cycled past, the men clearing the forest would laugh at her. But nowadays, they're all wearing face masks too.

On some days, Gugah is accompanied by her friend Sri, who carries a basket filled with bottles on her back. In the town, where many people can't afford to see a doctor, natural herbal tonics and medicines sell well. When I visited the clinic in Palangkaraya, there were only five patients. They were sleeping under stained mosquito nets, their relatives sometimes joining them in bed, or sleeping underneath it.

But because the Javanese surgeon who was posted here has started demanding sums for treatment that only very few people can afford, in the interim many patients have turned once more to the *Dukuns*, the traditional men and women of medicine, who know a great deal about herbal medicine, to be sure, but who also use animistic or totemic healing techniques. They've also been known to deliberately frighten patients, or to massage pregnant women or people with fractures for so long that blood poisoning has set in. Little wonder, then, that the average life expectancy in Central Kalimantan is only around forty.

In such circumstances, the kind of development that we call 'progress' only happens in a very asynchronous manner. Constantly, new fault lines keep appearing between layers of cultural knowledge, between traditions, between teachers, and between enlightenment and superstition.

On both sides of the road are felled swathes of woodland, pineapple fields and little ponds where the settlers sit and fish with rods. People are also selling mangoes and eggs by the roadside, and petrol in red containers and even water in blue ones. You can get your bicycle repaired or buy a parasol to shade yourself from the sun. Whatever people hoard in their houses by the side of the highway finds its way to the verge to be sold.

The small police station looks like it's been transported here from a model railway set, and given the tiny number of vehicles that are registered in this area, one might well ask what traffic there is for the officers to control anyway? A few kilometres further on, another low building appears out of the smoke. This is the small jungle brothel, set a bit apart from the road and very inconspicuous. Here, five girls wait for clients, one in a rocking chair on the veranda and four on the single sofa in the parlour.

The girl in the rocking chair is wearing a long, traditional robe with golden threads shot through a red fabric. It's got a long slit up the skirt, a sign of sinfulness. As she's dozed off, she doesn't realize that the slit is gaping wide open, revealing the entire length of her brown leg. Indeed, it's impossible to over-look a glimpse of eggshell-coloured panties. But when I make to slip past the building, the girl's eyes open to narrow slits, and she awakens as a knowing woman who makes no move to straighten her garment, but rather basks in this moment of shamelessness.

Inside the hut, the other four girls are huddled round a bamboo table. In the main, they spend a long time just waiting. They play patience, sell a dullard of a farmer who shuffles past their door a Diet Coke, and watch him as he plods off and crosses the road. One day he won't come anymore. And one day also the little whorehouse between the dry rice and dwarf pineapple fields will go up in flames. Not many people will have experienced great passion here, but quite a few will probably have lost their virginity. They will count its demise as a loss, certainly.

'Come in,' the girls beckon to me as I stand in the doorway.

I'm led into the building and given a Coke. Behind impro-vised screens, I can make out some stained bed sheets, and pillows in a faded red.

I sit down in the far corner, which they've created by pushing several partitions together. We play cards and drink Cola. One by one, the girls leave the room and go off to do something somewhere, then drift back, rotating to make my choice easier.

Somewhere in a corner on the far side of the building, someone's crawling over the floor. It must be some kind of sex game, but it sounds like someone cleaning. The girl who emerges from there wipes the palms of her hands on her dress. The man involved doesn't appear, though. We play another round of Mau Mau, compare the size of our hands, and put our forearms together to compare the colour of our skin.

'Nice complexion!'

The prettiest girl pulls a sad face when I make a move to get up and leave. No thanks, I say. She asks me whether I really don't want to go with her. I shake my head. She says that actually she can't comprehend how anyone could go to bed with any of the five of them. That almost persuades me to follow her. When I finally set off, she gives a long sigh like a sailor's wife. Out on the street, there's not a soul standing, walking or driving past. The sun is searing its way steamily through the haze. At least the brothel has good transport connections.

The only place where there's genuinely nothing is Tangkiling, that village at the end of the road from Palangkaraya; in fact, even the road doesn't end properly here. It ends without really ending; rather it fizzles out like it's too exhausted to go any further. It's mustered all the energy it can manage, and now it's all played out like the soil.

And yet this place is the bridgehead into the jungle, into the nothing-but-jungle. Only here does the legendary land of the aboriginal inhabitants of this wilderness unfold – the 'forest people', as their name literally calls them, the Orang-utan, who nowadays are hunted and displaced, penned in by the encroachments of the transmigrants or abused as pets. In former times, by contrast, they were revered as a separate people. Among the

Dayak, the indigenous people of Borneo, there is a taboo against incest with, or mockery of, animals. Anyone who transgresses puts their whole village at risk of being turned to stone.

The first wild orang-utan I set eyes on is standing upright under the glistening midday sun, high up in the snow-white skeleton of a dead tree. He's just torn out the aerial roots of a bromeliad to make a lining for his nest, and close by, soon after, he breaks two dead limbs off another tree and hurls them to the ground. Yet none of what orang-utans do – throwing down branches, hammering on rotten stumps, or felling trees – is done out of blind destructiveness. Rather, such noisy behaviour is used by the great apes as a way of communicating and marking out their territory. You can often recognize the domain of a particular orang-utan from the evidence left behind by the muscular force of his arms.

It's claimed that orang-utans are only just as sociable as a mammal needs to be. They're certainly much more solitary creatures than chimpanzees or gorillas, and, I reckon, more melancholic too. Adult males especially are such loners that meetings between them are only observed about once a year. They use their long calls, signals that can be heard for kilometres, both to attract females that are in season and to demarcate their territory from that of rival males. Because the females stay largely silent, it's clearly left up to them to decide whether to mate with the males. They, in turn, only accept females whose fertility they've assured themselves of beforehand.

I make my way through Tangkiling, an untidy, improvised settlement, and in no time find myself leaving the far side of it. In the river, women are washing clothes and children are bathing. On the far side of the settlement, snapped branches and heavily damaged tree crowns and young plantations bear witness to the destructive fury – though others call it construction talent, the urge to build – of the orang-utan. Their domain, if they can still be said to have one, begins here, beyond the Palangkaraya Road, which ends like it's just trickling away into a patch of dark jungle earth.

Recently, the women who have left their washing to flock round me tell me, another foreigner came here, another European. This Swiss priest made no bones about the fact that his mission was to open up, even subjugate, Asia in general and Borneo in particular to 'the one true faith'. Having learned a fair smattering of Chinese back home in Switzerland, enough at least – or so he thought – to get by, he stood up to preach at an improvised pulpit somewhere in the vast expanse of China, and delivered his sermon in a horrible mishmash of Swiss German and Chinese. But in any event, he preached for about an hour and a half, and after giving the Blessing, he strode off with his head held high, until a couple of lads came running after him, calling out; 'Mr Jesus, you've forgotten your hat!' Throughout his sermon, they thought he'd been recounting his own life story!

Deeply disillusioned, he'd quit China to come in his black cassock to spread the Gospel among the wild men of Borneo. Unfortunately, though, he got lost in the jungle and after several days, now emaciated and with a rough beard, arrived at the river, where he tried to hail passing boats for help. However, he looked so dishevelled, with his white skin and his black robes, that the locals took him for a ghost and wouldn't dare go near him, and so the Good Lord let his servant die of hunger in a bush on the riverbank.

'We laid him out in that hut over there,' says a young man. 'But what are we supposed to do with him? Apparently, his brother's coming to take his body home. Wouldn't you like to pay your last respects to him?'

As I approach the bier where the unfortunate man is lying in his cassock, with a long beard, hollow cheeks and deeply sunken eyes, it suddenly dawns on me who this brother is who's expected to arrive there, and whom I'd really rather not meet again. 'Yes, yes, yes,' I vividly recall, 'interesting, interesting.' So I bow briefly to these mortal remains, turn around and make every effort to put as much distance between me and the deceased, this revenant, as fast as I can.

The road to Palangkaraya lay before me once more.

Kamchatka

Ashes and Magma

You wake up and realize you're flying over a brain, red and deeply furrowed and bizarrely formed, with meandering nerve tracts; you're cruising over it at 31,000 feet, and it looks like an organism. You're on your way to a spot, 8,000 kilometres from home, across a geological formation consisting of loftily towering rocky massifs, deep chasms and tectonic stratifications laid bare. It's picturesque. And alien. You feel like you ought to be singing sea shanties, feeling homesick and watching junks sail by.

But on the in-flight television screen, the little symbol of the aircraft only proceeds infinitesimally slowly and jerkily along the dotted line of its simulated flight path, as it creeps through eleven different time zones. The Russian government plans to reduce these to eight soon. On another channel, a group of Polish female sumo wrestlers suddenly appears, followed by rally cars racing in Uganda, an Indonesian badminton player and finally a parade of Father Christmases. The world is multifarious and far-off. Then the cabin lights are switched on, and the stewardesses start coming round with trays of fish in a shiny sauce.

The harsh landscape of Russia is now beneath you. Spread your wings and somewhere ahead of you is Siberia, while directly below you is Manchuria, and in the dry stream beds lurk the mounted warriors of Genghis Khan with their battle standards.

Through half-closed eyelids, the businessmen examine the ethnic diversity on their meal tray. They haven't left Europe yet, but neither have they arrived in Asia; in this culinary no man's land, the prevailing idiom is 'crossover'.

It's also the names of the places you pass through, words with the mythical resonance of Samarkand, Surabaya, Havana, Damascus, Dakar, Timbuktu, or for that matter Kamchatka. The name has a rhythm to it that's like the tune of a military march, sung by a male voice choir. A vista opens up in the word; it expands as you say it. That's a good thing. Because in reality, the wide open spaces are becoming ever more constricted. Overpopulation, wars, waves of migration, natural disasters, resentments and epidemics are pushing them ever closer together. And the cities are expanding ever more carelessly, not merely by swallowing up the grey zones of the outskirts, but, far worse, by making the villages somehow city-like, turning them into places that act like they're metropolitan and have metropolitan needs to be fulfilled.

Villages don't respond anymore to the needs of villagers, they only acknowledge townsfolk, and so we're gradually becoming claustrophobic. We never get out of the city anymore. And so our journeys take on the nature of leaps into the unknown. We follow a reflex to break out into the open. It's as though our lives have got stuck in the elevator. But scarcely have we freed ourselves than we rush out in search of a word, a much vaunted word like: Kamchatka.

Viewed from above, the clouds have the beauty of animal pelts. Their surface seems to positively stretch out to be touched, and the slightest brush, say by the flat edge of one of the plane's wings, slices through their form. They rear up, roll slowly over to the other side of the aircraft and their edges flutter off into the atmosphere.

After we'd been underway for about two hours, I raised the blind on my window just enough to let some milky light in, but not so much as to wake the snoring colossus sitting to my left. Barren land now lay below us, dry river meanders in dust-bowl valleys, withered steppelands, a blanket of filth stamped flat and stretched out like skin under a microscope or wallpaper – yet at the same time like nothing I'd ever seen before. The sun was wilting on the horizon, seemingly undecided whether to rise or set.

We flew on to the sub-Arctic landscape, a sparsely populated terrain which up until 1990 had been a restricted nuclear test zone and so inaccessible to outsiders. Since then, the capital, Petropavlovsk Kamchatski, has been steadily shrinking. Once upon a time it had easily 300,000 inhabitants, but today that number has fallen by over a third, and the people that do still live here don't like to hear you refer to this as 'Siberia'; after all, that's too reminiscent of gulags and enforced exile.

'We call ourselves the Far East,' a woman on the plane says sharply, before snatching up a copy of the Russian *Hello!* magazine and immersing herself in an article about Amy Winehouse having a nervous breakdown. I glance around the plane. So, these are the people who are already working or living or dwelling in Kamchatka, or who have some other reason for visiting this eastern outpost of the Russian Empire.

Two aging men, corpulent and with grey crew cuts, who are drinking beer after beer and conversing loudly above the roar of the engines, recline their seats and look at one another through their little piggy eyes like lovers. They hold each other's gaze, like nothing else in the world really matters. Then they wink at one another, coquettishly and theatrically, to show how much they are on each other's wavelength, and feast on some fruit jellies and peanuts. On one occasion, they whisper something to the flight attendant that makes her disappear, blushing, behind the partition curtain, where, as it turns out, she exchanges her short-armed bib for a less revealing stewardesses' uniform. The atmosphere in the cabin is raw, earthy, stressful and only sporadically jovial.

Then the west coast of Kamchatka comes into view. The outline of the mountain ranges, with their ribs of snow-capped ridges, looks like it's been sketched by a rather inept hand. Then the scene is enveloped by cloud, but in those places where the cloud cover has been thrust up from below, forming the odd towering cumulus stack here and there, you know there's volcanic activity going on underneath. When the cloud cover begins to clear, the first thing we catch a glimpse of is the Opala River, followed by the black cones of the volcanoes around Petropavlovsk: Mount Avachinsky, Mount Mutnovsky. For a moment, we're alone with them in the layers of thin cloud, into which they release puffs of steam and gas from their fumaroles: below is a foam of cloud-cream and above it a feather-light veil of gauze, and between them the two matrons with their fumes and their smoky aura, saturated with volcanic ash. They smudge their dirty exhalations up into the pillows of cloud above.

The broad, curving expanse of Avachinsky Bay unfolds in front of us. The landscape that comes into view at the foot of the volcanoes is patterned like the bark on a tree trunk. The wasteland between the watercourses and the lakes, the dark spots indicating small community farmsteads, made up of a haphazard collection of barracks and sheds, the meanderings of the roads, which obligingly hug the contours of the mountains, the rivers, the volcanoes Avachinskaya Sopka and Koryanksky; this entire natural patchwork is orchestrated by a force that has only found its most visible manifestation in the fire-spewing mountains.

Kamchatka lies on the Pacific 'Ring of Fire'. In the east, this zone of generally unstable geological terrain runs along the Aleutian deep-sea trench and its foothills extend all the way down to California. From the south, the thicker Oceanic tectonic plate is slowly pushing itself beneath the Asiatic continental plate, turning the whole of the Kamchatka Peninsula into a site for the discharge of subterranean energy, which finds release in the form of volcanoes and geysers. This landscape, which geologically speaking is one of the youngest in the world, is constantly being shaken by the shifting of the earth's tectonic plates.

Earthquakes occur here sometimes as often as several times a week, and whenever things begin rattling or shaking, this only serves to remind those living here of their mortality once more, and of the fact that they inhabit a young, a very young, piece of land, one that hasn't yet been completed, and demonstrates to them beyond all doubt that we inhabit a living planet with immense energy at its core. Geologists warn that a catastrophe is bound to take place here in the foreseeable future. The city will disappear, the victim of a volcanic eruption or an earthquake, but still the locals remain here, telling themselves: not now, not today, not in our lifetime. Where else are we supposed to go? they ask. They live quite different lives to the rest of us, more aware as they are of the limited time at their disposal.

It takes nine hours from Moscow to traverse the Russian continent by plane to the furthermost point of land, where, since time immemorial, people have known little of their masters in Moscow, and wish to know even less. So this is Kamchatka, then, a peninsula off the coast of continental Russia, at the farthest reaches of the country, of which for a long time even Moscow had only a very sketchy impression. A trio of volcanoes is the trademark of this region.

Seven months in the grip of frost each year protects Kamchatka, at least temporarily, from the effects of its seismic energy. But, even so, fear of tsunamis, which are also a consequence of seismic activity, have among other things resulted in the capital Petropavlovsk Kamchatski being built inland from a large bay rather than on the broad, almost uninhabited coastal strip.

The landing here made by the Cossack Vladimir Atlassov in 1697 is generally regarded as being the discovery of this peninsula in the Russian Far East. However, many other people whose names have not been recorded and who left no trace behind them – most likely fur hunters – must have arrived here before him. But it was only in 1724 when Czar Peter I summoned the Danish explorer Vitus Bering and commissioned him to find out precisely where the Russian Empire came to an end, discover where the landmass met the sea, and sound out the possibility of more land to be annexed, that the foundation stone was truly laid for exploration of the farthest reaches of the empire. Bering duly set out, but the czar died a year later, long before the Dane came back with the results of his expedition in

1730, which then failed to stir the interest of the Czarina Anna Ivanova or anyone else. Only Bering himself was more convinced of his mission than ever, and set about making preparations for the Great Northern Expedition, which he embarked upon in 1733, but never returned from. He died on the Commander Islands east of Kamchatka.

Until the end of the nineteenth century, several expeditions visited Kamchatka, driven at first by economic interests, primarily associated with sable hunting. Ultimately, though, like everywhere else, the indigenous people – the Chukchi – ended up being suppressed by a brutal campaign of conquest and exploitation by the empire until the twentieth century, when they were deemed worthy of ethnographic study just as they were dying out.

Nowadays, if you climb one of the mountains near Petropavlovsk and survey the sweep of the bay with its wide port entrance, its scattered settlements and housing estates, which sprang up with no town planning regulation, and its utterly lacklustre appearance, then the green strip of the almost completely unsettled coast – which turns its face, unblemished by any cosmetics, to America – strikes you as being pretty much unchanged since the days when the first explorers set eyes on it.

The first Kamchatka expedition of 1725 did not establish the settlement of Petropavlovsk. When it was founded in 1740, the future capital of the region was nothing more than a garrison town. Catherine II the Great tried settling farmers here. Those who arrived, however, preferred fishing and still do to this day. The czar's bureaucrats despaired at the mentality of the unruly peasants, who failed to make any headway in either arable farming or sheep-rearing. Instead, they devoted their energies to salmon fishing, and even today nowhere else on earth has such rich stocks of all the various species of salmon as here, where wild salmon occur in such abundance that it is even used as pet food.

Likewise, nowhere else on the planet has such a thriving population of bears. But whereas the early trappers battled their way through the harsh winters, through the deprivations of a life lived in woodland bivouacs and mud huts, the hunting parties of modern times arrive here on private planes from Moscow, sometimes even shooting their prey from helicopters, before disappearing back west again. Other hunters concentrate their efforts on obtaining bear gall-bladders, which in China are reputed to have aphrodisiac qualities. The result is that you will sometimes run across bear carcasses out in the wilderness which have only had the gall bladders removed.

Less than twenty years have elapsed since Kamchatka was an inaccessible, forbidden territory, a military exclusion zone. In the Cold War, the largest submarine fleet in the Northern Pacific was based here, and the anchorage of the fishing fleet, cut off from the mainland, did not even have a railway connection to the rest of the world. At that time, then, it was a weird place, peopled by those with security clearance and separatists, a place without a public face.

And then the sheer strangeness of the place takes hold of you, and suddenly you're far, far away, unreachably detached as though you're in exile, with no possibility of an early homecoming, abandoned and shunned. It's then that the strangeness envelops you; you keep on encountering it, and, whichever way you turn, it will always show you the same uncomprehending face. It will reject you and discard you, causing you to lose yourself in the great realm of apparitions, on paths that lead nowhere, between the houses with their peeling, blistering paint, the plaster eroded by salt water, in the grandiose sadness of a settlement that doesn't wish to be housed but which, between its attempts to entertain, administer and feed its inhabitants, has found no language in which to communicate.

The houses stand around haphazardly, as though they've simply been scattered over the land. Some of their façades have been given a pinkish-blue coat of pastel paint, possibly because nothing else here is pastel. On a piece of wasteland which looks like it's been skinned, a funfair has taken up residence. But no one's running the dodgems, and there aren't even any lights on. In the four almost identical snack booths standing in a line, four saleswomen wait to serve customers four sorts of virtually identical salmon rolls. The city's monumental buildings, which house the municipal authorities and various university departments, are unimposing in their grey concrete rendering. The most impressive edifices here, though, are the shopping malls, garish cathedrals to consumption, which are bereft both of people and of any common sense and which appear somehow intimidating, like satellites hijacked from another world which might one day lift off and fly away.

Outside the city gates, disgruntled young soldiers are milling about aimlessly. They've recently been transferred here, and are trying to assuage their misery by downing large quantities of alcohol and staging nightly bouts of aggression. And when you visit a restaurant here, you're inevitably confronted at the entrance by a stuffed brown bear, rearing up on its hind legs and with its cubs at its feet, set against an artificial habitat made of papier-mâché. Such grandiloquent manifestations of sentimentality come across as fits, as acute attacks of lyricism, that have taken the wrong form and become fantastically exaggerated, when all you want to do is give your own life some sort of structure.

Seen from the outside, my hotel is a dull box with a peeling façade, but once inside, you step into a lobby which likewise contains a stuffed brown bear defending his painted domain with bared teeth. The rooms are furnished in the Old Russian style, with heavy gold brocades, and in the drawer of the bedside table there is a handbook proudly listing four services the hotel can offer its guests: a wake-up call, laundry, an iron and a shuttle bus to the airport. There follow five full pages of proscriptions and regulations, such as 'Cooking of vegetable soup is forbidden' and 'Guests are not permitted to keep any birds in their room'.

In summer, the city wakes at 5.30 in the morning. The air is clear at that hour, not yet laden with the smog produced by the heavy traffic, while the neon signs are still lit up, beaming their simple messages in crisp Cyrillic script out into the dawning day. At this time, the birds' calls are still louder than the sound of little cars' horns, and the first lights are coming on in the rows of dismal prefabricated houses on the estate that covers the hillside. But from the empty windows of housing projects that were never completed and have been left to go to ruin, black night still yawns as though it were truly at home here, and the pink light radiating from the morning clouds bathes this sad location in a glow of kitsch.

The streets are populated with drunks tottering home, bleary-eyed taxi drivers and workers on early shift. These people all seem thawed-out; emerging from a long, hard winter, they blink in the sunlight and blossom for a very brief spell before curling up and hibernating somewhere once more – in the sheds housing discos or in gyms or in the cinemas, whose brightly-lit frontages look like illuminated portals to the world.

From 6.30 onwards you can get breakfast in the hotel, consisting of a fried egg with a topping of crab meat and red caviar, with white bread and the Russian version of 'Livin' La Vida Loca' blasting in your ear, which sounds even crazier here than when it's sung by Ricky Martin. Service is provided by a uniformed martinet, who stares at me through the serving hatch for minutes on end before she finally starts bringing over plate after plate, with glacial slowness. There are desserts on offer, too, all of them looking like they've been liberally dipped in the pots of make-up Russian women are fond of using.

By the time dawn has faded, I'm out on the streets again, passing under gazebos that are crammed as full as storerooms, with tin cladding protecting them on the side exposed to the weather. The market is full of people dressed in bright clothes and wearing garish make-up, as though they feel obliged to counter the gloominess of the city's architecture with their own personal show of gaiety. But it only makes the buildings look all the sadder. It's rumoured that wealthy citizens donated their gold teeth and jewellery so they could be melted down to make the gold cladding for the onion-domes on the new cathedral; and indeed, the new building that is rising from the foundations of a former theatre displays a misplaced magnificence that is only rivalled by the neon advertising signs.

At the market, serried ranks of women stand by the barrels of salmon caviar that they're selling. They stick little piles of the eggs on the backs of customers' hands for them to sample. Each of the women here has her own recipe, which has to do with a particular salt content, or a special way of preserving the caviar. In terms of hygiene it all looks highly dubious, not to say downright dangerous, but then again would the market women have been plying their trade for the past thirty years if they'd been in the business of poisoning their customers?

I'm looking at a deaf couple walking along the pavement. The man has stopped, let go of his wife's hand and is refusing to go any further. She's giving him a good talking-to, her silent lips moving energetically. He shrugs it all off. Their gestures become more expansive as they give vent to their feelings. The husband launches into a gestural tantrum, his pudgy hands scything through the air in broad sweeps. He seems to be an oddball in all sorts of ways. The woman recoils exaggeratedly, like in a silent movie, but he's not finished yet. First he thrusts his fist up into the air, then, three times in succession, abruptly draws an imaginary line between himself and his spouse. Then he turns and walks away, leaving her standing there. But after just a few metres, he hardly knows which way to turn. Synchronised, they once more turn towards one another – separated, yet incapable of being so.

Petropavlovsk is known to many people by the soubriquet of 'the dirtiest city in Russia'. Small wonder, then, that everyone who lives here is constantly wanting to get out into the countryside. Yet there's a fundamental difference between discovering a city from the countryside and vice-versa. No, Petropavlovsk is the way it is precisely in order to make the surrounding nature appear all the more captivating and unsullied. And since the whole of Kamchatka, which in any case is twice as big as Germany, only has a fragmentary road network totalling just 130 kilometres of tarmac roads and, after seven months blanketed in snow, only experiences a brief flowering during the Bacchanalian summer, the natural world looms large here. It begins immediately behind the city, in the form of groves of Erman's Birch trees growing on marshy ground, low scrub and fir woods, which are home to the occasional Shashlik Café. In summer, the waysides are covered in dust, and even the tree by the silver-bearing spring, where people have tied little scraps of cloth for themselves, their wives, their lover or future wife, is permanently coated in a film of yellow dust from the road.

But up on the slopes, they start sparkling again in all their glory, the birch trees, which are much loved in this dark region as bringers of light. The silver of their trunks is still shimmering through the dawn – a natural wonder that shines out boldly like some precious metal against the all-day twilight that prevails here.

For days, we've been venturing out every morning into the wilderness of the vast, indifferent landscape with its isolated settlements. Busty women with blonde and brunette hair on one and the same head and wearing Mondrian print T-shirts wait at the blue-painted bus stops. If you talk to them, their faces open up and they launch into a gurgling Russian, which my interpreter Nastya translates into a richly coloured German for me, while at the wheel Sergei has proved to be 'man of a thousand stories', who has even rehearsed his punchlines in English.

From both sides, the bushes crowd in on the carriageway, as if there was something worth seeing there. But all these dirt tracks do is lead to the horizon straight as a die, and sometimes an old boy will pass by on his bicycle, or you'll catch sight of a soldier peeing in the undergrowth, in a cloud of mosquitoes.

And then, suddenly, the view opens up onto massive valleys, their floors covered in vast tracts of uncultivated land as if the sole purpose of the landscape was to act as carpeting leading up to the foot of the volcanoes.

Sometimes, in the villages, you'll come across a line of eight women, one after the other, standing by their little trolleys with *pierogi* containing all kinds of filling – potato, bacon, cabbage, onions, minced beef, fruits of the forest or apple – kept warm under hot cloths. The lorry drivers saunter up to them, most of them bare-chested or in vests, or soldiers or weekend warriors in their camouflage fatigues. Somehow, all scenes round here take on the colour of the surrounding terrain.

On the third day, we pick up two hikers, Yelena and Kolya, who are wandering along lost in the morning sun. She's chubby-cheeked, enigmatically self-absorbed and shy; everything she says is delivered slowly, and even when walking along she's deep in thought. He's a gaunt, clever lad whose remarks are quick and brief and who has fine powers of observation. Yelena's wearing a baggy flat cap, which takes on the form of her face, while Kolya has on a blue and white striped hoodie, a fabric more suited to kid's clothing, and a rapper's baggy pants.

'Where are you heading?'

Kolya points to a far-off hill. Where the power station is, he explains, he really wants to have a look round it.

'That would have taken them days without a car,' Sergei tells me when we've got out to stretch our legs by the roadside. 'There's no service stations, no food. Poor girl, her bloke's a bit reckless.'

We keep on winding up into the inhospitable volcanic terrain. The moonscape valley, where the yellow warehouse-like hall of the power station is situated, is surrounded by warning signs, corrugated iron huts, containers, rusty equipment and a few barracks for the workers, while further beyond the yellow block of a hotel for the more senior employees looms up.

There's no access to the site without permission, but Sergei wanders up, beaming and starting his patter even from a distance, to the barrier where the uniformed guard, in the company of his family and two dogs, has already begun laughing. The mood is that of a relaxed Sunday afternoon. Stories are swapped, the latest gossip bandied about and, before we know it, Sergei is in possession of the guard's pass. Our little party duly makes its way down the dirt track to the facility, passing air vents belching steam and ponds for collecting waste water – dark murky pools and toxic blue ones, which drain into the nearest river. That river is now dead. By now, Sergei has reached the plant itself: the turbines are humming, and at three points columns of smoke are rising into the air.

'I've visited here several times, and every time it's beautiful in a different way. It always gives me good but different vibes.'

The plant is situated in an upland valley encircled by the amphitheatre of the volcanoes; a really secluded location even for a power station. Hydrants are sticking out of the snow and pipelines are running in all directions. We step over pipes, go through a gate and descend a cinder slope; Yelena and Kolya are filming one another the whole time with both stills and video cameras. They've been together for thirteen years. When they're not filming each other, they're giving one another clumsy kisses or holding hands. Their mutual strength seems to be based on a shared weakness.

Yelena has lost both parents. In fact, she's so introverted that she only really likes to pull a single expression. She does it incessantly. Sometimes it's directed in a well-meaning way at her man, other times questioningly at us. These differences barely register externally. Rather, we have to interpret them in their context, and only Yelena's laugh is something where all nuances are neither here nor there, as she gives such unbridled vent to it.

One day, her face will become stern, and a crease of permanent bad temper will take up residence above the bridge of her nose, you can see it coming already. But on the other hand, a sense of bonhomie will never totally abandon her face. Although it may sometimes seem to be visited and swamped by dark moods, it's as much a mystery where they come from as her laugh, which is at its most candid when it seems to have no basis whatever.

But when Sergei's regaling us one of his anecdotes, which not even the arduous path we're walking along can prevent him from telling, Yelena's laugh comes across more as good-natured, maybe even a bit pitying, like she doesn't want to be a spoilsport. One of his stories goes like this:

'So this woman pushes her way to the front of the queue at the supermarket checkout, right, and announces: I'm pregnant. You understand: pregnant! Of course, the people behind start having a go at her, saying: we can't see anything! The woman replies: well, I can't help it if nothing starts to show after half an hour, can I?'

We're walking down into a funnel of earth. The ground has a mouldy-blue and rotten look – then takes on a yellowish tint changing to green, like a sponge resting against a wall, or a bad water stain, fungal bloom or tarnished enamelling on a bathtub. The rock beneath our feet is grainy and porous, it crumbles if you rub it between your fingers, and if you dig down into a hollow, it feels hotter to the touch. Here, you're evidently touching something that's in close contact with the earth's core.

Yelena stands there in her yellow T-shirt and bends over the steaming crevasses in the rock. In some places, groundwater is boiling and spraying up in little geysers, while in others it's just simmering and seeping up as though through perforations. The predominant colours here are sulphur-yellow and rust, mixed with varicose vein-blue and lichen-yellow. The various blue hues of the soil are all washed out. The air into which Nastya is exhaling her cigarette smoke is mustily hot. In other places, smoke is coming out as though through nozzles. The grass on the stream bank is a poisonous green, and the hillside has a reddish glow to it; the higher members of the plant kingdom have given this place a wide berth. The ground here is raw, stressed and porous.

Yelena looks at the seething spring and says:

'It's like in the fairy tale, a fountain of youth. You could dive into it as a mother and emerge as a young girl again.'

'And how often have you dived in already?'

She shakes her head thoughtfully:

'We women from the North are preserved by the cold.'

A rip in her jeans has been carefully darned, while the appliqué designs on her mustard-coloured T-shirt, which matches this landscape so well, have rubbed off, and where the fabric has become threadbare, it's been patched up with new stitching.

It might be like this: her shyness has driven her into the arms of the first person who recognized it. She's learned everything from him and treats it now like secret knowledge. It's probably not the case that she yearned for him and him alone. It's just that now she didn't want the others. Even now, in every moment of weakness she still clutches his hand. She likes the fact that he's a soldier. A soldier is a respectable man and, in her eyes, is a bit like a modern knight.

Kolya is originally a Belarusian, but he joined the army, spent a year in Ethiopia and finally returned to Russia, where he's currently serving at a base in the northwest of the country. Although he tells his wife stories about Ethiopia, he keeps quiet on the subject of Ethiopian women. For at even the merest mention of them, she starts ranting about these women with their African morals. When he was there, in this Ethiopia place, she cried every night, apparently. But life's good for her now, she says. Sure, they haven't got much money, but they're allowed to live on base with their two children. A friend who comes from Petropavlovsk recommended Kamchatka as a holiday destination and invited them to come and stay in his small flat there. But no sooner had they set off than he had to leave the city. Now they're living in his flat outside Petropavlovsk, but have no one to tell them what they might get up to hereabouts. They've been into Petropavlovsk twice, but they both agree that it's not exactly a pretty city.

'So, what else have you done?'

Yelena blushes.

'We've been swimming.'

That evening, when we drop the couple off at a miserable settlement of huts and she puts her hand up to her mouth, ashamed that everything here is so poor, she says:

'Today's been so packed with experiences that I don't know how I'll ever cope with it.'

And Kolya gives us a very stiff and formal bow and says:

'Thank you, Sir!'

When I ask them whether they'd like to come out with us again tomorrow, he gives me a crisp salute with his fingers to his temples and repeats:

'Thank you, Sir!'

So the next day, we're all back together again: Sergei, the ascetic with the shining eyes, a good knowledge of yoga, an endless fund of stories and a boundless enthusiasm for every hill; Kolya, the intellectual soldier, with his ridiculous outdoor hat, who pays more attention to nature than the society he's living in, and who captures everything on film; Nastya, with the tied-back tuft of blonde hair, who's always translating, rushing around all over the place arranging things, and who energizes the whole of the group with her mood; Yelena, with her calm, unwavering gaze, which in her embarrassment often flips over into a look of irony, and with the quiet voice which sometimes sounds a bit whiny; and finally Galina, a ladylike friend with a picnic basket, who is there to help us out in case we have any problems with the authorities. We eat our lunch on the tailgate of our jeep: salmon, tomatoes and gherkins, red caviar, sausages, white bread, smoked meats, and to drink some of the pure spring water that we filled our bottles up with on the journey, and *kvass*, a drink that's fermented from rye bread.

After drinking our fill, we lie back in the meadow and look at the clouds – the famous clouds of Kamchatka – like pictures in a museum. Some people come here just to see them, reputedly the most beautiful clouds in the world: the cauliflower clouds, the lenticular clouds, the UFOs that look like swollen sago, coarse grained with strong grey cell walls.

Today, for example, the paintbrush-stroke of the foehn has distributed the clouds around the sky with a broad brush; only a few feathery clouds have escaped and are floating weightlessly, as though they were trying to transfer the landscape design to the sky. Snowflakes are lying in the midst of a lush green, while the meadows shine greenish-white. It sometimes looks like the volcano has spat out snow and it is flowing down to the valley between the lava ridges. Now the panoramas open up before us. We climb up a mountain where the high plateau is rocky and you can scarcely feel the sun, and from a single vantage point count no fewer than nine volcanoes, nine individuals, who sometimes appear dramatic and at other times inconspicuously beautiful. Inexhaustibly, Sergei expresses his awe at the beauty of both the extinct and the active fire-spewers, giving us their names, reading them out enthusiastically from a list, all twenty-five of the active ones along with all the countless dormant and extinct ones.

Whenever you find yourself away from Sergei for a moment and then come back to him, he's invariably in the middle of a story set in the natural world. Just now, he's telling us one about a female cook in a camp who suddenly found herself alone with a bear. She screamed, and the bear withdrew. Hours later, she was still screaming, and kept on doing so for several more hours after that. When the camping party got back to base, she was still screaming, but more quietly; by this time she was completely drunk, having downed two bottles of Martini between the screams.

We hear a cuckoo call.

'Wait.' says Nastya and starts counting. 'How long are we going to live? Seventy, eighty, ninety …'

It turns out we're going to live to 120, and we start moving slowly across a high plateau. Sometimes, the path eats its way through two-metre high drifts of dirty snow. Then, at other points, the fields lie open to view, strewn with boulders. When the cuckoo falls silent there's nothing to be heard but the whirring of insects, and every now and then bizarre bird calls, the like of which we've never heard, interrupt the sighing of the wind. Tall electricity pylons stride rustily across the mountain ridge, while beneath the overhead power lines channels of fast-flowing meltwater shoot past, their banks populated with plump birds that shake their feathers dry and then walk off through the fresh snowy air, which is tinged with the aroma of sulphur.

As we walk along, Yelena tells me her thoughts on Nastya in pithy, gnomic utterances, such as:

'Northern women absorb the silence of their native landscape.'

In fact, that's the only sentence she utters. It's meant to lodge in my mind as some kind of aphorism, and I look at Yelena, her mysterious, slanting eyes set above her high cheekbones, her severe mouth, from which this sentence emerged, yet which when it voiced it was neither severe nor calm.

Yelena and Kolya have been together for thirteen years, then, but they still kiss one another like they're attempting to fill an empty space. Even so, Yelena occasionally allows herself little playful allusions, which, given her secretive nature, she makes sound even more cryptic than they actually are. After I remark that Sergei's swimming trunks look like a kitchen curtain, she laughs and replies:

'It's best living without any curtains.'

And when I call Yelena *Mischutka* – 'she-bear' – she says: 'I'm only going to become *Mischutka* tonight.'

Saying this, and lost in thought, her gaze comes to rest on a point in the distance. It's not where her husband is. It's probably not where any man is, only some vague knowledge into which she's not prepared to initiate anyone, a yearning only she knows how to deal with. Then – and this happens only very fleetingly – her eyes flit across at me to try and catch a reaction. As shy as she is self-conscious, she is the sort of woman who, underneath her shyness, is aware of her attractiveness – indeed, may even be conscious that her shyness itself is alluring – and combines the two with great dignity.

'My kitchen is as small as the interior of this truck,' she says, 'and the cake that I'd like to bake for you would be larger than my oven could accommodate.'

Like in a fairytale, she transforms her affection into cakes!

Today, we've been underway for hours when we suddenly come across a barrier – another restricted zone, this time protecting the secrets of a brand-new kind of hydroelectric power station. Galina is the legal advisor of the firm that runs this plant, and as our chaperone, she holds up a piece of paper with a barcode on it at the checkpoint, until a voice crackles out deafeningly from this call-post in the middle of nowhere, and our car's allowed to pass.

We haven't got far, though, before a violent shaking and swaying of the bushes by the side of the track betrays the presence of a hunting bear. As we stop, it crashes off deeper into the undergrowth, snuffling and grumbling. On impulse, all of us perform to gender stereotype: the three men in the car leap out and from the crest of a slope try for a while to follow the trail left by the bear as it makes its way through the thickets below, shaking bushes and the crowns of saplings as it passes. The women, meanwhile, stay in the vehicle, making noises of concern and alarm that fall on deaf ears. Even the bear seems to know its allotted role, and doesn't do anything unpredictable, rampaging off into the distance.

We follow the narrow, almost overgrown, track running through the compound until, after rounding a bend, an unimposing building comes into view. Behind the abandoned-looking company building, a solitary worker is sitting, his torso bare, and scaling a fish. His questioning eyes wander from face to face.

'Hi Kostya,' Galina calls over to him, 'have you got another fish for us? Or even a couple, maybe?'

Without answering, the man reaches for a long-handled net, leads us all down to the weir and, sweeping it through the water against the current, fishes us out two netfuls of very young salmon, scarcely bigger than sprats, from the fast-flowing stream. As we are leaving, Sergei thanks him by handing him a two-litre plastic bottle of beer.

We press on further into the compound until finally, tramping through heavy undergrowth in the midst of the wilderness, we encounter a waterfall. Walking across the rapids on stepping stones, across the smooth streams of racing water that only froth up briefly when they hit prominent rocks on the lip of the falls before plunging headlong into the abyss, we each find our own outcrop and sit there in silence on our separate rocks in mid-stream, each of them sparsely covered with moss. Yelena has rolled up her trouser legs and hasn't ventured far from the bank. From his own perch in the middle of the rapids, Kolya takes a picture of her. She looks at the camera like a mermaid, but, for heaven knows what reason, asks me why he's taking it. Sergei, meanwhile, is playing the gamekeeper, clambering onto a jutting ledge and scanning the bushes by the riverbank for any signs of bears. The rest of us teeter directly above the place where the river sweeps over the edge. Yelena only raises her voice to warn us, with maternal fervour, to watch our step.

Later that afternoon, we will penetrate further into the wilderness and find a feeder lake for this waterfall, its waters calm and with low scrub along its shore. There, we stop and grill our little fish on an open fire, and enjoy a meal of rye bread with red salmon caviar, apple, biscuits and pralines. When we've finished, the men take a dip, while the women relax in the meadow; we're all content that nothing happens but that everything simply is.

Back in the car, as evening falls, the five women start singing, and find themselves in complete harmony.

'This song's about yearning for a true friend,' Nastya announces, and pitches her voice way down low.

I can hear the yearning in her delivery.

'Now I'm going to do the song about the black cat that only brings bad luck to those who believe it's an ill omen,' says Yelena. 'Wait a moment and I'll sing it for you.'

She starts off rather weakly, but recovers and ends up giving quite a strong rendition. The others clap along in time; even Sergei, at the wheel, can't help joining in. The road running through the birch woods is so straight that you can easily drive it with no hands. He chooses and announces the next song:

'This is the song about people who were born on a Monday, and now want to abolish Monday because it brings them nothing but bad luck.'

During the refrain, one of our tyres bursts. We skid into the gravel bed beside the road, our tracks swerving wildly as Sergei applies the brakes; there's a strong smell of rubber. As a fine drizzle of rain sets in, Kolya changes the tyre, while Nastya has a smoke and Yelena looks at the sky like she wants to disappear into it. She strolls slowly down the road ahead, just occasionally waving her arms to ward off the mosquitoes.

Sergei walks round the truck, giving it a professional once-over, but doesn't pause for a moment in his storytelling. His stories are basically like those from the *Decameron*. They have titles like: 'The time a friend challenged me to overtake him, but I declined'; 'The time a priest slept through Mass'; 'The time the kids planned to cheat at their schoolwork, but the teacher switched their assignments just in time'; 'The time my first wife left me for another man'; and 'The time my daughter was taken to be someone else's because she's so pretty'.

'So, you were married once, then, Sergei?'

He gives a comically theatrical sigh: 'You know how highwaymen say "Your money or your life!"? Well, women take both!'

By the time the new wheel's fitted, the sky has grown dark. Today, it looks as though Kamchatka is recuperating in the rain. The atmosphere descends from the firmament and covers the land.

In these conditions, even the grey frontages of the buildings in Petropavlovsk are in tune with the weather. Lights are burning everywhere, and the exhaust fumes of adulterated diesel turn many of the falling veils of rain blue. When it appears, the sun looks as though it's shining from the depths of a Gobelins tapestry. The city has spent a whole day growing light and only now has it really found its mark. Like it was never meant for bright sunlight.

We drive to Petropavlovsk along the coastal strip, and enter the city just as the street lights are coming on. The way it looks right now, the city seems charming. So, I wind down the window and, mimicking the sounds of the words I've heard other people saying elsewhere, call out:

'Kakaia brijälist!'

Everyone in the car busts out laughing.

'What does it mean?' I ask.

'It means something like "What a stunner!"'

Fair enough, then. Under the trees outside their run-down apartment, we take our leave of Kolya and Yelena. I repeat the ritual of the previous day:

'So, tomorrow would you like to …'

Yelena beams at us in delight, while Kolya gives a laid-back salute and nods.

'Strange couple,' Nastya says as she's driving me to the hotel. 'Still so into one another after thirteen years.'

'She still acts jealous, too.'

'Right, though he's the one who'd have cause to be jealous,' Nastya replies.

She'd asked Yelena about the death of her parents, apparently the result of an accident she only hinted at. This left Yelena all alone, far from Kolya on his exotic posting in East Africa. And then came the death of her friend. What friend, I asked? She'd just blurted it out under pressure, Nastya said. This male friend had been a comfort to her in the period when Kolya had been stationed in Ethiopia; he was a guy who lived without any visible means of support, and who like her had no friends or other relatives, and had become an accomplice, an enthusiastic companion on trips, a second man in her life – and a lover too?

Had she got romantically involved with him? Had she wanted to break free of her marriage?

In any event, Kolya came back from abroad, their marriage turned out to be solid after all, and three months after Yelena's marriage had got back on an even keel, the friend had thrown himself under the local train. He'd only been cremated a couple of months before they came on holiday here.

'So, did Kolya know …?'

'Oh Christ, no, he hated the bloke right from the off, anyhow.'

The next day, we set off in a more sombre mood. Kolya's still wearing the American rapper's hoodie, and Yelena's still got her mustard-coloured top with the sewn and mended appliqué designs. Once we're on the road, a grand succession of birch woods, heather-covered hills, grassy plains slip by, while in the tundra zones we see Swiss pines and Alpine groundcover plants.

Time and again, nature retains its immensity through things that we humans are incapable of perceiving within it: the landscape which stretches to here from the distant wilderness, the zones of untrodden land that build up to this single spot, the foothills, the lines of ridges receding into the distance … Nature itself obtains this magnitude from the long time during which it is required to wait in the darkness of winter before the lush richness it now suddenly indulges in, and through human beings, who live bent double in their burrows and now emerge from them and straighten themselves up for two warm months. Stray dogs and ravens are also on the move. All movements ultimately come from this process of waking up.

The people who share their collective fate are different from villagers and townsfolk elsewhere, those people who are caught in fine-meshed networks. Here the ways of reaching an understanding with others are short. People don't wish one another a good day, but instead simply go up to one another boldly and start talking, and because there are few channels of information here, they set about exchanging rumours, just like in the Middle Ages, passing on reports by word of mouth, and interpreting what they see.

The *pierogi* seller stands there well wrapped up against the chill breeze and says: 'The travellers who come by sea now and pass through here are all red. It must be hot where they come from; at least, the sun must shine there a lot.'

Our route today takes us in another direction. At one point, beneath a hill, we spot a *Chum*, the traditional tent of the native wilderness dwellers in this region, which is covered in birch bark. But mostly, after driving for hours, we find ourselves arriving in villages that are no less remote. These settlements comprise of three blocks of rented flats and a few half-improvised huts with their own patches of garden. We plunge into the gaze of people who look like they've been built into the façades, like these men here lying smoking on their windowsills with bare torsos or white vests on. When I was young, such people were still to be seen all over. In the meantime, it seems, they've all decamped to Russia.

The few country roads hereabouts have rusty motorbikes with sidecars bumping along them, but their seats are ostentatiously upholstered with bearskins. Sometimes, residents will paint a single house entrance in a village in bright colours. This marks it out as the location of the regional store. Occasionally, they'll also paint a frieze of flowers on the windowsill, but real flowers don't make it as far as this. Many houses have already been abandoned, many windows nailed shut, while others have had plastic film stuck over them. In many places, the grass has grown halfway up the ground floor. All around are vast tracts of waste ground.

A couple of old women trundle by carrying plastic bags full of two-litre beer bottles. Most men here sport the military look, because this kind of clothing is cheap and durable and doesn't mark you out as belonging to any particular social class. The older men have also been known to appear on the streets in their dressing gowns. They all look like they're embedded in the house frontages.

In the first of the two shops in this settlement, they've run out of sugar, but in the next we're able to buy it loose, in a small cellophane bag. A chainsaw is buzzing somewhere in the distance. The inhabitants of this little spot in the middle of nowhere all have winter faces, even in summer. Washing is hung out to dry against the back external walls of the flats, while kids play football round the front. Behind, there's a row of old wooden houses with dark façades. They're built like the chalets on allotments, but stand there as bonny and presentable as little ladies who take pride in their appearance. A tethered horse is grazing by the roadside while another is running free and trots off.

Two women are sitting on an apartment balcony watching us. I start a conversation by calling up from the street:

'How many people still live here?'

'Less than a thousand.'

'The winter's just too long, right?'

'Nine months of it.'

'And how do you keep the cold at bay?'

'We glue over the gaps. We're at it all the time. If someone comes into a bit of money, the first thing they do is buy some modern European PVC windows, like those over there' – saying this, they point at the neighbouring house.

'How come no one farms the land here?'

'Anyone who owns land does farm it, but most people don't own any.'

'So how do you all earn a living?'

'Mostly from fishing in the river.'

'Incredible!'

They guffaw hoarsely. In fact, their lives are whatever they can wrest from a constant intake of alcohol, a form of survival in a barely habitable spot which they call their own.

Later, at a kiosk, we discover a handwritten invitation to an evening that's 'For Adults Only'. How we'd love to be there when the itinerant stripper peels off her fur coat! There's also a badly secured road sign by the side of the street, showing a man hanging upside down from a zebra crossing. There might well be a man hereabouts, but surely not a zebra crossing? One shop window contains an amateur painting on wood, badly faded by the sunlight. It shows a naked woman with a dog sitting on her lap. Beneath the shop window, great colonies of larkspurs are growing rampant.

We stop to have our picnic at the edge of a former cornfield. But instantly the sky grows black with midges and we beat a retreat in the face of the aggressive swarm that's emitting a sound like a chainsaw. We drive back to the little village and, on the patch of grass right next to the fork in the roads, set up our table, with five chairs, and lay out white bread, gherkins, tomatoes, red caviar, *qvass*, seakale salad, dried plaice, Russian sweets, and biscuits on the tablecloth. We present a curious image of decadent townies who have come to one of the poorest places imaginable to feast, as the residents lean out of their windows and gawp uncomprehendingly at us.

Sergei proceeds to tell us all about the various indigenous tribes of the region, paying special attention to – as he puts it – the lumpen, heavy-boned and libidinous women, and finishes by saying:

'Unless you've had sex with a Koryak woman, you can't say you've really seen Kamchatka.'

Everyone keeps their thoughts on this to themselves.

Yelena asks whether we've also got mushrooms in our forests in Germany.

'Oh sure, and every autumn I always used to go out into the woods and collect them.'

She beams at me and holds out her rough hand:

'Have you got the White Mushroom with the broad white stem and the large brown cap?'

'No, we don't have that one. We've got the Birch boletus.'

'But with the White Mushroom, the stem stays white even after cooking. And do you drink rosebay willowherb tea as well?'

'No, we don't.'

'Here, we even turn tree fungus into a tea.'

'That's not something we do back home.'

We agree that one day I'll go and visit her in her garrison town in the north of Russia, and that she'll bake cakes for me in the tiny kitchen of her apartment, that she'll cook for me, and that we'll go out in search of the White Mushroom, and ...'

'This lake is called The Dead Lake,' Sergei says, pointing out of the window.

'Why?'

'Because you never see anyone swimming in it.'

'So why's that?'

'Because it's called The Dead Lake.'

All the same, Kolya strips off his clothes and flees from the next swarm of midges by diving into the shallow water. Sergei's keeping a lookout for bears, so I decide to join Kolya. Silently, we swim next to one another out to the middle of the cold lake, whose brown surface is reflecting the mountain ridge, while, on the other side, the meadows ascend majestically between the hills. On the bank, Sergei starts singing a Russian song, and presently the women join in. After a hundred metres, Kolya decides that swimming any further would be too dangerous. He won't brook any objection on my part. Like some imperious landlord, he determines that we must turn round now, and then announces that this is no place for women to swim. Yelena duly puts her trousers and blouse back on.

'A man asks a Japanese visitor,' Sergei pipes up when we're all back in the car, 'what it is he likes about Russia. The Japanese answers: the children. And what else? asks the Russian. The children, comes the reply again. But you must like something other than that! the Russian exclaims. No, says the Japanese guy, everything the Russians make with their hands goes wrong.'

Yelena laughs her indulgent, knowing laugh. But her tone changes when she thinks of her own two children.

In the evening, the four of us stand and survey the great indifference of the ocean. Three rocks, covered in seagull guano, are being battered by the surf, and when the waves reach the shoreline, they push their crowns of foam up onto the volcanic sand in an orderly fashion. There are no stones, mussels, bits of wood or other jetsam on this beach, and the sky has conjured up a few puffy clouds – just for decoration, it doesn't mean anything serious. The bay is long and with no curve, just one huge horizontal, which only deviates at its far extremities. Behind us, we've got two volcanoes and a broad strip of low scrub and dwarf pines, and beyond it a sea of mixed wildflowers in a meadow. Yelena rolls her trouser legs up to her knees and says, before taking her first steps into the zone where the waves are breaking:

'I've never seen the sea looking more beautiful!'

Her mood is still oscillating between euphoria and solemn, introverted rapture. Then she snaps out of her reverie and starts running. Now she's beautiful. Now she's whooping for joy, for the first time in ages by the sound of it.

Finally, her husband ends up carrying her by piggyback from the beach, where she's cleaned all the volcanic sand off her wet feet, and back to the car so she won't get them dirty again, her little pudgy feet. It's clearly done her, a mother, a power of good to be treated like a kid again.

In the evenings, we no longer bother asking if the others would like to join us for the next day's outing, we just ask what time they'd like to be picked up. On the final morning, Yelena emerges with a basket hooked over her arm. She's spent the previous night baking *pierogi* and meatballs and salted noodles. She must have cooked everything she could lay her hands on, and when I bend down to greet her, for the first time, along with the cooking smell, I breathe in a faint aroma of a soapy perfume.

Approaching midday, and we're trudging through the monstrous scenery around Mount Avachinsky, crossing coagulated mudslides to reach the cooled lava bed left by the volcano's last eruption in 2001. On that occasion, it began by spewing out ash, followed by lava. The ash hardened to form tufa, and the lava became basalt. Ahead of us lies an uninhabited valley full of boulders – porous frozen lumps of rock – which is fringed by the green slope behind, covered with lichen, saxifrages and dwarf mountain pines, and filled with the high-pitched chirrups of birds and insects. A band of clouds has formed over the mountainside, and the dingy snowfields look like they've been besmirched by the dirty clouds – a sight that seems to predate the creation of nature.

Kolya, with his stout walking boots and the gait of a route-marcher who knows his way around mountains, has penetrated deep into the lava field. Sometimes, he crouches down for ages examining a plant down in the valley, and sometimes he's filming the petrified lava flow, and then he suddenly disappears from view behind the massive boulders that have come to rest on the fringes of the old river bed.

Yelena and I are left alone, and she touches my forearm. Her gaze has darkened from within and become more insistent, like it was wishing in this instant to be understood unconditionally, with no words being spoken. For the first time, there's something conspiratorial yet, at the same time, urgent in her eyes, and as I hold her gaze questioningly, she pulls an envelope from her pocket. Right, I get it. I'll take it, say nothing about it to anyone, and once I'm back home I'll search out a Russian exile who'll translate it for me, whereupon I'll reply, and the seriousness of my response will be leavened by my mentioning the White Mushroom.

However, she immediately withdraws the envelope and slips it back into her inner jacket pocket. But the imploring look hasn't gone from her eyes as I look into them.

'*Idi sjuda*,' she says in Russian, which I take to mean 'come with me'.

We teeter across a boulder field. Nastya is sitting on a rock, smoking and engrossed in one of Sergei's stories. Kolya has ventured so far down the cooled lava bed that he's scarcely to be seen anymore, and so we clamber on, ever upwards, to the sound of the wind humming, the boulders clicking, and the chirping of individual birds, on past a subsidiary crater that is showing signs of activity in the shape of erratic little puffs of smoke coming from its fumaroles.

This time I follow in Yelena's footsteps, captivated by her sense of purpose and still in thrall to that look of hers, which was like a promise. All around the sulphurously steaming side crater with its springs and geysers, green algae and horsetails are growing in abundance. Whenever a little cloud of sulphur smoke wafts up over us, we wave our hands in front of our mouths to try and wave it away and emit hacking coughs. In truth, it's just a shallow pit, a seething beige-yellow depression in the ground, on whose rim Yelena crouches, while the cloud of smoke billows around her. For a second time that day, she grabs hold of me, this time taking hold of my hand and pulling me towards her, and so I squat down next to her, while she, half whispering, recites a few lines of Russian verse, something formulaic or liturgical. I have no idea what she's saying. The deaf-mute couple on the street in Petropavlovsk spring to mind.

Her eyes briefly seek mine. Now there's something frenetic about her gaze, which has nothing to do with me. Then she puts her index finger to her half-open lips, pulls out the envelope again and tears it open at one end. Out of it she shakes a gossamer-fine cloud of ash into the breeze, some of which is carried down into the little crater, though most of it is blown beyond it, over the horsetails and algae, and scattered to the four winds. Yelena folds over the envelope twice and puts it back in her jacket. Finally she folds her hands, whispers a prayer, and it's all over. The acrid sulphur cloud shoos us down the mountainside. We keep descending, and where the vegetation is coated with dust, we're doubtless both thinking of what direction the ashes blew in, even though there was only a breath of wind. Then Yelena repeats her gesture, putting her index finger up for a second time to her closed mouth.

When we join up with the others again, she immediately throws open her arms to hug the unsuspecting Kolya and folds him into her embrace. He looks so young and immature in her arms, clamping his lips to her thick earlobe and clinging on for several long moments. She pats him soothingly on the back.

We spend our final evening together in the unused-looking surroundings of a hotel's open air pool; the pool itself is in the process of being filled with sulphurous thermal water via a hose. We settle breathlessly into the water. Kolya dives headlong into the pool, as Yelena dons a black bikini and swiftly plunges her stocky body beneath the milky surface of the water, while Sergei tirelessly fans the general mood of bonhomie. We drink beer from plastic cups and rampage around a bit. One time, Yelena gives my hand a squeeze under the water.

Piped music is switched on. Lots of instruments are involved, which sound terrible in their sheer jollity. They're led by an accordion, followed by the skipping sound of massed strings. The evening resounds with this happy sound. Later on, we're joined by a couple of Russian oligarchs; they're corpulent but muscular, and are carrying plastic bags full of bottles of drink.

They've also got a couple of pretty, purely decorative women in tow, who stretch and pose for one another by the poolside like nude models. When three more businessmen duly appear, all with white towels wrapped around their midriff, and start talking incessantly on their mobiles as they stand in the warm water, we decide it's time to leave.

Under the bushy trees on the poor estate where they're living, we pause for a while before taking our leave of Kolya and Yelena. We stand around the car and the men embrace one another with hardly any body contact. When I open my arms to Yelena, she approaches, her skin glowing with a light golden tan, and presses herself into my embrace without reserve, like she belongs there and wants to stay there forever. Then she turns to Nastya and asks her to translate:

'We've been through a period with lots of black stripes. We could never have imagined that we'd find such a white stripe here.'

Then she favours me once more with her plump body, which she knows people like to embrace, and stays in my arms. Meanwhile, Kolya's gone into the house to fetch some presents.

'I'll miss you,' I tell her.

When I open the presents back in my hotel room that evening, I discover that they're a pennant from Kolya's submarine base, a green metal key fob with the unit's emblem on it, and a blue and white striped sleeveless vest. It fits me all right, but looks like a wrestling singlet from a bathing resort on the Côte d'Azur in the 1920s. That's her present, I realize. I wear it for a whole night and then another, until it feels beyond retrieval. Yes, I'll miss her all right.

Mandalay

A Dream of the Sea

I grew up in that hilly landscape which on maps is called the Voreifel, and which devotees of the area like to refer to as 'Tuscany on the Rhine'. That's long since ceased to be a way of talking up the place, and is now just downright misleading. Our village, which was still a very rural place at the time, goes by the name of Oedekoven, which, as the mayor once explained to me, supposedly derives from the Germanic god Odin. Legend has it that the god once stopped and rested a while, as even deities sometimes have to, in a nearby wood.

The forest in question wasn't far from our house, and from one point on the gravel path that traversed this mixed wood before emerging into a meadow, you could look down into the valley through the sparse trees and catch a glimpse of the outlying villages and ministerial settlements on the outskirts of Bonn, which was close at hand. One time, when I was about seven, and was walking along this path with my mother very early in the morning, we turned down into a dip, and such a dense shroud of dawn mist blanketed the valley that I began to suspect I hadn't been told the whole truth about our village, and started grizzling:

'Why didn't you tell me we lived by the sea?'

In those days, I believed that the sea had a special power. There, far removed from cities, I fancied life must be different, clarified somehow by the constant sight of the water. Once I'd discovered the mystery of art galleries, I would search out depictions of the sea in the Old Masters, who weren't able to use photos, but instead had to work entirely from nature, and found myself astonished, for instance, by the seascapes of van Goyen with their dusty sheen on the water, and by the artist's evident skill in blending the sky, the land and the ocean surface together, like they were all made from the same material. I was also completely bowled over by the unfathomable, pagan Romanticism of Claude Lorrain's landscape paintings, where the valleys are deeper than any in nature and the horizons are sweeping.

Later, as a student, I learned about the phenomenon of dissimilitude, that is of falsification of the truth in nature, and discovered in Claude Lorrain's *Aeneas and Dido in Carthage* a kind of bashfulness towards the sea, which hinted at respect and a sense of helplessness, almost as if the painter had been afraid to produce an accurate rendition of the ocean, unable to look it in the eye, so to speak. In this particular work, the sea off the peninsula jutting into the Gulf of Tunis looks like it has been woven, like some ancient artefact, while farther out, it shimmers like a piece of blown glass.

Just as every fire reflects the sun, so in Claude's works every stream is supposed to recall the sea, and every puddle to allude to the ocean, and wherever waterfalls appear in his paintings, they really do seem to unleash the destructive power of breaking waves. Yet when Claude's gaze comes to rest on the surface of the actual sea, he's at a loss, and clearly finds himself incapable of imparting any motion or sparkle to it. Even where the oar blades of the galleys are dipping into the water, there are no splashes visible, and only a little bit of sea foam froths around the ship's keel. Nor is there any surf breaking on the shore, no reflection of the sky in the water. No, the fact is that there's more of the high seas in the wine glasses painted by many still-life painters than in all of Claude's depictions of the ocean.

So why should the thought of a bank of fog in the Voreifel or an oil painting by Claude Lorrain put me in mind of Burma? This mysterious country was for many years accessible to foreigners only for a week at a time, and even then just to visit four specific places. It was during that period that I was there. You were allowed to go to Rangoon, Pagan, Mandalay and Inle Lake. The rest of the country was the preserve of wild animals, pagodas, Buddhist monks and occasionally some pasty-faced apparatchik from the GDR, tramping through the jungle with his thick Saxon accent, in comradely solidarity with the socialist brother state of Myanmar. Anywhere you set foot was surrounded by forbidden places, lines of demarcation to the unknown and the inaccessible. So, from any given point in the country, you looked out as if from some vantage point at what was *terra incognita*.

In some places here, there are twice as many pagodas as there are people. You sit yourself up on the back of an ox-cart, sway across the steppe pastureland and stop in the sunset at one of these magnificent buildings, which seems to have blossomed and spread out from a golden bud on the roof. Inside, there's an incessant ringing, and from far-off the clang of a high-pitched bell lisps through the air. But in his shadowy niche, the selfsame Buddha sits there four times over, so that he can gaze out to all four points of the compass and bestow his blessings on them. Monks sit cross-legged and doze around his knees, holding incense sticks, and the ashes pile up in front their own laps.

Soothsayers also cower in the Buddha's shadow:

'Will you live longer than eighty? No, sadly that's impossible for you,' one of them tells me.

Sadly. For the first time in my life, I find myself hoping I'll make it to eighty-one. But while I'm still trying to come to terms with my short life expectancy, the enlightened one dunks a bitter, strawberry-shaped fruit into some salt, and his eyes say 'Just go ahead and cry!' I pass him a wafer-thin flag of gold leaf in an envelope as a gift. He bows. The proper decorum has been observed; things have been 'agreeable to God'.

The artisans worked away for hours in their dark pens, hammering the paper packet with the little gold nugget inside with their mallets until they'd turned it into this glinting scrap of gold leaf. The soothsayer picks up the leaf and, murmuring softly to himself, proceeds to stick it on a statuette of the Buddha that's only the height of a person, and which has lost all trace of its facial features beneath all the gold that's been placed there; now all that's visible through the accretion of gold leaf is the Kajal eyeliner on the lids of his eyes.

'Sadly,' the soothsayer repeats, 'no older than eighty' and then adds: 'During your lifetime you'll get on well with three of the four elements. Water will never be your friend, though. Never.'

Sadly. I'll burn my lifesaver's certificate, then, in the friendly fire.

'Everything that means you harm will come at you from a southeasterly direction.'

'And what happens if I turn round?'

This kind of hair-splitting won't do me much good. The seer doesn't say as much, but I can tell from his eyes. My ox-cart has left by now, but the steppe is steaming, warm and grey. I stuff a splinter of betel nut wrapped in a leaf into my cheek, salivate and proceed on foot. Every time you swallow, a warm sensation fills your stomach and you feel a bit more intoxicated. When you spit, it comes out a fiery-red colour; your saliva forms droplets on the leaves and trickles away into the sand.

After a lifetime of betel nut abuse, old people's teeth start rotting in their mouths. But chewing the nut does at least keep hunger at bay, and that's sometimes an important factor, not just because people are poor but also because Burma, as George Orwell found, has the rare gift of turning every appealing dish into an unpalatable one. Meat comes to the table covered in a greenish fur, the unidentifiable mush of vegetables smells of crocuses and stagnant ponds, the little flecks of colour in the rice turn out to be insects, and all the while we're being given sideways glances by the government functionaries in civilian clothes seated at the next table, who are making sure we don't get on too friendly terms with the locals.

Anyone who cares to get up at five o'clock can watch people panning for gold in the river, and observe how they put their heads together over the pans, while little girls wash and brush down oxen in the water. But at this hour, the snuffling and calls are muted. The pearly white face of a stone idol, half faun, half gryphon, looms over the bushes covering the cliffs above the river, and behind, in the old wooden monastery building, the barefoot monks are already on the move, like orange and rust-red splashes of watercolour. As they begin their bell-ringing and prayer, or simply sit studying holy scriptures in silence, the young woman truck-bus driver on the road below jams a thick, green cheroot in her mouth and flashes a beaming betel nut-red smile at the first passenger of the day. O happy day!

Burma has lived for too long with its back turned to the outside world for its people to have any inkling of quite how neglected and shabby the country has become, and how taken aback we tourists are when we get there. Taking any form of transport is an arduous affair, accommodation is pitiful, and the restaurants are questionable, but, then again, in the capital Rangoon there is The Strand, that magnificent hotel from the colonial period, which is on a par with its two sister establishments, the Oriental in Bangkok and Raffles Hotel in Singapore, with suites of rooms panelled in dark wood and antique fittings, with blood-red upholstery and lounges in which the aroma of a century of espionage and secret diplomacy and the memory of panama hats still linger. These are my favourite kind of hotels, the ones where you get steeped in their history when you stay there. That's what The Strand is like.

When I arrived, there were no single rooms left, so I agreed to share with a British woman called Belinda, who was travelling on her own. Our room, with its red furnishings and dark furniture – more of a set of rooms, in fact – was so extensive that we could almost have avoided meeting one another entirely. She walked in, declared it far too large and oppressive, and immediately closed the curtains, like she needed to protect our domain from the prying eyes of strangers.

'Shall we go and eat?'

We took a seat in the sprawling dining room of the hotel, with wood panelling all round the room, along with pieces of colonial memorabilia and a set of rituals resurrected from the past. The waiter pushed the chair into the backs of Belinda's knees as she went to sit down, and she gratefully acknowledged this attempt at politeness.

As a conversational opener, she opted for 'the poverty out there', which she found 'depressing'. I countered with a gambit of my own:

'On the other hand, it's very picturesque.'

'You cynic!'

I explained that feeling sorry for the miserable living conditions of most people in the world was only one side of the coin. The other was that many travellers would surely feel disappointed not to encounter images of poverty at their destination. She shot me an indignant look before replying sharply:

'I'm sure you're considering this from some loftier intellectual standpoint than me, but all I can say is that the sight of poverty makes me sad.'

I expounded on my theory that very few things made a country so multifaceted, such a feast for the eye and so baroque as poverty. Before shaping up to reply, she paused for a moment, to give me a chance to feel ashamed at what I'd just said. Then, for safety's sake, she decided to let it pass and contented herself with giving me that indignant look again.

'Don't you think that feeling superior boosts your own sense of well-being, though?' I asked.

She didn't deign to grace that with a direct response.

'These countries are so far away,' she said, 'and even further where their inner lives are concerned. We've only just opened the door a crack on these people, who are so friendly, and on their culture, their food …'

She says it with a stern look in her eyes, laying stress on every sentence she utters, as each of them has involved labour and great effort on her part. Yet although her words still sound magnanimous, in the next instant her thoughts have turned to the off-putting tendency of the Burmese to try and swindle her at every opportunity, and she duly embarks on some long and involved calculations of what she should have been charged for railway journeys, museums and rickshaws. Though all her figures come from some old travel guides, they can still be measured against the current exchange rate and then recalculated with the aid of a pocket calculator. She's also got a fund of stories about how she refused to let herself be diddled and managed to get the better of this or that transaction.

No, she finally announces, she'll never 'get her head round the price of things' here. So she'll only feel really at ease in large hotels with a fixed price list. But when there are gaps in the menu ... And when so many waiters are hanging about with nothing to do, like they are here ...

'You're missing half the menu, though. There you go.'

She scrutinizes the waiter like he is the menu.

'So what *have* you got, then? No duck? What, no duck in Burma? But I've noticed the odd duck wandering around outside. Just the odd one, mind ...' she gives a hollow laugh.

But the waiter doesn't give her the satisfaction of bursting into tears. Instead, he clumsily spills ice cubes over half the table.

'No problem', Belinda reassures him, and sweeps the ice cubes off her lap, sending them clattering down onto the wooden floor, where they skid away and are gathered up into a tumbler by two girls in traditional dress.

And Belinda? She knows the hospitality profession inside out; after all, she herself has a top position in the service industry sector, a realm where people's job titles somehow always seem to be comprised of terms like 'corporate', 'assistant', 'manager' and 'center'. There's no pulling the wool over her eyes, and she's not about to change her attitude in Burma either. She'll always view all the constantly changing landscapes, social structures, and moral situations she encounters in her career through the same eyes, and at the end of the day distill everything she's seen here down to the standpoint of the initiate, who can say she's been there and so has the right to speak when others would do best to hold their peace: 'Burma is … all the people there want to do is … religion makes them … their attitude to poverty is comparatively …'

All that can be said for her self-importance is that it stimulates an aggressive sexuality in me, as I discover when she saunters back into the bedroom from the bathroom in her skimpy pyjama shorts.

We spent that night sitting up in our high beds, drinking bottled beer and chatting, and the mixture of her fussy, imperious nature and her vulnerability in an alien culture somehow made her so attractive that I found myself constantly holding my bottle out to clink with hers. In turn, she confessed to me that up till now she'd simply had 'no time' for a man in her life. Later, we talked about what other people would surely do in our position. But we never got round to it.

The following day, I assuaged my guilty conscience for having stayed in such a lavish hotel and enjoyed such bossy company by buying myself a cheap ticket at the railway station for the journey to Mandalay. And so I took my place in cattle class alongside the peasants, workers and assorted vermin.

Burmese State Railway compartments consist of two benches made of light-coloured wood facing one another, each with room for three skinny people – or in the case of those opposite me, a married couple with a turkey. The turkey is an ugly creature, which spends all the time looking disdainfully out of the window and avoiding eye contact. Beneath its head, its red lappet dangles like a tumour. The couple who own it, on the other hand, are very attractive and animated. At first, it's only the husband, with his large, deep-set eyes, who ventures to give me a beaming smile. His eyes stay glued to mine unwaveringly, like he's flirting with me.

His wife Mariam is a dormant beauty, who clearly has no inkling of how attractive she is. Her skin is the colour of the earth, she's heavy limbed, her eyes linger for a long time on things before she looks away, and when she goes to pick up an object, her hand hovers over it before touching it like she's about to canoodle with it, and she caresses it before she uses it. Also, her smile seems to emerge from deep inside her. But when it finally appears on her face, it spreads out and doesn't leave until it's flooded every last corner of her countenance. You can't stop looking at her.

When she shakes my hand, it remains there in my palm like some item she's put down, soft and yielding. The growth of her fingernails has carried the last bit of red nail polish she applied to well beyond the middle of the nail. Whenever she nods, or the train rocks, the flesh of her face moves up and down slightly. Only her eyes redden.

'Where are you headed for?' I ask.

'Home,' says the man, 'to the war zone.'

'What war?' I ask, and call to mind the scene from the film *Masculin Féminin*, where Jean-Luc Godard asks the beauty queen 'Miss 19' where there are wars going on now, and she can't give him an answer.

'A war's been going on for decades on the border between Burma and China,' he replies. 'But we're very self-contained there, so the outside world doesn't know about what's happening.'

'Who are you, then?'

'We belong to the Kachin people.'

'What's the war about?'

He starts counting on his fingers: 'Well, previously it was against the British, then the Chinese, then we were in alliance with the Chinese against the Burmese government, then against the army, then against the rebel leader Prince Khun Sa, then we fought against the government to gain our independence ...'

His finger hovers in the air above the hand he's counting off from ...

'And that's the lot,' Mariam finishes his sentence for him and laughs.

I remember seeing Prince Khun Sa's photo in a news magazine. This drug baron of northern Burma had been pictured posing proudly with his private army. He was half Chinese, had formerly served as an officer in the Chinese Nationalist Army, and for decades controlled the opium trade in the 'Golden Triangle' of Burma, Thailand and Laos. In 1994, his HQ was stormed by Burmese forces and the drug trade in the region was reorganized. But the Burmese authorities turned down a request from the USA for his extradition. Khun Sa retired from the drug trade and began dealing in precious stones, and lived for another ten years and more in Rangoon under heavy protection.

Yes, war's a long established facet of life in Khin Maung and Mariam's homeland. They are both bookbinders and run a little workshop together. We've got a long journey ahead of us, and they use the time to explain their circumstances to me, with Mariam contributing just as much as her husband, and just as proudly, as her husband: even the British never encountered such a big problem colonizing a region as they did in the north of Burma. The name 'Kachin' is an umbrella term for various different ethnic groups, such as the Lashi, the Lisu, the Maru and the Rawang. The Kachin, who also lived in China and India, adopted Christianity in order to set themselves apart from the indigenous Burmans, who were Buddhist. Whereas in earlier times in their region, the Communist Party of Burma had fought loyally for closer ties to their Chinese neighbours to the north, up to 1993 the Kachin in Burma, with their Kachin Independent Army, had battled the government, and even nowadays the armed struggle was still going on to secure independence for their province and to combat the opium and diamond smugglers.

Khin Maung and Mariam lived in a village north of Myitkyina, in a district that was closed to foreigners and not far from the border with China. Myitkyina is a centre for the mining of gold, jade, and amber, yet farmers, who practice shifting cultivation, also bring their produce to the market there, and the local Kachins are still organized into tribal groups under chieftains. The railway ends there, but the road continues on into China and India.

Mariam gets control of the unruly turkey by grasping its neck. Khin Maung is gripping a linen sack full of sugar between his knees. Flies have taken up residence on it in their hundreds. Outside the train, expanses of black earth come into view, and the bell-shaped pagoda roofs shine in white or gold, and in so far as anyone has a new acquisition, it's just a peaked cap. The country here smells of sorghum and rotting vegetables. But everyone's still wearing a relaxed smile.

Huts stalk across the surface of marshy lakes on rotten pilings. You can almost see epidemics developing, and because the windows remain open all the while, every time the train stops, insects swarm into the carriage, drunk on the miasma of decay. Mariam holds an empty bottle of Western perfume, a gift from a tourist, to her nostrils. Little horses pelt, panting, down an alleyway. Tattooed boys in traditional *longyi* puff clouds of smoke from their green cheroots, while men in checked sarongs squat idly outside blue-painted huts, with their dogs and kids before them, ox-carts trail behind horse-drawn buggies, and far-off in the distance a loudspeaker van blares out music seemingly composed of knocking and whining sounds.

Schoolboys come down the road, arm in arm. There's a smell of dried fish in the air, and standing back on the platform, as if in respect for the train, is a group of farmers, cattle herders and monks. A clanking of horse harnesses can be heard, before it's drowned out by the thundering of ancient heavy lorries. Then as the train moves off silence asserts itself once more, broken only now and then by the cry of a gold prospector on a riverbank. Immediately, fellow prospectors crowd in on him from left and right, pressing to look into his pan and pointing meaningfully with their index fingers at the little pool of silt gathered there.

'We should be in Freetown,' says Khin Maung. He's read in a newspaper that in Freetown, Sierra Leone, recent heavy rainfall has washed away topsoil and exposed diamonds. People have been rushing there from every corner of the country, armed with primitive tools like spades and shovels, nets, sieves and pans, without a clue what to do. They're also bringing weapons with them. There have already been some serious clashes, and the government has had to deploy troops. Khin Maung has read that report like it relates to him. But isn't he living in the middle of a war himself?

A Burman mother on the other side of the corridor is jiggling her little girl on her lap. Every time the child screams in delight, she apologizes to everyone around her for the noise.

'Oh, don't worry, that's the sweetest noise.'

Hearing this, she places her hand flat on her chest with relief.

'Is it, indeed?' she asks incredulously, like she's never heard such a thing before, and looks at her daughter with fresh eyes.

The only other foreigner in cattle class is a Canadian, who went to a monastery in northern Thailand to try and get over his dependence on heroin, but ended up fleeing after enduring tadpoles in the bath water, lice in his bed, awful food and accommodation like a prison cell.

'They chain you up. If you try and get away, they beat you with a rubber hose. There's nothing meek or mild about that place. Just filth, violence and tyranny. But there is a fish pond in the courtyard and mango trees where you can sit in the shade and play your music.'

He's on his second trip to Burma to try and prevent his relapse into drugs. Running down his arm, he's had the word 'hellian' tattooed – a dweller in hell.

When I ask Khin Maung what the purpose of his journey is, he opens his large, soulful eyes wide and says nothing.

'The purpose,' I repeat, 'the purpose of your travel.'

The look he gives me is one of amiable dull-wittedness, and Mariam assumes an expression of serious introspection behind her frozen smile. And that doesn't change even as he begins listing what he bought in Rangoon: paper, glue, various knives ... He'll bind a book for me, he says, with gold embossed letters on the cover. And months later, it really is delivered to me – it's blue, with our names on it, and every line looks like it's been meticulously set by hand.

Now that he's got plenty of work lined up for the foreseeable future, he tells me, he ...

... still won't tell me why you've made this journey, then?

It takes quite some time, plus lots of exchanged glances between them and satisfying themselves that they're in agreement with one another, before the charming couple finally divulge what they've been up to. It turns out they've taken their excursion in order to do something scarcely permitted, basically because it's so senseless: for once in their life they wanted to see the sea, wanted to take the short journey of a few kilometres from Rangoon to the ocean and revel in the sight of the water. That was all.

'But there are shorter routes from where you live to the coast.'

'Ah, but it's easier to get permission to take a trip to Rangoon.'

In the capital, though, they'd run into a police roadblock and had been stopped from going any further.

'Why was that?'

Khin Maung laughs again. Only a foreigner could ask that.

He has some quite different questions: What happens to things that were once reflected in the surface of the ocean? He'd once read that their presence still remains there – the sunken ships, the silhouettes of freighters, even bottles that had been bobbing on the waves. Can you still see them, feel them, he asks me?

His questions are positively poetic. My answers aren't. But that doesn't dim his enthusiasm in the slightest. Why, he even wants to know, should the sea, of all things, be a simile for love? I explain:

'It appears boundless, its colour is that of devotion, and it looks static but it's constantly in motion …'

'But it can rage sometimes.'

The married couple sit there, their knees wrapped in their palms, sit there like mirror images of one another between their ugly turkey and their sack of sugar and refuse to accept the sea as a simile. Maybe their love is a seascape in the style of Claude Lorrain? Is that what I should see?

I tell them how, towards the end of the nineteenth century, the writer Franz Grillparzer travelled to the Adriatic to see the sea for the first time, which he couldn't appreciate properly in photos or early moving film. I recount how we readers waited with bated breath for the outcome; after all, this was a poet, a man of words, encountering the ocean in its original form for the first time in his life. And what does he write in his diary?: 'It's not how I imagined it.'

Khin Maung gazes contentedly out of the window. My Grillparzer story makes no impression on him, but we journey on, chatting and sharing.

'What's the sea like where you live?' he wants to know.

'We've got two small ones,' I tell him. 'They mean well.'

'And what do they look like?'

'Sometimes just like fog in a valley.'

The friendly expression never leaves his face, and the reason for this – however strange it may sound – is that I, the foreigner, am the one who can accredit everything I say, and so he all he does is sit there like a moderator and nod in assent to his wife. She needs to share in our mutual understanding. This she does indeed do, and when we spot a group of monks walking along the embankment, she calls out: 'Monks', and when it's water buffaloes, 'Buffaloes'. And that's all it takes to establish complete and cordial communication between us.

'What's your final destination?' I ask. 'What kind of village do you live in?'

'It's not worth mentioning,' says Khin Maung. 'It's so small.'

We can see from the train that poor people in Burma live in bamboo huts which get swept away by the monsoons, whereas the rich live in houses made of teak. Only very few villages have electricity, and Khin Maung tells me that in many cases people's only means of getting provisions is to walk for hours to the nearest markets.

'But do the Burmese live in houses, or huts?'

'We live in war,' Khin Maung repeats.

From our compartment window, we see villages whose poverty has even taken on an idyllic appearance. I fall to wondering whether the couple's home village is like this: a cluster of huts on pilings grouped around a pond, with wooden troughs for the cattle feed, surrounded by groundnut fields and palm groves, blessed with the black, fertile soil, graced with pagodas strewn liberally across the plains? It's clear people can make a living from farming here, and what they don't possess they cobble together out of scrap.

We see two workers taking turns to hammer a red-hot horseshoe on an anvil, alternating with lightning speed; we spot a lone peasant under a Palmyra Palm, praying to the tree spirits and hoping to appease them before he climbs up into its branches to harvest the fruit with his machete. We notice a potter bending over his wheel and shaving off clay so as to get the right shape of water jug; we see bamboo-mat weavers soaking the strips; gold beaters using mallets to flatten little packets of paper containing grains of the precious metal and transform it into gold leaf; women stirring and applying the protective cosmetic paste called *Thanaka* – made from water, bark and sandalwood – to their face; and women with their heads smothered in sweet tree-bark shampoo conducting their hair-washing ritual. And when the train stops, we catch the sound of handbells and flutes drifting over from the nearby monastery complex, as if this is the sound favoured by the gods, the aural equivalent of candlelight.

One can also hear prayers being chanted in unison, by voices that sound like they're arguing. They always intone the same thing; they always do the same things in the same sequence. This is the sound, then, of the prayer mantra, which never varies and which always follows the same cycle, like the mantra of work. Indeed, the mantras of prayer and work somehow belong together, given that they both concern eternally mythical realms of human activity.

Meanwhile Khin Maung has uncorked a bulbous bottle covered in smooth leather, and pours me and himself a small measure of rice wine into two tiny glasses that he unwraps from newspaper.

'Twelve hundred years ago, the Kachin left Tibet and emigrated to the north of Burma,' he announces. 'When the Great Spirit distributed the scripture among the Kachin, it was given to them on a piece of leather. So the Kachin carried the scripture under his arm, but in his excitement he sweated so profusely that the leather had to be dried out over a fire. But while it was hanging there, the rats snatched it, chewed on it and dragged it off into a rice basket. The Kachin retrieved it and tried to save the content of the scripture by soaking the rice and drinking the water.' Having successfully reached this stage of his story, Khin Maung gives me a beaming smile before continuing. 'And that's why the wise priests still drink rice wine today before they begin their prophesies, and in so doing gain access to the truth. Your good health!'

Mandalay, that rebellious settlement oriented toward the modern, announced its presence outside the window with the first outlying suburbs of a growing million-inhabitant metropolis, yet one which cannot yet shake off its village past. These little hovels gradually give way to the urban sprawl on the banks of the Irrawaddy, a river some people call 'The Refresher'. The city has been flooded with Western products, like the purple bobble hats worn by old men, comics, kid's bikes with stabilizers and oral irrigators. And yet its streets are still full of rumbling ox-carts, along with ancient tractors, wagons and rickshaws, and unstreamlined cars from China.

We exchange our final questions and answers. I'm not permitted to travel beyond the limits of this city, and Khin Maung and Mariam sit here in their red traditional garb, with their turkey and sack between their knees, and their amazing food, which they unwrap from sheets of newspaper – and with their inflamed eyes, which keep a lookout for everything, they'll await whatever comes.

'Why are you dressed in red?'

Khin Maung grows serious, for despite being a Christian like most of the Kachin, he's still keen not to miss out on Buddha and the animistic spirits, and this polytheism hasn't in any way diminished his faith. Christ and Buddha are jointly responsible for the Hereafter, he reckons, whereas the spirits mainly operate in the Here and Now. That's why he and Mariam also pay an occasional visit to the spirit sisters, the half-beings, who act as mediums.

'The red stands for the blood of the earth and for the migration of souls that awaits us.'

'And for water?'

'For us, water represents rebirth, the most important factor in the cycle of life.'

And Mariam adds: 'We've long prayed to heaven for Indra, the god of war and thunder, to split the monsoon clouds asunder with his diamond thunderbolt and draw rain from them.'

So, their trip to the sea was more of a pilgrimage than an excursion. They'd wanted to start by praying in the Shwedagon Pagoda, then journey to the shore and approach the ocean. But then a power had blocked their way that was neither God nor Nature, and yet which was as potent as both: the power of the state. The only liberty it granted us was to sit together in cattle class on a train and try and get over all our failures and frustrations. They won't get to see the sea, and I won't get to see their village.

Mandalay is the place where we'll part in a clumsy embrace. They'll try to re-enact the kind of embrace they've seen in films, and I won't know how much body I'm meant to hug when embracing the wife of a Burmese Kachin bookbinder or rather when I'm taking hold of her rounded shoulders and just drawing her a couple of centimetres closer to me. So we embrace one another here, at this intersection of two impermeable borders. Each of us disappears behind a wall that is impenetrable for those left behind.

I wished we'd been able to do the obvious, natural thing and stand by the sea, travel to their village and stay there, but this time our parting isn't culturally determined but politically. I haven't been able to give them a vicarious experience of the sea that they never got to see. My sea is a different one, and likewise I'm left to search for their village in their eyes, in the texture of their hands, in the glances they give one another, their fabrics and utensils, but I search in vain.

And so we remain gazing intently at one another, because the only thing we have left is to try and decipher the reality of the other's existence, and our eyes just will not disengage, as I stand by the carriage window on the platform at Mandalay station and the train carrying the couple starts to move off; they've only raised their hands slightly to wave goodbye. Khin Maung's passion is still palpable, and Mariam's beaming face still lingers in the air, and when they've finally both disappeared from view something intangible still remains on this platform, something I can only see as art. It is the aura of a border, which has just revealed itself to be impassable and yet permeable all the same.

Lake Fucino

Wasting Away

Around the mid-1980s, a young woman with a dark pageboy haircut was labouring long and hard on her research in the Austrian National Library in Vienna. Every morning she'd heave a weighty pile of books onto the same desk, and every evening, she'd lug them back to the same returns counter. She didn't let anything distract her. The only people who heard her voice were the library staff who handed out the books to her and collected them again in the evening. No one invited her for coffee, nobody chatted with her, and because I sat two rows behind her, I can say with certainty that she made no moves herself to invite anyone over to her desk, or to go and fetch anyone from theirs. Her skin was pale, but even so she still wore white face powder, never appeared without her Campari-red lipstick on and, even in her late twenties, must already have been dyeing her hair. Jet black.

But it wasn't her rather eccentric appearance or her forbidding, almost sneering, manner, nor indeed her fixation on her work – which was less zealous diligence than it was a burning fury, a self-immolation – that kept any of her fellow brain-workers from pestering her. Rather, it was that she couldn't help but give off an air of awkwardness and hysteria, a sense that she might well be fanatical or ecstatic, or, at the very least, unreasonably and desperately at odds with life. I didn't use her real name very often, since she couldn't stand it, and so we settled on 'Clarisse' as being the one that suited her better than any other. Curiously, I can recall her smell better than I can her appearance – a disembodied, mildewy odour that was somehow the carrier medium for the smell of churchy types who have remained unredeemed.

I'd been working in this library for some months, during which time we'd taken note of each other's presence, nothing more; months in which I studied her neck for the most part, her white-powdered, naked neck, which supported the black helmet of hair like the stalk of a mushroom supports its cap. And so the months went by, until one day I came back from my lunch break to find a note on top of my papers. On it, scribbled hastily in thin, violet-coloured ink, were the words: 'Our man from Cairo has arrived at the station'.

The next time I got up from my desk, I stole a glance as I passed hers just to check that she wrote in violet ink. So, that evening, I came and leant on her desk and asked:

'So, what now?'

She was writing about Kafka, but you couldn't call it research. Rather, Kafka was imposing his will upon her, casting a spell on her. Nothing and no one could resist it. It was a case of taking something too seriously beyond all measure, a classic case in fact, given that she was taking Kafka more seriously than he ever took himself in all likelihood. It was a hostage-taking, with herself as the hostage.

Kafka was hollowing out her life and moving around in it, and when she referred to him as her 'spiritual father', she did it deliberately in order to do down her birth father, a man who'd come to Austria as a guest worker from the Abruzzi – in her words, a contemptible little man who'd never felt at home here, and who'd had a questionable relationship with her when she was a child. Yet there was also something questionable about the way she spoke about it; it sometimes seemed as though she really wanted it to have been the case, so she'd have grounds, after the early death of her mother, for severing all contact with her father too, so she could make room for Kafka.

We saw each other regularly for a while. With her, it was always unconventional, always stimulating. We slept little, and theoretically nothing was out of bounds. One time, she explained the meaning of the motif of hunger in Kafka: it wasn't hunger in a material or social sense, nor did it have anything to do with desire, desperation or longing, but rather the 'Hunger Artist' in Kafka's famous story of that name was attempting to reinvent himself, to drain his existence, so to speak, so that he might ultimately be able to slough it off like a dead skin.

'It's all about self-abandonment as the prerequisite for self-creation. In order to find himself, he must first lose himself. But he can't do that all of a sudden, just like that – instead, he has to be rid of every atom of his former self, piece by piece. It's not just a simple dialectical process, you understand. He's someone who only becomes a person by becoming nothing. Or rather whose existence is sealed by his non-existence, his self-destruction through not eating.'

'Got it.'

I was at pains to appease her. That night, it had got so late that she'd had to sleep over at my place. Or rather, I'd eventually fallen asleep. In the middle of the night, she swung herself on top of me, straddled my loins and panted in my ear that we should make a baby now, a baby that would release us and become the focus of everything. Drunk with sleep, I managed to talk her out of the baby, though not the idea of release as such.

Even so, that was the only moment when she gave any indication of being delusional or alarming, and her ensuing humiliation and my resulting caution combined from here on in to create a distance, which had its origin in the moment of greatest intimacy between us. From this point on, we could no longer interact unconventionally. Something had arisen which was genuine, but which was also larger than our messy relationship.

So we drifted apart. I left Vienna, and pretty soon she stopped writing, and because we had no mutual friends, I didn't hear any news of her either. No trace of her Kafka study ever came to light in the academic world.

Then one evening her father phoned me, which in its own way was awful, since my mental image of him oscillated between the labourer from the Abruzzi and the sexually predatory patriarch. It took him ages to get to the point, though you could tell from the underlying tone of agitation in his voice that his call would take a bad turn, which he was spinning out mainly in order to spare himself.

Clarisse has ruined herself with her Kafka study, he told me. At first, of course, he'd been proud that his daughter would be a *dottoressa*. He didn't understand a word of what she was writing, but at some stage things had clearly gone off the rails. She'd given him a volume of Kafka to read, and he'd actually found it 'interesting', and sometimes the writer could even be 'genuinely funny', but the effect it had on her was ...'

'So what effect did it have?'

Two months ago, it seems, she'd applied to be admitted to a

religious order. And indeed, the sisters in the convent did take her in for a probationary period before it gradually dawned on them that she hadn't joined the convent to serve God but to starve herself to death. Of course, that was completely beyond the pale and so the abbess ruled that Clarisse should be dismissed from the convent. When her father came to pick her up, she was emaciated and utterly deranged.

He couldn't send her back to the library, and leaving her alone in her flat was too risky, he reckoned, so he'd loaded her into the car and taken her home, to the Abruzzi.

'You know Lake Fucino, right? Well, on the other side – on the south side of Lake Fucino, that is – Campobasso's up in the mountains there.'

'That's where you're from, then?'

'Yeah.'

'Have you still got family there?'

'No.'

'Is that where you're calling me from?'

'Yes.'

'And what do you want me to do?'

'Can you help us?'

He said 'us' – a quite different plural form from 'our man from Cairo', whom I should never have heard about again.

When I set off two days later, it was with some very mixed emotions: the father's voice on the telephone had sounded pitiful, and the thought of leaving Clarisse alone with her father in a village in the Abruzzi was unsettling, but it was also a sense of adventure that impelled me to purchase a railway ticket to Lake Fucino. So, I was driven both by concern and by the idea of seeing a part of the world I'd never been to before.

Lake Fucino was a familiar theme in a body of literature where Italy was still referred to as 'Arcadia' and was redolent of lemons and cemetery angels. Wilhelm Waiblinger, the young and disturbed friend of the poet Hölderlin who died in Rome, once wrote in a letter:

> What a southerly colour there is to the lake! What a beautiful blue, mixed with violet and greenish hues! What a sensual, magnificent, yearning enchantment in the lovely mountains … You can have no conception of the clarity of this lake. The charming surroundings are reflected in its surface not only as indistinct masses but also in the most delicate outlines, with all their colour tones and details, and rocks and cliffs shimmering in the most delightful way in the still, limpid water. You feel like you're no longer floating on the water; it seems to be another, much more refined, thinner, more spiritual element, an element akin to light on which you're being borne, and upon which the reflection of the azure-dark southern sky is resting.

I delved further into the Bavarian state library in Munich in search of more literary vignettes of the lake, and found that other, less rhapsodic writers than the young Waiblinger maintained that no rivers ran into the lake or flowed out of it, and that it drained into subterranean chambers; they also claimed that its vegetation was drab, and that a gloomy tranquility lay heavy over its surface. Sure enough, in watercolours by Edward Lear, it really does look like a pool of water that someone's just spilt, fascinatingly dead in appearance.

'Get off at Avezzano,' the woman at the station ticket booth told me when I bought my ticket. 'That's your nearest stop.'

Fine, then – I was off to Avezzano, that unfortunate place which was transformed by an earthquake in January 1915 from a charming mediaeval town into a collection of temporary huts. Of its 13,000 inhabitants, barely 2,000 survived. Then, during the Second World War, the town was bombed by the Allies, who were trying to hit German units. In actual fact, Avezzano had been an important stronghold of Italian partisan resistance. It was razed to the ground by this 'friendly fire'.

My train made its way across the Brenner Pass, through the countless tunnels of Emilia-Romagna, and across the plains of Tuscany and Umbria. Once the foothills of the Alps were behind us, what a sense of relief there was in the imperceptible, calming transformation of the landscape to a much softer one. Here the terrain mostly comprised round-topped hills, with only the odd cone-shaped prominence, often with its top flattened off, rising up, all on its own, alongside winding river valleys or from desolate hollows. These isolated prominences were like host animals to remote settlements, fortified from ancient times, which clung to their flanks and which for the most part had been hewn from the rock of the hillside. Almost all the old villages here had sited themselves in this way on the summits of hills or the slopes, with only the modern towns – unimpressed by old notions of defence and with their industries dependent upon water – electing to locate themselves by rivers.

The first hint of the Abruzzi Mountains is given by the light they cast – a light that bleaches out the most distant hill ridges to simple outlines, makes the intervening uplands in the middle distance rise up blue from the *sfumato* of the valley mists, and causes the closest stretch of land to the viewer to appear all the more colourful by contrast. Every zone of this typical terraced landscape, which sometimes displays line upon line of tree-lined ridges receding into the far distance, has its own colour, its own way of dissolving its complexion in the whitish-blue of the far haze and sky, its own structure. Far-off, all one can see is a bluish expanse, whereas closer at hand some grey-brown shapes begin to emerge from the green and black of the fields and meadows, and right up close you can make out the rich variety of asymmetrically-shaped cultivated plots, untended tracts of land, interspersed bits of wilderness, and overgrown streambeds overhung with bushes in blossom and willow branches.

But where the table mountains recede, their extended ridges peter out into gently declining slopes, and the wave motion of the hills comes to a stop, then that other form of landscape begins to form in isolated pockets, grandiose in its simplicity: that of the plains and the high plains. Here, a moonscape stretches away on both sides of the lonely roads; it's got a character all its own and there are virtually no settlements here, in fact it's almost devoid of any traces of human activity at all. Time and again, we come across fields of thistles and simple saxifrages carpeting mountain passes, and only on the more distant plains, where the gentle folds of the mountain sweep down from its dramatic heights, have farmers planted one or two fields of wheat or corn, which are liberally sprinkled with poppies and cornflowers.

Large tracts of land have remained undeveloped here, or were simply abandoned. The slopes, which look like they're covered in steppe vegetation, and the distant cornfields lie there so indistinctly in the haze that it's almost as if the primordial seas still covered this region. Other fields, on the other hand, were actually cut from the wilderness and now sit there as simple geometrical patterns like patches on a landscape that knows of no other such accurate figures.

Over large stretches, this landscape seems to positively suppress all signs that humans were present, but then suddenly an isolated farmstead pops up, or a bar, or a shop, and the alleyways run down between the few houses like open corridors that have been built to link the various different rooms of a single house. For just as the outer suburbs of towns have sometimes pushed outwards into and through villages, so the network of alleys, staircases, and horse stairs in these mountain villages often obliterate the division between public and private space.

While people were safer from attackers up on high ground in former times, nowadays these villages are endangered by their very remoteness and isolation. Yet forms of settlements are also ways of life. For instance, that's why you'll encounter more communal festivities among mountain-dwelling people, as well as more communal tasks like baking and washing, carting around burdens on donkeys, or balancing them on one's head – all habits that have disappeared down in the valleys, thus also causing various forms of conviviality, social intercourse and communal life to become less close and binding there too.

In such landscapes, it's like you're stepping into the backgrounds of paintings by Piero della Francesca or Perugino. In the allegorical paintings on the reverse of Piero's double panel portrait of Federico da Montefeltro and his wife Battista Sforza, just such a richly diverse, almost overemphasized, idealistically elevated landscape appears, with several towering hills, which are so characteristic of the region in which they were created.

And as Perugino's pictures became more classical and stereotypical, he levelled the richness of these landscape forms to a standard view that he kept on repeating over and over again. In this, two hill ridges, adorned with long-stemmed peonies and alders replete with delicately powdery foliage, run from each side to the middle of the composition, while along the centre line, a sweeping plain meanders its way into the idealistically hazy blue depth of the painting, where you can just about make out a lake, on whose shores people are hunting or working, and where shepherds have their grazing lands or are watering their animals.

The views are still there today, and you can see the same kind of scenery, dominated in the west of the lake by the humpbacks of the sandstone hills, which climb up to the Apennines, while in the east and south the landscape is characterized by the more precipitate contours of the limestone mountains with their terrace and plateau formations. Where the bare rock crags emerge above the green valleys and streams and overhang the wooded slopes, you instantly recognize the uniformly coloured grey stone which is predominant in many of the smaller local settlements and which assimilates the house into the surrounding rocks.

Because many smaller streams flow into the principal river of the region, the Tiber, this has become the main transport artery here. Both the railway and the main highway follow the course of its valley, while smaller routes run alongside the rivers that flow between the reservoirs and the long valleys in the less accessible regions to either side of the main river valley.

I sat in the train and followed the Tiber valley heading south. If the trip had ever had a purpose, it had disappeared in the interim. In the beginning, there had been a motive, nothing more, and at the end there would be a situation, nothing less. In between lay the promise of an experience, which attracted me like the thrill of being fearful. I pictured myself sitting with Clarisse somewhere in the mountains behind Lake Fucino, looking down on the water and thinking over what to do next. But that wasn't for real.

Instead, Arcadia, the landscape of ancient Italian pastoral idyll, turned out to be real. For this 'green heart of Italy', as the poet Carducci called the region in his famous verses, really is still home to sheep farms and shepherds, who drive their now much-reduced flocks from Puglia and Calabria along the legendary '*tratturi*' – the ancient drovers' roads.

The Tiber divides the region in a north–south direction. The strips of land along its banks have not remained unaffected by the modern world, and yet through this current landscape shines the ancient one that Pliny the Younger celebrates in his incantatory description of the upper Tiber valley:

The character of the country is exceedingly beautiful. Picture to yourself an immense amphitheatre, such as only nature could create. Before you lies a broad, extended plain bounded by a range of mountains, whose summits are covered with tall and ancient woods, which are stocked with all kinds of game. The descending slopes of the mountains are planted with underwood, among which are a number of little risings with a rich soil, on which hardly a stone is to be found. In fruitfulness they are quite equal to a valley, and though their harvest is rather later, their crops are just as good. At the foot of these, on the mountainside, the eye, wherever it turns, runs along one unbroken stretch of vineyards terminated by a belt of shrubs. Next you have meadows and the open plain. The arable land is so dense that it is necessary to go over it nine times with the biggest oxen and the strongest ploughs. The meadows are bright with flowers, and produce trefoil and other kinds of herbage as fine and tender as if it were but just sprung up, for all the soil is refreshed by never-failing streams. But though there is plenty of water, there are no marshes; for the ground being on a slope, whatever water it receives without absorbing runs off into the Tiber. This river, which winds through the middle of the meadows, is navigable only in the winter and spring, at which seasons it transports the produce of the lands to Rome: but in summer it sinks below its banks; towards the autumn, however, it begins again to regain its strength. You would be delighted by a view of this country from the top of one of our neighbouring mountains, and would fancy that not a real, but some imaginary landscape, painted by the most exquisite pencil, lay before you, such a harmonious variety of beautiful objects meets the eye, whichever way it turns.

I got off the train in Avezzano. It was still early morning, and exactly as one might expect at that time of day: women in curlers were sweeping the pavement while men sat chatting over the pink pages of the *Gazzetta dello Sport*. At the first bar I came to, in the station concourse, I asked a solitary newspaper reader the way to the lake. He begged my pardon. So I repeated my question: 'The way to Lake Fucino?' He folded up his paper and, staring fixedly at me with an amused but good-natured expression, replied:

'*Ci porto io*'– 'I'll take you there.'

So we ended up chugging up the mountain in his little blue vehicle with the farting exhaust until we came to a large square where the man parked his car and insisted on accompanying me to the parapet overlooking the valley.

'*Ecco il Lago Fucino*,' he announced with a proprietorial gesture.

And I saw the lake in the subjunctive mood, the lake that could have been; as it was, it lay there like a gigantic piece of marquetry composed of green and brown inlays, with sharply cut parcels of land following the course of paths and broad carpets of scrubland, wheatfields and acreages of vegetables with just the occasional farmhouse on their fringes.

Lake Fucino is no more, '*non c'é piu il lago*,' said the man standing beside me. Dried out, not by time but by human agency.

I sat for a while on a bench above the valley and surveyed the scene: somewhere, the sun was shining constantly on the plain below, or spots of light flitted across it, and, just as though the valley floor was still water, the fields petered out towards the edges of the depression, giving way to sparse and then denser settlements and finally running out altogether. But when the plain is shrouded in mist, from a distance it can seem as if the lake has returned home, back to its bed.

Over the next few days, I increasingly lost sight of the original purpose of my visit, so fascinated was I by the lake that wasn't a lake. I visited the local library to read up about Lake Fucino, then went to sit for long hours like a pensioner, staring out over the plain. Apparently when the lake did still cover this area, it was well-stocked with fish, the lake on whose shores the Marsians, and later the Romans, grew olives, vines and fruit. Although its climate was considered quite harsh, before it was drained the lake by all accounts only ever froze over five times, the first of which was in 1167. The way its water level rose and fell baffled both the locals and the historians. In 1752, it was said to have become so shallow that you could make out the foundations of the ancient town of Marruvium, and statues of Claudius and Agrippina were salvaged.

And so now we're standing on the spot where a dream was realized, that is, where it was buried – a dream that antiquity began to dream and which the modern period brought to fruition. The earliest plan to drain the lake, which had come into existence after a landslip, damming the River Sagittario river over an area of 155 square kilometres, was devised by Julius Caesar, who believed reclamation of the plain would, first and foremost, ensure a huge supply of corn for the booming city of Rome. This plan never got off the ground.

The same vision prompted the emperor Claudius to revive the plan and start to put it into action in AD 44, a massive and onerous undertaking on which, according to the accounts of Roman historians, 30,000 labourers, most of them slaves, were employed excavating subterranean drainage channels.

Eleven years later, the construction work was finished and Claudius and his entire court decamped to the area to inaugurate the grandiose project. Rostra were erected, festivals held, and at the high point of the proceedings the floodgates were opened. Yet all that happened was that a trickle of water started running through the culverts, and the level of the lake fell by only a few centimetres. The emperor and his retinue returned to Rome in great umbrage.

And so work began all over again. When this round of construction was over, even more extravagant festivities and games were laid on. Right at the head of the main drainage culvert, a banquet was set out, once again rostra were put up and decorated, and an orchestra of shawm players clamorously proclaimed to the world the triumph of this new feat of engineering. But when the sluices were opened this time, the weight of water that flowed down the so-called 'Emissary' was so great that it washed away the stand where the emperor's party was sitting, almost drowning Claudius, his wife Agrippina and their son Nero. Lake Fucino came within a hair's breadth of altering the course of history.

Later, the emperors Trajan and Hadrian renovated and extended the drainage system, which continued to serve its purpose until the sixth century, at least when it wasn't getting blocked, or vandalized by Barbarian invaders. Thereafter, the princely dynasty of the Colonna, who lived in this region, along with the Holy Roman Emperor Frederick II and Alfonso I of Aragón, attempted time and again, without success, to clean out the 'Emissary' and drain the lake.

The person who finally achieved this feat was the private citizen Alessandro Torlonia in the nineteenth century, who commissioned architects from France and Switzerland to study the old blueprints from the time of Claudius and to try and correct the mistakes that were made. From 1854, new work began on draining the lake, by first locating its deepest point, then lowering the drainage channel by three metres, and finally resiting the mouth of the 'Emissary' further to the east and nearer to the lake itself.

To carry out his scheme, Torlonia assembled an army of convicts, casual labourers and local peasants. 'Either I'll drain the lake, or it'll drain me!' he declared. Contemporaries reported how the workers would stand hip-deep in mud, Stygian figures who looked like they were descending into the pit of hell.

Twenty-one years later, this round of work was finished. In return for his achievement, Torlonia laid claim to the reclaimed land, dividing it up into 497 parcels of 24 hectares apiece, most of which he donated to Abruzzese miners and people from the neighbouring provinces, who thereby suddenly became landowners.

The drainage of the lake profoundly altered this area of central Italy, and it is quite impossible to imagine the kind of landscape that would otherwise be here today, or, as the historian of antiquity Heinrich Nissen put it at the turn of the nineteenth century, namely that it would be inconceivable for anyone to immerse themselves in the natural beauty of this country 'without at the same time being aware of the deep scars that humanity's ignorance and rapacity have inflicted upon it'. And so it is perfectly understandable in the light of the draining of Lake Fucino how German historian Ferdinand Gregorovius began to have grave concerns about the survival of the lovely Lake Trasimene: 'Now they're trying to ship it off to the sea as well, so that they can reclaim farmland and pasture, and who knows what new murderous capitalists and drainage specialists are creeping around its delightful shores, calculating what it will cost to turn this wonderful piece of natural poetry into industrial prose.'

There's no denying that reclaimed marshland is, in the main, particularly fertile, and if it's possible for farmers to engage in a profitable form of agriculture anywhere, then land consolidation, straightening of byways, and the shared deployment of farming machinery make it feasible here. By contrast, up on the lower slopes, or even right up in the mountains, individual fields sometimes lie around like exposed playing cards amid a desolate landscape of scrubland, boulders and isolated trees.

The typical landscape formation in this region is a ridge covered in light, fuzzy vegetation, with translucent cliffs up on high and scrub, boulder fields and patches of pine forest below, and sprinkled with isolated fields cut out of it, which in many cases only grow enough to provide for the needs of the family, and which are often close to the farmstead. Below them stretches the silvery-grey of the olive groves, similar in their flow and colour to the boulder fields, and as they get closer to the valley floor, they're increasingly interspersed with meadows, colourful fields and moist black tracts of arable land fringed with mighty willows and enclosed watercourses. Finally, in the valley the landscape becomes completely mellow. The fields fit together like pieces of intarsia woodwork, their colour grows more intense, and the paths and roads run straight as a die.

Without more ado, I hitchhiked from the far side of the dried-out lake over to Campobasso. It was easy. In the countryside, people have no qualms about picking up strangers. By the time a couple of kilometres have passed, they aren't strangers anymore. The last of my lifts dropped me off at the door of the 'Locanda', the only house offering 'bed and breakfast'.

Once upon a time, Campobasso had around 2,000 inhabitants. In the meantime, though, its population dwindled to just the old people. A smaller group had decamped to Rome, while a larger group had emigrated to Canada and the USA. Later, their faces were to gaze out at me from the sepia-toned photos that filled the town's only guest house. All around the world, the Abruzzese form well-known expatriate communities. This wild province of high mountains, peasants and bears can barely support its population from farming anymore. Those who remain behind form part of a dying community, and into some of these half-abandoned villages, with their tumbledown build-ings and farmhouse settlements that are only patchily provided with street lighting, the *Vucumprà*, refugees from Africa, have now started to move in. They're called this in unkind mimicry of their accents when they hawk carved wooden elephants from their homeland in the markets hereabouts. So it is that in vil-lages in the Abruzzi, the last of those who stayed behind are encountering the first who manage to effect an escape.

I was walking across the dining room when I spotted Clarisse and her father sitting in the little courtyard behind the house. He rose and morosely shook my hand. When she caught sight of me, Clarisse shot up from her seat, blushing furiously like she was in the middle of an argument, and simply said:

'At last, you're here!'

I only had a dim memory of how she'd once looked, but now her complexion was feverish. She'd abandoned her hair to the incipient grey, and her get-up had gone from being simply care-less to almost totally shabby. She took hold of my elbow and steered me across the dining room – giving me a conventional but demonstrative peck on the cheek on the way – and out into the open. The guesthouse owner gave us a sullen look as we passed. A dusty reception, I must say! On the narrow street outside, we took a right turn, then right again, virtually cover-ing the whole village in the process.

'Everyone seems strange to me,' Clarisse hissed.

'How do you mean, strange?'

'You don't know them. They're completely different people. You've never had to deal with people like them.'

'Forget them. Then you'll find some peace and you'll be able to …'

'It's because of the first evening that they're like this. It's all down to that first evening.'

On that occasion, apparently, she and her father had gone to the dining room of the 'Locanda'. She'd greeted a couple of the people there; the atmosphere was tense and embarrassed. Still, she'd managed to pull herself together, curtsied to the landlord and shaken hands with all those present.

'Right, we'd better get ourselves a room', her father had announced at length.

'What room?' she'd asked.

'Our room.'

'But we'll need two.'

Indignant looks were directed at her from all sides, and people shook their heads quite openly. Coquettishly, the landlord had dangled the room key on its wooden fob in front of her nose. When she made a move to knock it out of his hand, an old man had stepped between them and tried to act as an intermediary. She could give it a go, he suggested, at least for the first night.

'That's it, then, is it: just give it a go?!' she'd shouted, then turned to the room and shrieked at the top of her voice: 'I am not sleeping in the same room as this man!'

Other people are prone to exaggerating what they supposedly said when they were furious, but if anything, the opposite was the case with Clarisse. You could be sure that her scream would have been piercing, but also that, after her declaration, she'd have cursed them all to hell.

'What business is it of yours, anyway?' she'd doubtless yelled at them and then called the landlord a 'web-footed inbred' in German, whose 'rectum' she hoped would be afflicted by the 'bloody Lombardy squits'.

I shook my head, but not out of disapproval, nor because I didn't believe her, but more at the bizarre constellation of events, and the disaster zone that was her father.

But she too misconstrued my head-shaking.

'What, you think it's normal too, do you? A grown-up daughter sharing a room with her father, sharing a bed?'

'No,' I said, to humour her.

'They're all abnormal here. Well, not all of them. But they're all in each other's pockets, that's for sure.'

I couldn't help but smile again, but this time because of the figure of speech she used.

But she grabbed my hand indignantly and dragged me down the street, with that fanatical look in her eye that I knew of old, accompanied by her necrotic wheezing and bustling. In that instant, I got the feeling that I'd been summoned down here primarily to be the recipient of this outburst of rage. Keeping a tight grip on my arm, she led me across a dirt track to the little village cemetery, the most idyllic spot for miles around, with a fine view of Lake Fucino in the distance. There, she let go of my hand, and gesticulating extravagantly to either side, began to prance down the gravel path between the tomb sculptures, the moss-covered stones and slabs, pointing to this or that head-stone and declaiming:

'Maria Passa, Francesco Farinello, Pietra Farinello, Sergio Farinello, Guido Passa, Eleonora Passa, Mauro Farinello, Massimiliana Passa, Pippo Farinello, Gloria Farinello ...'

She wheeled round to look at me; I was following several paces behind her and reading the names out to myself as she rattled them off:

'A village of two families, you get the picture now? They're

all related to one another: Farinello, Pass, Passa, Farinello …
They're all here …'

She clutched at her head and made a screwing gesture against her temples with her fingers, in a very Italian-like way.

'They're degenerate … loony!'

We sat down on a bench and looked out at Lake Fucino. To be on the safe side, neither of us broached the subject of Kafka. But I remembered how she'd once said that in order to find himself, the writer first had to lose himself. And there in front of us, in all its down-at-heel symbolism, lay the lake that wasn't a lake anymore, and beside me sat Clarisse, wittering on about there being nowhere anymore, nowhere – no library, no convent, and least of all this village – no place under the sun she'd be able to call home. And I gazed out over the land that the drained lake had uncovered, lying there all meticulously parcelled out, luscious and fertile enough to make you despair at the sight of its beauty.

Clarisse is no longer with us. She finally found a way out after all, an exit from her own life.

Gorée

The Door of No Return

The Isle of the Blessed has a basement. You know this to be the case, but you can see no sign of it as you cast off in a small boat from Dakar harbour and head for this fortress rock just three kilometres offshore, that terrible idyll which was originally simply called Ber and, later, Ila da Palma. Then the British occupiers rechristened it Cape Coast Castle, and finally, it was the French who were ultimately responsible for naming it Gorée, the 'good harbour', or Gorée la Joyeuse – 'Gorée the Fortunate'. However, that was already at a time when the ships with holds full of chained slaves were plying the Atlantic route, and hardly anyone who made it to Gorée considered themselves fortunate.

Nowadays, the ferry from Dakar to Gorée departs every twenty minutes. The women in the boat in their magnificent *boubous* balance loads of tropical fruit, sugar, sweet potatoes and other produce on their heads. Their destination, this rocky island which once had some fifty thousand people living on it, is now home to only about a thousand. This morning, some of its inhabitants are lazing about in hammocks, while others are strolling down the alleyways under the waving washing, or lying in the meadow above the free-roaming sheep, or just sitting around in an atmosphere filled with the screams of children and seagulls.

This legendary islet at the westernmost tip of Africa measures barely one kilometre long and three hundred metres wide. From the boat, we could easily see the whole of Gorée laid out before us. Greta had the complexion of a Southern European woman, but could trace the roots of her family back to African slaves, so before our visit, she'd been at pains to put me in the picture about the significance of the island.

In 1444, Gorée was occupied by Portugal, and then by France, but subsequently also by the British, the Dutch, the Danes and the Swedes, and then once more by the British, who ran a trading post here for a while. In all, the island changed hands seventeen times; a fort more than a residence, a citadel whose black cannons still loom over Dakar harbour.

The Portuguese took control of the Ila da Palma in the course of searching for the fabled goldfields of West Africa. Barely a hundred years later, a local trade in human trafficking began, and right up to the abolition of slavery in 1848, the island served as a key base for the transportation of slaves to the Americas.

After North America was 'discovered' and demand arose for manpower to work the plantations there, as well as in Brazil and on the islands of the West Indies, the slave trade boomed. Between the sixteenth and the nineteenth century, a total of twenty million slaves are believed to have been sold and transported from West Africa to the New World. They also disappeared into the silver mines of Mexico and Peru, the tobacco and cotton plantations of North America, and into the sugar cane fields of the Caribbean. The Dutch sent them to their colonies of Surinam, Berbice and Guyana, and the offshore island of Curaçao soon evolved into the most important slave market in the world.

'Meanwhile, back in Gorée,' Greta explained, 'the slaves became a kind of currency. For instance, the price of a house was reckoned in slaves, and a fine Arab horse cost twelve or fifteen of them. But horses were much in demand in times of war, and so many slaves didn't find themselves caught up in the transatlantic trade, but instead were bartered within Africa.'

'Was it a lucrative business?'

'And how! Slaves were the valuables of the age. In Africa, you could get hold of one for a small quantity of brandy and cheap trade goods to the value of five guilders, and then exchange him in South America for ten times that much in sugar. And then you could sell on that sugar for many times that sum again in Europe, where confectionery was by this time no longer a preserve just of the upper classes. Plus, it changed people's eating habits here completely, and incidentally also gave rise to the dentistry profession. It took no time for the European slave-trading concerns to start establishing their own plantations in Africa.'

But recently several scholars have raised the possibility that the business of supplying the ships in Gorée with victuals and agricultural produce for export was actually a more significant economic activity than trading in relatively cheap slaves. All human life assembled here on this small fortress island: white slavers, prosperous Africans who themselves took part in the slave trade, and even rich slaves who kept slaves of their own years before the first Europeans arrived on the continent. Many slaves at that period quickly converted to Islam, because an edict decreed that no one had the right to enslave a Mohammedan. The fact that today around 80 per cent of Senegalese and 50 per cent of African people as a whole are Muslims reveals quite how intimately and enduringly even religion was bound up with the slave trade in this region.

Our boat was by now entering Gorée Bay. The harbour here consists of little more than an enclosed area of the shore where a boat can put in. In former times, this was also where ships were fitted out for the long transatlantic voyage. Nearby, a market grew up, where gold, ostrich feathers, clothing and wax were traded, and because of the pleasant conditions here, even some freed slaves moved to the island and lived cheek by jowl with their brothers and sisters who were still in bondage.

Many of the ships that unloaded their cargoes here and then took slaves on board came from Liverpool, the European centre of the slave trade. Here, human beings were exchanged for much sought-after European goods, such as textiles, iron-ware, tools, glass and weapons – all commodities that over time either lost their appeal or prestigious status, with the result that this kind of trade ultimately declined. On the other hand, in certain aristocratic circles, it was deemed a mark of status to own a slave. And then there is the unforgettable story of the Viennese woman from the time of Mozart who had her African husband stuffed when he died and exhibited in a museum – all with his consent.

'I gather that around a quarter of the three thousand or so people on Gorée Island at that time were mulattos. How come?' I asked Greta.

'White women were forbidden from setting foot on the island. So the European masters there took native wives, and in the eyes of the law, the moment these women died or the men returned to Europe, they were considered divorced. So the mulatto offspring remained behind, and mulatto women in particular became important intermediaries between the two cultures. They had their own houses built, and in many cases even took slaves themselves.'

So we duly landed on ground burdened with a heavy historical legacy, setting foot on the sun-warmed cobbles, only shaded here and there by bougainvillea bushes, palms and baobab trees. We glanced up at the houses with their columned porticos, and on the verandas there really were mulatto women, sitting in steamer chairs, with red bougainvillea flowers behind their ears and their eyes closed above their cleavages. The scene is straight out of the novels of Pierre Loti, pure oriental kitsch – or like a glowing canvas by Delacroix set before the distant coastal strip leading to Dakar, with its basalt spoil heaps under a haze of smog.

Sure, you can easily stumble into the miniaturized world of colonialism, captivated by taboo sensations. It really oughtn't to be so beautiful, this place they call The Dachau of Africa, it shouldn't blossom in the glare of the sun, and its walls shouldn't be exuding the aroma of warm volcanic rock. No, the atmosphere simply ought not to be so free and easy, or the romanticism of the empty palaces so lyrical. A museum just shouldn't be like this, a monument of 'World Heritage Site' status, and a place which by common assent is supposed to belong to a closed chapter of history.

There are places which compel the casual tourist not to behave like one anymore. Places where idle rambling just has to cease. Sites of obsession, scenes of pure mania. In short, there are places that evoke involuntary memories through a sequence of inescapable and obtrusive images which detach themselves independently from the firm ground of consciousness, and non-places which generate nothing but oblivion. At present, we can observe the proliferation of such non-places, which are little more than depositories for people.

And it is the places of helplessness, to which no experiences attach and which fulfil no need, which rather feed the urge not to exist. They are sites of obliteration. You don't need to be conscious in order to have seen them. No engaged look takes them in, no care maintains them, and no history finds its origin here. The traveller finds no access to these places, instead he has to transpose them into a book, a film or a television show, put them in another context. Under these conditions, then, this harbour might not appear just as some squalid little landing place, but rather become the promise of 'faraway places'. And beyond it would lie the world.

But it is the fate of Gorée, this inescapably African place of human potential, to be the repository of another kind of memory, and if it hadn't revealed itself so spontaneously, a certain expression on Greta's face would have sufficed for me to identify the aftershocks it could still cause in the agitation I saw there. That look on her face was haunted by the awareness that human beings were sent to their destruction from here, and that they were intended not just to experience it, but to do so as consciously as possible. They were to be transmuted into the endless here-and-now of their misery, an enduring sense of being present that would coalesce into a proof of their existence: indeed, they could not manage to detach themselves from life, and we later generations now consign them to some notion of a historically remote, almost literary torment.

Yet how can one make it vivid and urgent and real – the pain that went to the very core of their beings, that struck them dumb because it was the prelude to their devastation, and their transformation into nothingness and non-existence; the pain that was like some intrusion of the silence of the grave into their lives? How can we hear it above that screaming pain, that vital, full-throated, demonstrative form of pain they also felt? How might one preserve the motion of passing away against that from which Rousseau (and after him also Nietzsche) claimed language originally derived, namely the motion of the scream, the interjection? Did the dying man have no language? And what impulse toward communication remains when the tortured person wants to proclaim his oneness with his physical body?

We were approaching the heart of the settlement. The Maison des Esclaves, built in 1776–78, is now an exhibition space, showcasing the trade in trafficking human beings, and full of dungeons where slaves were held awaiting transportation. They all passed through here. When Nelson Mandela visited, he insisted on being shut in one of the cells; Pope John Paul II apologized for Christians' involvement in the slave trade; Bill Clinton just apologized in general, while his wife Hillary had herself photographed by Annie Leibovitz for *Elle* magazine; and George W. Bush stayed for twenty minutes, during which time he spoke about 'past wrongs'. But the most compelling act of contrition here was by Brazil's President Lula, who apologized for his country, which imported more slaves than any other and which only abolished slavery in 1888. The consequences of this have shaped the present: almost half the population of modern Brazil is of African origin.

Anyone who has ever entered the House of Slaves must have done so in a very sombre frame of mind, yet must have been, at the same time, involuntarily touched by the allure of the place, its repellent beauty. The slave owners also lived here in well-appointed and comfortable surroundings on the *Piano nobile*, which was accessible by a curving external staircase painted in antique pink and looking for all the world like it could have been designed by Antoni Gaudí. From the salon on this floor, beneath the massive wooden ceiling, you can look out through a large window over the balcony to the ocean beyond.

Underneath the *Piano nobile*, separated by just a few floorboards and joists, the slaves lived penned in and chained up in crowded conditions. They were only permitted to leave their quarters to work or when they were transported. In their quarters, they waded through a sea of excrement that was only cleared out when it had reached a certain depth. Sometimes these cellars were mucked out, but at other times just sluiced with sea water. Undernourished slaves were literally force-fed with a paste made from beans and palm oil. From time to time, someone would come and drag out the corpses and throw them to the sharks. The terminally sick and the frail were next in line.

Greta stood there in silence, inwardly projecting everything she'd read about this place onto the walls. Gorée attracts lots of visitors, who, drawn by the TV series *Roots*, come here in search of their ancestry. This series was what first made them aware of the significance of having forbears at all, and then of the fact that they had come from this place. Among the visitors are those who just stand and gaze in wonder, those who have taken on professional assistance to help them trace their roots, people who touch the fabric of the house and claim to 'recognize' it, and people who instantly feel that this is their place of origin, who feel at home in a place they have never actually set foot in before. There are also more matter-of-fact visitors, who enter one of the cells and close their eyes, call to mind the images they've seen of past times and sincerely believe that they are now bound to be imbued, overwhelmed even, by those last images of Africa that the slaves themselves also saw before being transported.

Greta was taking short, halting steps. She didn't take any photos or point a video camera at the complex. I wondered what internal images she was storing of the *porte sans retour*, the 'door of no return', through which the wretched slaves walked to get to the ships' holds. The buyers would have the black 'ivory', as they called the slaves, paraded before them so they could examine their muscles, bones, teeth and even assess their mental condition. After the sale was concluded, their bodies were branded, and through the gap afforded by this narrow opening in the wall they could glimpse the open sea. Then they were loaded into the deep bellies of brigs or schooners, vessels that had been specially modified for transporting slaves, with extra decks added to provide more accommodation, though in the process this also created appallingly cramped conditions.

Their hands and legs in shackles, the slaves were herded across a plank into the ship's hold, where they were first required to unload the cargo the vessel had brought to Gorée, before being shown their place on one of the decks. The excrement and vomit of those working above dropped through onto those lying below. Anyone who could manage it hurled themselves into the sea; many of those who couldn't despatch themselves in this way died on the transatlantic passage. Less than half of all those who embarked from Gorée ever reached their intended destination on the far side of the Atlantic.

In addition, the slaves were gripped by fear that the Europeans were going to eat them at the conclusion of the crossing. This terror sparked a number of slave revolts, which were reported in a variety of different ways in the eighteenth century. The ringleaders of the very few such uprisings that were staged were publicly tortured to death.

In 1685, Louis XIV of France had enacted the *Code Noir*, the 'Black Code', a measure designed to prevent the unlawful misuse of slaves, yet the way in which this codex was framed only succeeded in legitimizing the degradation of non-European races. In effect, it came to form the legal basis of the slave trade. Although it spelt the end of unlegislated trade of this kind, sadistic and arbitrary cruelty by slavers could scarcely have been more brutal than the hypocritical legality of the codex's clauses. For example, Article 38 stipulated that a fugitive slave who had been on the run for one month should have both ears cut off and be branded with a fleur-de-lys on one shoulder. If he should manage to escape for another month, he would have his hamstring cut and be branded with a fleur-de-lys on the other shoulder.

But even in regions outside the jurisdiction of the 'Black Code', cruelty was no less rife. Nowhere in the world was the ratio of slaves to Europeans as great as in Curaçao, where moral standards became brutalized to a state hitherto unknown. Slaves were whipped till their flesh was raw, and owners were required by law to cut their slaves' Achilles tendons if they should make any attempt to escape. At the second attempt, one leg would be amputated. Women slaves, on the other hand, were forced to suffer sexual abuse and made to serve guests at banquets while dressed in just a serviette. Their mistresses would show them off as pretty acquisitions and rent them out by the week. If the slaves fled into the jungle, they found Indian bounty hunters waiting for them, who earned a living from hunting down slaves.

However, the official end of slavery did not in any way mean an abrupt cessation of human trafficking. Instead, this period witnessed the growth of so-called 'freedom villages', where former slaves would settle in apparent liberty. But in actual fact these settlements were recruitment camps set up by the French to create a pool of indentured labour, which businessmen could draw upon. They would pay a one-off sum, for which former slaves would commit to work for their new masters for anything up to fourteen years. Nor had the motives of the abolitionists at the start of the nineteenth century been entirely selfless, either – much of their involvement in support of the outlawing of slavery was driven primarily by thoughts of their own salvation. In this part of the world, it was only when the first president of the independent Republic of Senegal came to power in 1962 that such activities were done away with entirely. In neighbouring Mauretania, meanwhile, slavery was only officially abolished in 1980.

Nevertheless, Gorée's decline really set in after the official ban on slavery gained widespread acceptance in 1848. When the end came, Gorée was home to five thousand people, most of whom returned to the mainland after emancipation. A sleepy torpor now settled over the island. The palaces either stood empty or were squatted in by homeless people. Anyone with ambition who wanted to get involved in business or politics left for the mainland, leaving behind on the island a small community of homebodies, old people and invalids – until slavery made a comeback, though this time in the form of nostalgia, in maintaining the museum and preserving the place's cultural heritage. The island revived once more, in the spirit of this dark legacy. But now it's really capitalizing on the business of remembrance.

The fact that it enjoys such an idyllic location, criss-crossed by car-free, cobbled, narrow alleys, and that there's still such a concentration of charming old colonial buildings situated between flowering shrubs under ancient trees, and that wild animals roam free on the island, and that music seems to come from every window, and that it's home to many artists, either classical painters or avant-garde artists who assemble sculptures or souvenir goods from recycled bits of refuse – all this has made Gorée into a souvenir in its own right, one that you can walk around; a Bohemian attraction, in which all traces of the past have been prettified, diluted and dissipated by this relentless urge to memorialize.

Yet there is another tendency at work here: this time-honoured effort to envision the history of a place where it actually unfolded also renders people amenable to being distracted from the actual scene of events into new forms of remembrance. One effect of constantly being exhorted to feel empathy for what those who suffered went through is the assuaging of our own conscience through his cathartic act. Anyone retrospectively empathizing with the victims cannot possibly be complicit in what the perpetrators did. Thus, the reality that you encounter at sites of remembrance always has something synthetic about it.

The fundamental question posed by all travellers is: 'Where was I?' It's what you're wont to say when you've lost the thread of your story, and it's also the phrase that springs to mind when you're trying to pinpoint the thing that made a trip a real experience for you: a look, a building, a situation. But as soon as you've visited a memorial, forgetting sets in. However picturesque a place may be, it can also be profane, prosaic. Only in conditions of the very closest spatial proximity do you become aware of the real distance that separates you from what you were looking for; and so it was on this morning, as I wandered through the island of Gorée, which rises lyrically from the sea, and found I could barely contain my sense of joy and foreboding.

In a little shop Greta unearthed a reprint of David Boilat's *Esquisses sénégalaises*. In 1853, this artist set about trying to capture the scenery hereabouts. He prints barren landscapes peopled by savages, all of whom have European facial features. It seems as though the Old Masters were incapable of reproducing or accurately portraying the unfamiliar. All they did was colour Europeans brown and give them fuller lips. Not only did they patently fail in their attempt to look beyond themselves and yet still identify something familiar in the exotic, they didn't even manage to depict what they observed without distorting it. In the same way, Gorée revealed itself to Greta and myself as a place that affected us precisely because it eluded our attempts to grasp it, and yet which in a strange way seemed to approach us once more as we were sitting in the little boat taking us back to Dakar, leaving the island behind us in the gathering mist.

On the coast road to the north, billboards educating people about the dangers of AIDS and churches both proliferate. But the true cathedrals of the Third World are the petrol stations, with their sprawling forecourts, dazzling logos and their streamlined appearance, which makes them look like spaceships that have just descended from orbit. No doubt about it: they're the great representational buildings of the energy sector.

Pretty much everywhere here, the landscapes are on a vast scale. An isolated tree, a hut roof projecting into the sky, a sand dune – these all serve to emphasize the general flatness of the terrain. Little dust devils whip across the plain, while a group of boys with sticks herd three goats. You've constantly got sand grains in your teeth, and even if you close your mouth, it gets in through your nostrils. Severely emaciated horses and goats trot, step by step, along the roadside, their sore eyes gazing fixedly at the barren fields.

The generations and the sexes squat down together in the shadows cast by the round huts, and at the general stores along the way the shelves display a range of goods that have miraculously found their way here: a pile of grubby yellow blocks of curd soap, brightly coloured buckets, alkali batteries, four jam jars full of ratatouille, a plastic gun and a pack of cards. A siren sounds, its pitch growing ever lower until it becomes inaudible, with no one having attended to it. Perhaps all these low-frequency sounds are there all the time throughout the world. It's the same with goods; they get disseminated to the far end of supply chains and fetch up somewhere in the desert.

Saint-Louis, near the border with Mauretania, thrived until 1902 as the first capital of Senegal. A fort like Gorée, a military stronghold on the coast of what was then Senegambia, this 'New Orleans of Africa' – as people came to call the city that grew up on the island between two arms of the Senegal River close to its estuary – experienced periods of boom and bust in quick succession. When this modest place lost its status as capital, the inhabitants of Saint-Louis went out onto the streets waving flags to demand annexation by France. Its prosperous citizens moved to the new capital Dakar, while the old and the poor remained behind. The city's public buildings were allowed to fall into disrepair, while the private palaces of the rich also went to rack and ruin, the white and ochre-yellow of their façades gradually fading. These two colours eventually merged midway in the spectrum into a dirty indeterminate shade; the complexion of decay.

Senegal's connection with France goes back to the year 1664, when the French West India Company secured the concession to exploit African colonies in the service of the nation. The town rapidly developed into the most important administrative and commercial settlement in France's West African Empire, with rubber, cotton, ivory, gold dust, palm oil, coffee and cocoa all being traded here. The slave trade flourished, and civil servants and employees of the great commercial enterprises took up residence in the tile-roofed private villas, with their wrought-iron balconies and their cool inner courtyards. The French merchants and colonial officials consorted with freed female slaves and local women. Before long, Saint-Louis was the most significant French settlement in the whole of Africa, and in truth it really was ideally situated, for it was here where the trade routes to the Atlantic, to Mali and on into the Sahara – great arteries for the movement of both people and goods – all met.

Increasing numbers of merchants thronged to Saint-Louis from France, using it as a springboard for opening up the rest of Africa, mining mineral resources, planting groundnuts and establishing rubber plantations, so further stimulating the traffic of human beings. Saint-Louis became the capital of Senegal in 1840. But just eight years later the slave trade was officially outlawed, leaving France in possession of two slave islands, Gorée and Saint-Louis, but divested of all legal rights to operate them as such. What was to be done? Was the best thing simply to give up and withdraw? But that would be tantamount to capitulating. Accordingly, in response to the aggressive colonial policies of Britain at that time, it was decreed that Saint-Louis should be expanded to become the centre of French West Africa, and as a result, the city became a site of both humanistic high culture and of misery and oppression.

Although slavery had been officially abolished, to all practical intents and purposes it endured for another century. It developed covertly in Saint-Louis, as the position of domestic servant was created to cover all manner of subservient duties – this role was largely unregulated, making it a very attractive proposition for the ruling classes. Thus began a period in which the number of slaves in the city far exceeded that of free men and women.

We found a room in the Hôtel de la Poste, a crumbling building from the colonial era. The hotel was as beautiful as some flamboyant cliché. The veranda, constructed completely out of bamboo, and roofed with straw and with rattan furniture, was managed by a barman wielding a fly-whisk and wearing a red *képi*; it took him a while to appear at our table, but eventually he served us long drinks in tall glasses with such a passion that you might almost have thought one of the Ten Commandments read: 'Thou Shalt Make Long Drinks'.

After our drinks, Greta wants to go up and rest in our room. She finds it too hot to go out around midday. We turn off the air-conditioning, though, as it's too noisy. Instead, we open the bathroom window to try and get a rather faint draught to blow through. Then we lie back naked on the bed, waiting for tiny beads of sweat to form, only just about feeling the airflow, which doesn't seem to want to move either. Outside the window, four vultures are tussling in a treetop. But even they are going through their lazy routine like they're in slow motion.

In fact, two distinct districts go to make up Saint-Louis: the coastal area with its administrative buildings, its fading old-style hotels and hidden palazzi, and then – reachable across the Pont Faidherbe – an offshore island, in actual fact more of an extended sandbank with straight alleyways and low houses of a light hue, with wrought iron grilles on the windows, balconies and inner courtyards. But most of them lie empty.

One time we were there, a Muslim dignitary came walking down one of the alleys holding a little boy by the hand. As he passed an abandoned house and read the graffiti on its walls, he shook his head disapprovingly.

'Don't go in there,' he said, 'a spectre lives there!' The architecture here is offbeat. There's rubbish lying around everywhere. Somewhere, rotting carrion is creating a miasma. The better-maintained houses sit in their own compounds; none of them were built directly on the seafront. But some of the flower beds hereabouts are as precise as a Turkish woman's eyebrows. We stroll through a ruin; in its courtyard, an enormous turtle has become stranded and died. Next to it, there is a tortoise tethered to a chain, hissing furiously and tugging on its shackles. Despite the searing heat of the sand, it refuses to give up.

The part of the island that faces the sea is a slum. The canals in its interior are full of detritus that has long since begun to rot. But its outer fringes are lapped by the foaming surf with its pure white crests. Dugout canoes ride the waves. Some of them, piled high with fish, are being hauled up the beach out of the tide, where men with crates on their heads come running up to carry off the catch.

The architecture in this second part of the island resembles that of the other, only transformed into filth, without any buildings worth speaking of. Instead, standing crumbling amid piles of refuse and abandoned appliances and toys are mean little shacks with chairs where a person can sit or lie down, living organisms with the appearance of rubbish tips. In the sheer variety of forms of decay here, man's ability to coexist with all the things he needs, consumes and discards has been honed to a fine degree. Symbioses are in evidence everywhere you look.

A girl of about seven sitting on the beach suddenly hoists her dress up above her waist to expose her genitals. Everyone around screams. She didn't do it for money, she did it for us, proud to call something so beautiful and shocking her own. But when she sees the effect it's had, she does ask for some money and sulks when she doesn't get any.

Greta announces that she's captivated by the 'dithyrambic' spirit of the place, by the musicality of its atmosphere and colours, its abundance and indulgence and its sheer exuberance in decay. Even so, the next morning, she wakes up and tells me about a dream she had. When the real world takes on phantasmagoric features, dreams can often feel dull by comparison, and as your day unfolds it can happen that you do little more than log the kaleidoscopic welter of impressions offered by the world outside.

For example, Greta never misses a single animal that crosses our path: not the cranes in the tops of the tallest trees, nor the geckos spiralling up the trunks or pooing in the hotel swimming pool, the black pig rootling around in a little stream of filth, the aardvark galloping over the hill near the market, the dried fish butterflied and hung out to dry like Christ on the cross, the dog lying in the roadside ditch with its ears bloody and weeping open sores, the birds with their unfamiliar cries, the butterflies and their exotic coloration – and all of this at every moment in close proximity to blood, earth, bark, mud, ashes, piss, effluent, secretions, things intrinsic to, bound up with, associated with or related to death, and like everything creaturely with its face turned towards transience – forms that the Western world's obsession with hygiene has largely effaced.

This is a unique place, for sure, unique also in the way it gathers all its life up into one foaming wave crest and sets it free to dance on the seething Atlantic. All the same, I can't shake off a feeling of déjà-vu, this impression of a place I've visited before, but in a quite different way to the US tourists returning to their roots on Gorée – more immediate, more sensual.

Every morning we venture out once more into the cacophonous atmosphere. Every morning there's the old man playing the same melody on his goatskin-covered stringed instrument; he continues until we pop a couple of banknotes into the soundhole of his *kora*. Occasionally, he'll accompany his playing with chanting that sounds querulous, argumentative and discontented but which is, in fact, all about love – a song that was made up somewhere out in the desert and which sounds somehow wrong when played near a hotel.

Sometimes we'll stop and listen for a while as a second musician, this time a guitarist, joins in. There's a captivating simplicity about the tonal interplay between two stringed instruments, enhanced by a recitative voice breaking in. They produce sounds like those heard in nature, only then to conjure up mood pictures that sound like they've been painted by the plucking of a mandolin. It's as if the emotions of the players first have to gain a foothold, and acclimatize themselves, and then can begin to vary, taking on height and depth. Theirs is the quintessential exhilaration of musicians.

'We never practice,' says the older musician. 'Music's part of my physical constitution, and it makes my spirit grow. We don't discuss it, we just improvise.'

'Pure traditional music is a source of truth,' the other chips in, and launches into a rhapsodic declaration of love for *griot*, the musical language of the legendary keepers of the oral culture, who preserve the legacy of traditional West African classical music through long song cycles, recitatives and ballads, which among certain noble families are passed down from generation to generation. This music conducts an antiphony with nature. We may not be able to hear it, but it resonates within the inaudible aspects of the music all the same.

We've made our way through the detritus, over ditches and down narrow paths, and have not been aware of any curious, outraged or astonished looks directed at us, but rather fixed gazes from watery, weeping eyes, into which any expression, be it of shock or amazement, would only seep very gradually and then remain there. Eyes in which encounters with the unfamiliar would find an invisible reflex, such as can be triggered by encountering death or set off by illnesses that cause flickering vision.

'If you contract this disease,' a sufferer from this so-called 'river blindness' tells me, 'the maggots work their way right up to behind your conjunctiva, where they mate and reproduce visibly. That's when your eyes start shimmering from all the seething activity going on inside them.'

At the market, manpower is no longer on offer, but instead the remnants of European surpluses, Chinese mass production, and cheap manufactured goods from the Far East. Alongside these are the home-produced textile handicrafts, while pharmaceutical products range from modern medicines to indigenous animistic cures. A long line of stalls offers snake heads, songbird beaks, turtles' feet, lions' paws, bat heads and the internal organs of crocodiles. Everything is effective in some way or other. There are even animal body parts here which are barely preserved, nor are they embalmed, but instead surrounded by a stench of decay and swarms of flies; the vendors are coy about what beasts they originally came from. They just smile at us and say:

'Souvenirs.'

There's even a white man at the Saint-Louis market who performs a routine behind a curtain that involves him baring his expansive white belly and gyrating it to the accompaniment of the Beatles' song 'Get Back'. One man is prepared to give him two mangoes for his performance with the one proviso:

'Just keep your gut covered!'

Someone at my shoulder offers me some product or other. I decline, smiling. Whereupon the man takes my hand.

'I want to thank you for the polite way you said "no". It shows me that you're no racist. Look here, at our two hands, black and white together, that's how it should be …'

And into my hand he suddenly slides his 'present', a silver wire bracelet.

'And think how lost you would be if you didn't have this

bracelet ready to slip onto your lady's arm – beautiful as she is – when she was ready and waiting to go out to a club …'

The conditional tenses he uses are spellbinding; they make his little speech so poetic.

But the much-vaunted lady in question, who's right beside me, interposes a sharp 'No'. 'No presents, damn you! Take your rubbish back and clear off!'

Undeterred, he shimmies his considerable bulk up to her, slips the bracelet onto her arm and laughs; half an hour later, she's still weak at the knees wondering what retribution might befall her for having bought it.

The truth is that the street vendors here aren't bothered about what people might actually need. Rather, their sole concern is how rich they reckon their customers are. That's how they end up trying to sell an individual electric hotplate to a backpacker, a crude pair of sunglasses to a glasses wearer, a black wig to a blonde woman, and black shoe polish to someone wearing suede shoes. After all, don't these foreigners have the where-withal to buy all this stuff?

When we turn down the chance of buying ourselves some fans, the saleswoman, who has a huge iridescent fly perched on a wart on her upper lip, calls after us:

'Don't think you can forget me that easily. I'll appear to you one day and you'll cry … you'll found a village that's always shrouded in darkness … You should … '

And so it goes on. Finally, our resistance worn down and we buy a bottle of *bissap* – a watery, dark red juice that tastes of tea and fruit combined – and a bundle of teeth-cleaning sticks.

'I'll give you a sweet for the mature lady!' a lad shouts out.

His sales pitch persuades me to buy the sweet.

Then there's the seven-year-old mouth-organ salesman, draped all over with instruments. He's carrying one in his mouth, one in his hand and one in a box. Every time someone turns him down, he sighs into the harmonica in his mouth. It sounds like the blues, or a collection of blue notes that have been waiting patiently in the mouth organ precisely for that moment of disappointment.

Yet amid all this chorus of itinerant salesmen, market traders, canvassers and guides, I still can't shake off my sense of déjà-vu. But it's not Gorée, or the slave trade architecture, or the legacy of the exploiters, human traffickers, colonial masters and oppressors that's making all this seem so familiar and inevitable. It's something else which I can't put my finger on.

Sitting alone on the hotel veranda, looking down on the street, I can observe the basic modes of local life. People here organize themselves into personal microstructures. They don't consume in any centralized fashion, but go from shop to shop, nor do they think in a centralized way, but go straight from the church to the local soothsayer and then on to the totem seller. They create vertical systems, with farmers employing farmers and nursemaids having nursemaids of their own …

A delegation of boys who guide blind people appears in front of the veranda. After them come the footballers from the prostitutes' quarter. And then the match sellers announce themselves:

'Isn't it us that you've been keeping an eye out for all this while? Well, here we are! *Un cadeau*, please, *un cadeau!*'

The hotelier shoos them all away with his feather duster.

'I beg your pardon, monsieur,' he says before adding – no word of a lie – 'they're the descendants of slaves.'

That may well be so, I tell him. But, I continue, nowhere has the memory of slavery gripped and unsettled me like it has in Gorée, the centre of the African slave trade. And it's absolutely true: in the Maison des Esclaves, we'd been reduced to silence, as had our fellow visitors, who'd just stood there, overcome by the injustice, the martyrdom and the thought of the terrible voyage …

The hotel owner gives an ironic smile, and then addresses me in all earnest, as soberly as any academic:

'*Écoutez,* I don't want to disappoint you, and you've experienced what you've experienced. Also, there's nothing we can do about it, but American and French researchers have suggested that Gorée didn't actually play an significant part in the slave trade at all.'

'But there's all this talk about millions of slaves being shipped from here, and of the "Dachau of Black Africa"!'

'Yeah, those researchers have been publicly denounced here as "Holocaust deniers", but there's no denying their theories were based on sound evidence. Between 1700 and 1850, only just over 427,000 slaves were transported through Gorée.'

'So what does that mean?'

'It means we're talking about less than 5 per cent of the total slave trade! So, in contrast to Saint-Louis, say, Gorée was, if I can put it like this, a relatively unimportant "source of supply".'

I could have replied that that was an obscene statistic, could have trotted out the customary cliché about figures telling us nothing about people and their experiences and suffering; I could have advanced arguments about families being split up and enforced deportation, mentioned the phrase 'individual fates', or asked what it meant to him to live in the capital of slave deportation. I could also have asked myself why I'd followed this remembrance trail in Gorée and not in Saint-Louis, where there was no such slavery commemoration industry. I could have considered whether the idyll of the world heritage site somehow kitschified my act of commemoration, whereas the plain, unattractive presence of African poverty in Saint-Louis hadn't even prompted me to memorialize slavery in the first place.

But instead I just nodded to him in parting, disabused and chastened, rose from my bamboo chair and wandered back inside the hotel, where I was drawn in passing to a small framed photograph hanging on the flower-pattern wallpaper. The first person I recognized in it was Philippe Noiret, then Stéphane Audran, and then the rest. It turned out that Bertrand Tavernier had shot his film *Coup de Torchon* here in 1980. That was all I needed. The first port of call for memory isn't real history, but the cinema. I was still standing in the corridor looking at the photo when Greta appeared and announced:

'You won't believe the dream I just had! Well ...'

Hong Kong

Poste Restante

There was shattered glass lying in the courtyard. Alarmed but lethargic, your ear reconstructed the story behind what had happened – ebbing away in a scrabbling on the ground, and prior to that a scream, and before that the recollection of being woken by an explosion. Your ear sweeps back to the silence before the fall. To a time when there was no courtyard in your consciousness, and no alarmed agitation either. And then came the silence of the fall.

There's a clinking, shivering sound on the cement paving as the glass is swept up outside. In amongst the clatter of the broken fragments, two girls can be heard laughing in turn. Someone must have opened a window in the laundry opposite, because all of a sudden you can quite clearly hear the washers and tumble driers belching their steam out into the courtyard. In the midst of this rhythmic thudding, a man's voice calls out and the girls respond. Then silence descends.

Outside, a radio is switched on, the traffic noise dissolves into a monotonous *basso continuo*, only interrupted now and again by the shrill blast of a horn. The stifling heat of the street even penetrates through the closed window. But when I close my eyes, the red earth of China appears – it really is red, too, and in mountainous regions is piled up into neat sheaves and cubes that look positively unnatural.

In comparison, Hong Kong is one big overstatement, with signs everywhere, and with the buildings all around the harbour and at the airport looking like they've been constructed out of cigarette packets or packaging material for rolls of film and crispbread. As I'm drifting off to sleep again, I see clouds piling up on the skyline. Then it starts raining, inaudibly, and the cars' tyres slice through the puddles with a melting glissando.

I sit up, swing my feet onto the floor and, leaning over from the edge of the bed, switch the air-con from 'cool' to 'very cool'. Instantly, the cover of the unit shudders and, from the grating, long filaments of dust, stuck together in a damp film, flicker out towards me in the airflow. These hotel rooms may well be in high demand, but in fact all they do is testify to the absence of everyone and everything. No one was here. Their chairs are never heavily used, their blankets never touched and their pictures never looked at. The taste of their décor is not that of any individual, and if you were to ask anyone what he'd done behind his room door, he'd only be able to describe the ways in which he'd been absent from it.

It's still morning back in Germany, and people are breathing the air of the working day. In the corridors of office blocks, women carrying files are dodging men carrying files. And in the bright sunshine, someone is crossing the empty car park to retrieve something they'd left behind on the back seat of their car – more files. From the distance, these movements look like episodes from a charade, performed as though they were preceded by a conditional like in a children's game: if you'd walked across the car park, you would have … you wouldn't know – an anticipated and imitated story.

A boy comes down the corridor wheeling a tea trolley; with every irregularity in the floor surface, bottles clink against bottles, spoons against saucers, and cutlery rattles on dirty plates.

'Get stuffed!' someone outside bellows.

I trudge to the bathroom. The oppressive humidity surges towards me with a smell of warm adhesive and mushrooms. As I approach, before the mirror steams up, it reminds me of my face. I stick a toothpick in the frozen corner of my mouth and sit down on the side of the bathtub while the sink fills. The light is as colourless as the water, the contours blurred, and the plastic shower curtains are matt like frosted glass. Gradually, the mirror clears; now you can make out the curtain in it and the extractor fan, mended with black insulating tape, on the ceiling. Then I catch sight of my knees, covered with scars from childhood and a patch of inflamed skin, no doubt caused by an insect bite. Beneath the last coat of plaster on the ceiling, greenish blisters are beginning to appear; coated in dusty paint slapped on without any primer, they seem on the point of crumbling. We are all made from the same material.

There's a newspaper on the table, an exercise book, brochures, pictures of a roof terrace … the water in the bathtub has left a taste of bitter almonds in my mouth … the open hotel brochure proudly displays a photo of the breakfast lounge, the 'Five Diamonds Bar', flanked by images of casual guests and smiling, uniformed Chinese staff. Right at the back, the head chef is standing in front of a mirror – a king, a gourmet.

Someone opens the window in the room next door, then closes it again. An empty plastic cup drops down a chute into the yard. These rear courtyards are like chicken coops, all fenced off and covered with muck, not to mention soot-black from all the exhaust emissions, coal-fired ovens and grills. All around the yard is a system of emergency exits down fire-escapes and corridors, but at the same time there are tripwires in the form of washing lines that are frequently hauled up and taken down, hung with hand towels and pyjamas that have turned grey. The clothes are gathered into the interior of the building by a single arm that appears from under a blind jammed in a diagonal position. Once a year, the mayor makes a point of visiting one such rundown backyard. All you can make out in the picture accompanying the report of his visit in the newspapers is an affable man standing in his light suit in the darkness, surrounded by others wielding cameras and umbrellas.

It's half-past four.

From the foot end of the bed, which is just eighteen inches away from the TV, I wait and watch while the picture resolves itself amid much crackling. The screen goes from anthracite-black, to grey, to dark blue, to blue; then flecks of yellow, red, light green, and purple begin to emerge against the blue. Clothes now appear, but the dazzle off them colours the faces of the people wearing them. Cheeks redden in an instant, while eyes darken to a shouting violet. Foreheads and hands sometimes look brown, and sometimes the colour of aubergine or even curry; the television doesn't seem to be able to decide – first it imposes a uniform brown patina, then changes the skin tones in quick succession.

Three Chinese men are proceeding through a mountainous landscape; their lavish ancient costumes are extravagant, with wide sleeves, hats with intricately embroidered edges, and shoulder pads and bodices cumbersomely stiffened. They are conversing affably and walking stiffly in a circle on their high wooden sandals, endlessly thanking the woman who has appeared in their midst.

Quarter-past five.

Then the woman starts talking to the men. She is perfectly composed. Even though she's the empress, she regards the men kindly, and they in turn indicate that she is an acceptable woman and very prettily turned out, with her gay headdress and her dainty little steps. The woman tells them that it mustn't happen, that on no account should it be allowed to happen. Saying this, she shakes her head, then repeats it, and again a third time. No, the men answer in measured tones, no. And now they're laughing and resuming their perambulation; rest assured, they tell her, it won't happen, on no account, they're all agreed on that.

Now the face of one of the men is shown in close-up – a decisive, melancholic and pronouncedly comic face that one's happy to take a closer look at. Then a group of servants with trays appear on the scene, and in the next frame it's raining.

The laundry belches another plume of steam into the courtyard.

Now the empress is wearing a diadem, scaly and domed like the skin of a pineapple. Her companions are nowhere to be seen. Maybe that's why she's so agitated, because she's twisting her upper body this way and that and peering about so comically that she's scarcely recognizable as the empress anymore. She's quite out of breath and keeps listening intently – perhaps there's some kind of conspiracy afoot? Then, coming to a sudden decision – it's plain to see that she feels she's waited long enough – she comes directly towards me, so close that I can make out every last curve of her nose, the cracks in her lips and all the minutest details of her face, which look like they're composed of graphic little bits of shorthand, and even the whitish fleshiness of her raised hand, above which she's just in the process of pursing her lips. Frozen in this photogenic expression, she falls silent. And as the screen fades out from this image, really elegant, sharp and colourful graphics start to appear, briefly forming writing before dissolving once more, then repeating this cycle all over again until the orchestra is past the crescendo. As the picture fades and the music starts to build to another climax, it too is faded out.

The day has done its duty, the head chef is still smiling in the table drawer, all the shards of glass have been cleared from the courtyard, and the image on the television screen has dwindled to a dot ...

In the foyer of the Shamrock Hotel, the bags of guests who are checking out are covered with a net and secured with a padlock. Open up, store some more luggage in the net, close up, open up again, remove some luggage, close up once more: presiding over this procedure is Mister Fo, as the name badge on his lapel indicates. He arrives every morning at seven and leaves every evening at seven, and spends more than half of his working day keeping an eye on the luggage in the net. Once upon a time, he provided room service on the ninth floor, but then some guests complained, mainly about the noise he made at night. Since then, Fo has been responsible solely for the luggage. Three times a year, the air-conditioning gives him a bout of bronchial catarrh and he has to take a week off to recuperate, for which he isn't paid. As soon as he can breathe soundlessly again, he's back at his post.

When I stepped out of the lift into the lobby that evening, Mister Fo was nudging the bellboy sitting beside him, but on catching sight of me his facial expression reverted to normal, namely completely expressionless. His face, now reduced to an abstract entity, betrayed as little character as that of an ideal clown. At reception, they took my key without looking up. Then, quite unexpectedly, Fo stood up and yanked open the glass door for me. Flopping back down into his faux leather seat, he gave his companion a look of ironic deference, finally revealing he was human after all.

I took the next Star Ferry, and in an effusion of idiotic communicativeness poured my heart out to a Canadian called Stephen. From below, the ship's engines were thudding through the deck, as the ferry slowed down a hundred metres off Kodak House.

Here's the story. I start telling him about Ricarda, but I run aground. For one thing, she's an irrelevance now, and secondly it seems to me that everything is already starting to dissolve into objects, body parts: these were her lips, her arms, the colour of her skin was such-and-such, the smell of her handbag lining, the taste of her tongue in my mouth and in the air. She sat in her bed and gave me a dreadful look, in other words a tolerant look. I'd ordered her like she was some fish in a restaurant, and no sooner had she arrived than I wanted to get the hell out. But before I left, I turned to look at her once more, so as not to miss seeing the tears rolling down her cheeks. What on earth was Stephen supposed to make of all that?

I got off the ferry; it was still sweltering, so I steered a diagonal course across the square, dived into the nearest shadow and from there into the air-conditioned space of the post office. You were permitted to loiter there, looking at the free brochures. The Chinese official at the *poste restante* counter leafed through my passport to the very last page, before turning back to the page with my photo on and looking up at me. The picture had been taken that summer in a photo booth in Urbino. I was pulling a silly face, because Ricarda had been standing next to the booth at the time and trying to make me laugh. I wasn't laughing in the picture, but looking kind of optimistic.

The official furrowed his brow.

'Is there something wrong?' I enquired.

He turned over the page.

'What's your nationality?'

I turned to page one for him, where it states: 'The bearer of this passport is a German national.'

'What's you nationality?' he repeated.

Once again, I showed him the first page. He compared my face with the photo once more.

Then he pointed to the name of the German provincial town on the official stamp, the date, the stamp itself, the validating signature of the passport office employee and the director, important office-holders – clearly concerned in his own mind to exaggerate the importance of people and dates, places, terms, and roles.

So this Chinese official sat there, staring at the signature of the Rhineland passport office director, which snaked off in an unbroken line right towards the edge of the page. It was evident that he couldn't envisage any living individual who might match this signature. Eventually, he turned his back on me and started looking at the deliveries under 'W'.

The moment I left the post office, the place was closed behind me. There was a group of tourists out on Connaught Place. They had their heads tilted back and were looking at the skyline and trying to decipher the names on the various buildings, the same way as visitors to churches identify depictions of saints or gallery-goers spell out the signatures on paintings.

I sat down on the edge of a flower tub and flicked through the pages of an English-language magazine. It was a fortnight old. The first thing I read was three paragraphs of an article on the nervous breakdown of an actress, who had won fame some years ago for a nude role. Then came a report on how women found themselves repeatedly taken in by polite fraudsters who came cold-calling at their doors. And under the rubric 'Culture' there was a piece about a plane crash and an artist who'd recycled the bits of wreckage into an installation. The red upholstered seats of economy class hung in trees like works of art. The caption to the picture talked about the work being an expression of 'human failure'. The magazine's 'Green page' showed several pictures of frogs, in the grass, on leaves, and underwater too, where they laid spawn in the mud.

I took a table at the window of the next best restaurant and, as I ate, found myself involuntarily thinking of Fo. He started his day sitting in his chair, then he was busy rummaging around with the net over the luggage, then he'd leave and walk out into the rain on Nathan Road. I wondered what kind of tiny hole he might live in in this city, where every square metre cost a fortune? I pictured him in front of his television, or leaning over his sink. When I called to mind the mocking faces he pulled, I marvelled at him, the way I marvel at everything dead; my first impression on seeing a picture of a corpse in a newspaper is always how exemplary it looks.

When I summoned the bill, I noticed the name of the restaurant on the letterhead: 'Toad In The Hole'. I had drunk three
San Miguel beers, and so I placed the money all the more carefully, with the coins piled up neatly, on the saucer provided. At
the pier in Kowloon, I hailed a taxi, since by that time it was
half-past eleven. Back in my room, I switched on the television
straight away, washed my face while the picture was warning
up and re-entered right in the middle of a yet another difficult
dialogue being played out on screen. The protagonists were
deeply troubled about something, shooting each other questioning looks, gazing into the distance when they spoke, knit-
ting their brows in concern and casting their eyes down in a
sceptical internal monologue. This was the 'TV Jade' channel. I
had no wish to see any of it.

On TV Diamond there was a programme about the dangers
of throwing things out of high-rise buildings:

'... every year, hundreds of people in Hong Kong are killed
by falling objects, which people have thoughtlessly hurled ...'

The commentator's voice sounded anxious, like a mother's.
Then a picture of a drinker appeared on the screen, who was
first shown sitting in his chair in front of the TV and getting
agitated before hurling a bottle backwards over his left shoulder out of the open window. Then silence. Cut to falling bottle.
The mother's voice broke in again, before the imminent catastrophe, desperately warning viewers of the danger. The word
'victim' was mentioned several times. Then silence again, and
for thirty seconds nothing but a blank, blue-grey screen. Then
the trumpet concerto by Charpentier suddenly breaks in, and a
violin, quill and artist's palette come together to form a logo ...
Once more, a female voice-over announces:

'Now it's time for the arts. We're taking you over to *Masterpieces*. Today's programme is brought to you by "The Mild One", the cigarette with the lighter taste, and "Pabst Blue Ribbon Beer", the original strong ale.'

TV Pearl was showing a film in Mandarin. But the action and settings were far removed from the reality of the streets here and as formulaic as an American movie; mothers cried when they learned about their daughters' impending weddings; after women are beaten up by their husbands, they get on the telephone; when one person hangs up abruptly, the other looks into the receiver and presses down repeatedly on the cradle; dying people reveal secrets and signal that they're dead by staring fixedly into the distance; and you can tell just how evil the bad guy is from the way the camera zooms in on him. And so a few archetypal situations were played out: a reproach, an apology, an accusation. The music soared to great heights. Faced with the prospect of complete emotional hyperbole, I switched off and arranged my insensate body on the sagging mattress. I recalled Ricarda's shoulder, narrow and bony, and the way she smelt of leather …

The following day, I was on the ferry to Victoria well before midday. The official behind the post office counter shook his head. Stepping out onto the square, at first I was at a loss what to do. I strolled between the houses, stood in the entrance to a bank and rolled up my trouser leg to inspect my knee, which had discoloured around the small inflamed patch of skin. I took the tram for two stops up the hill, but it was no good. So I alighted, turned back and took up position in a park, sitting behind a hedge.

Later, I shifted to a little grandstand and watched some boys playing football. The match was played in an atmosphere of silent professionalism. On both sides, there were no celebrations when goals were scored. I sat there for two hours. By the time I left, the teams had changed their line-up on several occasions, and the score stood at 8–7. There's something very unmodern about sport. You can achieve its pace and its aims by other means without any fuss – say, by jumping over a bar or running a distance. And yet how satisfying it is that sport is still being played at all.

I took a bus to Prince's Building; though it took me twenty minutes, I realized when I got to the restaurant there that all I'd done was come round the corner. Beneath the window, taxis were waiting two-deep for hotel guests. A man wearing a straw hat was sweeping between the cars. Several times he was hit in the back by taxi doors being flung open, but he kept on sweeping, unconcerned. A man in uniform was leaning against the outside wall of a telephone kiosk and talking on the phone. He looked up at me.

In the farther distance, an unlit neon sign was advertising an amusement park. Small delivery vans parked under the trees. A basket of pastries was lifted out of the back of one of them; immediately rain started blowing in. Nearby, a man in bare feet was working on an engine, while a businessman with a suitcase paced indecisively up and down in front of the taxis. The first driver in the queue waved to him, but he didn't respond. Now, from far in the back somewhere, a car horn was sounded – a gap had opened up because one taxi driver had popped into the hotel lobby beneath where I was sitting to have a quick rest. Only after his cab had been put into neutral by his colleagues and pushed right up to the bumper of the one in front did he emerge bandy-legged from the hotel lounge, shrugging his shoulders in resignation. Two of the other drivers immediately went up to him. The uniformed man had by now hung up the receiver and made to intervene in the dispute between the three drivers, as a fourth wiped raindrops from the windscreen with a Kleenex.

Four women with open mouths paraded past my table. The Angels of the Annunciation. The announcement on the radio suddenly broke off and someone started playing variations on the theme of 'My Hat, It Has Three Corners' on the trumpet. I got up and walked through the restaurant to the toilets. Twice I passed a sign with the legend 'Private'.

A confection of coloured tiles and marble-clad walls that look in the mirror. Fifty wash basins, fifty mirrors, fifty soap dishes all at the same height, ten paper hand towel dispensers, plus hand driers and skylights all create a coldly endearing atmosphere. A man who's in there picks up his guitar from the floor and walks out. I turn on a couple of the taps. Gradually the skin grows accustomed to any temperature. It reminds me of something forgotten, the passage of the seasons, the way it passes over a treetop and conveys itself to materials, to stone, leather, wax. Nothing, only the light swims on the skin. Locking myself in the first available cubicle, I sit down on the lavatory seat fully clothed. How delighted I am to be here.

And how beautiful the city is! When was the last time I could cross an avenue, stand on a square and look up at the sky, and see all the buildings around me soaring up into the ether and pointing out into the great expanse above wherever I turned? And where did I last see cascades of banners plunging down the façades of buildings, then taking flight and wandering off over all the rooftops? A thin strip of artificial light shone through the crack between the top of the door and the ceiling. It was very yellow, indifferently yellow, and slashed across the edge of the door like those ethereal bridges in Renaissance paintings that saints use to ascend to heaven. Then I went back to my table, laid my knife and fork on the plate and dabbed my mouth with my napkin. Its hem was instantly soaked with blood. But when I looked again, it wasn't blood after all, just a set of red Chinese characters spelling out the name of the restaurant.

As I left the eatery, darkness was beginning to fall between the buildings. Determined to visit the post office again, I set off for the harbour. At this time of day, the traffic was so light it was like the streets had been closed. The official from my first visit was back behind the counter. He only seemed to remember me when he saw the photo in my passport. Then it took him barely twenty seconds to deal with my request.

His look was set to expressionlessness, but even so the ghost of a smile hovered around his lips. I stood there at the counter, scanning the piles of tied-up letters on the shelf, just like all those who just can't believe that they have been forgotten. The official, too, stood quite motionless next to this still life of uncollected letters, postcards, telegrams and special delivery items – a bundle of trapped voices clamouring in all the world's languages to be heard. Some had grown old, while others had just been overtaken by the present.

It was pointless.

So it's out onto the square once more, which now has the atmosphere of a cathedral where the sexton is gradually lighting the candles. I waited until a beggar had sidled up, bent double but with the theatrically agonized bearing common to both genuine and pretend paupers. Even genuine beggars have no option but to act out their poverty to their best ability. But instead of giving him a response, I inadvertently kicked a can so violently across the tarmac that it flew through the air and left a tiny, sharp dent in the hubcap of a parked car. The beggar decided against approaching me.

As soon as I began to concentrate, the emotion welled up in me. I'd been left in the lurch. I saw myself tramping the streets, like millions of others, in clothes that grew ever shabbier. I'll shuttle back and forth a few more times on the ferry, and eat mangoes, and the juice will dribble down onto my shirt collar; to cool off, I'll start sitting in the air-conditioned draught at the entrance to department stores; the stains on my clothes will tell the tale of increasing neglect, and behind it the other story, invisible, which I'm staring into, first on a daily basis and then without any time or measure. Now I'm resting, and have, like all those who've ever gone bust, attributed my woes to a single, key episode in my life. I'll sit at the Star Ferry Pier and accost tourists, ready to reel off my hard-luck story and give them sightseeing tips. The ferries will cast off, and I'll be left behind in my disreputable clothes. The tourists will think: 'He's still talking away to himself, telling himself his story, but he seems completely *compos mentis*.' Maybe they'll start imagining how my story continues. The image of a stranded paranoiac gripped by his obsessions, always going on about the same people, the same situations.

At home, Ricarda sits up in bed, breathless; her grey eyes are expressionless, she draws her knees up to her body and hugs them, thin arms, round knees, and lowers her head, her eyes fixed on me. I'll never be rid of this image. For a moment she keeps still, feeling my embarrassment, which rises up her body, alienated and dispassionate.

Instead, I find myself in this skyscraper graveyard, sleep-walking. Cut off from my own past, and with no connection to people or the chain of events that have brought me here. Gently and therapeutically disengaged from myself while I'm still alive, exposed to viewpoints, unforgettable moments.

That same evening, I wandered through Wan Chai, disappeared a couple of times into bars on Lockhart Road, staying for almost two hours on both occasions, and making the fleeting acquaintance of one of the hosts:

'Come inside, sir, come inside.'

I looked at him uncomprehendingly. Seeing this, the host slumped back into himself and shook his head. As I came through the hotel lounge, the night porter saw from the intense concentration I was giving to walking that his guest was drunk. I waved him away peremptorily and lurched into the lift with a movement that I hoped would appear casual, even when I stumbled halfway through executing it. Upstairs, I didn't wash or undress. Just once I dragged myself to the end of the bed to switch off the heavily snowing TV.

Crusts of bread with butter; the kids sitting in the back; eat up, says the motherly mouth; you'll get home just as the streetlights are coming on, it also says; his fame spreads far and wide, over the lanes and the sports fields; the path to school is lined with asters; water is dripping from a pipe into a barrel where, fluffily bloated, a mole is floating. The girl unbuttons the boy's shirt over his midriff so far that her cool hand can get right inside it, and then slips down under his belt to his genitals. All the while, the boy's face is suffused like he's running – a distraught face that later takes on a look of amused resignation.

The boy only comprehends his childhood in the minutest isolated elements, say in images from the periphery of larger events. Or in nature, when he lay on the floor of the forest and imagined: if I play dead and make myself just like the wood, then it'll forget me and go back to how it was before, when it just existed for itself. The wish to be overlooked, to be forgotten and to learn what happened next.

The following day I ventured beyond Nathan Road, penetrating deep into the alleyways of the exclusively Chinese quarter. Here the apartment blocks are even closer together; their façades are crumbling and outside the doors stand huge piles of rubbish and other waste, which the derelicts rummage through and leave strewn all over the place. Occasionally a lorry comes by and washes down the pavements. The water evaporates off the hot asphalt. Then the veil comes down again and the rubbish is lying around like before, only now thoroughly drenched. The woman on the hoarding advertising Good Companion Cigarettes looked down dismissively at me from her perch ninety metres above.

That afternoon, I crossed three metropolitan zones: the quarter between Nathan and Jordan Road with the night market and the Star Ferry Pier in Kowloon; Connaught Place with its pier; and the harbour loop road between the New World Centre and Harbour Village on the Victoria side. My skin exuded streams of sweat, opening itself up to the heat and soaking up the dirt, then contracting again in the coolness of shopping malls, service counter areas and waiting rooms, sealing the grime in.

In today's paper: no news from Germany. In the back section was the Pen Pals column. Under 'Interests', you could read 'cycling, cooking, making clothes'; 'making friends, picnics, listening to the radio'; and 'outdoor games'. I became embarrassed, even though I was the only person in the room. I looked out of the window until the feeling passed.

Turning over the page, I came across an advertisement for an Escort Service. The powerful heads of local women were perched on narrow shoulders, their collarbones as delicate as chicken bones, and all with fierce looks on their faces. The old ones in buttoned-up silk pyjamas scarcely look at you, and name you every name like a price. Although in reality they're never touchy-feely, on the television they appear sailing boats across the waters of the harbour and singing imploringly 'let's keep this Hong Kong clean'. Today, I longed to be treated with the warmth of advertising, too.

I noted down the address and telephone number of the Escort Service and lay back on the bed. Another image from childhood came back to me: the biggest boy in the class, hand in hand with his mother, who always brought her son to school, so the teacher could hit him with a ruler. As the boy approaches the school, his mouth opens ever wider, pleading and whining, but the mother knows no mercy. She's a widow. The ruler whistles down onto the calves of the big boy, who thrusts back his knees in ecstasy ...

Through the window I could see as far as the New Territories, a region which at that time was under lease to Hong Kong from China, and which formerly had been marshland, where peasants planted rice or ran chicken farms. But satellite towns have been growing up there for a long time now, and the shacks are a thing of the past. Villages of two hundred skyscrapers rise from depressions and bays, without any limits or any centre. To the right and left of the unmade roads a kind of science-fiction rurality is developing.

I waited in my room until eleven o'clock, deliberately killing time so as to give the post office ample time to sort the newly arrived letters. So I lay abed behind closed curtains for ages, pulling up my knees and fending off room service twice:

'No, I'm not ready yet.'

And the second time:

'No, no thank you, no.'

The breakfast room was already closed, so I stalked into the restaurant, ordered rice and two eggs, ate half of it and then went back to my room. The girls from housekeeping had finally given up. A sweet smell of rotting mangoes was coming from my bin, so I chucked the magazine on top of them. It landed with the back cover facing upward. A woman's profile was set off against bleached hair, and her open mouth spoke to the dark brown ceiling of the room: 'My colour is cream hair colour'. I pulled my notebook from my bag and jotted down on a fresh page: 'my colour is cream hair colour'.

The steam from the laundry was hissing from the mouth of a pipe into the courtyard and rising up again through the duct. The two Chinese ironing ladies watched it. I too was looking up when, at a very high altitude, a small aeroplane crossed the clear blue sky. The sunlight was reflecting beautifully and playfully off its wings. But as the aircraft climbed, the wings clouded over, and the fuselage plunged into the darkness of the more distant sky, creeping upwards, shrinking and gradually dissolving into the blank tableau of the atmosphere. The speed of the city, by contrast, is that of the observer's eye, which by turn finds itself repelled and attracted and moves on relentlessly.

I reached the post office with one leg limping and dragging. In the interim, I'd clearly become less of an irritant to the official than I had been at the beginning. His 'No' was as much an integral part of his job as putting on his blouson at the start of the working day. Now he began shaking his head when I was still five metres away from his counter. But I fancied that he'd started to feel a bit sorry for me.

The street behind the post office ended in a scuffed-up grass bank strewn with refuse and various shredded, bent and scrunched-up objects. Up on the platform above, a few pensioners were gyrating in slow, narcissistic movements. Old women in pyjamas and hair nets gesticulated at something invisible and with military precision dissected the air first into cuboids and then into strips, always speaking from the strength of their own body axis. I clambered up the bank to watch them.

On the park bench to my left, their instructress was drinking a can of Schweppes. Next to her was a sword in a scabbard, a large ritual sword with a heavy blade. As soon as she caught sight of me, she put the can down and advanced on me with both arms outstretched. The invisible had taken on a tangible form, namely mine. The entire group turned on its collective axis to face me, with Kabuki faces, a gaze concentrated in the root of the nose, and a lunge-step which involved lifting their feet slowly from the ground and bringing them down again noiselessly.

'Go away!' hissed the old lady at the head of her troop.

I stepped back two paces, teetering on the edge of the bank.

'Go away! Away!'

An index finger suddenly projected from her shooing-away arm, flying down the bank and on across the city, maintaining a certain height over the sea and over the horizon, and on around the curvature of the earth. Then her arms were flung wide again like they'd been hit by a gust of wind or a wave. This wasn't my park.

I beat a retreat down the same road I'd come along. On the first billboard I passed, three girls in short nightdresses were bending over an oversized newspaper. They were all laughing uproariously; this was the first time in Hong Kong that women hadn't avoided my gaze. I could still see the sword lying on the park bench. At the beginning of a *tai-chi* session, it is lifted up and displayed to the assembled group like some religious monstrance.

The television was screening European football matches from the year before, and Chinese operas in 1950s costumes and settings. Today, I found myself missing the charm of TV advertising, the genial ingratiation of posters, and the intimate superficiality which took its cue from Western consumer culture.

Overnight, my knee swelled up so badly that I couldn't leave the room the next day, nor on subsequent days. I didn't call a doctor, and for a whole week, room service supplied me with all my needs. Mister Fo even dropped by once, a real act of friendship, since his allotted place was in the lobby, and besides we had nothing to say to one another. Even so, he'd bought me a pound of plums from a shop called 'International Fruits', and declined to have any himself.

I spent most of my enforced leisure learning poems off by heart or gazing at the ceiling, where I found my interest drawn primarily by the frosted glass lampshade, at the edge of which there was a pale shadow, around ten centimetres long, which I found myself at a loss to explain.

Travelling, it occurred to me at that moment, was like projecting your homeland onto a foreign wallpaper. There, you can find the house that you left and put out of your mind, and feel the anchorage that you wanted to cast into oblivion. You overturn the shelf, you tear down the curtains, but it's no use. When you're abroad, home puffs itself up ever more theatrically: Leave me, it says, destroy me! Find something that isn't the same old familiar routine! And then you find yourself lying in a hotel room in Hong Kong and feeling as though you haven't left home at all, but that everything's been transformed into your childhood room; the last straw is that you see on the room service waiter's menu the description 'Wintery salads' and you burst into tears.

When, after a week of being bedridden, I'd finally regained some sense of balance when I was standing upright, I propped a chair up on my bedstead and investigated the lampshade. It was hanging so loosely from the ceiling that an animal could easily have crawled in through the narrow gap on the right-hand side and met its end there. I switched the light on, and the shadow darkened visibly, but only like a shrivelled leaf on a St Martin's Day lantern. So I unscrewed the whole casing from the ceiling and peered inside.

What had once been a gecko had, under the influence of heat, light rays and hot air, been transformed into a husk, a simple gecko structure, a stick figure made of gecko bones, hair-thin at its extremities, but as intricately structured as the living animal. The heat had burned off a bit of flesh every day and evaporated it. Now there was nothing left but the time-scoured skeleton of a reptile that had strayed into the wrong place and come to grief there.

So, was that 'my Hong Kong', then? Where was I really, and what remained? While, viewed from my sickbed, the city had melted into a diffuse mass of impulses, only the empty PO Box and the gecko had any real presence, and for all I knew maybe there really was some connection between them. It struck me then that, seen from a certain foreign standpoint, your own home can be the ends of the earth, and this being the case, these far-flung places, these ends, aren't portals through which you can exit this world. Yet at least sometimes it can seem that way, I thought, and left the next day without even bothering to go to the post office again.

The Amu-Darya

On the Frontiers of Transoxania

From history, short-maned horses burst forth, steppelands stretch into the distance and morasses loom threateningly. Travellers throughout the centuries have gravitated to this river, which marks the border between northern Afghanistan and the former Russian Empire – modern Tajikistan, Uzbekistan and Turkmenistan; their journey was arduous, with many of them suffering great hardships and failing to reach their destination because they were waylaid by ambushes, privations, malaria, worm infections or epidemics. Mulberry and tamarisk trees were the first harbingers of the distant river. Traders travelled across the sand dunes in caravans, while other caravans approached from Transoxania, the land on the far side of the Amu-Darya. Their camels were laden with canisters of petrol, one of the many commodities that people on the Afghan side of the river obtained from the former Russian territories.

A mythical landscape clusters around the banks of the Amu-Darya, which in ancient times was also known as the Oxus. In the ninth century AD, the Persian poet Rudaki, renowned as the 'caravan leader of poetry', fantasized that its craggy banks felt like silk beneath his feet, and that its waves leapt right up to his horse's bridle for sheer joy at the sight of him returning home. Travel writers down the ages talk in hushed whispers of this river and its environs, not only because it was so difficult and dangerous getting there but also because the sights that met your eye when you entered this world-renowned region were said to more than compensate for all the hardships along the way. You conjure up a mental image of the natural conditions around the river, its vegetation, cobbled together from fragments of old tales and stories passed down by word of mouth. But in your mind's eye it's all still devoid of people, the landscape still has no faces and the origins of the river still lie shrouded in enchanted mystery – at least, travellers who once made it to the banks of the Amu-Darya certainly speak in these terms.

Marco Polo visited the source of the river, high up in the Pamir mountain range, and on 19 February 1838, the British army lieutenant John Wood also found himself standing at the same spot, on the 'Roof of the World' as he called it, above the Bam i Dünjah lake, or the Sir i Kol, as the Kirghiz people call the body of water that is the source of the Amu-Darya. As the astonished Wood reported: '... before us lay stretched a noble but frozen sheet of water, from whose western end issued the infant river of the Oxus'. The beautiful lake, he wrote, 'took the form of a half-moon'.

But from here, it's still a long way down to the valleys of northern Afghanistan, and the traveller asks himself: how can you possibly hope to traverse all these barriers – the mountains, the rivers, the various battle fronts – and finally cross the vast steppe, where all movement always seems to be aimless? That's what makes it so alluring. And when a person like Robert Byron successfully reached the Oxus, he was so totally enraptured he couldn't help but look down haughtily on all the other poor wretches in the past who had perished in the attempt.

For a long time, the area around Kunduz was greatly feared. Thanks to its marshy terrain and unhealthy climate, people were wont to say: 'If you want to die, go to Kunduz.' But since an urban culture began to develop there in the 1970s – with indigenous tribes and ethnic groups from outside the region combining with international hippies to set up museums, cinemas, theatres and all kinds of sporting and entertainment venues – the place that was traditionally known for rice-growing, silkworm cultivation and the mining of lapis lazuli and rubies has earned itself a new motto: 'If you want to live, go to Kunduz.' So it was that a thriving, artistic and liberal city arose, where Koranic scholars, Indian Sikhs, bikini girls and potheads happily rubbed shoulders.

We leave behind us the tanned hide of clay walls that are threatening to burst after being subjected to winter frosts followed by the raging heat of summer. Outside the city gates, the fields have been flooded to try and make their rock-hard surface a bit more yielding to enable water to soak down into the soil, while on the banks of this man-made lake oxen stand, arching their twitching backs as children brush them down.

We pass the first sand redoubts of former refugees, who fled back here, to their homeland and peace, along the road from Kandahar. But what did they find when they got here? Fields that had reverted to arid steppe, derelict or shot-up houses with their connections to electricity and the water supply cut off. So they regrouped, erected their makeshift houses on the edge of a stretch of water, and are getting on with the business of survival.

The steppe stretches out like a desert, and the settlements sit in it like oases. Nomads pass by, selling camel skins, goat cheese and cloth. Kids swarm about, carrying containers of water on their heads. They vanish into the endless waste, like they've disappeared over the curvature of the earth. Every so often, there's a hamlet – a bush with a few huts round it, an enclosed courtyard with a well and an oven cheek by jowl. Old people who have learned to fight for this life and then for their very existence, young people who are almost collapsing under the burden of the life they imagine for themselves, conveyed to them by images, all of them growing up on deserts, rocks, dust – on virtually nothing.

We turn once more onto the wide black road, which runs across the pale yellow landscape of the steppe. Now there's an old man with us in the car, with a voice like an organ; he knows the hidden tracks that will take us to the shy Uzbeks, and he'll be able to find a way to get us into one of their villages. We drive for a long time. On the horizon, we see what could be distant haze or maybe the curve of mist-covered hills – who knows, it may even be a mirage. After twenty minutes, we encounter the first bend in the road.

We turn off from the metalled road and drive into this nothingness. On we go, over humps, across dips and over hills, we're driving in a cloud of dust and sand, then it's downhill across the soft ground of the steppe, which yields like pressed straw underfoot.

Finally, there's a bulge, a slight swelling in the horizon line. Those are the sheep herds, guarded by one young shepherd who's asleep on a sand hill and another who's trotting around in a circle on horseback in leisurely fashion and three fierce dogs, whose job it is to tackle wolves and jackals and who are always spoiling for a fight. Then again, when the war was going on, the wolves ate the corpses of people that lay scattered around.

The shepherd knows that, he slips off his sand hill and takes a couple of steps towards us. Under his long felt coat, he's wearing a pullover, a padded green jacket and a pinstriped waistcoat. He uses the long crook he's holding to lean on, and to protect and herd the community's sheep. There are around seven hundred all told in this region, guarded by anything between ten and fourteen shepherds, and constantly threatened by tarantulas, snakes and wolves.

Where does he sleep?

'Somewhere on the steppe.'

Where does he get his water from?

'It's six hours with the herd to the next watering hole.'

'And is the herd safe?'

'Sometimes rustlers will come along and steal a couple of animals. But what can I do about it? So we just steal some back to even up the score.'

'And what would you do if I stole some of your sheep?' our friend Turab asks him.

'I know karate', the shepherd replies, with a face that has never joked in its life, or at least looks that way.

'What do you eat?'

'My bread, with a bit of fat that I carry with me in this jar here.'

He shows us it.

'Why do you choose to stay around here,' Tuareb protests jokingly, 'rather than finding yourself a sensible job in the city?'

'I can't leave.'

He learns where we're from.

'You live in a good country where there's always plenty of rain.'

'What do you earn?'

'I get a tenth of all the newborn lambs in any one year. If I'm in luck that may be as many as fifty.'

'How old are you?'

'No idea. Twenty-one, maybe?'

'But you haven't even grown a beard yet!'

'Maybe you tell me how old I am, then?'

Conversations among Afghans often run like this. They start talking straight away about each other's circumstances, about quite personal matters in fact. They never refuse to respond to a question or answer one with another question. They share their history as readily as the air they breathe.

We proceed through the steppe on foot, and for a long stretch all we can see is solidified sand dunes and dusty hollows – and then all of a sudden we're ambushed by children who come running from all directions, appearing as if from nowhere. They're clutching plastic submachine guns and toy Kalashnikovs; it's the first things they spend their pocket money on here, having no conception of disarmament.

Then suddenly there's a change in the atmosphere. The air becomes clearer, and ahead of us we see taller vegetation. Cotton fields come into view, and some maize. The Uzbek tribal villages are situated behind straw palisades, with their dwellings laid out defensively in squares and their well-trodden connecting paths, dusty thoroughfares which the camels are led along. All the buildings here look like African mud-brick architecture, no different to, say, Mali or Burkina Faso.

We remain outside the gates, waiting to see if we'll be allowed in. There's a ceremony in progress somewhere nearby. In traditional fashion, a bride is being led on camelback to the house of her fiancé. We can hear the clatter of a motorbike, but for all that, we really are on the fringes of an isolated civilization that's sealed off from the surrounding world, yet which at the same time is in danger of choking on its own poverty. While we're waiting, a boy, accompanied by a mangy dog, drives a camel with a matted coat past us, followed by an old man riding a lady's bicycle.

Eventually an elder from one of the farmsteads bids us enter. He doesn't take off the absurdly modish sunglasses he's wearing – less practical eyewear than status symbol. Behind our little party trots a boy holding a pitcher of hot water and a bowl for us to wash our hands in.

The inner courtyard of the settlement contains all the vital functions of the tribe within one confined area: the well and the fireplace are here, as are the barn and the workshop. The latter building is empty as we approach, since the women, who assemble here every day to weave Uzbek carpets, have all withdrawn into the interior.

The foreman of this estate was interned in Kunduz prison for a long spell. He mentions that he was tortured there, in passing, like he's just ensuring, for the sake of completeness, that he doesn't omit to touch on this fact, which is a commonplace for many people in these parts. As he's speaking, his turbaned head looks down at the ground, and his slender hands stroke the unfinished pieces of woven material in front of him, brightly coloured textiles, which are finally assembled by the deft fingers of children into complete carpets. Even the soles of the kids' feet here are decorated with henna designs drawn on as part of the celebrations just past. The senior village elder offers us tea:

'Wait, I'll drink mine first, so you don't need to worry.'

In former times, people here were given to singing the praises of caravan tea, which actually came from China:

'It's got creases like Tartar boots, curly locks like the dewlaps of a mighty ox, spirals like mist rising from a gorge, and it shimmers like a lake caressed by the blue of heaven ...'

As we're drinking our tea, the children stream out to convene the Elders' Council, and in no time, there they all are – twenty-five men, most of them wearing turbans and long cloaks, with dignified, profoundly serious and sometimes even melancholic faces – and then through the crowd of elders strides Nadia, the Afghan exile, her hair hidden beneath a scarf but with her face uncovered, heading for the community hall, where she will hear the council's petitions.

The community assembly hall has only recently been completed, and is the pride of the village. In a fit of either presumption or idealism, it has been decorated with light blue cloud motifs. In these surroundings, it looks as strangely newfangled as encountering a jacuzzi in a nomadic settlement.

We sit in a circle on cushions. More men keep crowding into the room from outside. Boys squeeze between them, carrying dishes of pistachios, almonds, dried fruits and pulses. There are also some sweets wrapped in cellophane on the plates. All these refreshments arrive without us hearing any command for them to be brought in. Later, Nadia tells us that there was a great flurry of activity behind the scenes to try and assemble the makings of a proper meal, but that they couldn't find enough ingredients.

As soon as she starts to speak, the room falls silent. The elders – with countenances showing they've entered their twilight years, their fear of the future and their adherence to the last vestiges of tradition – gaze into Nadia's open face and see how radically times have changed. They all knew her father. That doubtless makes it easier for them to listen to her now. Nor do they need to learn to trust her – they do so already. But their requests are exhaustive and, when measured against Nadia's ability to deliver, really quite excessive.

Suddenly, the light in the room shifts abruptly into twilight mode. The elders bite open an almond or two, but keep their gaze focused on Nadia's face the whole time, trying to divine what she might donate to help them sink a well, build a school or pay for a doctor to staff the local clinic, because there's no one running it at present.

Most illnesses hereabouts are contracted from the water. Sometimes animals will die in a well and contaminate it, and sometimes uneducated farmers will throw a cadaver down the shaft just to get rid of it. Malaria is rife, too. Nadia listens to all this, as patiently as if she's hearing it for the first time; all these stories have the same basic pattern. Numerous pairs of eyes are glued to her every facial expression, unblinking. Many of the faces are finely chiselled, while others tend toward Mongol, Asiatic features. Nobody begs, nobody complains, nobody wrings their hands, tears their hair or loses their composure.

Where their livelihoods are concerned, in good years they can keep themselves afloat for six months by selling carpets and live-stock, while for the second half of the year they have to live on what they've managed to grow themselves. The farmers are in the fields or tending to their animals from the crack of dawn. They breakfast on tea and bread, and milk as well when it's available.

I'm simply reporting here what one of the farmers said at the meeting. Everyone in the room was taking a discreet but definite interest in what I found intriguing, and scarcely had I put pen to paper than all eyes were upon me. As far as they're concerned, all they're recounting here is their everyday lives. Why would that be worth writing about? Maybe because there's a high risk of treading on a landmine while you're working in the fields? True enough, but then it's not exactly easy dealing with the wolves, either.

The most fortunate farmers are those with an ox-plough and who have a cow of their own that they can rely on for milk. Farmers like these can sometimes even afford to buy fertilizer.

'But doesn't the milk taste better without fertilizers?' I ask, and everyone laughs, delighted that all foreigners seem to think the same way.

The conversation now turns to arable farming – the harvests, and the late sowing of rice. Behind a school, we discovered a couple of poppies. Where, we want to know, might the seeds have been blown from? In any event, no one had spotted a poppy field from the road.

'We don't grow poppies here,' the local superintendent announces with a deadpan expression.

'But we've been told you got a forty-kilo yield off your fields,' Turab calls out and everyone laughs again; the man to whom he addresses this remark rewards him by slapping him matily on the back several times.

Yet if we somehow imagined that there was a secret source of wealth in these villages, we'd be barking up the wrong tree. Tilling the fields is backbreaking work, and time and again drought destroys the harvests. The kids get up at six o'clock to go to school so that they can come back in the late morning to help their parents again, either picking cotton or looking after the livestock.

In the meantime, Nadia has begun to draft the proposal for a new well on a page she's torn out of an exercise book. As she does so, the oldest villager resumes his account of the daily life of a farmer. After a lunch usually consisting of rice, nothing else is eaten until evening prayers, when there's bread and buttermilk.

'That bloats your stomach and makes you sleepy,' says Nadia. 'We call it Afghan Alcohol.'

After supper, the men go and sit with the women, and knot carpets or swap stories. Sometimes, they'll even take charge of looking after babies so that the women can do their carpet-knotting in peace. Because men can take several wives, they also leave behind multiple widows. As a result, in many villages women play a vital role in keeping the community alive. The place we're visiting today doesn't have a television, and only the richest farmer has an electricity generator. So people go to bed early.

'Has the climate in this area changed over time?'

'Yes, generally it's become warmer, which means we get more pests, and that's hit the cotton harvest. Years ago, we used to get much more snow.'

Their faces, which are as tanned as pairs of shoes, are permanently etched with worry. They keep their hands, the chapped tools of their trade, folded in their laps, and even their feet look leathery and worn out. The tea tastes of the smoke of the wood fire it was brewed on.

Meanwhile, the proposal for the well is finished. Someone appears with an ink pad, and all but two of the men press their fingerprints over their names, which the secretary has written out in block capitals. One of them even has a wax seal. Then another farmer approaches Nadia and whispers:

'Help me, get me a moped!'

Finally, Nadia is left holding a grubby proposal sheet, smudged with candle soot and covered in inky fingerprints – a draft from which a well will result within the foreseeable future. The senior elder of the village then presents us with three sumptuous robes, draped over his forearm, in violet and green, just like those worn by the Afghan president. Quite impossible to refuse this gift, especially after he's delivered a little speech:

'It's true that we have nothing, but two things that we possess and will never give up are our humanity and our pride.'

We travel on northward, now moving across the steppe as the crow flies, straight towards the border, in order that we might set foot on the riverbanks that turn their back on war-torn Afghanistan. Caught up in the all-pervading atmosphere of imperturbability here, we too have begun to move more slowly – or does it just seem that way because this endless plain makes all movements across it small-scale and slow?

As evening falls, the shepherds herd their sheep into pens, while the cowherds drive their cattle along beside the ditches, between the rice paddies or parallel to the road. At one point on the route, three boys have set up a small bicycle repair shop. They're wearing cardigans that match their turbans. Their friends, who come rushing up when we stop, show their red henna-dyed hair beneath their embroidered skullcaps. An old man catches an escaped lamb and lobs it over the walls of his compound.

Otherwise, everything is quiet on the road and only the fact that we pull over and stop gives people's activities some focal point. They come running in our direction from even the most far-flung huts, and even the cattle drovers and their animals pause for a moment to look at us, as the sun spreads its opulent late afternoon light across pools of water standing in the fields.

The lads tell us that they're unemployed, and swiftly add that they have 'no future'. Two of them had only recently come to this region, their parents' homeland, from the Pakistani refugee camp in Peshawar, but now, as they put it, 'we're dying of boredom here'.

And it's a fact that hardly any group finds it as difficult assimilating themselves into the poverty-stricken home region of their parents as young people, who have left behind the utterly different world of the Pakistani transit camps and are now supposed to make a life for themselves without electricity whist living alongside a road in northern Afghanistan, in the company of two thousand five hundred other families. They smile their most engaging smile, but you can see it's already choked with traces of fatalism:

'It's so boring here,' the youngest of them says, 'I'm sick of life.'

Now they're thronging in from the grazing paddocks and the rice paddies, the little kids with their widows' faces, approaching us in what look like pyjamas, attentive but as mature as shrivelled buds. Who talks about the undiscovered potential of these kids? If you ask them about their 'free time', as we call it, they look at you with astonishment. You have to explain the term to them; likewise, they find it hard differentiating 'playing' from 'eating' or 'tending livestock'.

One of the children nuzzles up to its mother like a goat kid. Young animals have a habit of expressing their love like it's some vital function. There's nothing about this child that wouldn't also apply to a baby animal, whose tenderness does not come across as practised, but as needy for affection as the day it was born.

But we have to press on. If you follow this road for its entire course, you find yourself in China. We cross the 'Three-Waters-River', pass rice terraces, okra fields and shallow scrapes in the ground, where camels and sheep are watered. We turn off onto dust roads, where little girls are running to school, and that's where we're headed too – a school that nowadays takes in eight hundred children from twelve villages. All these children are required to help out on the farms, bringing food to their fathers in the fields and looking after the animals. Some of them have to walk a full hour before they reach the sign at the school entrance that bears the motto: 'Knowledge And Skill Help People Get On'. What is to become of these children, and what of the people here who find themselves displaced by the ravages of war, destroyed, killed or driven into exile? They will be condemned to grow ever poorer, their harvests will dwindle, basic commodities will become scarce and their village communities will be swamped by refugees.

The pastel glow of the sunset spreads across the steppe: alone against the backcloth of the opalescent sky, the camel driver stands with his eleven animals, the youngest of which is two and the eldest six. We approach him in the ditchwater hues cast by the early gloaming.

'Ai ha!'

The camels slow momentarily, look round at their driver and then trot on.

He stands there leaning on his crook and gives us the same shepherd's look he gives his animals. Yes, he tells us, they've all got their individual characters, and moods too. And no, he doesn't always accompany them: when they start trotting, he'll sometimes run after them. They become particularly temperamental in winter, kicking out and biting one another. You've got to watch out than that they don't injure each other. No, they don't have any natural predators, only the landmines; jackals will only go for smaller sheep, and snakes don't trouble them either.

'No one can defeat a camel!'

In the interim, the camels have slowly made off.

'Aren't you worried that you'll lose your camels while we're standing around here chatting?'

He gazes patiently into the grey-blue haze of the darkening steppe. Then he just shakes his head.

It's a good ten minutes before he finally picks up his coat and takes his leave of us, saying he really ought to go and look after his animals now. Then he promptly heads off in the opposite direction to where they went. Only later do we learn that he also tends a flock of sheep, which have long been grazing somewhere out of sight. He was too polite to pass by without exchanging a few words with us. As he's leaving, he turns around once more:

'You want to see the Amu-Darya, right?'

'Yes, we do.'

He just keeps nodding as he walks away.

By now, all that's left of the sun is an orange-grey shimmer on the horizon. The camels trot off to the pitch-black quadrant of the sky, while the shepherd dwells in the lighter zones. And now night falls with a silence so profound that it even muffles the barking of the dogs and the bleating of the camels, whose hooves leave no imprint and make no sound on the cushioned ground. The new moon rises, and Nadia says:

'On the first night of a full moon on the steppe, it's traditional to kiss your fingertips and make a wish.'

We do it.

The next day, not far from the end of the road, we come across a run-down frontier post, where a border guard is standing outside a hut. There's a little shop here too, with a straggly-bearded derelict leaning against the balustrade; maybe he's a hippy who came here and never left, or a Sufi mystic or a mental patient. All around, between the huts, lies abandoned military hardware rusting in the fields. All in all, a blind, hopeless place built around a border barrier and manned by a couple of marooned, forgotten people.

The road ends in front of a gate through which we're permitted to enter the port facility – or to be more accurate the graveyard of junk that now occupies the site where a thriving port must once have operated. What the destruction of war has left behind, combined with loads of rusty bits of metal gathered from the surrounding area, now lies piled up between warehouses, loading ramps and a monstrous crane gantry. It rises up above the brackish water of the sluggish river with all the operatic drama that people in former times must have experienced when confronted with the first great machines of the Industrial Revolution. The effect is like one of Luchino Visconti's stage sets, transposed to the world of machine poetry, like an allegory of a hundred years of technology grandly rusting into collapse. And the arm of the great crane points blindly across the river towards Tajikistan, as if it had been frozen in this pose.

The Amu-Darya is grey from the clayey soil it washes from its banks. It seems to have acclimatized itself to its surroundings. Its banks are silty; on the face of it, the water appears to flow quite sedately but in fact there's a powerful undertow, which only now and then reveals itself through flow marks left on the bank. Not long ago, a man on horseback tried to reach safety by fording the river to Tajikistan. The rider and his mount battled heroically, locals reported, but both drowned all the same.

Broad strips of mudflat remain where the river has ebbed, shot through with tidal creeks and crumbling ditches. Upstream from here lies the little makeshift ferry, which crosses the river on request. Over on the far side in Transoxania, at least according to travellers, another world begins, as evidenced by the greenness of the landscape and the towering chimney stacks. Once upon a time, a paddle steamer even ran from the Russian bank, while the Afghans used sailing boats, which took them as far as the Aral Sea.

When we get there, the ferry has just tied up over in Tajikistan, between a couple of nondescript industrial units and containers, which echo the spirit of the Afghan side of the river: a posthumous landscape, the landscape left behind when all events have drained away, remaining as a place-holder for an absent history. But no sooner have we turned our gaze eastward than we notice that the steppe is still there, the yellow-green steppe that stretches away endlessly into bleak vastness.

It would take nothing to enliven this confused mess of mud, ruins and war debris. As if he were aware of this, an old man on crutches suddenly appears over the harbour wall. His potato face gapes at the dust-grey sky like he's trying to get scent of something. A flock of birds rises up with a great screech, at the same time as children can be heard screaming in the distance. Then there's near-silence, just the sound of something metallic clattering in the wind. A gust carries voices over to us, and even the birds nesting on the crane make a few desultory noises, so grating that they scarcely sound like birds any more. Footsteps can be heard walking away on the gravel. One of our companions has spread his prayer mat out on the mud and is performing his devotions with his eyes turned upwards. All at once, a holiday quietness descends over the place, an unreal atmosphere like the exhalation of time between two wars.

Our little group makes its way carefully down to the water's edge. The jetty is deserted and devoid of any signs of life, like no one's crossed here for years. Nothing here is beautiful; but for all that, the sheer concentration of certain objects – the stone slabs, the rusty equipment, the bushes and the weeds, the rubbish and other detritus – makes it seem as though it has all purposely coalesced into this elaborate constellation to create an impression of unsurpassed blandness.

Of all the attractive non-places I've seen, this one has a particular allure. Clear off, it says, there's nothing here, turn around, don't look at me, don't retain any memory of this, stop being here, just go away. I dip my hands into the yellow-grey and milky shimmering water of the river. It's like plunging them into cold, liquid opal, and someone's about to tell me that there are Hellenic and Buddhist statues lying on the riverbed, thrown in by the Taliban, and that bodies regularly floated past here, which is why the water might still be host to infectious diseases.

The harbour wall is covered in luxuriant yellow lichen. There's a pontoon floating in the water but in all likelihood no one has landed on it for years. The only thing on it is a blue plastic chair, facing the steppe on the far side. If you turn around, a moment later you'll be saying: I only imagined this place.

In this moment, an arrowhead formation of migrating birds rearranges itself as it flies over the river. There are plans to build a bridge here soon. The only people to object have been former Afghan and Russian soldiers, not only because of their old animosity, but also because they know full well, as do the powers that be, that the main beneficiaries of such a bridge would be the drug smugglers.

And who isn't casting envious eyes over there, where, further downstream, a few scant gold deposits still attract prospectors, or where raw opium is processed, which just through the act of crossing the river multiplies many times in value? A kilo costs three thousand dollars on this, the Afghan side of the Amu-Darya, whereas it's worth ten thousand over in Tajikistan, a mere five hundred metres away, and one would be naïve to imagine it's only the Tajiks and the Afghans who are fighting for a slice of this trade.

One of the most influential people in these parts is an American citizen. Nobody knows anything more about him, or is willing to divulge them in any event. The only thing I can get out of two locals is his nickname: 'White Ibrahim'. One of the Afghans who has attached himself to us tells me about a German diplomat who smuggled seventeen kilos of opium out of the country undetected in his luggage; he sprayed his stash with a scent that the drug-sniffer dogs found repellent.

'How do you know that?'

'Because it was me who sold him the drugs.'

Now we've got to the far side of the landscape, we follow its imperative and turn away, turn round, turn about-face. It's a multiple turning away from a landscape which comes to an end, which draws a line called the Amu-Darya under itself.

The steppe welcomes us back once more in all its desolate magnificence.

The night spreads far and wide. Is that now the most silent silence? It's as if someone has lifted a glass cloche off the steppe and replaced it with a sphere that descends from above and goes down into the earth and creates a far more widespread and solemn hush than before. Pure atmosphere mingles with our silence. And something resonates within it like breathless anticipation. And into the silent realm that is open to the skies above, from below there now comes the noise of a single dog barking, way off, a sound that has only been instigated to make the silence all the more palpable.

The silence of the steppe: the minute you hear a noise far-off, you're up close to it – in the distance, that is. But if the steppe stays quiet, all you've got for company is your own breathing or the sound of your own footsteps. In other words, you're totally absorbed in yourself. And that's a rare place to be.

Toraja

Among the Dead

My friend Hannes was a diminutive dandy with a noble-looking cranium, thick black swept-back hair, and a ring with a skull on it. Above and beyond being my friend, he was also my mentor, who would occasionally deliver mumbled monologues on such subjects as the portrayal of death on Mexican sacrificial mounds, the mummified corpse catacombs in Palermo or the necrophiliac wood engraver José Posada and his prints of the *Dance of Death*. Hannes was an avid collector of images of death from anywhere and everywhere: in folklore, scrapbook pictures or in kitsch items from the turn of the nineteenth century.

His entire flat, in an old building with winding corridors, a real warren of a place, was peopled with skeletons – grinning, dancing, riding, grave-digging, guarding, copulating, always grotesque figures with large, reproachful eye sockets. Friends and visitors had differing views on the collector's passion that had brought this assemblage of objects together. Yet Hannes, who wasn't much given to introspection, had little interest in the theory behind them; he was merely objectifying his own fear. His real motivation in assembling this collection, rather, was to observe the human imagination in its preoccupation with letting death run riot in the world while remaining somehow oblivious to its own mortality.

As a direct result of this, Hannes set great store by everything corporeal. It was just that he invested greater trust in the
body in its spontaneous manifestations of life than he did in
any moral code. He ascribed a certain intelligibility to functions like sex, puking, shitting, pissing, coughing, farting,
blushing or getting an erection; blood, semen and other bodily
fluids, they all meant something to him, they were all quite literally expressions of life.

Then, one day, I was preparing to set off to Southeast Asia
for a year, where Sulawesi – or Celebes, as the island was still
called back then, just as Jakarta had once been called Batavia
and Ujung Pandang Macassar – was also on my itinerary. I
said goodbye to Hannes, who got up from his desk, which was
covered in death's-head netsukes, to let me hug and kiss him
farewell, and in return he dispensed the following advice:

'If you really do make it to Sulawesi, then you've got to go
to Toraja Land, in the Rantepao region! You'll see the famous
pile dwellings there with their brightly painted saddle-shaped
roofs, and if you get the chance you must attend one of their
funeral ceremonies. They've got a couple of the most original
death cults in the entire world there.'

For sure, I'd heard of those tall pile houses, swooping
dwelling-ships with bamboo roofs and built entirely without
nails; they also boasted painted friezes on the gable ends, extensive carvings and buffalo skulls hung on the façades opposite
the rice stores. The Toraja were a fabled people, descended
from a race of Cambodian seafarers who had fled their original
home on the coast when they were threatened by Muslim inva-
sion and made their way into the interior of the orchid-shaped
island, where they finally settled in a series of remote valleys.

They fell between various religions. Though basically animistic, espousing the belief that the dead lived on in the places they had inhabited in life, they did assume some elements of Islam into the practice of their religion, and likewise some Christian elements too with the arrival of the first missionaries.

I travelled most of the long route from Ujung Pandang, the capital of Sulawesi, to the highland region of Tan Toraja sitting on the roof of the public bus, amidst pieces of luggage, two cages containing valuable turkeys, and three youths playing cards, whose interest in me quickly evaporated when we found we had no language in common. The only person I struck up a reasonably fluent conversation with was Michael, an earnest student who was heading back home to attend a family celebration.

'So, what brings you here?' he asked me.

'I wanted to disappear.'

'And are you managing to?'

'Like a shadow.'

'But a shadow doesn't cut stone.'

We kept on talking in this curious vein. He bade me farewell in a very cosmopolitan way when, at the first bus stop on the territory of the Toraja region, I clambered down from the bus roof to try and find somewhere to stay. I was very close to getting sunstroke, and for the next two days the severe sunburn that I'd suffered while sitting up on the roof laid me low with a fever in a *losmen*, one of those family guesthouses you find throughout Indonesia.

Determined to press on into the more remote village areas, I set out on foot on the third day. The rice paddies were shimmering so brightly in the sun that it hurt my eyes; the fresh, bright green of the new plants seemed to be alive with the constant breeze that blew through the grasses and the monochrome paddyfields. Nowhere was the elegant asymmetry of Southeast Asia displayed better than in this landscape, and I ventured, sometimes walking and sometimes hitching a ride from one village to the next, ever deeper into the rural life.

But one evening, as I was walking down a narrow sunken lane overgrown by high grasses on either side, I was pulled up short by an apparition: there, motionless on the crown of the farm track in front of me like a great white buffalo, stood the unlikeliest of vehicles – a limousine. The wide-eyed Indonesian driver, who sat with both hands gripping the steering wheel, really was wearing a chauffeur's uniform, and he too was paralyzed with astonishment, perhaps because the sight of me coming along this hollow lane was just as surprising to him as he was to me, sitting there in his UFO.

I started to approach the car, but halfway there the rear door was opened, though I couldn't hear or see much else. The driver turned his head to face me, but did not signal to me in any way. When I finally drew level with the open door and bent down to peer inside, I was met by the sight of a slim American dressed in a white suit sprawling elegiacally across the back seat, clutching an ice-misted glass of mineral water in his left hand and wearing the expression of someone truly decadent and elegantly depraved.

After a brief exchange of words by way of examination, which I evidently passed, my bag was stowed in the boot and I was permitted to sink back into the air-conditioned depths of the back seat alongside the American, sipping ice-cold water and giving him my take on travel.

As I did so, the man, a heart surgeon with an abundance of money and phobias, kept casting glances out of the window, like he was duty bound to do so. But he soon grew bored of this. He was mildly interested, but clearly quite pleased with himself in a disgruntled kind of way, and in the one week of annual vacation he had remaining had hired an Indonesian chauffeur to drive him through the jungle. The driver came from nearby Rantepao, but was resident in the USA at present as a student, so he no longer came across as quite so Indonesian.

'Anyhow, I'll start again,' the driver said, at which the doctor gave a pained smile. 'So there's this guy sitting on a pump at a gas station …' The doctor smiled at me apologetically. 'And jerking off.' The doctor shrugged his shoulders indulgently, as if to say okay, in for a penny … 'And this woman comes along and says: "Tell me, is that normal?" No, the guy replies, it's Super.'

'Very funny,' said the surgeon lugubriously and sank back into the protection of the limo, which, I later learned, he didn't like to step out of, even when visiting temples.

But when he did get out on one occasion, to take a photo from the top of a hill, the chauffeur lost no time in rattling off his litany of woe to me: he scarcely got anything to eat, and definitely no meat on any account, he wasn't allowed to smoke even out in the open, he was required to tell gags on a running basis, and on top of all that it was by no means clear what his passenger wanted from the trip. I must admit, the idea behind this journey was a bit of a mystery to me too; he seemed to be deliberately avoiding all the well-known sights and taking in everything else from the protecting cocoon of the limo.

When the surgeon came back, he asked the driver:

'What shall we go and see next?'

Ineptly, the chauffeur began to describe a nearby temple, and the surgeon listened with half-closed eyes, while pulling a face. The tireless man behind the wheel brought his florid narrative to a close with the flourish: '… an unforgettable moment!' But the traveller would no doubt just let this wash over him as well; scanning the paddyfield landscape for some fixed point, he asked:

'And this evening?'

'This evening we'll climb Mount Pedang, where you'll get a view over the whole of Rantepao, and we'll see the sunset too. And this will be another unforgettable moment.'

It now dawned on me that this was the whole point of the trip. The surgeon found himself in the merciless grip of the chauffeur, who was leading him round by the nose; the driver had found the magic formula by which he could keep dragging the lukewarm traveller around, making him endure the hardships of a long-distance journey: namely, the great promise of moving from one 'unforgettable moment' to another. Ultimately, then, he'd be back in his hospital in his home town of Denver, Colorado; the operating theatre doors would swing shut behind him, but he'd still have these personal 'unforgettable moments' packed away in his hand luggage, and he'd tell his colleagues about the trip, and as he recounted it he'd begin to find everything he'd experienced 'unforgettable' himself for the first time. For, after all, who wouldn't wish to snatch a moment worthy of this description from the stream of experience, and how might one tempt a person who had no time for any conventional tourist sight or anything of architectural, cultural or historical significance? With a nameless and unforgettable sight, that was how.

For the duration of twilight, in the company of the clueless medico, I enjoyed the splendour of an unforgettable sundown, which in fact on that particular evening turned out to be eminently forgettable. Banks of cloud stolidly closed over the horizon and refused to part to give us an unrestricted view. And so the sun set morosely. I took my leave of the surgeon and also bade farewell to his driver, who gave me a complicit smile as we parted.

And, without turning round, I made for the first obvious *losmen* on the main square in Rantepao.

'Hey, Mystère!'

This piercing and pushy, imperious sound is constantly in the air whenever you enter a square here. 'Hey, Mister' is what they mean … 'come here, buy this, listen, buy me, be mine …' But this time it had an ironic tone. Michael, my serious-minded travelling companion from the bus roof, had caught sight of me and was hailing me from the veranda. That evening, we dined on *pili pili* with a heavy peanut sauce, and the next day I went with him to his grandfather's funeral, which was due to take place in his home village half a day's journey away.

By the time we arrived, the ritual of slaughtering buffaloes had just begun. For two years, the family of Michael's grandfather, who had been eldest man in the village, had stored the old man's embalmed body, while saving up money to buy water buffaloes – fifty of them no less, and expensive white ones at that – which in the Afterlife would embody strength, influence and prosperity. While the female family members performed loud lamentations over the corpse, the men sat up on a raised dais and looked down on Golgotha, the place of the skulls, where the magnificent beasts were being sacrificed beneath the slashing knives of their slaughterers, who wielded them in dance-like arabesques.

The blade opens up the animal's neck. The bull rears up like some swaggering hoodlum and gives a haughty stare. Initially its reaction is one of perplexity, displaying unbridled joy like a dog greeting its returning master, leaping up, stretching and flexing its body in the air. Then, with a violent twist of its head, it notices the pain of the wound, tries to correct its stance but can now only dance clumsily, much to the amusement of the seated onlookers. It lowers its head, as if searching for something on the ground, or wanting to plough the ground, then flings it back like it's in a catatonic fury. This movement only serves to open up the wound still wider, like a wet mouth, before the animal presses its neck down once more between its front hooves like it's trying to stem the flow of blood.

But the blood spills out all the same, and the animal's musculature, spasming violently, manifests itself first as a shudder, then a shaking, a trembling and finally just a faint flickering motion across its flanks. And the buffalo bull falls to the ground, slumps down, bellowing into the pool of blood that's flowing out of its own massive bulk, with its eyes wide open, displaying pathetic astonishment, and a swishing tail and panting lips. And there, lying in a puddle of foamy, frothed-up blood mixed with gravel and saliva, the light in the beast's trusting eyes finally falters and fails.

Eventually, death passes across its features like nothing more than a minor discomfort. The kids cut the switches off the tails of the colossal stranded beasts, and tread with their big toes on the animals' death-dulled eyeballs, pressing them down into the sockets. Later, they dig the eyes out completely, and play a barefoot version of marbles with them. But before long they're all covered in sand and won't roll properly anymore. So they swish them around individually in a dish of water. Sometimes, the buffaloes' backs keep on twitching after their death. The body appears to have abandoned itself entirely to the flight of the soul, and just dies away to nothing.

The men look on unmoved. An easy thing to do provided you're not the young man who cleaned the afterbirth off the new-born calf when it emerged from its mother's womb, or who led the young animal out onto the pasture and watched it grow to adulthood, or who nursed it through sickness and lavished it with tender care, who put its nose ring in, and who, finally, led it by this nose ring to the slaughtering festival. Only as it's dying does the animal perhaps exhibit anything unfamiliar, which was hidden deep inside while it was still alive: a temper, a feverishness, a wantonness. This fervour that evidently lay dormant inside the animal is totally out of place, the young man reckons, and this readiness to twist its body as far as it will go, to the utmost degree, ultimately makes the animal seem quite alien to him.

We were sitting up on the gallery, eating meat from the freshly slaughtered buffaloes with black wild rice, drinking fermented palm wine from a bamboo tube, and testifying through our presence to the importance of the deceased. The cacophony produced by the wailing laments of the mourner women, the death bellows of the buffaloes and the cheering of the children did not abate for quite a while. At around two in the morning we went down to the river to wash ourselves:

'The spirits have taken the fat off our skin into the rivers,' Michael whispered, which I didn't understand but which I could feel nevertheless.

Later we climbed up the chicken ladder into one of the saddle-shaped hut roofs, disappearing through a hatch cut in the carved frieze. The loft-space smelt of warm blood, which was still steaming up off the sand below. The aroma of the slaughter had got trapped beneath the eaves. Two candles burning in candle-holders next to our bunks illuminated a dreadful picture of a bare-breasted Andalusian woman riding on a donkey, a painting which Michael's parents had hung up ten years ago, since they feared that the guest who had once given it to them might return and wonder where it was.

We were already lying in bed when Michael suddenly sat up again:

'Do you want to meet my grandmother?'

We each took a holder, lit the candles, and groped our way into the adjoining room, where she was lying immediately behind the door in a cot, embalmed for a year now, and with her torso so caved-in it looked like she'd been eviscerated. Her cheeks glowed with a yellowish-brown patina. From her closed eyes, the old lady stared into the light cast by our candles.

'You can take photos,' Michael whispered.

Only when enough money had been collected to purchase an appropriate number of sacrificial buffaloes – and under no circumstances should there be fewer than twenty – would the family be able to bury the old woman. Then she'll have been properly provided for in the Afterlife, and only then will they begin to mourn her death, as keenly as if it had only happened yesterday.

The next day we escort the oldest man in the village – whose black coffin is splendidly adorned with a white cross – on his final journey, a loose procession that wends its way through the rice paddies, a rivulet of mourners, which sometimes became strung out and at other times came together in a cluster once more, where a stream was difficult to ford. As the coffin made its way across, it swayed about on the shoulders of the pallbearers before straightening up once more. But all the while the sun was shining, the larks were singing and the idyll was perfect.

A good hour later, we came to the foot of a cliff, where human skulls lay piled high, while above, in niches cut into the rock, wooden idols stared down; one of them depicted a missionary wearing a solar topi. My guide, though, had declined to come with me.

'I've got a sick child at home,' he explained, 'it's best I don't walk past the cliff burial site.'

Now the coffin was lifted into one of the recesses in the cliff face and the ceremony was concluded. The long period of waiting for this moment finally, then, had an end. A sense of relief hung in the air, and on the return journey Michael expounded his theory of why Western women had larger breasts than Asians: it stood to reason, he maintained, since the former had originally carried their babies around on their backs, that in order to feed them they had to be able to sling their breasts over their shoulders. He burbled away happily to himself on the subject as we walked. The procession had dispersed by now, and a disordered ragbag of small groups made their way back to the village, and as the veiled sun sank behind the line of hills, I sensed that an 'unforgettable moment' was in the offing in these final hours.

A few days later – in the meantime, I'd pushed on to the north of Sulawesi – I began my homeward journey by taking the night bus to Ujung Pandang. Eight hours' travel lay ahead of me, which I'd have to endure on the back seat of this ancient, rugged vehicle with its peeling yellow paintwork and its leatherette upholstery in ox-blood red. The passengers got onto the bus carrying woven baskets, canisters, rattan furniture, sacks of cloves, huge clusters of colourful plastic bags, fruit and eggs. Water ices, slices of coconut, sticky rice, and biscuits were passed through the open windows, and the *pater familias* sitting next to me spread a rug out over his own lap and those of his two small sons. Then he put a handkerchief up to his nose, as did other locals on the bus, because many Asians can't endure the smell given off by Europeans.

The bus hadn't been rocking through the night for very long before one of the boys next to me sicked up his water ice, closely followed by his brother. They didn't vomit out their food extravagantly, nor did they cough it up; rather, what they had eaten simply fell out of their faces and into the rug, which their father had clearly laid out for this very purpose. It wasn't long before the woman on the seat in front of me followed the kids' lead, and from the front of the bus too came the soft gurgling sound of people being sick. The slipstream carried the smell of vomit out of the window, where it swirled around and re-entered the bus two windows further back. All this, however, did nothing to disrupt or dampen the cheerful atmosphere, or the ebb and flow of chat and laughter.

The next time the bus stopped, the children were given their next portion of water ice, and I fell to wondering how I might explain to the father that this would in due course go the same way as all ice. But the terms 'stomach', 'empty', 'nausea', or 'get well soon' didn't seem to be in my Indonesian–German dictionary; instead, all I could find was a series of obscure archaisms and hilarious misspellings, including the mysterious phrase 'a stunted footprint', which I've never encountered anywhere else, before or since. So, when I tried to get my meaning across to the father by miming it to him, all he did was smile benevolently at me, say 'no harm done', and, when the next wave of nausea announced itself, roll the sick-rug up a bit more so that the boys would have a clean piece of material to relieve themselves into.

In the meantime, night had drawn in, and the stars were so low in the sky that you could have mistaken them for light on the hills. The kids had fallen asleep. Anyone who got up to stretch their legs in the corridor took care to lift their feet up high to avoid the streams of vomit on the bus floor. The driver hurtled down the dirt roads at breakneck speed. He was keen to get the journey over and done with as fast as possible; after all, he only had to set off immediately again at dawn to do it in the opposite direction. For ages, we didn't see any street lights or settlements, but just kept heading directly towards the faint, distant point of light that danced in front of the speeding vehicle. I hunkered down on the step next to the driver; he was happy to let me sit there in exchange for a few pleasantries and the sense that we'd help keep one another awake.

Nevertheless, I found myself woken with a start from half-slumber by a sudden bang, dull and metallic in equal measure, and when the driver reacted by abruptly swerving to try and compensate retrospectively for the force of the impact, I hadn't yet regained my senses sufficiently to brace myself, and was flung across the bus floor.

The bus came to a halt on the edge of a maize field. The gravel road shone brightly in the glare of the headlights, the bank was a lush green colour and the sultry wind tasted in its top notes of flowers and grass. Yet in the right-hand ditch was a black gents' bicycle with twisted handlebars and a sack lashed to its carrier, while on the left-hand side of the road lay its rider, an old man, who'd been killed on the spot. He was bent, too, contorted into a *Figura Serpentinata* like on a Mannerist sculpture, with his bare head twisted toward the moonlight and an unfocussed, vacant face. A wet patch was spreading across his crotch.

The other passengers now stumbled out into the road behind the driver and me. One of them went up to the body and turned it over out of respect; the old man's face was frozen in an expression that looked like a pantomimic rictus of toothache. Others only glanced over briefly at what had happened, shook their legs or stretched themselves, while the *pater familias* walked over to the ditch to clean off his sick-rug.

As there was nothing more to be done for the dead man, a few maize leaves were laid over his face, the bike was placed at his side like it was his wife, and a note made of where the accident had taken place, so that we could inform the police when we got to Ujung Pandang. Then we set off again.

When we arrived in the capital of Sulawesi in the early hours of the following day, it was my birthday, so I indulged myself by opting, for the first time in ages, for the first good hotel I could find. It was all I could do to maintain my composure when, after taking my passport and noting down my details, the receptionist extended his hand across the counter and said:

'Happy Birthday!'

After showering, I strolled down to the main post office, took delivery of fifteen letters that were waiting for me, and opened them one by one lying on the soft hotel bed, reading them slowly so that I didn't get through them all too fast. The last letter was from a familiar address in Cologne, and I laughed the instant I pulled it out of the envelope and saw from the decorative border that it was a wedding invitation.

But at a second glance, it turned out to be a death notice, which succinctly and starkly informed me that my friend Hannes had passed away a month ago. Nothing more, no explanation. The funeral was of course now long past, but I read the few words printed on the card over and over again, trying to fathom what had happened, but I got nowhere. For the first time, I looked homewards and saw nothing but emptiness; I pictured a funeral parlour, where all the mourners were turned away from one another, I saw the cortège, with everyone looking at the ground, and the tear-streaked faces, and I imagined someone putting on a Charlie Parker record at the graveside. We had our rituals in Europe too, after all, and Hannes was a mischievous character who'd be bound not to observe them.

I could never have guessed it, but now it struck me that I'd been gravitating towards this piece of news right from the outset, down a flight of steps, from the killing of the buffaloes and the attendant rituals, through the viewing of the mummified grandmother, to the dead cyclist by the roadside. Hannes would have approved of the theatricality of the story, not least because of the abundance of cadavers and corpses, the slaughter and the puking, and the stupid phrases in my bilingual dictionary, and because of the simple, slightly sentimental symbolism: a dead man is left lying there, while the others journey on.

I didn't leave the hotel again that day, because this terrible 'unforgettable moment' just dragged on and on and seemed to have no end.

Tonga

Taboo and Fate

Black clouds were said to have billowed up over the Pacific, and the water in the ocean boiled up into a seething white foam; fishing boats and ferries supposedly sought shelter in bays, while people on the shore fell to their knees and prayed. They streamed in their thousands into churches to take confession, and many priests were reported to have claimed that the 'Day of Judgement' was at hand. And that was even the case here in the capital Nuku'alofa, apparently, whose name literally means 'The Abode of Love'!

'Precisely because of that,' says the old man who's telling me what is was like in March 2009, when one of the underwater volcanoes hereabouts – of which there are thirty-six all told – erupted, an event that heated the waters of the Pacific and sent fountains of steaming water shooting up into the air, where they dispersed in a sulphurous-yellow haze.

'That's how it is nowadays on the Pacific Ring of Fire,' he tells me, evidently quite proud of the belt of volcanoes that exerts an elemental hold over the lives of the inhabitants of Tonga.

After all, this kingdom stands only a few centimetres above sea level. Not far from here, in an easterly direction, yawns the 10,882-metre-deep Tonga Trench, a chasm in the ocean floor where every year the Pacific tectonic plate moves by as much as twenty-four centimetres beneath the Australian plate, threatening the island realm with tsunamis. What's more, it's also become so prone to hurricanes that it can sometimes take several days for news of the extent of the damage to reach the mainland from the affected islands.

'So why is Nuku'alofa called "The Abode of Love"?'

'Hard to say,' the old man replies, without elaborating further.

One hundred and sixty-nine islands and two coral reefs comprise what is officially called the 'Kingdom of Tonga', a place which Captain James Cook dubbed the 'Friendship Islands' or 'Friendly Islands' in 1774. And indeed, that's exactly what they were, at least until the early nineteenth century. Thereafter, Europeans' impressions of the place took on a more bitter tone, as by that time the Tongans' own experience of the new arrivals had also grown more sour and because an almost fifty-year long civil war, which only came to an end in 1852, had spread terror throughout the islands. Two-thirds of the population are said to have been killed at that time, with cannibalism even making an appearance, and still now cultural historians with an interest in the fate of these paradise-like islands ask where this propensity for violence came from, and why this peaceful world is repeatedly disfigured by outbreaks of savage brutality.

When he landed here, Captain Cook chose the most beautiful bay, in actual fact a whole system of bays and spits of land, interspersed with patches of bright blue water where dark patches of algal bloom float, drifting out into the intermittently grey and shining blue, dazzling and turbid water of the open ocean. The shores are densely covered with scrubby bushes, but the tip of every spit is home to a palm grove. Even nowadays, this is a landscape that shows virtually no signs of human agency, remaining wild and untamed except for the little spot that has been cleared and tidied up as a memorial to James Cook, and where a tree had had a sleeve put round its trunk bearing the inscription: 'Here stood formerly the great banyan Malumalu-'o-Fulilangi or Captain Cook's Tree, under the branches of which the celebrated navigator came ashore.'

We are a quite different breed of traveller. We don't have to wrest the impressions we glean of the world from situations of danger, nor even very often from mere discomfort, and should we ever by chance find ourselves flirting with danger in our travels, then it's only as a result of governments having declared an area a no-go zone – like Burma, Murmansk, Kamchatka, Bhutan, or the Forbidden City in the centre of Beijing, say – or because wars have made them inaccessible. The good thing about it is that we can no longer merely judge by appearances. Whereas earlier travellers were able to offer sweeping statements about the life and nature of other countries, all we can do – at best – is capture what they're like at the moment we visit them, and recount how they appear in our heads, and how they interact with our individual personalities.

On the flight from Sydney to Tonga, I sit in an aisle seat with May, a native of the island, next to me, in a sleeveless top. She's folded her strong brown hands in her lap and is staring solemnly out of the window. Her face is broad, with a mass of rounded individual features, like her nose, her chin and her cheekbones … and her arms are so smooth that the glare of the evening sun as it sets over the ocean finds its final reflection on her skin, where the grey-blue of the sky mingles with the brown of her complexion to produce a nameless colour.

It's almost midnight by the time we descend the aircraft gangway and walk through the warm wind of the Polynesian islands towards the airport terminal; we can taste the salt-water tang in the air for the first time. To both sides of the little whitewashed cube that houses the passport and customs desks, queues of bulky people press forward, calling and waving, and others who are still descending the plane yell boisterously and wave back. Our baggage is spewed out of a hole in the wall and stacked up and sorted by a frantic but not very systematic operative, who fends off all attempts by the owners of the bags to get at their luggage. The customs official cuts a cheerless, authoritarian figure, but what can he do? We're in Tonga now, and sending us back would be no easy matter, and, anyhow, several hundred kilometres of South Pacific until the next bit of mainland is a pretty effective fortification when all's said and done.

Outside the terminal, a clutch of strangers are hanging around waiting for a communal minibus to take them into town: a bad-tempered French married couple, a homecoming Tongan with no relatives left here, a woman in a wheelchair who cheerfully explains that she wanted to come back to the island of her birth one more time before her death, and an Australian couple, he with the glazed expression of an alcoholic and she with the spherical head of a native Tongan. The French woman coughs and issues orders to no one in particular, while her husband, either because he's embarrassed or because they are already too much at odds with one another, looks on with the smug demeanour of someone who's got more important business to attend to than arriving at a Pacific airport in the middle of the night.

Then a friendly, warm rain sets in, and the Haitian minibus driver reduces his speed from forty to thirty kilometres per hour. So we creep through the night until we find ourselves driving through a nocturnal scene by Gauguin. The scene outside is just like one of his paintings, with the palms not in groups or serried ranks but standing isolated and dotted about the landscape as though all other vegetation – banana trees, sweet potato plants and tomato vines alike – should fall in line with their wilfulness. Groups of men in skirts, some of them staggering, cross the unmade road in front of us.

The riots that took place here in November 2006 – when the democracy movement erupted into violence and shops were set on fire, and both supporters of the movement and opponents could only look on helplessly as the wind spread the fire across the whole of the city centre – left the old heart of the city completely in ruins. Now, the food stalls there are well lit but protected by bars; that's how these Chinese-owned businesses guard against looting. The vendors wait behind their grilles like workers in a fairground coconut shy. The living rooms of the little houses are mostly lit by neon lamps, while dogs roam around outside. The next shower that arrives is blown horizontally past the windscreen by a sudden gust, and in the hotel lobby, the receptionist announces triumphantly:

'So – what do you reckon to this weather, then?'

The hotel is a dilapidated old complex of interconnected wings that at some stage were augmented by a half-mildewed main building. In the semi-darkness, I can make out various courtyards, lawns, open loggias constructed out of bamboo; I also notice that the walls are discoloured with fungus. I can hear the sea, and the Vanu Road, along which a couple of cars are slowly approaching, and I can hear two boozers in the next-door room crashing about, and their toilet door slamming.

Yet the feeling that now takes a stronger hold of me is one of agoraphobia: being cut off on the far side of an unbridgeable ocean and marooned in the most remote of foreign places suddenly feels deeply oppressive. It's like I'm cooped up in this vastness, sleep-deprived, yet still harassed by traffic and regularly startled. How can one possibly feel so trapped where everything is so boundless, so free, and so released from the constraints of the mainland, even released from the constraints of my own homeland? If you were to draw a diagonal line from there right across the globe, you'd end up here in Tonga. So, isn't it a good thing that you don't encounter the same experiences here, just the reverse side of the same globalized world that's been given a bit of a folksy twist?

The last time this island realm came to our attention in the media was at the millennium, when European television stations wanted to celebrate the first day of the new millennium in fitting style and Tonga, being situated in the first international time zone, offered to sell them pictures of its sunrise that morning. In point of fact, this honour really should have gone to Kiribati, a nation comprising a few tiny islands, and right through the middle of which the International Dateline ran until 31 December 1994, at which juncture someone decided to shift the line further east. But what lay in store for Europeans beyond this demarcating line that they couldn't have found somewhere else? So here was a new day, a new year, century, millennium, heralded as it had been since the beginning of time by the breaking dawn, and all you needed to do was go out into the street in Europe twelve hours after sun-up in Tonga to see it live for yourself, breaking over the millennial horizon. However, anyone who found waiting too onerous, or too tardy or sentimental or who somehow didn't find the experience genuine enough, always had the television, which in turn would not be called 'television' if it didn't have the ability to peer into the far distance to see what the rising sun looked like, the self same sun that had just set over Europe. But in any event, people hereabouts are given to saying: 'Time begins in Tonga.'

So, because the first sun of the new millennium would be rising over this island kingdom, the rights to capture the event were touted around to the highest bidder, and we came within an ace of enjoying a premiere at the advent of the new millennium: namely, a sunrise with a commercial break.

On my first day in Tonga, I was also keen to see the sunrise, twelve hours before it occurred back home. On the morning I sat waiting for it, the full moon was still visible at 6.30 a.m. Then a bank of cloud rolled across it, extensive enough to completely blot it out. On the opposite side of the sky, the day announced its presence with a grudging hint of brightness – like it was undecided whether to grow light – borne on a cool breeze. At this hour, people were already kneeling down to pray in the neon-lit cubes that are church interiors here, while Chinese shopkeepers were already waiting behind their counters, and cocks were crowing.

But on this particular morning, the sun showed itself only once, as a delicate red cross-hatch effect in a slate-grey bank of cloud, glimmering faintly before vanishing entirely. Then it returned, glowing like a toaster, before it promptly disappeared once and for all. Day broke at a leisurely pace and somewhat lackadaisically. Still irresolute about adopting an unequivocal mood, it wandered aimlessly like a person who has just got up, still heavy with sleep, before finally putting another quintessentially South Pacific weather situation on the agenda: the preamble to tropical rain.

Even so, the minute I set foot outside, I found myself caught up in the sheer verve of the place, the unflappable way its life revolves around a sea frontage that actually isn't one, but rather port installations visited by a stream of ships covered in great rusting flakes of paint, with other smaller and newer but still battered ships following in their wake. An atmosphere of letting oneself go, of patient waiting and acquiescence pervades the scene, a feeling of exposure and permeability to the onward march of time. Rubbish is strewn everywhere, but how could it be otherwise, given that the wind catches it, whisks it from outdoor dining tables and overflowing skips, from children's hands and from the quayside. Such an agglomeration of unattractiveness becomes so concentrated that my eyes start to water and I walk ever deeper into the dark wall of cloud that's looming until rain does actually begin to fall, saturated, warm and incessant, and I take shelter along with three plump, friendly women beneath a plane tree. We get ourselves four coconuts and drink their milk, nodding our approval.

Every morning I walk for twenty minutes to a small Beach Café, as it calls itself, even though there's no beach anywhere to be seen, only a dingy harbour breakwater where a few half-rusted barges are anchored, while others are in the process of being reconditioned. Every day I do the same thing, not just for the sake of ritual but also because I want to see what else is going on each morning. There's no better way of getting into the routine of a place than by imposing a routine on yourself while you're there.

Besides, I like sitting on the tiny, wind-battered veranda

made of corrugated iron and drinking coffee and a juice mix of melon and pineapple, and eating buttered toast with orange marmalade. In the general run of things, the landlady is quite severe with me and wishes me 'Goodbye' rather than 'Good morning', but this morning, when 'New York, New York' came on the radio, she started swaying along with her two-hundred-weight bulk, and singing aloud: 'If you can make it there, you'll make it anywhere,' though there was no one in the world for whom these lines could have been less fitting than her.

Then she approached the table and asked me where I was from, or rather where I was from and how come I'd ended up here sitting at this table. I answered:

'If I can make it to here, I can make it to anywhere.'

She laughed, put her hand on my shoulder and let it rest there, while translating what I'd just said to her friends behind me in guttural Tongan.

'Are you alone?'

'Aren't we all?' I replied, thinking that we'd found common ground for friendly banter.

'No,' she replied brusquely, and answered the quizzical look I gave her by adding: 'The Lord is always with us.'

'Oh sorry, I'd forgotten about Him,' I responded.

'You should never do that,' she chided me.

I promised I wouldn't.

From the next-door table, a woman in her seventies dressed in bright red and wearing golden earrings looked over and shrugged her shoulders sympathetically.

'That's how it is here,' she said. 'You must have seen it for yourself: the place is full of churches and there's three masses on Sundays, all packed full. People still believe in God here.'

Because she clearly didn't anymore and wasn't attempting to convert me, I went over to her table, offered her my hand in greeting and told her my name. Kerry, who had once worked as an anthropologist and had since made a living writing crime novels with her female partner, said 'pleasure' and then turned to wave to a local woman who'd just that minute driven up in a large sports car.

'Dorothy, darling, if it isn't yourself, back from the islands!'

I went back to my table. From here I had a panoramic view over the neighbourhood: I saw an old woman standing in the receding surf and gathering in fish traps; a flatbed lorry transporting soldiers and blue plastic chairs; an old man lifting up a stone slab covering a drainage manhole and plunging his hand down inside; a massive female truck driver crossing herself behind the wheel; Cassiopeia's Café, with men coming out of it sporting bouffant hairdos and skirts while women, with their majestic heads, showed their gold teeth when they laughed; a peasant woman carefully putting earthy manioc roots into a basket lined with banana leaves; two people arm in arm, with each of their limbs fully tattooed; a woman in the prime of her life sitting in state on the back of a pickup truck in her wheel-chair and gesticulating to a group of her friends, who have gathered round in a large gaggle at her feet, as the truck moves at a sedate pace down the road. And the wind is leaving behind its traces, too, bending the palms, parting the banana bushes, tearing signs from the nails securing them, blowing over bicycles, making coconuts drop from the trees, and catching hold of the large clam shells that have been used as ashtrays on the veranda and sending them skidding across the tarmac below, in a hail of mother-of-pearl splinters.

Rubbish everywhere, and people sniffing all around me, but even the kids in their contrasting light and dark blue school uniforms half-raise their hands to me in greeting as they pass by, and the clouds are once again setting the tone and grumbling away, and the clam stew tastes like a concentrate of the air here. The women all have flowers in their hair and the men have little tree air fresheners hanging on their rear view mirrors.

And then there's the quaint things – called 'sites of interest' – that you run into when you're wandering round here: Railway Road for instance, the dreariest thoroughfare in the kingdom, is renowned as the only one-way street in the country. People come here specifically to look at this sad place, with its petrol station, its car-hire firm, and undeveloped lots along the street, and say: Look, it's our only one-way street, and they view it with different eyes, and at the end of the street, on a square patch of grass, a marble memorial stone has been erected with an inscription commemorating the day of the street's extension to this point.

Another curiosity is the palm tree that people on Tonga have discovered, a really unusual specimen whose trunk divides into three separate crowns high up – a Siamese triplet among palms. This is the only one of its kind in the kingdom, and it's on land that belongs to the Mormons, who immediately built a new church nearby.

Then there's the magnificence of cemeteries here; the tomb of the royal family is more like a mausoleum, segregated from the other graves by a fenced-off area three times the size of a football pitch. Steps lead out to the gravestones, which are guarded by statues. In the hierarchy of piety, the next most important graves are those of Tonga's mayors. Pink sashes were draped around their houses, front gardens and fences when they died.

Tongan cemeteries have the effect of lavishly-decorated building sites; the ones that have little white heaped-up grave mounds with scarcely a plastic flower in sight are the graves of the poor. The wealthy have high grave mounds, covered with flowers and with a screen at their head end, decorated with multicoloured geometric patterns. These are people who will want for nothing in the hereafter. As you stand here, you can hear the screaming of piglets being slaughtered as part of a burial rite.

In village cemeteries, the rich are also interred under high grave mounds with excessive sprays of artificial flowers and tall display walls that look like plush blankets, while the poorest citizens often simply have a low bump in the ground, strewn with a couple of plastic flowers, or are even laid to rest in their own gardens. So it is that people's unequal financial circumstances are maintained right up to the threshold of the afterlife. But doesn't the Bible tell us that the Kingdom of God belongs to the poor? Or, to put it less pointedly: couldn't one grant people the freedom to be poor and even the choice to be that way?

Only the sepulchre of the royal family rises from the earth with pediments and steps like an Inca temple. The ruler of Tonga is George Tupou V, the eldest son of His Majesty the late King Taufa'-ahau Tupou IV, who reigns over one hundred and seventy Pacific islands yet is still only a monarch on demand. Years ago, the powerful democracy movement on Tonga forced him to declare his abdication, which he did, but without stipulating exactly when he will stand down. Some people maintain that he's a womanizer. Yet because royal protocol stipulated that the only suitable candidates for marriage were two rather elderly ladies, he elected not to marry, choosing instead to surround himself with pretty young things. This also served to quell any rumours that he actually preferred men. The king loves technological innovations of all kinds, especially those that have helped the Tongan authorities pinpoint foreign poachers on the fishing grounds, bring their boats into harbour and slap heavy fines on their owners. Yet on other occasions, the crown prince is content to sit at home dressed in a silk suit and Italian shoes and play boogie-woogie on the piano.

I, however, am still sitting on the edge of the cemetery when a colossal man arrives, dressed in the traditional *ta'ovala* mat, which is woven from pandanus leaves, and surrounded by his black-clad family, and says to a woman on the veranda:

'You know, my mother passed away just recently, but she was old, so it was no surprise,' and everyone bursts out laughing, even his daughter.

I suddenly realize that the woman is May from the plane, and when she in turn recognises me, her smile grows a bit wider. Then the party turns away again and goes off to the cemetery to confer with the deceased. They discuss the funeral rites, which include burning various parts of their own bodies, lacerating their cheeks or giving themselves head wounds. It is thought that rituals like this can help cure a person who is dangerously ill, overcome the pain of death, and support the deceased in the afterlife. As part of the ceremony for healing the sick, low-ranking relatives will cut off a finger or a joint of a finger. To help speed recuperation, human sacrifices even used to be made for chieftain's families. The German naturalist Georg Forster, who travelled to the Pacific with James Cook, noted that many people on Tonga had fingers missing, sliced off as a sacrifice to cure a high-ranking person who had fallen ill.

Likewise, it was Captain Cook who brought the word 'taboo' back from this region and gave it to the rest of the world. A whole range of phenomena can be taboo here: places, foodstuffs, actions, and even people or particular relationships between people. For example, fathers have a taboo attached to them, according to which their children are forbidden to touch their heads. Nor are they allowed to eat his food, and if a brother and sister are both in puberty at the same time, they are not permitted to sleep under the same roof. Moreover, the ancestor-spirits mediate between all the living, whether for good or for ill. For Sigmund Freud, ancestors were basically projection figures who embodied the 'collective clan consciousness', one of the very oldest forms of consciousness. It is no different on Tonga.

The state of *feitama* – that is, pregnancy and the preparations for giving birth – also has a taboo associated with it. The whole family participates in this process, with the result that there is no such thing as a private sphere or any secrets during this period. Husbands share the state of pregnancy with their wives, following various eating taboos and himself displaying symptoms of morning sickness and vomiting. Pronouncing certain things taboo helps lay the first foundations of the super-ego, which furnishes society with a kind of protectorate formed from the spirit of collective proscriptions.

The man who sits staring at the sea out of the rolled-down window of his pickup truck, which he has parked at the roadside, has a facial tattoo on his brown skin. He stretches his hand out of the window for me to shake. I do so, and we remain clasping hands. Over the next few days, we are to become inseparable. He will drive me all over the island, offer me a plot of land, and introduce me to his wife and two of his children. He will share his life story and his food with me. But the very first thing Douglas does is assure me in no uncertain terms that he really is called Douglas. He even pulls out a piece of paper with his name clearly written on it. He once played professional rugby in Australia. To prove it, he shows me a fearsome surgery scar running right round his right shoulder. I say:

'I believe you.'

Whereupon he tells me the story of a man who refused to believe him.

Douglas is missing the little finger of his right hand.

'Is that a rugby injury, too?' I ask, pointing at the stump where his finger had once been.

'No,' he says, shoving his fist inside his jacket. 'Look at these mangoes all over the place. We don't know what to do with them all. We've even taken to feeding them to the pigs.'

Douglas has four children; he lives according to traditional principles and is bringing them up strictly. His wife is standing on the lawn outside their little house like an idol, a self-absorbed beauty who is extremely shy, and yet who has a gracefulness that makes her statuesque body seem somehow dainty. Douglas has followed the dictates of his culture to the letter; any other course of action would have been unthinkable: the wife's family chooses the husband. It's crucial that the family should love the husband. He suddenly stops recounting his story. He doesn't want to spit it out. Maybe he's frightened of looking foolish? Did they laugh at him in Australia for being a primitive South Sea islander?

At the wedding, he continues at length, the bride receives the special third cup in the *kava* ceremony. Ultimately, the bride and groom sit on the laps of their respective maternal uncles.

Kava is a drink prepared from the aromatic root of a shrub, and is said to have an intoxicating effect, but Douglas is having none of that. Drunkenness isn't good, drunkenness is the work of the devil.

'What about *Moemoe*?'

I'd heard about this act of obeisance, but this appears to be another subject that Douglas isn't comfortable with, or maybe he's not willing to let me in on the deep mysteries of local rituals. It's all very personal.

'It's true,' he grudgingly admits. 'The feet of the person due respect have to be touched with both the palms and the back of the hands. That's the ritual.'

He was employed as a rugby pro for long enough in the Australian outback to know that practices like this are seen by outsiders as native superstition, but for him they're vital, and he's passing it all on to his children as well. They'll be brought up according to the traditional code of laws being handed down from the older generation to the younger.

And yet, in some regards the coming generation is more old-fashioned, and more sentimental, than their elders, who have seen so many things come and go, and who all have the same reaction towards the beauty of the islands and the way outsiders apply the word 'paradise' to them – a word they can no longer stand hearing, they who have to live day-to-day in this paradise, which doesn't even have a refuse collection service.

We're sitting by the ocean with a view of the outrigger canoes and black pigs, who are snorkelling around in the shallows for things to eat. It's true: Gauguin was ultimately responsible for framing and assembling the collective historical memory of these places, which are now like Tahiti was in his day. We step into his paintings, and sometimes just outside, into the spaces that can open up between his picture frames when they are hung together.

Then Douglas and I set off into the island's hinterland. You might imagine that the more precious land became in such a geographically limited space, the more pedantically everything would be parcelled out and enclosed. But in actual fact, borders tend to be primarily demarcated by people in those regions where there's land aplenty. Here, by contrast, where the dimensions of all the islands are very small, the little houses often stand isolated on a green meadow, dotted around haphazardly and not separated from one another by any fences. The pigs dash about, the fruits drop, the colourful washing waves on the line like it's been hung there for decoration, and the flying foxes dangle in the trees like bunting, so densely packed they look like they've been left behind after some fête. Some of them even begin whirring around and squeaking in broad daylight.

'Those were the days,' says Douglas, 'when hunting flying foxes, as the white men christened them, was the sole preserve of the royal family!'

We've stopped in Kolovai, an idyll of a place; this loose community of colourful little houses and huts, scattered among the palms, really has the lot: butterflies fluttering up from the field like flying confetti, and hands waved in greeting suddenly popping up from the meadows. The fisherman are sitting around on the grass and mending nets, while a sculptor is busy chipping away at a wet, red chunk of wood. Kids are playing tag among the trees, and an old man is absentmindedly stroking broad vanilla pods hanging on a bush.

The farthest tip of the island is home to volcanic bays with sharp-edged, porous rocks, which tear your hand open if you so much as touch them, and blowholes, through which the surf blasts with such force that it creates fountains several metres high, over each of which a rainbow forms. Before me is the boiling sea, pressed into the rock as if through a valve. Sometimes, it only comes across as a sigh or a moan, but in the main it produces a blowing noise like an indignant snort, along with fountains of spume which time and again rise ten metres into the air before dispersing in a mist of fine spray.

Offshore, underneath the cliffs, there is a solid ledge of rock where the waves build up. The ocean sends its undercurrent to the shore, venting itself through the porous composition of the rocks. The wind lisps in the marram grass on the beach. This is the place where the Christians landed and became fishers of men. Even nowadays the smallest villages have four, or even six, well-attended churches.

Douglas sits down silently beside me. The sea lulls us both. Further. You feel like you want to venture out beyond the line of the horizon … I want to go further, I say, to a landscape that's even more remote and where this distance is even more palpable, because there's nothing beyond it.

Douglas replies:

'I know what you're looking for. On Wednesday the night ferry sails from Nuku'alofa to Ha'afeva. I'll get you a ticket on the *Princess Ashika*.'

When we get back to the car, there's an Australian couple waiting there, the same pair who were in the taxi that took me from the airport to the hotel on the first night of my stay. She's broad in the beam and big-breasted, with powerful upper arms and the dark, lowering face of a native Tongan, while he has the immutably stiff physiognomy of an alcoholic and is taciturn, because talking isn't worth wasting his breath on.

Stephen and Leah are mineworkers, who live in the outback a couple of hundred kilometres north of Sydney. Their job demands hard physical labour, which has led them to the conviction that nobody can put anything over on them. They're unashamedly anti-American and anti-Semitic and are dyed-in-the-wool conspiracy theorists, yet they consider their theories to be a private matter which they're not about to share with all those false friends out there. When Douglas calls the 9/11 terror attacks an 'unexplained mystery', they dismiss him like some hanger-on trying to parrot their opinions. The car they'd hired to get up to the promontory was pulled over by the police for speeding when it was doing forty kilometres per hour. The officers took the woman cab driver off to the station, and turfed out her two passengers. So we find ourselves obliged to give them a lift, and clear the back seat for them.

I ask Leah what work she does down the mine.

'I don't work down at the face. I repair the heavy machinery, the drilling equipment, power shovels and lorries.'

Leah's parents are from 'Eua, a neighbouring island. The couple have come here on a kind of pilgrimage, so that Leah can show her man the land of her forefathers, the fabled Tonga, which her parents – now eking out an existence on the Australian mainland – have told him so much about.

They stare straight ahead, it's like they prefer to look through the landscape. The thing about the forefathers is one explanation, until it emerges that Leah has never visited the islands herself before. Basically, their primary reason for coming was to get the family's blessing, at least, the part of the family that still lives here and who they're long overdue to pay a visit to.

'Do your relatives know you're here yet?'

'We've still got to call them,' Stephen says wearily, and glances across at Leah, who gazes down at her lap.

Douglas gives her a dubious look.

'They'll sacrifice a pig to celebrate your arrival, you know.'

'I know,' Leah says. 'I'm a vegetarian.'

She lives with Stephen. The family didn't choose him, nor are they married, but under her smock-top, her belly reveals a slight swelling that might well belong to a woman who's already four months pregnant.

'It won't be easy,' she tells Douglas, who's giving her a very severe look.

'When's the best time of year to come here?' Stephen asks.

'At Christmas,' says Douglas. 'You can go to church twice, and in between you can even eat for free.'

'What about all these Chinese, then?' Leah says, pointing at a sign advertising a hotel. 'They're writing their names in Chinese characters already!'

It turns out that she hates the Chinese, too, who do business everywhere they go and who, like the Americans, 'give nothing, it's all just take, take with them'.

'But in the paper yesterday, there was …' Douglas starts to object.

'Forget the paper,' Leah interrupts this mere novice in conspiracy theories, 'you know who controls them, after all.'

'As a rule,' I tell her, 'it's women who tend to give things, even to strangers … a smile, food, jewellery even. Men keep themselves to themselves more.'

'But I'm here for you,' Douglas says.

'That's true,' Leah agrees, 'yesterday a woman wanted to give me a chain. Just like that: I'll give it to you, she says to me.'

'Just like that?'

'I'll give it to you out of love, is what the woman said to me. But then you've got to give me some money in return for my love.'

Leah only had ten dollars with her. So, that's all my love's worth to you, is it? the woman had asked indignantly.

'That's a bad example,' says Douglas.

The shadow of an impending visit to his relatives loomed over him, as well. At least 'Eua, the island they're having to visit, is only two hours away by ferry.

'Why haven't you at least called them yet?'

'We will do.'

Leah looks serious and pale and her eyes shift uneasily as she reads the words from Douglas' lips. In this moment, the landscape means nothing to her.

During their lunch break, workers here flake out on the ground under the palms and rest, while the kids play tag round the bus stops, and those who venture out to sea do so in tiny boats where seven or at most nine of them sit hunkered down, making the little sloops lie low in the water, and one person among the crew constantly has to bale out.

The Tongans have their Stonehenge, too, an alpha-sign made of volcanic rock. You go through this archway and come to a tall stone slab, in the shadow of which one of the ancient kings of Tonga, who was two and a half metres tall, is said to have leant, as shown by the impression left by his body in the stone, and then you can walk on further into a dense, dark wood full of spiders' webs and unfamiliar flowers, and further on towards the sea, which you can only hear from here but not see. Leah took a few apprehensive steps down this path, but quickly turned back.

'It's haunted,' she said.

'That's your relatives,' Douglas whispered.

And doesn't she have every reason to be afraid? In cases like hers, there have been plenty of stories of corporal punishments, mutilations and imprisonment. The violation of taboos has to be avenged, otherwise it wouldn't be called taboo.

We make our way back. Our gaze grows numb as we watch the receding waves. On the gravel path to her hotel, Leah turns around one last time, like she wants to say something. Then she seems to think better of it.

As evening falls a couple of hours later, four well-built women descend the path just outside my room, notice me standing at the window and give me a wave. I wave back. One of them beckons to me, inviting me to join them. I shake my head, at which she squats down and mimics a riding motion. In former times, the women here offered themselves to strangers for a few rusty nails, and sailors praised their tirelessness. Even the degeneration of charm into vulgarity that I've just witnessed is actually quite genial in its own way.

In 1803, a merchant called John Turnbull landed on the island of 'Eua. The natives had little to offer except foodstuffs and a few tools, but in exchange for these few odds and ends demanded valuable items like scissors and axes. When the English sailors refused, the natives had three women – who were clearly war captives and the prettiest they could muster – brought to the vessel, and offered to sell their services to the crew. But in his log, Turnbull calls them 'stocky, masculine and with hard features', and none of the sailors wanted anything to do with them, which baffled the natives, who had gone to some lengths to bring them to the British.

At this stage, Europeans were primarily interested in trading with China. Yet they had few commodities that were of interest to the Chinese, with the exception of furs and whale fat, which together with all manner of whale by-products found a ready market in China. And so the Europeans extended their whale-hunting areas to cover Polynesia, which in turn led to bitter trade wars with indigenous whale hunters, conflicts which were marked by skulduggery and extreme violence that poisoned relations between natives and foreigners. If one also takes into account the fact that an unprecedented wave of Christian mis-sionary activity reached the Pacific region at the same time, it is easy to imagine the Polynesians' confusion. Who was the quintessential Westerner, they must have asked themselves: the unscrupulous whaler and exploiter, or the missionary fisher of men, who proclaimed brotherly love and shared humanity?

And that wasn't all. Precisely the fact that Captain Cook characterized the inhabitants of Tonga as peaceable, friendly and helpful and spoke of the abundance of natural produce available there, and because it was generally known that mis-sionaries were well established on the island, led whale hunters to beat a path to Tonga in particular, so exacerbating the con-flicts between peoples.

In addition, Europeans spread infectious disease to the islands of Polynesia, and once slave traders had also found their way to the region, the arrival of the white man once again proved disastrous for the indigenous civilization. But despite that, or maybe precisely because of it, Tonga is the only state within Oceania never to be colonized by a European power.

'Indeed,' Georg Forster exclaimed while accompanying James Cook on his second voyage to the South Pacific, 'if the learning and erudition of individual men have to be bought at the cost of the happiness of entire nations, then it would have been better for both the discoverers and the discovered if the South Seas had remained forever a closed book to unruly Europeans!'

Sometimes, the idyll looks down upon a car park. This is the case looking out from the Beach Café: every morning the manioc sellers lay out their earthy roots on cloths on the quayside, knock holes in coconuts, display bundles of vanilla pods and pour *kava* powder into bottles. And every morning the fishermen wait for sloops to take them out. The arrangement of the stalls is always the same, the cars stop in the same places, and the same hands shake one another in greeting. Tourists flock here for the market's immediacy, in search of sights worth seeing and opportunities to take snaps; by contrast, travellers come here looking for the permanent and the everlasting. You have to have spent a long time in a particular place, visiting the same haunts over and over again in order to discern its true spirit.

Kerry, the anthropologist and crime writer, is already ensconced at her little table outside the café by the time I arrive today; she's dressed in red and dripping with gold jewellery again, and is also sporting a pink ribbon for Breast Cancer Awareness on her lapel. With the beady-eyed alertness that can equally well characterize both ladies and wild beasts, she's keeping a close watch on the car park, the quayside and visitors to the café, and immediately waves me over when she sees me.

'Sit down, keep me company, I'm writing a postcard. Tell me, who were those two people you were with yesterday? Friends? I've never seen them round here before.'

I tell her about Stephen and Leah, their conspiracy theories, their resentments, and their fear of her family.

'The woman's a local, you can tell that straight away. Simple people. People like that used to be called "dirt-eaters" on Tonga. Don't be shocked.'

She picks the raisins out of her muesli and lines them up, one by one, on the saucer under the bowl.

'So, she's come here with her boyfriend, pregnant I'm guessing? I thought so. Oh dear, that could get tricky. Yeah, the dirt-eaters can be brutal if you violate their traditions.'

A sports car draws up right in front of us. An Indian beauty of forty or more slips out, wrapped in a formal green and black sari, and with lithe movement floats up the steps to the café.

'Dorothy, meet my new best friend ... what's your name again? Roger.'

The two friends immediately lapse into a private argot. I catch snippets concerning an appointment, money, some former advice and a warning.

Dorothy announces 'I must go inside, I've got to wait there at a window table.'

The moment she's disappeared, Kerry's head comes right up close to mine, so close I can smell her face powder.

'Some really shady business goes on in this café. Did you see Dorothy? She's as poor as a church mouse, but she's dressed in her glad rags and has hired that car; she's meeting a man here who wants money off her for brokering a leasehold. In the café, I ask you! I've warned her already. And in cash, too, can you imagine?'

She throws herself back in her seat like someone who can look back on a gratifying tradition of smart-aleckry, but what she says is true: because foreigners aren't permitted to buy land here, just lease it for fifty years, at which point it either reverts to the owner or the leasehold is extended, some dodgy dealings have evolved between Westerners wanting to get away from it all and native landowners.

It clearly bothers Kerry that from her seat outside on the terrace here she hasn't got sight of the second entrance, which Dorothy's would-be business partner might use to enter the café.

'Excuse me, dear, I'd better go inside and give Dorothy some moral support. She can be such an airhead.'

When Douglas drives up a moment later, he hasn't got a ticket for the *Princess Ashika*, but in its place he has a suggestion.

'I've been thinking and wanted to ask you, now that we know one another a bit better, why don't you come with me to 'Eua, my home island? We're burying my great aunt there at the weekend. That way, you'll get to see the real Tonga and witness a genuine funeral ceremony with my own family. You'd be very welcome to join us.'

The two islands now known as 'Eua and Tongatapu were named Middelburgh and Amsterdam by the Dutch navigator Abel Tasman. 'Eua was the second island of the kingdom that James Cook landed on, a small, nowadays largely neglected island largely untouched by tourism, where people are left to their own devices and on which reason has so far failed to impose order.

Douglas recounts some of the other advantages of life on 'Eua:

'On 'Eua we always say: Just keep calm. It's not nearly as hectic as on Nuku'alofa …'

'… and the top speed for cars is fifteen kilometres per hour, and hefty people waddle comfortably along the pavements, and I've never seen anyone there make a sudden movement. That's just the way it is: the farther away you get from the centre of things, the slower the pace of life.'

Two days later, the little aircraft begins its descent to the island of 'Eua. The pilot puts his plane down on the grass next to the runway, because it's safer than landing on the rutted tarmac. The paths running off into the palm groves between the huts are a bright cinnabar-red colour. Sometimes, the women here rub a bit of this soil into their washing water and use it to dye their hair.

We can tell we're approaching Douglas' parents' house from the purple sashes that have been draped around the white-washed wooden sheds in the compound, as a sign of mourning for his grandfather's sister.

'She was eighty plus, I think,' Douglas says.

He doesn't really categorize people by their age. The oldest of the mourners is Douglas' mother, who has a fine-featured face etched by austerity and is wearing a shawl decorated with a blue and yellow flower pattern. A Hammond organ is tootling away in the background on the radio. All the sheds surrounding the meadow have been cleared and laid out with mats with the designs of peacocks, coffee jugs or rhombuses woven into them.

The women are sitting in a circle preparing for the interment. Even the professional mourners are draped in bast-fibre mats, which make them look like scarecrows or Christmas figures from the Krkonosze Mountains in the Czech Republic. Douglas' mother puts tapioca served on pandanus leaves in front of me, and next to it a little pile of finely chopped beef, including the fat, gristle and bones.

'Now say your prayers and eat.'

I fold my hands and lower my eyes. The meat has a doughy taste, and there's country music playing on the radio now. My gaze is drawn through a back door, to the open fireplace behind the house, surrounded by a pile of coconut shells and more upholstered chairs in a circle. From this afternoon on, no more radio music will be allowed. Instead, there will be communal singing of spirituals, the whole night through until ten o'clock the next morning. That's how long the deceased great aunt's family members will have to keep the fire outside going, while others tell all the good stories from her life. Indeed, a young girl with a very deep voice has just begun to do so.

I go out and sit in the open. From the steps of a shed for housing guests, I can see the black and brindled pigs. A boy is grating coconut flesh coarsely, skinny dogs with scarred faces are panting in the grass, there's the bleat of women's voices and an old woman comes singing through the finely drizzling rain; she stops, noisily snorts up her mucus and lingers a while under the flat green canopy of the mango trees.

An hour later Douglas has mobilized his lethargic cousin Winter, along with the family car. From the glove compartment wafts the aroma of vanilla pods, green ones and black and brown flecked ones. The little tree air freshener on the rear view mirror can't compete.

Underway, Douglas's commentary is all on the one topic:

'Look at all these coconuts. See how rich the soil here is! We've got any amount of mangoes, so many we're even feeding them to the pigs. We only need money for electricity and fresh water and for the kids' schoolbooks, everything else literally grows on trees. Look how much *kava* we've got; I've never seen this much *kava* on Nuku'alofa.'

Here and there a few plots have been cut into the sparse jungle of coconut palms, mango trees, weeds and other undergrowth and planted densely with vanilla and *kava* bushes – land for cultivation chopped out of the bush, and which nature, from all sides, is constantly trying to reclaim, with rampant undergrowth and encroaching branches everywhere.

Presently we find ourselves climbing a cliff high above the sea. A good five metres from the edge, Douglas stops dead and keeps tugging at my shoulder to pull me back. Far below us, birds wheel out from the cliff-face, and spume froths between the black volcanic boulders.

'I get dizzy easily,' Douglas explains. 'Even when I'm sitting in the sea and put a diving mask on and look at the bottom, it makes me giddy.'

Suddenly, this colossal man seems quite delicate. We carry on along the cliffs. The cliff tops are rounded and grassy, while inland the land sweeps away in loose folds, like careless drapery. Here, on the most beautiful spot on the island, high above the sea where one only has the wind for company, there once lived a German friend of the old, plump king of Tonga. This mysterious German built his house in complete solitude, cut off from everyone, and set about raising pigs.

But after a few years it emerged that the man had six passports and twice as many aliases. Also, a U-boat which he was in radio contact with was once rumoured to have surfaced in the bay. When these stories began to seep into the public domain, the authorities picked up his scent and he was forced to flee. The king, greatly perturbed, took swift action and summarily had the mysterious German's house razed to the ground. It was as if, by doing so, he was wanting to expunge his memory of the man too. Under the house, a vast hole came to light, presumably a dungeon of some sort. But for whom? Soon after, the fugitive was shot in the back on a neighbouring island. No one ever found out who he really was.

We drive back to his mother's house, where the mourning party has by now dispersed. They're all waiting for the arrival of the coffin, which is supposed to come on the ship first thing that morning. Douglas sets off to do some condolence visits.

In a village that's been very much left to itself, I find myself likewise left to my own devices, amid free-running hens, free-running pigs and free-running strangers. Here, too, there are scarcely any fences. Throughout the island, everything lies strewn about like on some opulent lawn, with pigs and huts and columns of smoke and stories and songs. Today we've had all kinds of weather, none of it very long-lasting. The clouds are scudding by.

If you were to ask me what my ideal footpath is, it would be one of the paths here: light or reddish-brown earth, without any demarcation, and palms dotted about irregularly and piglets crossing it now and then. You hear the wind, the shouts of children, an axe, a cockerel, and in the fields to either side stand the mango trees with their broad-leaved canopies. The huts are surrounded by flowerbeds that are home to the most exotic plants, and butterflies of an unimagined size and colour flutter round the banana bushes. The voices of the old women crack in the wind like flags. You hear our own footsteps, you stop and it is perfectly still and complete.

We take the family car to the harbour and park by the bollards. Men lurch up like they're staggering under their own weight. A large group of black-clad, mat-bedecked people, solemnly bowing to each other and respectfully greeting one another, gathers at the quayside.

When the ship docks, Leah and Stephen are the last people to disembark, before the coffin is unloaded. They sidle up, pale and earnest, to a group of locals who make not the slightest move towards them, but who immediately close ranks around the couple, so that I lose sight of them. In a great throng, they walk off down the dirt track, and I ask myself how they're planning to square their own conspiracy theories with the great system of taboos.

The ornate coffin is the last thing to come off the ferry. Where the ship's ramp meets the quayside, they're all standing there in black, and in the grotesque bulk of their bast and mat cloaks, which they sometimes roll up laboriously. Douglas especially, who's wearing a mat that looks dirty and frayed and keeps on popping open, seems to have changed character entirely. He appears comical, and when the women start fiddling with his mat cowl, he gawps at them like a village idiot. But at one point both of his hands, with all nine fingers, are pressed up against a gate on the breakwater. His niece looks at him, I look at him, and then she and I look straight at one another. A taboo wouldn't be a taboo if he were simply to tell us what had happened at that juncture.

The coffin is loaded onto a decorated truck and immediately covered with mats. The women sit up alongside it as it sets off on its final journey in a slow-moving convoy with a police escort. It will come to a halt finally on the lawn in the middle of a great feast, where the guests will contribute their good memories of the deceased and the bereaved will contribute the food. Throughout the whole night, until sunrise, they must stay by the fireplace, since it is the family's duty to keep all the funeral guests supplied with nourishment on a running basis.

Finally, at dawn, when the visitors' stories have dried up and the spirits have all departed, the fire may also be extinguished. Justice has been done to the deceased. It was a lovely send-off, a worthy feast, and now the departed may rest in peace.

Next morning, when I walk into my familiar Beach Café in Nuku'alofa, Kerry is already sitting there. She's busy picking out bits of spaghetti with her fork from a fish stew, and waves me over.

'You've heard the news, I suppose? It was bound to happen sometime. I warned about it time and again …'

'Warned about what?'

'The *Princess Ashika* sank on the overnight sailing to Ha'afeva. It's been less than a month since she came into service. They've only picked up fifty-four people alive, eighty-seven are still missing, but the toll's rising by the hour. Trouble is, who on earth here had a regular ticket, who was a registered passenger?'

'How did it happen?'

'The police are acting very professionally, they're not jumping to any premature conclusions or issuing statements. But I hear the ship wasn't even properly seaworthy. Anyone who had a berth below deck will have drowned. They haven't even been able to salvage the bodies. But the men standing at the railings and the smokers are probably the only ones who've survived. Did you really hear nothing about it?'

I tell her that I've been on 'Eua at the funeral of Douglas' great aunt, though originally I'd been intending to sail to Ha'afeva on board the doomed ship.

'That's how stories go in this part of the world,' Kerry says. 'You miss your own death because you've been at someone else's burial.'

Over the following days, the number of dead rises to one hundred and twenty, and the authorities ask publicly how it's possible that there should have been so many unregistered passengers on board.

Then the same old pattern as everywhere: an incident had taken place and now the hunt was on for the moral high ground, and for someone to take the blame, carry the can, no stone was left unturned and no cesspit left undrained. The king was told about the catastrophe, expressed his deep sympathies and a few hours later went off on holiday to Scotland. The democracy movement immediately came out onto the streets to stage public protests and to reiterate what they'd been saying for years, namely that it was high time that the monarch abdicated.

'We don't need a king like this.'

But on the road to the airport, there's still a prominent poster of him, just as before, with his image and the slogan: "King George Tipou V – Icon to the World"...'

'When are you off back home?' Kerry wants to know.

'Monday. An hour and a half's stopover in Sydney, then it's on to Singapore ...'

'What, you're planning to catch an onward flight to Europe one and a half hours after arriving in Sydney? You can forget that straight away. The flights from here are never on time. They're driven away from Tonga by the wind. Either they're stuck here unable to take off in the first place, or they can't land, and are diverted somewhere to wait, or you're advised to fly to another island and pick up a flight there ...'

'So what does that mean?'

'Clear off as fast as you can. Now the Red Cross people are flooding onto the island as well. Doctors, journalists, relatives of the victims from the mainland. Who's to say when you'd next be able to get away?'

So, I grabbed a seat on the late flight to Auckland the following evening, days before my planned departure. In a back hall at the airport, I saw coffins piled up. People in bast-fibre mats were solemnly taking delivery of them and bowing to the boxes like they were bodies from which the souls had already departed.

In Auckland, long after midnight, I check into the first hotel I can find at the airport. On the transistor radio on the night porter's counter, a voice is reading the local weather forecast: 'Clouded skies with occasional rains, heavy winds up and single thunderstorms on all Tongan coasts.'

Kinshasa

Scenes from a War

If people are said to radiate an aura, then why not cities as well? Or at least an abiding impression, sometimes of promise, sometimes of intimidation. Certainly the quintessence of one city is encapsulated in its very name: Kinshasa. This aura is enhanced through newspaper photos and old pieces of reportage on the place, and encounters with people who came from there, whose faces would take on a very particular look at the mention of their distant home city: pained, saddened, forbearing, fatalistic, and fighting to suppress a feeling of rage.

Kinshasa's aura is a dark one, in which the prevailing tones are the hues of colonialism and military drab. And there was also a time when Kinshasa stood for boxing shorts, for the 'Rumble in the Jungle', for *soukous* or Congolese Rumba Rock. Following the triumphal success of this musical genre, the style of dress associated with it also became popular. By contrast, the Belgian colonial power's legacy here consisted of manufactured goods, architectural styles and companies.

Yet the recent war has virtually erased even these images and instead imposed its own: twisted bodies in roadside ditches, marauding bands of soldiers on the city outskirts, looting, rape, mutilation and murder, the unleashing of violence, and a bloody assault on the capital, at the conclusion of which a strong man called Kabila seized the reins of power.

'No photos, please', the flight attendant says, taking it upon herself to push my camera down. For a moment, through a gap in the clouds, I'd caught sight of what looked like a vast spa town, green, cut through by the delta of the River Congo, and overrun with sprawling development: Kinshasa in a state of war, charming but clearly to remain incognito.

'We are duty bound to advise you against undertaking this trip,' was the way the German Foreign Ministry had put it. But that sounded to me like a standard-form response. They were 'unwilling', indeed 'unable', to assume a responsibility that they did not have. 'Worst city in the world, multiplied by ten,' an Australian colleague told me, and now here was this steward-ess, acting like she had to protect the place from paparazzi from an altitude of three thousand feet.

Forget the romanticism of *Gorillas in the Mist*, or the eupho-ria of the 'Rumble in the Jungle' or the hope embodied in the Lusaka Peace Accord. The gorillas were butchered during the war, the splendour of the stadium where Muhammad Ali knocked out George Foreman is now faded and the treaty has been violated several times. In a city that has been fought over now for years, no one expects law and order any more, but instead vigilantism and anarchists, rebels, freebooters, child soldiers, occupiers, tribal enemies, petty criminals and their godfathers. You just have to come to terms with the law of the street, with landmine victims and the survivors of years of torture, broken prisoners and the mentally disturbed; in short, the whole spectrum of human flotsam and losers of history. And resign yourself to a country with 80 per cent unemploy-ment, widespread malnourishment and shortage of medicines – this is the home of the Ebola virus.

You only need to see the Congolese people, who hang out of the compartment windows of suburban trains every morning like umbels, or those who patrol up and down on the roofs of these trains, touting their wares, bartering or playing cards as the train rumbles slowly through Kinshasa's commuter belt. Try not to overlook the fates of any of these individuals, whose image sears itself on to your retina between two blinks of your eye, and empathize with them! Oh, forget it then – you're too slow and too sentimental!

You make your way from the aircraft to the terminal on foot, following a series of yellow markings. You'll come back this same way when you leave, but changed, that much is certain already, but what will stay the same? People will still be there on the viewing deck, looking down on the airfield and thinking of all the places that we, down below, are flying off to. One of them keeps waving.

The porters at the baggage reclaim carousels are heaving down pieces of upholstered furniture, wrapped in what seems to be kilometre-long strips of bubble wrap, beneath which pink floral designs run riot like frost patterns. After a long journey here from some cheap manufacturing site somewhere on the planet, this three-piece suite has finally arrived at the Heart of Darkness. But at the same time, on the far side of the arrivals hall, some very similar furniture that has been produced on the streets of Kinshasa is being flown out. The porters stand between the carousels, monitor this senseless exchange in the international movement of goods and keep watching a television lounger that's being exported, long enough to be able to picture the far-off living room in which this little piece of their homeland will be nothing but another item of seating furniture.

I'd come to the Democratic Republic of Congo, formerly Zaïre, to meet a musician. I wanted to make a film profile of the country's most famous musical artist, the spiritual father of Congo's urban, cosmopolitan youth who danced to his tunes in the clubs of Kinshasa, and whose one dream was that he might one day leave his exile in Paris and come back to his home-land, as less of a fellow sufferer but as more than just a tourist: Papa Wemba, the co-founder of *soukou*, that pan-African style of music, also known as Rumba Rock, which originated in Kin-shasa in the 1970s and went on to conquer the entire continent – the musical language of self-expression for a youth that now, two wars later, had nothing left except their music.

I wanted to know what had happened to music in the Congo during this period and was keen to see how this larger-than-life musician would fare when he entered the orbit of this con-flict, and to hear what this world ambassador of Afro-Pop, who was travelling in the full glare of publicity in the music-loving world, had to say about the president's politics. How much license would this untouchable personage allow himself, and how much of that freedom would he ascribe to his music?

The clouds were hanging low and colourless over the airport, and a cluster of baggage handlers dashing past forced me to take refuge beside a pickup truck, against which a friend who's been waiting here for me for the past two days is now leaning, ashen-faced. On the way here, the minibus he'd originally been travelling in had hit a pothole at eighty kilometres an hour, breaking both its axles, and sending the camera it was carrying flying four metres through the air across the vehicle, where it gashed open the head of the front seat passenger. My friend – and cameraman – was left with a nasty head wound, while our bodyguard sustained a compound back injury; the driver fled the scene of the accident. Three days later, the vehicle was still lying there by the roadside, by now stripped of its interior.

On the hotel bed, we gingerly turn over our bodyguard's massive body at which his groans grow louder, and by now even my friend is having trouble turning his head. Six hours later, both of them are lying side by side on trolleys in a hospital awaiting treatment. Then, one of them at least is fitted with an ivory-coloured neck brace and discharged. But by the time they get round to rolling the bodyguard into the bowels of the hospital, he's already spent three hours crying, even occasionally screaming, this colossus of a man. A cracked vertebra, the doctors think.

All the while, Papa Wemba, the country's most renowned singer, is waiting at the bar of the Hotel Memling, though 'waiting' isn't the right term; it would be more accurate to say he's in residence there, bidding those who come to pay homage to him on bended knee to stand up, having his hands and cheeks kissed, ordering newspapers to be brought to him in which his arrival in the city is Page One news, and perusing the cocktail menu.

As a young boy, he used to accompany his mother, who was a *Pleureuse* or professional mourning singer, to funerals, learning from her the high, melancholic timbre and the soft mellifluous intonation which no musical training has ever managed to spoil. He moved to Kinshasa, became a singer with the group Zaiko Langa Langa and steadily acquired the status of a god of African pop music. The then-president Mobutu indirectly helped his rise to fame by proclaiming *'L'Authenticité'*. This policy promoted indigenous music at the expense of Cuban music, rock, Western pop and R&B, which were banned from the airwaves; musicians were arrested, and the Congolese were encouraged to think of their national roots. At this time, the nation's top musician Papa Wemba blended folk music with dance rhythms, a style that became such a hit he was soon more popular than any president.

Whatever he touched turned to gold. People in the West sat up and took notice, and his records began to be produced in Paris. An optical illusion – perfectly understandable from the perspective of Kinshasa – made Papa Wemba appear to be seated at the right hand of Michael Jackson in the eternal musical firmament. Then someone – very possibly Papa Wemba himself – hit upon the idea of referring to his so-called 'magic touch'. He had the phrase printed on his business cards, and soon gained a reputation for being some mythical seer or guru. At the same time, thanks to the extremely flamboyant clothing he liked to wear, which made his concerts into fashion happenings, this pop star also came to be seen as a trendsetter in Central African couture. But he's not so keen on that label nowadays.

For in his own estimation, he is an important man of small physical stature, and with measured gestures and a talent for pathos. His indigo-blue silk blouse is embroidered with golden appliqué designs, his generously-cut trousers elegantly crumpled, and even his fly-whisk blesses every insect it shoos away. Wearing a jacket by Yamamoto, spectacles by Mikli, and with his mobile to his ear, he briefly puts the phone down and extends his left hand:

'Welcome to the Congo! Nuts? A cocktail?'

We sit and wait, in a way that one can only wait in Africa. Something will come, a messenger will bring something or some bit of news will arrive. Arrangements will be made, meetings fixed, both sides will smile and nod, both fully aware that everything discussed and agreed here is just so much waste paper.

Papa Wemba keeps telephoning incessantly. Delegations arrive at his desk. They bow, he sits. I enquire about a likely date for us to start filming.

'Garçon, more nuts!' he calls out to a liveried hotel employee, waving the empty dish at him. There's clearly no question of fixing a definite date.

'Where are the others?' Papa Wemba asks me.

I tell him about our accident; after all, we could use him putting in a good word for us at the hospital. He pushes the replenished dish of nuts across to me.

'Let me have a look at your work permit,' he says.

That's impertinent of him. Even so, I'm happy to present him with the quarter-pound of paperwork in my possession, all the exchanges of correspondence that have shuttled to and fro over the last few months between embassies, authorities and offices on both continents just to make this meeting over a cocktail in the bar of the 'Memling' possible in the first place. He shakes his head at all the letterheads, stamps and signatures, and continues shaking it as he pulls out a small piece of paper from the pile. This document, as it turns out, is missing the personal signature of the minister. So he shoves the whole pile back to me and, with no sense of the irony of the scene, adds the bill for the cocktails and nuts on top.

'First thing you need to do is get hold of that signature!'

In the lounge, a group of men in safari jackets are gathered around a television. President Kabila is addressing the nation.

On screen, he looks even fatter than on his posters or the lapel pin sported by the customs official at the airport.

Foreign commentators see him as a weak man who was elevated to his present position at the last moment by a group of marauding guerrillas, who are now fighting in opposition to him. Currently it's a state of complete anarchy, with militias from Burundi, Uganda and Rwanda occupying parts of the Congo. Kabila's troops have already been disarmed in the north of the country.

But the way he's talking there on the television makes him appear presidential, that's clearly one of the first tricks you learn in power.

'We want to involve Mobutu's supporters in government,' he's saying, 'but we won't tolerate a Nazi Party!'

The camera pans to show a view of the supporters of the 'Nazi Party', that is, the party of Mobutu's supporters. They're just sitting there looking stunned. They're evidently no longer opponents who are to be taken seriously, at least to far less a degree than the rebels who are fighting against Kabila's people in the countryside and even making Kinshasa unsafe.

The president now turns his attention to the occupation forces, though he doesn't call them that. How can he possibly countenance three mini-states numbering some six or eight million inhabitants apiece as serious aggressors within his realm of fifty million people? How could he allow them to maintain their long-running control over certain parts of his country? Condescendingly, he accepts the President of Botswana as an 'arbitrator'. But scarcely has this man left the room than he starts mocking him. The UN observer standing to my left shakes his head in disbelief. That's how this president is. Two weeks ago, he invited a camera crew over from New York for the first time to interview him. He kept them waiting for eight days. Yesterday, they flew back to the States empty-handed.

As it happens, at that moment the only other Western camera crew in the country apart from us is just checking out at reception.

'Have fun at the Ministry of Information,' the cameraman says to me. 'They don't appreciate the concept of information here, still less how much we love their country. Go on, have a guess how much footage we've managed to get after seventeen days here: eight minutes. That's the last time I come to the Congo!'

He's already heading out the door when he suddenly stops and comes back to tell me another anecdote:

'Just you be careful. There's a woman here who is friends with the Médécins Sans Frontières people and who's got a little flat in the city. Well, one time she let an acquaintance go out onto the balcony and view the town through his binoculars. For that, they both spent a fortnight in gaol on suspicion of spying. I'm telling you: never again!'

Meanwhile, I'm trying to find a new angle on the war. Articles in Western newspapers customarily begin with sentences like: 'Dopka is a dead village. The smell of burned thatch is everywhere.' Or: 'Night was falling when Dzara Dzeha caught sight of her murderers storming into the village.' Or 'The church is full of the bodies of the dead.' Instead of an analysis of policies, all we get is a scrapbook of massacres – that's the Africa of the Western media.

So, there's never any mention of the fact that the Congo is an occupied country, and that the relatively small neighbouring states of Burundi, Uganda and Rwanda have encroached and seized control of land as far as two thousand kilometres into Congolese territory. In 1996, after the dictator Mobutu had been toppled, Rwandan rebels were responsible for staging the victorious entry of the current president Laurent Kabila into the capital. Public opinion cautiously applauded this move at the time. Rumours that the rebels had murdered their original candidate just outside Kinshasa and only latterly appointed Kabila have scarcely had an airing outside the country's borders. In any event, the man who came to power in this way quickly fell out with the rebels, who in the meantime were able to disarm his troops in the north of the country but who, as a drunken freebooting rabble, have no prospect of seizing the reins of government. On the other hand, the political opposition has retreated so far underground for fear of reprisals that even if the people wanted to choose an alternative, they wouldn't know where to find one. So, the only alternative to Kabila is Kabila.

He, this unloved lame duck of a president, looms threateningly over the city's streets on high billboards. Yet however distant the war might seem in Kinshasa, the brutality of a president on a war footing is omnipresent. Seven people are rumoured to have been shot dead by his henchmen for simply failing to get out of the way of his motorcade quickly enough at a crossroads. There is a deep-seated fear of his despotism.

The first thing we learn is that Western eyewitnesses to the war or investigators of massacres are not welcome. But haven't we come here in the service of music? Only later do we learn our second important lesson: namely, that a reversed racism is now rife here. Whites are despised, harassed and subjected to increasing bureaucratic chicanery, with their passports deliberately being dropped in the mud at border crossings before being seized and retained for hours on end, and sometimes only retrieved by paying a bribe. Any white person who's still prepared to live in the country under such conditions is often here for altruistic reasons, and not infrequently even has some sympathy for the these acts of belated revenge. Yet even this painfully acquired sense of understanding, stoutly defended against the resentful criticism from their fellow whites, is held in deep contempt.

Papa Wemba, though, is loved. In his conversations with friends, local musicians or fans, the war is never mentioned and nor is the president. Instead, Wemba cruises through the city in his air-conditioned Mercedes, telephoning Paris, letting people pass him fruit and newspapers through the window, listening to his own albums, and sometimes even waving at the never-diminishing throng of enthusiasts on the street, who almost pull his car to pieces in their sheer ecstasy.

'You should film this,' he says.

Yes, sir! From now on, we spend our time taking hours of footage of his triumphal procession through the outskirts of Kinshasa, protected from harm by his fame. Now he's waving more frequently, too.

Does music work in opposition to the war or is it another world entirely? Does it represent a line of continuity in the history of the country, or has its bloodline now run its course? Does it speak of the victims and the poor, or just aspire to be bought by them?

'The poor should be left in peace,' pronounces Papa Wemba.

The sad truth is, though, that of course they're not left in peace, but instead have to pay the price for this war. Yes, that bothers him too, he says, brushing some bits of fluff off the flamboyant floral pattern of his *boubou*.

'I may be an artist, but I still read a lot about politics,' he adds. Yet when I try to probe deeper, he clarifies his position: 'However, that doesn't mean I'm about to take a political stance.'

'So there's no link between music and war?'

'Music should inform people about the war, and we have to win this war.'

He didn't say what he meant by 'information' in this context, or what winning the war would entail.

'I'm proud of my country,' he rhapsodized, sitting back snugly in the upholstery of his limousine, but I wonder whether he's only really proud of it because it spawned him. He doesn't mention the name Kabila once.

There are barely any Europeans, or any whites at all for that matter, left in Kinshasa. But one female BBC reporter is sticking it out. The authorities tolerate her presence because her reports are filmed but never broadcast, so at least she's maintaining the outward appearance that international reporting can go on here. Her office is on one of the upper storeys of the Interconti-nental. We ask her if we might be allowed to film a swift panning shot over the city from the hotel roof? No, much too dangerous, she tells us. Everything here is political, she explains. Even our visiting her office is politically charged – was the meeting pre-arranged, is there some conspiracy afoot here? It'd be safer if we just left again straight away. We feel our way down through the seamy, rundown building, which seems to breathe through its pile carpets; the heat is oppressive, the atmosphere no less so. We're in a place where no one would want to be.

But when all's said and done, life has this blind urge to keep on going somehow, and if there's still any dancing and singing taking place in Kinshasa, then it's a reflex reaction. In the courtyard of his town house, Papa Wemba stands in front of the guard of honour formed by his own youth band and instructs them, his brow knitted in concentration. The voice training of one of the two albino singers is a pet project of his. This white-haired giant of a boy with his pink-lidded eyes produces sounds such as I've never heard before in a high falsetto; his voice is as clear and pure as those of the *castrati*, and the gold-bedecked star of Rumba Rock really does stand there dumbstruck for a moment. Then he nods, asks to hear a vibrato and promptly turns his attention to the 'Fioti Fioti', the ensemble of short-skirted stage dancers and their new dance routine. All of them, boys and girls alike, tense up when they look into Papa Wemba's face. They're respectful, but timid with it, and anyone address-ing a question to him doffs his cap first.

We drive with him to the church where he used to sing in the choir as a boy, and now goes to attend Mass, strolling up to the altar in flip-flops and an Adidas tracksuit and telling the widows, the old ladies, the social rejects and the downtrodden day labourers that they can all make it if they really want to. This jars like it's been churned out by some party sloganeering machine in the US presidential election. Make 'it', indeed! – no one standing in this church nave looks like they understand the foggiest about this phrase, unless it has something to do with salvation.

So, is he going to reveal anything to the Congolese popula-tion except his own fame? Doesn't he have anything for them but his waving hand? Isn't he going to make any pronounce-ments about the war, except that it must be won?

The security barrier outside the Ministry of Information is manned by a group of adolescent boy soldiers. Two of them have stumps where there had once been arms. You couldn't exactly say that these young war invalids look like prematurely aged children. It's far worse than that. There's no hope for the future evident in their faces, it's like they've been indelibly brutalized. The childlike aspect of their features hasn't been erased, but all the tenderness has vanished, leaving only an impression of abrasiveness and ruthlessness. They've adopted this air of assertiveness among other soldiers, who like them simply had a gun pressed into their hands and were told to go off and defend their country. The first thing they had to do was prove themselves at some front or other, and now they're allowed to guard the propaganda headquarters with the grim faces of battle-hardened veterans. If they find themselves involved in some misadventure where a person mistakenly meets his death at their hands, President Kabila is wont to say: Look, they're still so young. What can I do to curb their excesses?

The ministry complex is deserted. The press hotel has also been empty for some time now, and fungus has started to grow on its walls. But in the basement of the main building, a few local journalists and cameramen are still hanging around, playing cards and flirting with the office girls while they wait for their next assignment. Most of the women are gap-toothed. Many of them have deliberately had their incisors taken out because men enjoyed oral sex with them more that way. Their faces are also disfigured by scars; repeatedly, they come over, wink at you for a second and incline their heads as if to say 'Come on, then!' But where – there's nowhere to go here.

At least there's a kiosk in the courtyard where they sell Fanta Orange, and where there are also a couple of young women sitting in the shade and waiting. They're too heavily made-up to be government employees, wearing a thick foundation that's plastered on like a mask to hide the signs that they're infected with AIDS. The illness has left scars on their faces but the women have just covered these up. Now their eyes, highlighted with kohl and eyeliner, are gazing out of their sockets with an even greater intensity of expression, and their cheeks glow feverishly from the thick layers of rouge they've applied, which looks wholly out of place on their dark skin. But there's something in that look that never focusses on what it's ostensibly directed at. They seem to stare into their own frailty, unable to disengage their inner attention from the prospect of dying.

We'll be able to obtain the permit we need, we're told, on the tenth floor of the ministry, the all-important permit without which our filming becomes a criminal act. Every day, I return to the ministry in search of the relevant official and his signature. As I wait for the lift on the ground floor, a workman keeps lugging cement sacks in on his back.

'You building something?' I ask him, after he's slammed the sixth sack down on the top of the growing pile.

He laughs, then giving me a conspiratorial look; bending down, he opens up a rip in one of the sacks with two fingers.

'No, it's just money,' he replies, his fingers riffling the corner of a stack of banknotes.

'All in cents?'

'Yep, this is the employee's salaries I'm bringing here. They're all payable in cents.'

The cash travels up in the lift with us. But at every floor we stop at, the doors open onto blackness. People get out and disappear into the total darkness, the sacks of money likewise. From office to office, the bundles of cash will be weighed with scales – given the rampant inflation here, this is the easiest way of counting money.

'So, you earn a pound?'

'About that.'

There's not a sound, not even a telephone ringing. Even on the tenth storey the smell of decay hasn't dissipated. The workman with the barrowload of money sacks has vanished into the depths of the dark corridors. I feel my way along the deserted passageways, navigating by the occasional rectangle of light that spills out from an occupied office.

Finally, in an administration office at the end of the corridor, I manage to track down the entire 'case' that has my name on it. It's hard to imagine what tortuous journey our documents have been on before ending up in this drawer. In the process, they've got covered in a light dust and dirty fingerprints. But it's all to no avail anyway. More documents, more passport photos are required, and more money will need to change hands.

Over the ensuing days, I find myself having to drop in daily on the ministry, where I drink weak coffee with a secretary, make some new friends, provide lists of topics I'm planning to cover, show immunization certificates and other official-looking bits of paper, forge a signature, and even hold out the prospect of a visit by Papa Wemba. And all the while, I'll know exactly where the information minister is at any given time, though he certainly won't have any idea how persistently I'm dogging his every step. Even so, it will ultimately prove impossible to bring the minister and my documents into contact with one another at any point.

On one occasion, I catch a glimpse of his face on a black and white TV screen, where he's sitting in the audience at a parliamentary debate. The secretary points out his face with her index finger:

'There! There he is! Now all we need to do is bring that man and these papers here together, and you can get started!'

I wonder if he ever got to learn of our request? For some days already, we've been filming illegally, sticking to Papa Wemba like glue, because we're guaranteed to be safe around him. For his part, he's adopted the camera as one of his trademarks; he likes to show his countrymen that he's travelling in the glare of global media attention.

We drive to his house on the city outskirts, and film him up on the veranda from our vantage point on the far side of his swimming pool. He waves to us. Then we set up the camera behind his back up there and look down into the garden. He waves again.

'As a small boy from the country, could you ever have dreamt that you'd end up here one day?'

'I always knew I would. Always. It's no coincidence – it was predestination. Always. And one day, I'll explode across the entire globe, too.'

'Predestination!' scoffs a local musician when I tell him the story that evening. 'He was fired from Zaiko Langa Langa. So he goes off and cries on the shoulder of his best friend, some loopy diplomat's son, who went out and bought him Western clothes, some really outlandish gear. And Wemba caused a sensation by appearing in this clobber on stages here. Ever since, he's been linked with fashion, though he can't stand it. Thing is, he owes too much of his success to it.'

Is it the case, then, that war brought the president to power, and fashion put the musician where he is? One of them dreams about ruling the country, the other about ruling the world music market. And the most intimate connection between them resides in the fact that the president, in refusing to grant us permission to film, is suppressing the production of images of the pop star, while he in turn is careful not to formulate any opinion about the president. So in their intimate state of separation, they cosily feed off one another.

I keep going back to the Ministry of Information on a daily basis for a while, and see the money courier with his sacks of cash again and walk past the empty offices and sometimes sit on a chair in the corner of the administration office, but I don't even get to discuss my request again. I become nothing but an applicant in a dingy ministerial corridor in war-torn Congo, a castaway who's been forgotten about and who months later might simply go feral and end up getting filed under 'any other business'. All roads end here, I can't go a step further.

A couple of years later, political reality caught up with both of them: Kabila was executed in his presidential suite by his supporters, his palace guard, the security services, maybe even members of his own family. No reliable account of what happened is forthcoming, and his son Joseph Kabila comes to power.

Papa Wemba's musical trajectory doesn't ultimately go global. Although he continues to present himself in interviews as a political force for integration, his influence has been outstripped by the passage of time. Instead, he's arrested in Paris

when it emerges that he's been arranging for Congolese com-
patriots to enter France illegally in return for large bribes and
has allegedly been at the head of a major people-smuggling
operation.

But when we leave Kinshasa on that autumn afternoon, the
president and the pop star are still secure in their positions.
Never have I been so glad to get out of a country, and consequently at the airport the world begins to fall back into its
familiar old pose: there are the furniture packers once more,
reliably sitting on the edge of the baggage carousel, ruled over
by Kabila, soundtracked by Papa Wemba. Their labour helps
feed both of them. But one certainty remains. As we follow the
yellow markings back to our plane, I turn around. How com-
forting: someone up there is still waving.

Chiang Mai

Opium

I travelled to Chiang Mai for the 'opium eating'. Ever since Thomas de Quincey, that's been the familiar expression. Notwithstanding that it's been ages since anyone actually ate opium, ingested it in the form of cough syrup or took it to combat the flu, as was common practice around the turn of the nineteenth century. Nowadays, people smoke it, inhale it, take it on board and let it rampage around; I'm of the view that everyone ought to have smoked opium at least once in their life. Everyone should appreciate what the brain is capable of, and anyone who says: 'Well, all I need to do is climb mountains, run marathons, dive off cliffs or even just run up the stairs fast' has no conception of how many dramatic changes the wild beast that inhabits our skulls can undergo.

I travelled to Chiang Mai in northern Thailand by train, crammed into the short box of a bunk bed, which was only separated from the corridor by a curtain. On a note which the conductor gave every passenger to read before the journey began, we were warned not to accept any offers of refreshments from fellow passengers. In many cases, these were spiked drinks, designed to knock us out so we could be robbed more easily. The only narcotic substance I consumed was a bottle of Tiger Beer, which Helen and Mark, two Australians on their honeymoon, got me from the buffet car.

There was also a madam on the train, who, spotting that I was travelling on my own without a female companion, talked me through all the beauties pictured on a brochure she handed me, whom she assured me were already waiting for me in Chiang Mai. She ended up telling me that my moral scruples were a real handicap.

'You're absolutely right,' I replied, 'but I can do as little to change them as I could a game leg.'

At this, she pulled a face like a wrinkled gherkin and beat a retreat.

When it began, very gradually, to grow dark outside, I pulled the window down and breathed in the air wafting out of the rainforest. At the station stops, people passed us coconuts, mangoes, pineapple and sticky rice through the open windows. I was so happy that I sang 'Guantanamera' and then Eric Burdon's 'When I think of all the good times I've been wasting having good times'.

I took a room in the 'Je t'aime' guesthouse, along with the newlyweds. It really was called that, but apart from the complimentary condoms in the drawer of the bedside table, nothing in the place reminded one of love. In the evening, a heavily suntanned Swiss woman with smoothly depilated arms and legs and a garrulous stream of chit-chat sidled over with her brimming glass and latched on to us.

I told her: 'Your limbs are so beautifully proportioned.'

'Thanks,' she replied. 'What was that again about proportions and whatnot, though?'

Then she started going on about places where we didn't happen to be right then.

'We did Singapore last week. We had such gorgeous weather

there, it was wonderful. We got tickets for the theatre in the evening. I'll happily go to the theatre if there's nothing else on, but it was lovely all the same, we saw Gorky's *Summerbreeze*.'

'You mean *Summerfolk*.'

'No, it was definitely called *Summerbreeze*. Whenever there's beautiful weather now, I always say: oh look, it's as lovely as in Gorky's *Summerbreeze*.'

The next day, Helen, Stephen and I decided to leave the 'Je t'aime'. One of the local drivers had pinned a homemade name badge to his chest with a safety pin; he reckoned the name 'Richard' suited him. Every day, he could be found waiting for customers on the street in front of the guest house. He offered his services to take us into the jungle, into the more remote 'tribal' villages of the 'Golden Triangle' and where, he explained, people still lived totally unmolested by the state and according to their own rules.

'For instance, if they want to have sex,' he continued, 'they have to marry the woman. That's why they often try it out with their relatives first. You can imagine what that produces.'

Hearing this, we called to mind pictures of cephalopods, and it's true, when we finally got to the villages, we did notice some deformities, children with huge feet, misshapen heads, simpletons who spent hours talking to an insect or dangling their fingers in front of their face like they were pulling the strings of a puppet, who didn't stop even when you put a coin or a sweet on the back of their hand, and if they were smoking, it was thick cigarettes rolled out of banana leaves.

'The government even allows them to grow opium. It's part of their religion and their traditional medicine.'

By the same virtue, Richard regards this as vindicating what he does by lending it some kind of ethnological credibility.

'At least life expectancy in these villages is twenty years longer than in other parts of the country.'

In the poppy fields, the plants were bursting with sap, their greyish-green, baroque-shaped capsules swollen and ripe. A couple of ill-tempered guards who were patrolling the perimeter of the field with blunderbusses stopped us from cutting diagonally across it.

The next village we visited sat tucked away in a valley bottom between two spurs of the rainforest. In a kind of social mimicry, it had taken on the colour of the surrounding landscape: the huts were made from the same wood as the trees, and were covered with their leaves, standing anchored between their trunks and connected by a network of paths. Chickens and pigs ran free, the men were out in the fields, and the women were sitting around and smoking. There was also a village elder here, with a congenial but still somehow malicious face, which, after mumbling to himself for a while, he would suddenly lift up, gazing straight into the eyes of his interlocutor with a long, searching look.

We drank his tea, listened to his complaints about the distant government in Bangkok, and sought his approval; we were just travellers passing through, but in his eyes we were also transient human beings. We would leave and disappear in our cities, we'd be superseded and swept away 'like bubbles in a puddle of water', as someone supposedly says in Gorky's *Summerbreeze*. We had his sympathy for being the way we were, but he reserved his self-pity for the eternal man, namely himself. He was subject to another law entirely.

Sitting there in his colourful striped knitted pullover, one hand clutching a long-stemmed pipe and the other resting on the back of a dog, and nestled amongst his blankets and his soot-blackened housewares, completely within his own jurisdiction, he really did turn us into what he saw us as: decadents flaunting their *ennui* at civilization. The fact that we wanted to smoke opium only confirmed his view: naturally, what else?

We spent the afternoon vainly attempting not to stand out in the village. We walked down to the river and back, settled ourselves into our hut – a pile dwelling that stood several metres above the marshland – skirted round the edge of the forest and smiled at everyone we encountered. The locals instantly recognized us as travellers from the hundreds of little signs in our gestures and clothing that betrayed our essential restlessness and curiosity, but which we ourselves were oblivious to.

In the evening we were summoned once more to the village elder. In the middle of his hut, around a pot of tea, mats had now been rolled out, a corncob lay by the fireplace and the sunken-cheeked, haggard man, who came in alone and sat down, wrapped in faded rags that had been dyed pink, was introduced to us as the 'medicine man'. Our first glance told us he was a drug addict himself; Richard told us that all the opium in the village was at the medicine man's disposal, and that he'd got into the habit of smoking around forty pipes of the stuff every day.

The first thing he did was to urge us to go out and relieve ourselves in the undergrowth, since we'd find it difficult later on. Then we took our places in a square around the fireplace. Anyone who wanted to smoke a pipe lay down in the right-hand corner of the hut with the medicine man, who was indulging in one himself. The village elder sat to one side and looked on, watching the opium first being taken out of a small tin, divided into portions, warmed between the fingers, rolled, and then placed as little pellets into the bowl of the long pipe.

After just one or two puffs, each tiny ball, boiling and bubbling, was used up and evaporated off into the evening sky. But its aroma remained, that fresh-smelling, mild and spicy blend of herbs and leaves, which had nothing smoky about it – that aroma clung on and spread out to become a general feeling of well-being, a sense of contentment, nothing more. This particular high wasn't about to take any hostages, and it wouldn't announce itself with hallucinatory ravings and phantasmagoria, nor would it ambush our consciousness from behind: rather, it was there in its full force right from the outset – weak, but clear and benign.

The medicine man lay a corncob in front of me and poured me a beaker of tea. I leant back with my arms crossed behind my head – how remote and quiet the world was!

Mark and Helen followed my lead, each of them likewise taking their hit; they were overcome, not overwhelmed.

With the second pipe, your distance from the ground increased and you gained a better perspective on things. We were friends. All the lines of life met under this roof, intersecting at their only possible point of convergence. In this moment, there was no hereafter. All you had to do was to descend into the depths of good vibes and stay there.

Stay.

'I knew a guy,' Mark began, 'who smoked mushrooms and reckoned he could see the world through the eyes of the mushrooms.'

'Is that a good thing?'

'Sure; if only for a change.'

'So, are you about to experience the world through the eyes of a poppy head?'

'Why shouldn't I try and see nature from the viewpoint of nature and look at me and you in the same light while I'm about it?' Mark insisted.

'I don't want to be the image,' I said nonsensically, 'but the seeing.'

Thus initiated into the mysteries of opium, we kept talking, meaningfully or senselessly, endlessly or not endlessly, since right then we didn't have the slightest sense of what was sensible or finite.

Richard sat off to one side, fiddling with the peak of his cap and pulling a wounded face. From the dark shadows in the interior of the huts, there were occasional flashes of light from the bright borders of the costumes the villagers wore, kaftan-like robes made from a heavy black cloth and decorated with colourful embroidered hems. The next pellet of opium was burning in the pipe, imploding in upon itself like a planet that was forming.

'It's always better at the end,' one of the villagers from the second row said, smearing a cigarette with opium. Another was chewing betel nuts and spitting out the juice. Women had also come to sit at the rear of the hut and watch us smoke. Tiny children were decked out in silver jewellery, swarms of bees were buzzing in a dead log, and from the forest there came a loud droning and rustling.

'Don't be concerned,' the village elder said. 'We've put up fences to protect ourselves from wild animals.'

We didn't feel afraid, we just wondered wide-eyed at the sense of spiritual order encapsulated in the idea of 'concern'.

Hours later, the village elder counted seven corncobs where I was sitting. We hadn't touched the soup that had been prepared for us in the meantime. The medicine man and the village elder are laughing about this, because lack of appetite is a classic sign of the opium eater; indeed, a number of motor functions are impaired by the drug. We crawled back to our hut on all fours, dragged ourselves up the planks leading to the entrance at a dizzying height of three metres and crashed out on out mats, Helen and Mark in one corner and me in the other.

The most immediate manifestation of opium-induced well-being is in the act of smiling. That is, you allow the corners of your mouth to diverge, complete their motion, and as a consequence of this movement you find yourself happy, faintly amused and content that your facial expression is following the sensation you feel; no, rather, okay with the fact that the sensation is following expression; no, that's not it either, just happy that one movement is following another, for there is no earlier or later, no cause and effect. Instead, everything's on this amplitude of happiness, which keeps extending farther and farther, driving the corners of your mouth beyond the bounds of your face, so that you've now got corners of your mouth outside of your self, which spread beyond the contours of your face and take off until they're flapping up there all alone in the night air. Ah, the night air! I was already deep in the abyss of a hallucination.

A drug trip is also about stripping away the surface appearance of things. The functional side of life crumbles into dust. How – and more to the point why – was one supposed to operate on this level of existence anymore? Why should one serve any purpose? And what does that mean anyway – a 'purpose in life'?

Some snatches of music waft over from the village. Music that doesn't sound like accompaniment. In this moment, the subject of the music is not the musicians, but rather the instruments. They're singing their inner life out of their bodies.

'That's where it comes from, then, the intrinsicality of instruments,' I say out loud, without me or anyone else remotely understanding what I mean. But has the sentence already left my mouth or is the body of it still stuck in my throat, was it forgotten there?

That's not the end of it: suddenly, the neglected world begins to crowd in on me. It's full of rejected objects and thought contents, this overlooked, suppressed, oughtn't-to-be world, and it's doing my head in trying to constantly mediate between the state of consciousness and the function of thinking. Now though, in this instant, everything is in a state of transition, in the motionless state of turbulence that is neither consciousness nor activity, but rather conception and creation of the world.

In such a state of swimming receptiveness for creation, and with my gaze trained on the delicate mantle of the universe, which surrounds the earth like a gauzy shroud, and in my rising sentimentality for everything that that creation entails, the smell of the air has a taste, the breath on the skin feels itself, and the forest gently and lovingly inhales and exhales. You find it impossible to walk, to urinate, to get an erection; motor functions are sluggish and superfluous. But it has to be that way, since everything you concentrate on now is becoming so profound – if 'concentrate' is the right word, that is, because you're drifting off and incapable of grasping hold of anything. Tempos shift radically, and an eternity opens up in the twinkling of an eye. But when so many impressions, internal processes and motions occur within minutes, then the tempo during that period, which appears to drag, must in actual fact be quick. So, a lot comes and goes very fast, but in ponderous movements, and people's faces are all naked and blank like a tree trunk that's been stripped of its bark.

'How many pipes can I smoke?' I had asked the medicine man, and he'd replied:

'If no evil spirit appears, you can smoke up to ten.'

'And what if an evil spirit does appear?'

'Then it will tell you to stop!'

'And what else?'

'Take care that you don't touch the fences, that helps you overcome any anxiety you might have about the spirits.'

I look out into the forest, where the wind is wafting over the treetops in a gentle swell, I see the naked women washing under the jet of water behind the huts, and at the bare-breasted old woman with a headdress. They're all, without exception, smoking opium, prepared to communally read the world from a skewed viewpoint. Reality viewed as if at first sight.

My stomach's itching. How original. I take great pleasure in scratching the extensive landscape of my belly with all ten fingers, up and down. The following day, the medicine man will inform me that scratching like this is one of the most characteristic things a person who's high on opium does.

But what if these images were to coalesce into an infinite loop, if they became a mania, a fixation that trapped a person's consciousness into the same old routine every time? This is the structure of fear, which resides in being caught in an escape-proof prison of recurrent thoughts and image sequences.

Many internal processes arrange themselves unbidden into a form of mental opera: everything screams, open-mouthed, even trees and molehills. Then they automatically morph into cartoon films, where everything becomes brightly two-dimensional and hectic and loud. Later on the world starts to look like a painting by Carl Spitzweg, and finally it changes into a silent movie. It then becomes a real effort to wrench yourself away from any of these visual idioms, as Spitzweg changes back once more into the cartoon film, and this in turn tries first to transform into an El Lissitzky picture and then a collection of technical modules.

Also, many things undergo a spontaneous metamorphosis into music – the autonomous development of soundscapes composed from the noises coming from outside, which then manage to free themselves and become independent. In addition, these are still accompanied by streams of images, a constant reciprocal association of images and sounds. So, if your imagination conjures up a hill, say, in your inner landscape, the music will follow with a crescendo; if the landscape becomes dramatic, the music grows soothing, transforming it into an Arcadian place with running streams, cows, sheep and shepherdesses: 'Oh broad valleys, oh hills, oh beautiful green forest, you my solemn place of joy and sorrow...'

An opium high is a form of microscopy, and if fear can be said to be palpable in any form, then it is as a magnification of trace elements, an elevation of trivialities to absolutes. I am already drinking the perfumed moisture of tears, it is already thinning to a foggy mist, already the light is breaking through the night like a tablet being squeezed through tin foil.

Tell me now, head, what was the name of the girl who sat at the far left desk in my first form at school: there was Maria Deussen, then Monika Schmitz, Michael Schlohbohm, Jörgi

Longwitz, Anita Heister, Ursula Bartmann and so on *ad infinitum*: the names come pouring in, one after the other, packed in dresses, trousers, particular patterns of cloth that no longer exist, textiles that have become threadbare, and smells redolent of old fabrics, mothballs and sawdust.

But no, my high wants to generate images, to flush them out of the vaults of my memory and wash them up to the surface and from there back down into oblivion again: Don't retain me, it whispers, forget me, off you go to your present existence. But if I were to pick up a pen right now to write down the names of my former classmates, the moment the tip of the ballpoint touched the paper, I'd no longer have a clue what I wanted to write. Instead, I'd become completely engrossed in the sight of the tip of the pen, shimmering there in its iridescence like an insect, and an inexhaustible process of entering the here and now would fixate on this ballpoint tip.

I lay in this hut, surrounded as if in a cocoon by the polyphonically rustling forest of northern Thailand, and whenever I rolled over, I found a different world on each side. I flipped over like I was turning over the pages of a book. On the one side my primary school, my route home, and the kitchen smells in the afternoon. On the other an Italian monastery beneath the knoll at Settignano: Don Gabriello in his bed, wearing a mealworm-coloured jersey … but in-between … I felt myself sinking.

First of all, images still kept appearing that were generated by an inner movement, and borne on emotion, then came more tenuously connected ones, between which a miasma spread, an atmosphere, a climate, an aroma, a sound. Soon after, all that was left was this 'in-between'. The connecting lines from one to the other started to flicker, tautened, and the braces between the modules became soft and flexible; the whole edifice of internal images stood on the verge of collapse.

It is Now: finally, the eye has arrived at a bird's eye view over the building block system of my own inner life. Nothing like intelligence exists there anymore. All that remains is the construction principle of impersonal connections, which follow their various paths, and in a benevolent act of acknowledgement unhampered by any limitation, it dawns on you: the personal is impersonal, and fear – or something that has been accorded the name of fear – is guiding and directing desire and aversion and instructing you: don't go from A to B, the most direct route isn't as the crow flies but the escape route. Everything supposedly inspired is nothing but a way of making detours, of avoiding things.

And so it was that I found myself looking down upon the model, the chemical model of my personal unreason, and I gave birth to the word 'I' as the symptom of a dysfunction. What was once called 'consciousness' was now nothing but a wound, fascinating in its originality, which had no supporting medium and which also would not heal. Only seven hours later did the phantasms finally dissipate, and I awoke out of a state of 'it thinks' and entered the illusory realm of 'I think'.

Orvieto

The Fixation

The *Trattoria Giusti* in the Via Giuseppi Giusti was the favoured eating place of many people who studied in Florence in the late 1970s or who, as perpetual travellers, found themselves stranded in the city. I was studying at the *Kunsthistorisches Institut* at the time and earning a living working as a tour guide. My friends there were two other students, an attendant at the Uffizi, a pharmacist's daughter from Siena and a Canadian journalist couple.

The only pieces of furniture in the Trattoria were two long tables, and there was no menu. You simply sat down at one of the tables, often among complete strangers, or with a mixture of strangers and friends, chose between fish and chicken and left the rest to the chef.

The first person from home to venture forth and visit me in Florence was a woman who – don't ask me why, I've no idea – went by the name of 'Matubi Hühnchen' – a large, blonde, shy woman who invariably responded to my witticisms by exclaiming: 'Ooh, you've got to laugh, haven't you!' Not that she ever did, mind.

Back home, she lived in a one-room attic flat above a confectioner's. All the other apartments were unoccupied; in other words, there were lots of spare rooms with beds and fusty old furniture, and when we wanted to have sex we always decamped to one of these other rooms. When we'd finished, Matubi would sit naked on the windowsill with the curtains open and breathe in the baking smells that wafted up from below, day and night. Her snow-white body and the smell of the confectioner's were so intertwined in my mind that, even in Florence, the aroma of warm baked buns and cakes always filled me with thoughts of summer love and homesickness. Yet this habit of sitting naked on the windowsill was the only truly liberated act of Matubi's that I could recall.

Nor did that change when she came to see me in Florence. Everyone around us was some sort of Bohemian, yet all the two of us could think of was that we missed the aroma of confectionery. So on the second night of her visit, when I'd drunk too much *Vin Santo*, I confided in her:

'I really just feel like talking wildly, no holds barred.'

To which she responded: 'There's plenty of time for that later.'

That second evening, I'd taken her to *Trattoria Giusti*, where we soon found ourselves surrounded by a group of American tourists. One of them, Peter, a painter, swam through European art like a biological cell through its surrounding medium. His main interest was in the Catalan informal artist Antoni Tàpies. He carried around a reproduction of one of his works in his wallet, and in the run-down Trattoria he was able to point out certain places where the fabric of the building had decayed in interesting ways that Tàpies would surely have found intriguing. Peter wanted to become a pupil of Tàpies, and to this end had already written him three painterly letters, liberally larded with artistic formulations and offbeat metaphors, which he hoped would persuade the master to invite him to Spain. All three letters remained unanswered.

In the meantime, though, Peter had also become interested in Greek philosophy and studied Plato's theory of art and the edifice of ideas in Neoplatonism. It all made for a very animated evening in the Trattoria. Drink was quaffed liberally, and the discussion flowed freely between such topics as impressions from our travels, biographical snippets, cultural knowledge and jokes, with everyone chipping in where appropriate. The only surprise at the end of the night was that no one insisted on exchanging addresses. So it was and should remain, then, this one-off, unrepeatable evening, at the very last gasp of which Matubi told me that there was no future for us and that she was going to go back home early.

Some weeks later my six-square-metre room had grown too cramped for me, so I moved into a commune with two American girls, an Argentinian girl and a Turkish guy. The girl from Argentina, Anna-Maria, was, in her dark splendour, one of the most beautiful women I'd ever seen. Several times a week in the afternoon, she entertained her lover, a squat Neapolitan called Luigi. He'd put on Ravel's *Bolero* and, as a master of his art, would arrange it so that that he and his girlfriend came to a climax in synch with the music, and as the orchestra reached a crescendo, so would they. The ensuing diminuendo would coincide with Anna-Maria's loudest orgasmic moan, and all the while I'd be sitting in my room beneath a reproduction of Jacopo della Quercia's 'Tomb of Ilaria del Carretto', shaking along in time to their exertions.

One day, there was a ring at the front door and a man's voice enquired:

'*C'é Riccardo?*'

And I responded, as arranged:

'Non c'é Riccardo!'

We were having trouble with the landlords, so we only let in people who gave the correct passwords. And duly, up the stairs came Peter, Peter the painter, who turned out to be a friend of one of the two American girls in the commune, or to be more precise, her discarded lover. The first thing we said when we saw one another was that we knew it, we just knew we'd run into one another again.

Since we'd last met, Peter had sold his return ticket to the US and was planning to stay in Europe to study aesthetics, visit Tàpies – who still hadn't replied – and devote himself to his painting. For the time being, he was eking out a living renovating apartments.

Thereafter, we saw one another almost daily and shared the crises that hit the commune: Anna-Maria found out that Luigi had a wife and four kids back in Naples, the Turk got involved in pushing drugs near the Ponte Vecchio, and the clash with the landlords reached such a pitch that we took a joint decision to quit the place.

At that time Peter was living in a Benedictine-Olivetan monastery in Settignano, in the hills above Florence, a building that had once housed fifty or more monks, but where now only four were left. Accordingly just four of the remaining cells were rented to secular guests, who were only outwardly required to abide by the order's rules: no music, no noise, and no women visitors in the cell wing, over whose exit hung a sign bearing the sombre legend: 'Clausura'.

The abbot, Don Carlo, was so short and pot-bellied that his monk's habit was clearly the only garb he could possibly have worn. He received me and gave me a soul-searching examination, which I passed without taxing my soul excessively. But when Peter wanted to take a photo of us both, because he liked the way the rubicund man of faith only just reached up to the height of my belt, the abbot demurred:

'I'm not a vain man, but you really mustn't take this photo.'

His proscription had all the force of an Old Testament 'Thou Shalt Not'. Over the ensuing months, I came to learn all the foibles of the other monks: Don Tarcisio liked to read out loud the instruction leaflets from the tablets and other medication he took, Don Lorenzo remonstrated with politicians on the television from a distance of two metres, and Don Gabriello had two collections, a public one of perfume bottles and a private one consisting of pictures of transvestites, which he filed between the pages of a hymnal that he kept well hidden.

Don Gabriello had become a monk when he was twenty-one, but by twenty-three he'd realized that it couldn't possibly be God's will for a young man to be confined to a monastery from such an early age. Consequently, he had found himself committing transgressions on a regular basis. Indeed, we only addressed him as 'Don' out of sympathy, as he'd never actually taken holy orders, so in fact was the only 'Fra' among the brotherhood. Peter and I like him best out of all of them, and sometimes of an evening we'd sit either side of his high bed, in which he, cocooned in a sheath of eggshell-coloured jersey, sat looking like a large mealworm and regaled us with smutty stories.

In the mornings, we'd go and put the tables out for the two women who ran the bar on the nearby square, and eat our brioche there, before Peter headed off into the hills to paint, while I went into the institute to immerse myself in the art theory of the Early Renaissance. Sometimes we arrived at the bar in the early morning and found the mother and daughter kneeling in front of the television, where the Pope appeared briefly standing on a red carpet. After a couple of months, Peter was finally flat broke, accepted a larger renovation job in Rome, and so the plan was that I would travel with him as far as Orvieto, stopping off in Siena along the way, where we wanted to go and see the famous horse race known as the 'Palio' around the city's main square.

On the eve of our departure, Peter took a couple of hefty swigs from a bulbous brown bottle of *grappa*, strapped all his paintings on his back and went from bar to bar, where he hoped to talk the bored owners into purchasing sketches in oil and watercolour showing corners of walls, haystacks and forlorn animals to decorate the walls of their taprooms, which were already covered with pictures. And the impossible actually happened! By the end of the evening Peter was blind drunk but had managed to offload most of his paintings, earning him enough to buy a ticket to Rome and pay off his debts. Don Carlo nodded in satisfaction: despite his handsome exterior, here was a good lad who wouldn't end up doing a flit while still owing him rent. He'd known it all along.

From midday that day we stood on the mussel-shaped Piazza del Campo in Siena, where the racetrack had already been cordoned off and the square was soon barred to any more visitors, as the crush was already so great. A Red Cross ambulance did the rounds, picking up people who'd fainted. All round the square, small groups sat playing games, eating, sleeping or arguing.

By the time the riders in their medieval costumes – each individual representing his quarter of the city and bearing the coat of arms of his *Contrada* – nervously embarked on their first lap, the crowd were already yelling their support for the 'Tower', the 'Ram', the 'Snail', the 'Wave', the 'Giraffe', the 'Panther', the 'Dragon' and so forth.

The race itself went down in history as the Palio that had seven false starts. The jockey of the 'Giraffe' *Contrada* was injured in the melée and had to be carried off the track on a stretcher by the Red Cross. But just before he reached the open maw of the ambulance, he suddenly jumped off the trolley, got hold of his horse again and went on to win the race. The ensuing uproar culminated in a pitched street battle between the 'Giraffe' and 'Tower' districts. Although Peter and I managed to jump over the balustrade separating the rest of the square from the race track and the back alleyways and escape into one of the side streets, that was precisely where the two main fronts of the battle had converged. So, we pressed our backs against a house frontage and let the two cohorts lay into one another in front of us with raised sticks and bare fists, while residents in the upper storeys poured buckets of cold water down onto the hot-headed brawlers.

A young woman, who like us had got caught between the two warring fronts, fainted at our feet. We caught hold of her just in time, propped her up against the wall behind and waited until the fighting had moved on past us. The crush suddenly abated, the girl came to, and with us supporting her on either side, she let herself be steered into a café in one of the side streets.

Bernadette had, it transpired, come to Rome as an American au pair, in search of some cultural life. Instead, she'd found love there, and then lost it again. Her stories only gave off faint whiffs of this lost love, and as she scraped her fingers through her long brown locks and gazed into our eyes, she convinced herself that life was fated to take another romantic turn, some *coup de foudre*, a piece of sheer craziness, like finding herself cast into the company of two strangers in the wake of a street battle in the summer heat of Siena.

As night fell, Bernadette still hadn't taken a step without us propping her up on either side. She'd given each of us a peck on the cheek, showing equal favour, and the instant either one of us nipped into a shop or went off to the loo for however brief a time, she gave the other such a passionate French kiss that he couldn't help but feel he was the Chosen One. Indeed, her kisses were profligate and intemperate, she fairly launched herself into each one, flinging her bare elbow round your neck as she did so, so that you couldn't avoid it and so she'd enjoy the experience all the more. Whenever she stopped kissing, she'd throw her head back and give a guttural laugh, which sounded a bit insane, a bit dirty, and a bit proud all at once, and sometimes she'd even wipe her lips with the back of her hand. She was determined to drive us wild, the both of us, and while she was kissing us, we were definitely also meant to feel her girl's body nuzzling up against us as our tongues intertwined with hers at the back of our throats.

Shortly before midnight, things had progressed to such a stage that there was no question of us going our separate ways. Bernadette made no secret of the fact that she really didn't want to be on her own. The idea was for us to find a meadow somewhere outside the city and spend the night together there. When we hesitated, she walked a few steps ahead, lifted her T-shirt almost up to her breasts, bent over and asked:

'So, which one of you wants me?'

Men are both drawn to and terrified of women like this, while also despising them a little. But Bernadette was radiating the promise of a warm summer night, and there was enough desire in her for two. Peter was a dog, game for anything, and spreading his arms out munificently like Jesus, ceded the decision to me. I, however, was a coward, and with a curt 'Just get on with it, you two!' beat a retreat. As I did so, I could read two emotions in Bernadette's eyes: regret at having to pass up on one of us, and contempt – ultimately melting into friendliness – for the bashful guy who was probably just afraid of the competition.

So, for her part, our leave-taking was so motherly as to be almost hurtful. Peter was quick to assume the role of the loyal friend who was still prepared to forego the pleasure; there were more important things when all was said and done. But in no time we'd agreed to meet up at twelve noon the next day outside the cathedral in Orvieto, and once that was settled, his lust was shameless and urgent. I headed off to the station. When I turned round to look at them one last time, Peter's hand was grabbing her bum as if to say: look, that's how you do it, and as they walked away she threw her head back and laughed at the night sky.

At the station, once I'd found out that the next train to Orvieto was only due to leave early next morning, I bunked down in the corner of the waiting room next to a couple of backpackers and slept for hours, though I woke in good time to catch my train.

It was just pulling into Siena station when a couple – with tousled hair and rumpled clothes – lurched onto the platform. Peter was clearly sober by this time, while Bernadette wore a blissful but deranged expression and was leaning against him, clutching his arm, with grass stains on her jeans. All Peter did by way of a farewell was give her a pretty peremptory kiss. And as the train pulled away, it was me who kept waving the longest at her as she stood there on the platform, beaming, enthusiastic, and finally sweeping her arms above her head in a wide arc – this slightly crazy young woman who was very much of her time.

On the train, the first thing Peter wanted to know was whether I was angry with him. When he found I wasn't, he took off his brown suede jacket and presented it to me. Yet when I asked him about his night in the meadow, he shook his head and grew taciturn, like someone who had gorged himself and now had nothing to show for it but a guilty conscience. It had been too wild, too crazy, he said, he'd lost all self-control, and that wasn't good.

It was still before midday when we pulled into Orvieto, that soaring town that seems to reach for the heavens. The cathedral stands at its highest point, scraping at the sky and alarming the populace with its outrageous visions. At one time, the local burghers must simply have jogged along, content in the knowledge that tomorrow was just another day. And then suddenly they found themselves confronted with Luca Signorelli's fresco cycle in the San Brizio Chapel in the cathedral and must have come to believe that hell had the most beautiful naked figures and Heaven the angels with the fluffiest wings. For when, one day, the Day of Judgement arrived, they'd suddenly find themselves handed over to the grizzled ferryman Charon by the hosts of heavenly soldiers and rowed across the Styx into eternal damnation. And they'd discover that they'd failed to inform themselves about the need for repentance in good time.

Luca Signorelli, who envisaged the Last Trump and set it down in paint, was himself an enigmatic figure who came to Umbria from Tuscany. He had an obsessive interest in anatomy, and his painterly imagination was fired by Dante, whose work may be said to have influenced or even determined popular conceptions of hell for many centuries. Signorelli is even reputed to have fallen from the scaffolding once while executing his frescos, but then again nobody's descent into hell is exactly featherbedded.

I told Peter all I knew about the fresco cycle: that it was begun at the end of the fifteenth century, that Signorelli was a contemporary, and perhaps also a rival, of Michelangelo, and that his work in Orvieto Cathedral was the largest, most ambitious depiction of the Last Judgement that had ever been attempted up to that time.

'Here we can see,' I lectured him, 'that only the young and naked and pure in spirit are admitted to heaven, which recognizes no class distinctions. The base and vile, on the other hand, aren't even let into heaven, but are simply massacred where they stand, while prostitutes are spirited away through the air by winged devils with athletic figures who torment them, and are spat at by demons. At the Apocalypse, the trees sweat blood, and blood also rains down from heaven, while the stars vanish from the firmament and the earth is consumed by fire. Skeletons emerge from the ground and put on new flesh. And they're all fit and trim.'

Despite the fact that Peter had spent months living in a monastery and was acquainted with the motif of the Apocalypse, Signorelli's work left him cold, particularly because of the anatomically exaggerated and decidedly un-sensual human figures, with their heads turned toward heaven. Repelled by the weak materiality of the corporeal and the painter's evident lack of interest in material things, he launched into a paean of praise for the great Tàpies, who precisely in matters of materiality ...

'You really ought to write to him one more time!'

In the event, then, we didn't spend long looking at the *Last Judgement*. Instead, Peter felt far more at home among the ancient ruins of the Etruscan period. In Orvieto, you come across these in walls and gates, burial objects and stelae. They sometimes look like they've developed directly from primitive art forms, so I, in my assumed role of travel guide, summoned up all the knowledge I had about the Etruscans:

'The most important monument from the height of Etruscan culture is the Temple of Belvedere, which is thought to date from the beginning of the fifth century BC. The podium of this ceremonial complex, which was purposefully sited to afford it a panoramic view over the Paglia Valley, is built on a natural rocky outcrop. A flight of steps leads to two lines of columns, behind which are three stone chambers, one leading on from the other. From the position of the complex, scholars surmised that this was where haruspices – seers trained in the art of reading entrails and other auguries – brought their human sacrifices. In addition, many terracotta artefacts from the Etruscan period were excavated here, primarily small decorative architectural adornments, along with the bronze figurine of a female dancer and a number of larger figural reliefs, in which the influence of the Greek sculptor Phidias and echoes of the Parthenon frieze were identified.'

The Etruscan burial chambers cut into the tufa rock cliffs around Orvieto, notably those at Crocifisso del Tufo and Canicella, yielded a particularly rich haul of finds. Yet even more was to come: when, some years back, a landslide dislodged a large chunk of the tufa outcrop on which Orvieto is built and sent it crashing down into the valley, it happened to expose one of the ancient burial sites, and the city's inhabitants tried to identify through binoculars what the chambers that were now laid bare contained. When Peter and I attempted to do the same, all we could make out was soil, ancient soil.

In the afternoon, we went for a dip in the river, and while I lay listening on the sandy bank, Peter, who was standing in the reed beds, recounted to me the twelve ways in which you could inadvertently drive the woman who loved you to give you the elbow. These included; always talking too loudly, having to have jokes repeated and explained to you, wiping your runny nose on your sleeve and giving a running commentary on it ... Never again have I encountered a guy who exerted such a magnetic pull on women.

I went down to the station with him in the evening, and as the train pulled out, his hand stayed sticking motionless out of the compartment window in farewell, even when the train began to tilt into the curve and disappear from view. Then, all of a sudden, there were two policeman at my side. They seized me by the right and left elbow, led me away and interrogated me in a small office in the station building; who was the man I'd just seen off? What had we talked about down at the river? Where did we come from and why wasn't I telling them the truth? From outside came the sound of birdsong, occasionally interspersed with the clanging of the level crossing bell as the barrier was lowered.

I submitted willingly to their questioning, answering them readily, precisely and exhaustively. To this day, I have no idea what these two policeman wanted from me. When they finally released me, I got the feeling that grilling me had simply been an amusing way for them to kill time, or maybe they'd just wanted to practice their interrogation technique on me, but in any event my train to Florence was long gone by that stage. I stayed one more night at our *Locanda* in Orvieto and set off on my return journey a day late.

Three weeks later, I met a German singer on the streets of Florence, and spent an evening with him and his coterie of expats and transients in the garden of the Villa Scifanoia in San Domenico, just outside Fiesole. This motley crew had taken up residence there and because the night was so exquisite, we just didn't want it to end. I only made it back to my monastery in Settignano as dawn was breaking the next day and had managed to grab no more than two hours' sleep when I was woken by someone shaking my shoulder. My friend Antonio, the Uffizi attendant, was kneeling at my bedside, repeating the same phrase over and over:

'*Tanti saluti di Bernadette!*'

At first, I could make no connection between his face, my room in the 'Clausura' and the name Bernadette.

'She was here,' Antono whispered. '*Una vera donna!*'

It seems that she'd arrived late on the previous afternoon and sat waiting for me on the low wall outside the monastery as evening fell. When night fell, the monks took her inside, and Don Carlo allowed her to sit in the refectory, outside the 'Clausura' and wait for me. Antonio came and sat with her to keep her company, entertaining her with his fund of funny stories. Even so, after a couple of hours, when he asked her whether she'd rather he left her in peace, she'd replied 'Yes' and then spent a while working on a drawing – here, he showed me it – after which he'd sat by her again in the dim light in the empty, echoing refectory, by the window that looked out over the distant city. At 3 a.m. she'd finally decided to leave; Antonio walked her out to the taxi and was rewarded with a kiss on each cheek.

The drawing showed one of the standard-bearers from the Palio in full costume. The flag he was carrying was emblazoned with Bernadette's message to me:

'Hi, lover! I've spent half the night waiting for you. It's two in the morning now. I've finally managed to shake off that pain in the neck Antonio, your Uffizi attendant friend, for a bit. I'll give him this so that you'll know I sat up half the night waiting for you. I've got to get back to Rome now. Then I'm flying back to Denver from Rome. Leave me not,' she signed off, 'Be here.'

And beneath she'd printed, all in capitals, her full address in the States, including the apartment block number and the floor she lived on.

Not long after, I left Settignano and returned to Germany. Bernadette and I wrote each other long, fond and convoluted letters – hers covered in a mass of little doodles and drawings, interrupted by clauses in parenthesis, and embellished with stars, annotations, footnotes and inserts, while mine were full of innuendo, double-entendres and excessive presumption. We kept up our airy-fairy and mutually titillating correspondence until the following summer. Then she sent me a photo, which showed her standing on the sidewalk next to a broad American boulevard, laughing. She was leaning toward the camera, and on the left side of her head, a ponytail dangled down as far as her waist. There was something unwholesome about the way she was laughing, despite the fact that a little dog was nuzzling round her feet and that she was bathed in strong, warm light.

Oh, Bernadette, I thought, that's you all right, and recalled how she'd collapsed into our arms at the Palio and conjured up the image of her stumbling onto the station platform, propped up on Peter's arm and with her jeans covered in grass stains, after several hours spent doing things that Peter had called 'not good, not right'.

A week later I got back to my place in the small hours – life back home had finally begun to pick up pace again – only to be greeted by a high-pitched yelp of delight that filled the room when I checked my messages on the answerphone: 'Guess who-hoo?'

So euphoric it was positively scary.

She'd done it! She'd finally done it, and she was free, free at last! She didn't say from what, but she was clear about the upshot: 'I'm coming!'

No later than twenty days precisely from then, she'd be expecting me at twelve o'clock sharp inside the cathedral in Orvieto, in front of Luca Signorelli's *Last Judgement* naturally, 'to reinvent history,' as she put it. There followed some brief chitchat, which was hard to grasp as it was evidently being drowned out by the street noise of Denver wafting in through her apartment window. Then came another exuberant yell: 'I'm leaving!'

Her voice, which had always been high-pitched and full of vibrato, already sounded like it was caught in the slipstream of a moving vehicle, and her sheer happiness burst into the deep German night of my room like a communication from another plane of existence.

There was no point calling her or writing her, she'd told me. She was already on the move.

'Just be there,' she shouted joyfully and hung up, though it sounded like she kept on talking all the same. I played the tape a second and third time. Fascinating. Whatever we did in Orvieto, whoever we were, it would have very little to do with the world we were leaving to hook up with one another again. My fantasy life was at something of a low ebb, and I was keen to exorcise the memory of the coward who'd wandered off to the station that time. It was summer. I dreamt of grass stains and bought myself a train ticket to Orvieto.

Climbing up the steps to the cathedral, which on this midday was shrouded in the same shimmering heat haze as the year before, I was overtaken by a brief spasm of unease at this reenactment. Wasn't life slipping back all too readily into a worn-out posture? The flight of steps, the façade, the sunlight, the smell of the warm stones were exactly as before. But my gaze took it all in much more sketchily than before; after all, this time I wasn't there to sightsee a church, a fresco, a *Last Judgement*, but to meet a woman.

But that's not how it panned out. No longer curious, but simply biding time and determined to get through viewing Signorelli's fresco as quickly as possible, I sat myself down on the front row of pews and cast my eyes fleetingly over the paintings, whose bold and dreadful power couldn't help but draw you in. In fact, the drastic and vulgar nature of these ruthless images, the way they so insistently strove after visual effect and impact, violated the sanctity of this space somehow. The local clergy had even given Signorelli religious instruction while he was working on the frescos. They been concerned to wring his conception of the work from him and trammel his creativity into pre-agreed lines. Yet he proved to be a recalcitrant pupil; hardly surprising when one considers how the principal work of Signorelli's teacher Piero della Francesca, the *Legend of the True Cross* fresco in Arezzo, depicts, immediately to the right of the altar in the High Chapel, a workman with one testicle hanging out of his tunic.

In one of her letters, Bernadette had told me how devout she'd been as a child. At the age of seven, during communion classes, the pastor had granted her remission for all her sins. All those she'd committed up to that time were absolved, he said, and in her mind's eye she'd envisaged the blank white sheet of paper that was her list of transgressions and thought long and hard about what new sin might be worthy of being the first one to be recorded there. She'd duly stolen the pastor's eraser, and was quite pleased with this new sin of hers.

While he was working on his fresco cycle, Signorelli conducted anatomical experiments with cadavers. He'd also painted his dead son, to keep his memory alive, and had learned how to use poses and facial expressions in order to portray people in crowd scenes as individuals. He twisted the corpses into unlikely contortions, experimented with the way they stood and the human body's centres of gravity, all the while tirelessly asking himself: what is a naked person? What does he signify?

In the *Resurrection of the Dead* scene, and above all in *The Damned Cast Into Hell*, his fantasy is dangerously unchained. Here he opens up the dungeon and the images burst out. In an daring mix of the heathen and Christian worlds, he expands the act of creation out into a cosmic anarchy. Deluges loom threateningly over the horizon, while the animal world cowers in terror, errant people wander across the plain, false prophets scan the firmament for signs of hope, while many human souls have already been possessed by demons. A blood-red moon shines dimly from the heavens, and the Antichrist is seated on his throne, heeding the advice of a demon. Soldiers in black uniforms are razing the Church of the Holy Sepulchre to the ground. Even the elements no longer obey natural laws and are now behaving erratically and randomly.

The sky is a murky soup, the stars have been wrenched from their usual path across the heavens and almost casually are setting the whole world aflame. The seas overwhelm human settlements, fire consumes the land, earthquakes shake the ground and people are seen pressing forward up slope and out of the picture, like they're attempting to break the illusion of pictorial space and step into the real world of the viewer, who on this day happened to be me, sitting on my pew and waiting to commit a sin that had come a long way from the original 'resurrection of the flesh'. And for sure, there on Signorelli's fresco, skeletons were rising up out of the ground and taking on corporeal form or blossoming forth into the full glory of their anatomical beauty, as yet still pure, conceived in God's image, but still flesh for all that.

When she was twelve, Bernadette had told me in one of her letters, she took part in a competition to find the prettiest doll. And hers ended up winning, even though it was the ugliest, and could only move its eyes. But its owner was everyone's favourite back then, pretty as a picture and with exclusively cute friends, and if all that wasn't enough, a perfect black dog called 'Arrow' too. Bernadette had her first kiss in the graveyard behind her house. No sooner had she been kissed than she resolved never to undergo such an intense experience again.

'Why?' asked the boy, who was four years older than her.

'Because it's a sin,' she replied.

'What's so sinful about it exactly?' the boy pressed her.

'I dunno,' she answered, 'but it sure felt like a sin. That's all I know.'

The next day, she spent ages trying to explain to the lustful boy what a sin was. As she was doing so, 'Arrow' was run over by a car. Whereupon she stopped talking to the boy entirely, and instead, with a guilty conscience, gave him the push instead.

Signorelli's pictorial spaces are dramatic stages, and he sees the end of the world in very theatrical terms, with the descent to Earth of the Antichrist, a scene that is evoked in the Apocrypha, in the chronicler Jacopo da Voragine's *Golden Legend*, or in the visions of St Brigitte of Sweden. It is a matter of ultimate questions and last things, with humanity required to awake to a new life. It is the end of the world; the Cumaean Sibyl points to her 'book of prophesies', where ships are shown teetering on the crests of waves, the ruins of ancient buildings stand as stark warnings, a bank of cloud the colour of spilt blood lowers in the sky, an impending firestorm threatens in the background, while in the foreground a throng of mercenaries and soldiers, devils and demons advances. But in all this, the aspect of the painting that appears so nightmarishly personal is the pedantic way in which Signorelli dissects a mass fate into a whole series of individual dramas.

An artistic soul, too artistic for her home environment of Denver, shone through the personal vignettes that Bernadette's letters sketched out for me. She wrote about her early boyfriends – handsome bores who wanted to save themselves for marriage, a slacker, a guy called Elwyn who she loved in a platonic way and with whom she went on seven-mile walks every day. But the inside of his mouth turned her stomach.

Later, she'd had a dog called Bronco. It was run over one time when she was out walking with Elwyn. She promptly made up her mind never to go out with him again, and as she was telling him this, she kept her eyes fixed firmly on the chamber of horrors behind his open lips. That made it easier to ignore his tears.

After this resolution and Bronco's death she also took a long hard look at herself and decided henceforth to live like an Amish girl, keeping her eyes lowered, wearing plain black and white clothing, singing folk songs and renouncing the world of technology. That did her a power of good. Friends in the city started to think she'd gone into a convent. But in actual fact, adopting a supposedly Amish lifestyle was just her surreptitious way of neglecting herself. She duly woke up one day in hospital. Days of her life had gone missing, and all she felt was a strong urge to eat some ice cream again. She conducted running battles with the nurses, the well-meaning, strong nurses with the calloused hands. She was determined to stay there, but all to no avail; in due course, she was sent back out into the wide world again.

'Since the age of fourteen I've been living in a state of disillusion,' she wrote, and after emerging from her spell in hospital she drifted into university, where she attempted a dual-track approach to her education, thinking in epicurean terms and avoiding the platonic. But Marlon, the only toy boy she could ever have imagined in her life, escaped the tidal wave of desire she felt herself being born aloft on in the nick of time and went to Europe.

In the *Resurrection of the Flesh*, Signorelli's figures are not seen climbing out of graves. Rather, these bodies emerge straight out of a barren field and take on fleshly form. On the open expanses, people gather, transfixed by the state of emergency, and seeking safety in numbers in this situation of general confusion. The only figures that stand separate from these knots of humanity are those who are beheading, tormenting or liquidating others.

On their way to the place of judgement, the damned are led through hell, where a woman stands burning in the infernal abyss. The naked bodies writhe in an orgy of disinhibition, given over to the excess which at the Apocalypse goes hand-in-hand with a surfeit of lust. On a bare stage in Purgatory waits inescapable damnation, and the mass of people, shot through with a complex rhythmic pattern like in bebop jazz, swells back and forth, and up and down, leaving us with the impression that nothing exists under this dismal firmament other than a despairing humanity, united only in their attempt to escape.

And what is humanity's lot here; more specifically, what is the fate of women in this world? Exposed to a sovereign form of sadism, they find themselves subjected to every kind of humiliation. Their nude state is not that of Paradise, but of pornography. They are thrown to the ground, kicked head-over-heels out of heaven with their legs splayed; they are shown being bound and beaten, run over and bitten, abducted and dragged by the hair. Their naked bodies, depicted in the willing poses of pin-ups, abandon themselves to the cruel fantasies of the *Last Judgement*. Yet their nakedness, as if in some biblical men's magazine, is already an integral part of their degradation, their punishment.

On the other hand, it is only in the context of damnation that these nudes possess any sexual identity at all. As soon as they have been raised from the dead or received into heaven, they begin to wear their naked form like an accessory. Only in damnation does their countenance become an animated human face, and their backside turn into an arse. What a chance I was being offered, here and now, just before my so hotly and obsessively imagined rendezvous, to renounce sexuality! But in the light of what had motivated me to come on this journey, I was firmly on the side of the Damned, and stimulated by the meat market of these supine bodies.

Come the early afternoon, and I was still hanging around the cathedral, sitting down occasionally on the sun-drenched steps outside the main door to warm up, and scanning the piazza, the steps and the entrances to the alleyways to see if there was anyone keeping an eye out for me from some hidey-hole. Then I went back in again to stand in front of the *Last Judgement* once more, where the tide of the Damned still hadn't receded, and a monumental miniature, showing a single couple, began to attract my gaze, ever more insistently.

It was the pair of figures whom Signorelli had placed immediately over the central axis of the throng of people. The woman is naked, with her blonde hair blowing free, and is being carried on the back of a flying devil. Her anxious gaze lights upon the eyes of the angel standing to the right of her, resplendent in his armour, while the Lucifer-like winged devil who is carrying her through the air flies on unimpeded, horned and cackling, down to the pit of hell. Yet, frozen in motion above the seething mass, with no clear provenance or destination, in this moment the pair still had the potential to be anything; even the monad of an ill-matched pair of lovers who have saved themselves from damnation and taken flight.

But there was no escape.

Bernadette did not appear that day at noon, nor did she show in the afternoon, nor in the evening, when the cathedral entrance was closed. In fact, she never came, and yet in her very absence she was actually present in the most appropriate way. I was disappointed and relieved in equal measure, caught the train back to Rome as darkness fell and from there continued my journey back home the next day. There was no news awaiting me there, and when a fat letter in a padded envelope finally arrived a fortnight later, I didn't bother opening it for several days – out of spite, for sure, but also because, standing in front of the *Last Judgement* in Orvieto that day, I'd grown tired of this correspondence, and decided to draw a line under it for good.

But when, in a weak moment, I did open the letter after all, an avalanche of inserts fell out into my lap: the photo of a girl at a prom; an empty packet of 'Lucky Strikes'; a piece of silver paper; a picture of a sleeping child under an alarm clock; a drawing of a knight beneath a tree and one of a hunted deer; two plasters; a sketch of a screaming woman holding a flower and standing in the middle of a field where all the trees were screaming too; a label reading 'Kalamata Crown Figs shipped by Jenny'; a photo copy of the address printed on the side of an eraser; a postcard with the logo of the Universal Postal Union; a piece of animal hide; a drawing of a traffic intersection with a level crossing; pictures of packers and flamingos; a colour photo showing exhausted fishermen in a boat; a copy of a painting of Dante by Signorelli; a snapshot of a summer party at a swimming pool set above an ocean; a clipping of a newspaper headline 'Ex-altar boy steals $15 from plates'; an illustrated copy of the book *Little Black Sambo,* covered in kids' scribbling; a white envelope inscribed with the word 'Bernadette', and inside it a blank, transparent sheet of white paper; pages torn from an old book on dog training; a list of foreign words and their translations – epigone: descendant, plethora; too full, provenance: foresight; taciturn: silent, élan: vigor; exhume: dig up, zeitgeist: ghost of time, obfuscating: to make obscure, nemesis: goddess of vengeance. The package also contained: a flag with a skull on it; an old card with the legend *Volkstracht von Schapbach*; sheets from a Chinese calendar; turn-of-the-century photos of children playing on a sandy beach; a drawing of a naked woman embracing a clothed man, and on the reverse a small woman riding on the back of a huge man; the draft of a logo for 'National Pornographic' magazine; a photo of Saturn; a skeleton playing the bongos; a picture of a Boeing 737–200; a drawing of a man holding in his arms a naked woman in the posture of the Deposition of Christ; a man and woman in front of an enormous heart; a woman standing screaming between pieces of furniture; a sketch of a rowing shadow beneath smiling stars, on the back of which were two men in a boat, pushing clouds along with the oars; some drawings with crêpe paper stuck over them; biblical quotations; a notebook full of illegible jottings, which on one page had notes under the heading 'soundless exercises'; a drawing of a cat tearing its fur out because it was being bitten by mice; more lists of foreign words; additional photos of flamingos; more sketches of planets.

The twelve-page, densely written letter that came with all this stuff had been franked in the USA. The handwriting was so regular in its messiness I found it as pleasing to look at as the hieroglyphs on an obelisk. Her imagination rummaged through the flotsam of her life, and I kept reading dutifully in the hope that this rambling narrative might ultimately offer some explanation of her failure to appear in Orvieto. But instead she kept talking about her feeling of disorientation whenever she woke from sleep, when her desire was at its height and yet her sense of shame was no less strong. To try and explain her confusion, she gave the name 'Saturn passing' to one aspect of this phase, though she also called Saturn 'the planet of wisdom'.

She wrote about a boyfriend she'd had at high school, Chester, the next in line of the Unredeemed, the Platonic ones. After he passed his high school leaving exams with flying colours, she decided give herself to him, completely. But then Chester, who waited so patiently, had to go abroad all of a sudden, 'and I really lost it,' as Bernadette put it. The letter went on to say that he returned as a 'spiritual guest'. This time the story ended with her finishing high school, determined to go to Europe and work as an au pair and get herself a real love life under the heathen skies of the Old World. It had proved impossible for her to synchronize living in the USA, going to university and a having a sex life.

So during the next strong phase of 'Saturn passing' she'd set off for Italy and drifted around.

'But when I look back,' she wrote, 'all I had left from that whole time was your address. Peter gave me a false telephone number and vanished without trace. So I came up to Florence to look you up, then to Rome, but you weren't there either, and then on to Orvieto, and Perugia – where on earth could you be? Finally I saw you standing in an oriel window on the road to Assisi. But because I was a hitchhiker travelling in someone else's car, I couldn't pull over and stop. So I flew back home with your words ringing in my ears. Had you spoken those words, or had Peter translated them for me, had they resounded in my head, or had I written them down from your thoughts?'

She didn't say what those words were, as her handwriting went totally off the rails at this point.

'I surrender. I submit. Daniel was the first man I gave myself to, but he always had more layers of clothes on under his clothes, and I could never really get to him properly. Peter was my sin. Those two had to come first in order to clear the world between you and me. It's all good. Don't be angry, because they led me to you, my first true love. I'm ready. Forgive me, it took me all this time to catch my breath. Now I surrender to you and to love and to life.'

She'd added her name at the bottom, a scribble that tailed off sharply to the right. No further explanation followed, but the presence of a third party was palpable in the lines she'd written. And that was the end of her letter.

A month later, I turned on my answerphone to hear the harsh voice of a clearly older American woman, who told me in a resolute tone that a 'travel agent' who'd been on the ball had fortunately refused to accept Bernadette's recent flight booking to Rome, because she seemed so distraught and confused. I should take my cue from him. He'd alerted the family, and they had decided to 'get this young lady into custody' and 'put her in professional hands'. At present, then, Bernadette was in an 'institution', and in urgent need of psychiatric care. The last thing she needed were my irresponsible letters, which, like last week's and the one from the week before, were no help at all, but only made things worse. 'For Bernadette's own protection,' she said, 'if you choose not to desist from such outpourings, we'll have no choice but to burn your letters. And we also reserve the right to take legal action against you if need be.'

At that point, I hadn't written a letter to Bernadette for the past eight weeks.

Years later I received an air mail letter from the States. My address had been printed on the envelope in capital letters, with all the painstaking care of a child clutching a pencil in its fist. The only thing inside was a reproduction of Signorelli's devil with the broad wings, carrying off a long-haired woman over the struggling crowd and into the fires of hell. A scribbled note below read: 'Saturn passing'. The angel of salvation in armour off to the right wasn't in the picture.

The North Pole

Contemplation

This July, the city has all the trappings of November. A half-hearted, chilly drizzle descends over Moscow, and beneath the pallid, swinish sky, even the colourful modern estates in the affluent suburbs, with their apartment blocks banked up like amphitheatres and the geode-like jerry-built highrises on the city outskirts – indeed, the whole human anthill that is the Russian capital – take on a uniform greyness. But in the interstices between buildings, the billboards advertising liquor and mobile phones sit up on high like Vestal Virgins and reign supreme.

On the streets beneath them, the careworn, even brutalized faces of both the new and the old proletariat – those who can still remember a time when politics claimed to speak in their name – are milling about. Back in the old days it was seen as a mark of distinction to have a face like this, a haggard, exhausted mien. In the meantime, impoverishment can be seen in people's clothes and beards. Every car contains a small family. In every bus window, you see a drinker with a boxer's nose. And in the gaps between the vehicles buildings with their ribs showing.

The first time we set eyes on one another – we little group of travellers who variously call our impending trip together an 'extreme holiday', an 'expedition', an 'adventure', an 'annual vacation' or a 'dream journey' – is in a nameless Russian hotel. I leave the breakfast room and go to drink my coffee at a window table in the anteroom. A wiry blonde woman of about sixty, but who looks somewhat younger, joins me, lights up a cigarette and, drawing on it with a pained expression, remarks:

'You and I should stick together.'

'Yes we should,' I reply, 'the thing is, though, I'm a non-smoker.'

'Well, get a load of that!' she chuckles. I haven't heard that expression in years.

To get to the airport, we choose the bus with an English commentary, sit together, queue behind one another at the desk, and take adjoining seats on the Tupolev to Murmansk, commenting on what we see out of the windows, and in the pauses between looking out, regaling one another with selected excerpts from our lives. Marga is Austrian and was formerly a flight attendant; she quit the airline she worked for on bad terms, but got a handsome pay-off and now helps out in a dance club. She's unmarried and childless and this is already her second trip to the polar regions. Before, she got as far as Franz Josef Land. That was three summers ago. The expedition leader on that occasion was Victor Boyarski, the most experienced of all Arctic explorers, a man who once reached the Pole on a dog-sled, and subsequently was received by presidents and fêted by the world at large. He'll also be heading up our trip.

'You'll like him. He's waiting in Murmansk for us. Let's see if he remembers me!'

Seen from the outside, the Tupolev is as sleek as a paper aeroplane. But inside, the cabin smells of smoke, all the springs in the seats have collapsed and my tray has lost its clip and only stays in position against the seat back in front of me because the vomit that a previous passenger deposited on it has spread over its surface and gained adhesion as it dried, holding it in place. When I finally manage to unstick the tray, the dried, congealed mass shatters into shards and tumbles into my lap. The seats themselves have seen better days, too. Where there should be upholstery, there's now bare metal, and the foam rubber filling has either crumbled away or been wrapped with black insulation tape to keep it from deteriorating further. In fact, only the heavily made-up air hostesses in their vivid blue uniforms and their aubergine-coloured wraps look so wholesome and fresh that they could have been imported from some other hygiene zone. The carpet under their feet is heavily patterned with Persian motifs, but is badly stained.

Marga looks out of the window.

'"As the crow flies" really does mean just that over deserts and Arctic tundra.'

Our fellow travellers, some of whom are clearly seasoned tourism snobs, chat occasionally to one another, putting on airs like they're God Almighty:

'Then we did the South Pole, then went through the Northwest Passage, and after that it was Patagonia, and two years back we climbed Kilimanjaro ...'

You can hear the conquistadors in their conversation, and picture a hand sticking little flags all over a map, but the tales only have value in so far as they relate to the person telling them, and people like this invariably take one bit of their story from the television, and characterize another as either 'indescribable' or 'unbelievable'. Evidently, several of the people here, finding themselves in extreme places, felt extremists themselves, and so neglected to answer the basic question all travellers should pose themselves: Where was I?

Marga complains that the springs in her seat are digging into her buttocks. The steward gives her a sullen look as he listens to her complaint, sensing an imminent attack on Aeroflot or on the Russian Empire as a whole. Then he shoots her a fleeting look of concern and shrugs his shoulders, a mere two centimetres up at most, by way of apology.

'What an *apparatchik*!' groans Marga and, advancing as the crow flies between two clichés, adds: 'the next moment he'll start crying, you wait and see.'

But she isn't really very worked up, or at least can't be bothered to take the matter any further. She far prefers spying out her fellow travellers from her inwardly superior standpoint and concerning herself with what they might be saying or thinking. From this vantage point she also casts her gaze on us:

'They'll probably be saying that I've hooked myself a toy-boy,' she whispers, briefly resting her slim hand on my forearm. 'I just know it. All you've got to be is unmarried and have no children, and the gossiping starts. I can hear them at it right now.'

At Murmansk airport, we are once more divided between two tour buses. The area around where we've landed is barren and undeveloped, and the airport terminal is not much larger than a filling station. But the broad, sweeping bay with its scrubland and bright silver-birch woods and meadows spreads out generously below us around inlets of the Arctic Ocean. From here, only the town itself comes across as grey and pragmatic, unaffected by a sense of idealism, a defrosted organism that swallows the light between its walls – in other words an individual of a city, original in its unloveliness. No sooner has the bus started up than a Russian travel guide stands up from the front seat and greets us:

'Dear friends. As we drive into town, I'll point out one or two of our notable places of interest.'

'Places of interest!' scoffs a cocky Berlin voice from the back seat of the bus. 'Can't wait to see those!'

In the absence of anything attractive about the city itself, the travel guide imbues every word she utters with the utmost charm. In fact, her words are more enticing than what they're meant to describe, and so it's her that ends up being the real feature of interest.

'On the right here you can see a town house with its garden. Then comes a *dacha*. And next door to it you have an example of standard bureaucratic architecture.'

She pronounces everything likes she's reading fluently from the works of Gorky, Gogol or Chekhov, only then to take any shine off her pronouncements by saying: 'You won't see anything special on the way into town. We grow normal vegetables here. In the city, you'll also notice one or two Norwegian filling stations.'

'The old dear's talking such a heap of shit,' the Berliner announces.

Beaming, the guide turns to her left and waves her hand in the direction of a scrubby hollow the bus is passing, an empty aisle of nothingness running between industrial complexes and high-rise blocks.

'Here you can see the Valley of Contentment, as we call it, where our athletes train for the Olympic Games.'

This calls forth a ripple of laughter in the bus. Valley of Contentment, indeed! A clump of birch trees on a patch of worn grass is the only remotely homely-looking thing about the place.

'Contentment! Now I've heard everything!'

'And this,' the guide continues tirelessly at the next rounda-bout, 'is the Square of Five Corners. But, my friends, you won't find five corners here.'

Today, a circus has set up its big top on this square, a circus that specializes in singing sea mammals.

'You can have seals kiss you!'

'I'd just as soon kiss the old dear,' the Berliner chimes in, still casting around for accomplices. His companion grins at this splendidly vulgar alpha male and seems ready to become a disciple.

'Now we're entering the city's northern district, which isn't so attractive ...'

'Just like you,' the Berliner shouts.

He goes on, gazing from afar out of the bus, to declare the place 'uninhabitable'. But the travel guide looks serious. She tells us how many people have left the city in recent years, and how hard it's becoming for those who remain:

'But then it's not always easy for you in the West, either!'

'Oh, she's priceless!' the Berliner calls out to the bus in general, then turning to the front, quips: 'People in *glasnost* houses shouldn't throw stones!'

He then pronounces everything that takes place within these walls to be a life not worth living. At the top of his voice; he couldn't care less if she hears him.

And what about winters here? She tells us about winters when it's been so cold that you can only stay outside for short spells at a time, and you find yourself having to break even shopping trips into stages. For the seven months that winter lasts here, shelters are even put up on the street so people can warm up quickly. Sure, sometimes far too much vodka is drunk in this season, but with this in mind, policemen are stationed in doorways to come to people's aid if a drinker turns violent. Even so, violence here isn't markedly worse than in other big cities; people are far more worried about potential food shortages.

'Allow me to clear my throat,' gasps the Berliner, and gives a hacking cough. 'I know what the score is here: it's a case of raise your glasses and cheers everybody, the management's sozzled!'

We're approaching the harbour, which used to be a nuclear exclusion zone. Nowadays, though, it's like a ships' graveyard, full of rusting barges, naval patrol boats, tugs and icebreakers. The shore is lined with policemen, who are young and yet still scowl, and in the harbour itself lie several high-legged floating cranes that remind you of insects. They're a permanent feature of the port. Beneath them cower the hastily welded rumps of new vessels taking shape, looking like metal sculptures by Jean Tinguely.

The bright red atomic icebreaker *Yamal* is a real beauty amid the dull-painted naval vessels in Murmansk harbour. On either side of this leviathan's bows, a grinning set of shark's teeth has been painted, a childish gag that has transformed this floating nuclear power station into a kind of toy Matchbox steamer. The gangway up to the deck is a walkway that leads diagonally up the side of the hull. At the top, jovial and full-bearded, waits Victor Boyarski, shaking everybody's hand as they step aboard. When he sees Marga, his expression freezes. Then he extends his long arm and shakes her solemnly by the hand. He's recognized her all right, but it's not exactly what you'd call a warm reunion.

Our sleep that night feels like a midday nap; after all, the sun never even gets close to touching the horizon. The ship smells of salt and diesel. The thick red paintwork of the *Yamal* has blistered in places, which have then hardened, broken, and been painted over again. The Russian ensign is blatting away on the mast, and the fog is so dense this morning that you can barely see fifty metres ahead. It's as if we've been caught frozen in motion, as there's no horizon line visible to give us any sense of progress. Not even the tone of the grey surrounding us changes; it simply remains unrelentingly grey between the sky and the sea.

I have occupied cabin number 39, which at other times is used by researchers, engineers or ship's officers; it's a bare, purely functional set of rooms. Any romanticism here is in the names: the fan is called 'Zephir', and the hairdryer 'Scarlett'. I slept on a sofa bed, made up for me by a robust Russian woman, a single mother from Murmansk. By its right-hand corner stands a Formica table, and a fresh, icy wind is blowing in through a small, open porthole. I sit down on a rickety office chair and stare out, happy that we've now irrevocably set sail into Nothingness. The feeling of doing something desperate, of not being able to dodge it any longer, that's the thing above all that gives this trip the flavour of an 'expedition'. Indeed, the very term 'research ship' serves to rein in any expectations of comfort we might have.

'So what?' Marga says when I chat to her the next morning. She's quite the old hand, and has seen it all before. She knows all about the cabins and the routines on board ship, and there are even some crew members who acknowledge her with glances. Yet she keeps herself to herself. It's only me whom she has rather high-handedly shielded from the other passengers, even physically putting herself between me and them, while at mealtimes she searches out a table apart from the others, where she'll sit and talk quickly and aimlessly about past injustices in her life, and tell me about stupid things our fellow travellers have said or done, and less frequently about the icy landscape that awaits us. Her attention takes on something of a manic air.

After two days I begin to widen my circle of acquaintances, moving to stand beside other people and switching my dining table. Those who are needy, yearning, and hungry for new images always form the most interesting groupings. At meal-times now, I mostly sit with Hanni and Victor, two well-travelled Swiss with tattoos from Burma and a Tibetan flag in their luggage, which they plan to raise at the North Pole. They're content just to stand at the railing and view the scene.

Up there, near the bridge, there are always a couple of travellers to be found, bracing themselves and narrowing their eyes as they face into the icy wind. The Berliner raps his knuckles on part of the ship's superstructure:

'"Want a safe and steady course?/ Then travel on the Iron Horse!" Well, this looks pretty fresh, doesn't it? All in one piece, and it's still working fine ...'

Everyone on this ship is visiting a different Arctic. The sailors cultivate stony faces which mask disapproval; after all, we're encroaching on their living space and indulging in activities that count for nothing here. They're here to earn a living, and have only contempt for those who think they're entitled to journey to the ends of the earth in comfort. If the Northwest Passage wasn't free at this time of year, during the summer, the icebreaker would be deployed there instead of being desecrated by tourism.

Others are following in Fridtjof Nansen's footsteps, or attempting to retrace the routes described in Arctic exploration journals from Robert Edwin Peary to Christoph Ransmayr. Yet others are here because they've already seen the Antarctic, just because they're wealthy, because they've been everywhere else, or because they've always dreamt of coming here … There's the industrialist, who calls the North Pole 'something else for a change', the middle-class traveller, who has been 'scrimping and saving' for years to afford this trip, the disinterested thrill-seeker, the gobsmacked, the reverentially silent, the unmarried teacher, the survivor from chemotherapy, and then again there's simply the guy with the damaged larynx, whose speech is barely intelligible and who has to have his food cut up for him with scissors. He's always cheerful, like he owes us that because we find it so hard to understand him; it takes a dreadful amount of effort on his part to make even a single, whimsical quip.

At seven in the morning, Viktor Boyarski rouses us with his unremittingly good-natured announcement: '*Dobre Uta*. Good morning, ladies and gentlemen, it's Tuesday the seventh of August and we're on the correct bearing, it's getting colder outside. You can tell we've left the Gulf Stream behind us now, as it's quite calm out there. There were some icebergs off to port a few moments ago, and we're expecting to pass the southern tip of Franz Josef Land, the famous Cape Flora, sometime early this afternoon. Get up in your own time. We've got a fantastic day ahead of us.'

In the Bering Sea, a light northwesterly is blowing. It's seven degrees above zero, we've still got five hundred miles to go and we're proceeding at a slightly reduced speed of twelve to thirteen knots, because of the fog. The Svalbard island group, which means 'The Cold Coast', looms up. The changes in the outside world are minimal. Sometimes the fog bank drifts farther away, then it pushes up close again and swallows us. The icebreaker sends out long, hollow-sounding blasts on its foghorn into the dense bank. Sometimes we catch a brief glimpse of the horizon, then it's gone again, obscured by the rolling clouds.

Up on deck, we take part in compulsory drills, practising getting into lifeboats or the helicopter the ship carries. Regulations concerning what we should do in an emergency are painstakingly gone through, and those who are slow on the uptake do their bit by asking obtuse questions, all so that we won't dwell on how long we've been ploughing through the impenetrable fog. The only thing to match the monotony of the aching cold, which polar explorers of the past must have felt acutely, is the monotony of the colour all around us.

'That dried food tastes awful,' says one of our number, after sampling an emergency ration from a lifeboat.

'If it tasted any good, it wouldn't last seven days,' replies Viktor Boyarski.

'Just like it was in Prussia,' chips in the man whom we've come to know as the 'Blocker', the manager of a savings bank branch in Bielefeld, whose friendship with several CDU backbenchers entitles him, he believes, to interrupt any conversation, which he does by laying his hand on the forearm of the person speaking.

Then we're sent back to our cabins like schoolchildren, where we wait in our emergency anoraks for the signal for the drill to abandon ship: seven short blasts followed by one long one – man the lifeboats!

Today, as it happens, we're all saved. Tannoy announcements inform us: 'That was satisfactory.'

It makes it sound as though not only the gaggle of passengers but also the foul weather have obligingly fallen in line with the crew's instructions.

The icebergs stand in shattered blocks, with glassy splinters at their base, as we drift into the zone of shelf ice, namely the ice masses which for millennia have been 'flowing' into the sea from the glaciers along the coast. We are witnessing the last days of shelf ice, a melting process that is exposing huge tracts of the ocean's surface, which for at least the past 12,000 years have been covered with a 200-metre-thick layer of ice. The life forms that occur here, and which were hitherto inaccessible, form part of one of the best preserved ecosystems on the planet. Here, between siliceous sponges, a whole new fauna developed, teeming with unimagined interactions.

Localised pockets of turbulence in the sky. In the midst of a vegetation whose morphological diversity is infinite and yet almost invisible, this voyage, which progresses through a narrow colour spectrum and in monotonous motion, is the materialization of a state of emptiness. Ultimately, even the vast vistas of ice are a landscape with no present. You see them approaching from far-off, and you see the world ending in them, and yet you still can't get enough.

I spend several hours every day now standing on deck. Nature spreads her silence over us, and before long all that anyone who stands by the rails long enough can hear is the sound of their own breathing. Occasionally someone will come up to you. For instance, a Russian lady approached me and began showing me every other page of a magazine article she was reading, a report on the beaches of the Costa Brava.

'Just like our resort of Sochi!'

She rummages around in her bag: 'Thank God, I'm no early bird!'

She says it like she's confessing a sin. 'Thank God!'

So mischievous. She initiates me into the mysteries of her SIM-card. I don't get it, as I have no mobile of my own.

'Hey, that's really old-fashioned of you. I like old-fashioned, mind. My father was a North Pole pilot!'

Her gaze wanders over the empty sea. The ice drift wreathed in plumes of ice-fragrance. What does the dull eye of the newly hatched eider duck see as, standing on a green patch in the midst of the ice floes, it finds itself obliged to come to terms with this habitat? In this icy environment it has the eyes of a mole, and is born with an expression of self-sacrifice.

Some years ago Viktor Boyarski and five fellow explorers from five different nations crossed the Arctic on dog sleds. He retains from this trip a physical memory of the state of utter exhaustion, and the boundless respect for those astonishing animals, the sled dogs. They are oblivious to the snow and cold. They can reduce their own body temperature in order to conserve energy, and even allow themselves to get buried in snowdrifts. Then all you need to do is pull them up in their snow holes by their leads once a day to stop them freezing themselves in with their own urine. At the end of the expedition, Viktor embarked on a tour to show off these animal heroes of his polar adventure to the whole world. However, two of the dogs expired at an airport in Cuba because it was too hot for them.

'Now you're in your mid-fifties, do you think your body would still be in good enough shape to do the same journey?' I ask him.

'My body would, for sure,' replied Viktor, 'but my head couldn't cope with it now.'

The *Yamal* keeps biting deeper and deeper into the polar landscape. Anything resembling nature steadily recedes. Vegetation becomes ever sparser, and most of the birds have disappeared by now. In the main, all that is left are elementary forms: crystalline, polygonal, tetrahedral. That's another process that's taking place on this trip: you let yourself be enclosed by the landscape; sit tight, and no sooner have you done so than it begins to gnaw into you, the interloper, searing your eyes, allowing the frost to penetrate, first through your clothes and then through your flesh. Everything that is tissue is transformed into a structure, deep frozen, spreading through living flesh like tetanus.

The ice offers a grand opportunity to convince yourself how indifferent nature is to man, and when you come across the remains of human habitation, the first thing you find is graves, graves with rusty crosses and sentimental inscriptions. Yet far more moving are the many invisible burial sites somewhere out on the ice that have been blown away and scattered to the four winds. The headlands, where the researchers sited their polar stations, are covered with rusty nails, shellac plates, exposed film stock, crockery, bottles and machined wood. Everything becomes a souvenir for later generations, a memento of the polar region. And all that's left here are these few objects gathered together by fate.

We swap stories about the expedition of 1912, when just three out of the original party of ten came back, one of whom had gone mad. We argue about Amundsen and Peary and the question of who really reached the Pole first, and what significance should be ascribed to the shadow on Peary's 'proof photo'. Even Payer and Weyprecht's Austro-Hungarian expedition of 1872–74 is a familiar topic to those who have made the North Pole their special subject of study. And it's true; this is a landscape replete with the words of those who lost their minds. Late summer stands as proud here as if it were winter, bestriding the land, ready at any moment to turn violent, and the mountains soar into the opalescent light of the sky, as bare and flayed as if they'd undergone radiotherapy.

Over dinner, Marga tells me about a cruise she once went on. At night, pale little boys in white tailcoats would appear; they had pitch-black eyes, never smiled, and only ever cleared dishes away, never serving them. If the passengers hadn't been distracted by dancing, they'd have been quite spooked. Also, according to Marga, these boys kept growing in number until the moment when the music stopped and all you could hear was the thumping of the ship's engines.

'When reality is usurped by the surreal.'

She stares at me with her large, blue, youthful eyes: 'Quite so.'

The first thing I do next morning is wrench open the little porthole; the sea air streams in like it's a liquid, and every morning it grows colder. The rapid changes in the sky ensure that every period spent out on deck is full of variety. The ship makes a soft bubbling noise, and it shudders like it's got convulsions, trembling and rocking. Sometimes it feels like we're living inside a sleeping dog.

Lying dormant in each and every one of us travellers is the desire, for once in our lives, to be the first to achieve something. With mountains, it's customarily the first blind person, the first one-legged person, the first without oxygen or the first from any particular country to climb this or that peak. Here, *en route* to the North Pole, one can still be a pioneer of mass tourism or instead a latecomer in the ranks of those who called this the 'Endless Ice' because they knew no better.

Outside the window of my cabin, the ice floes appear green or blue, sliced apart by the prow of the ship and pitched up vertically before they sink into the black water, get pushed under the ice pack and disappear.

The following day, the Zodiac inflatable ferries two polar explorers, a Norwegian and a Swiss, over to our ship. They'd set off on the first of May from the North Pole to retrace the route that Fridtjof Nansen took. After three and a half months, a few days ahead of schedule, they reached Cape Flora, where they're now waiting for a Norwegian ship to pick them up and take them home. On their journey, their rubber boat was buffeted from time to time by walruses, and when polar bears threatened to attack their bivouac, the two men had to drive them off with pepper spray. And now here they stand, looking rather embarrassed, on the podium of the *Yamal*'s conference room below decks, engagingly lost for words. The Swiss explorer's German is halting, and he's taught the Norwegian no more than a few phrases of the language. This is the first time they've seen any other people since May, and here we are, gawping at them like they're noble savages.

'Have you got any questions?'

When they go to sit down, both of them nestle approvingly in the soft chairs; they haven't felt so comfortable in a long while. Yes, they already undertook another expedition together before, taking fifty-four days to cross the pack ice off Patagonia, so they know what's in store for them when they finally get back to civilization. A TV camera will be waiting, lights will be trained on them, photos taken, and they'll be called upon to answer questions, which they'll be quite happy to do so and, always the consummate professionals, they'll point to a forthcoming report, a log of their journey, and eventually the questioners will move on.

They tell us about the landfast ice that they encountered, of the rise in temperature due to global warming and its effect on Arctic wildlife, especially the polar bears, which never used to venture as far as the North Pole. A tenacity that is as unforced as it is insistent shines forth from the eyes of both speakers. This is how people with a rich internal life look out at the world, men with an abundance of inner reserves. Some of the audience start to drift away. Now all the adventurers need to do is take a shower, pick up some provisions, and then go back and wait for the ship to fetch them from Cape Flora.

Just as they're leaving the stage, though, a small knot of passengers crowd round the men:

'How did you protect yourselves against the bears at night?'

'We set up tripwires around the tent, attached to fireworks …'

'Anyhow,' the Blocker abruptly launches into his monologue, 'last year we did the Northwest Passage …'

And so the two feral extreme explorers, with images of their weeks of crossing the pack ice fresh in their mind's eye, find themselves obliged to put on glazed, affable expressions and listen to what a savings bank branch manager from Bielefeld did on his vacation last summer.

The sea remains calm. A few chunks of ice drift across its smooth surface. Because the *Yamal* is currently at anchor, it's easy for us to see at what a leisurely pace the ice floes float past us on the crystal-clear water. Occasionally, we glimpse the flora of Franz Josef Land poking out above the crest of a bank of cloud. At such times, the travellers are wont to ask:

'Why can't we go ashore too?'

Rather than trust the expertise of the polar professionals, they suspect them of showing bad faith. An American woman in Birkenstock sandals says of the explorers:

'Sure, it's great that they've done all these things, but I want to do them too!'

She compensates for her displeasure by taking pictures of fog banks – with the flash on.

Then the two men are bade farewell with a round of applause and ferried over to the island in the Zodiac. All that remains behind are icefields, and snow gardens bathed in a floury light.

'Nobody could possibly return unchanged from a journey like the one they've been on …' says Marga.

I look at her, but I really can't get a handle on this woman. At times, her conversation is nothing but an incessant stream of small talk, but at others she can suddenly come across as genuinely unconventional. Invariably fast-talking, and with alert, darting eyes, she is needy without wanting to appear so. She's quick both to take offence and to take an arrogantly condescending or even indignant attitude towards anything and everything, yet in the very next instant she can appear genuinely interested, knowledgeable and enthusiastic in an informed way.

'I've got the photos with me that I took three years ago. If you want to come to my cabin to have a look at them …'

'I'll be sure to do that. In the next couple of days or so.'

'Are you worried about being alone with me in my cabin?'

'Of course I am. You're a scamp, you are!'

An uncle of mine always used that expression for unruly children. She threw back her head and laughed, which I found charmingly unrestrained. Then the laugh became something of a grimace and vanished in an instant. It was clearly more a case of her retrieving from memory the muscular contraction necessary for the act of laughing than of genuine laughter. It's symptomatic of the melancholic mood that's evidently taken hold of her right now that she starts telling me about a time when things weren't going so well for her. Three years ago on Franz Josef Land was one such time as well, but she'd managed to shake it off:

'When all's said and done, the sun rises and the moon sets for me just like everyone else.'

'Not here it doesn't,' I said flatly, given that it remained as bright as day even after midnight.

'My mistake,' she replied. 'If I seem a bit odd to you, please think nothing of it, it just comes from lack of sleep.'

She'd said something similar to me on the first day of the cruise, but then it was down to lack of food, and the fact that her blood-sugar levels were low. Even so, today she skipped another meal, and again the following day. She was nowhere to be seen on board. When she reappeared, though, she was very upbeat: sure she'd been out on deck! And of course she'd seen the amazing ice sculptures! She'd just wanted to be on her own for a bit, down on a lower deck.

And indeed, for half a day, it had been like we were passing through a gallery. Scattered over the dark surface of the water were the forms left behind by melting ice, sculptures modelled by heat, the wind and the current, all as quirky in their own way as Satie's *Gymnopédies*. The pallid outgrowths of the Arctic Sea, they bodied forth from its black depths and have been silently shaped by the wind and the waves.

'No,' Marga announced. She wouldn't be disembarking. She had a morbid fear of helicopters.

'Stewardess Syndrome, you know,' she explained.

No, we didn't know, but she just shrugged her shoulders like she was surrendering to a stronger power.

'Look,' she said, trying another tack, 'you've all seen that woman, haven't you, her over there who gets herself all done up like a tart?'

We all looked over in the direction of a bottle-blonde woman who was travelling on her own and who tended to stay aloof from the rest of the group; she was well turned-out, yet quite unselfconsciously kept primping and preening herself with all the insistence of a guillemot. Marga was convinced she must be a porn star who had retired from the business vowing that she'd never have sex again and that love held no interest for her any more. Now she was standing by the railing dressed as if ready for a film take, in a sable cap, a jumpsuit and a fur bolero jacket and staring sombrely at the monotonous sight of the glacier walls. The woman later turns out to be a widow from the Black Forest.

Now Marga's speech is sometimes quite confused. When she begins an anecdote over dinner, she speaks in a loud voice to draw attention to herself. She also wades straight into the story, insisting on everyone's rapt attention, but then she loses her thread, the story fizzles out without a punchline, it fragments into sub-plots or just runs into the sand, often with the words: 'Anyway, you know how things go, you plug away at things, and then …'

One time, four of us were sitting together; two Russian women had joined us. We were laughing a lot, but you could tell the strain it was putting on Marga.

'Which period of history would you most liked to have lived in?' one of the Russians asked.

'In my period,' said Marga.

'What, you mean today?'

'Absolutely. What would I have seen a hundred years ago? The beginning of women's liberation and the health food movement? Nowadays, I've got a ringside seat at the end of the world. Now that really will be something worth seeing!'

Saying this, she gives a rather sinister little laugh and looks at the ice, which at this point in our journey should be a solid frozen sheet, but instead is floating past us in isolated pieces. Marga's stories have no people in them. There are no bosses, or family members, no friends and no lovers. Only on the middle finger of her left hand does she wear a silver ring depicting two lovers intertwined.

'This ring is from Tel Aviv,' she tells us, draping her hand over the edge of her diary, which is filled with her large, regular and rather tedious-looking handwriting.

For the whole of the next day we don't set eyes on one another. But on the evening of the following day, she appears at dinner dressed all in snow-white and lays claim to a window seat simply by nodding her chin at the chair she wants to occupy. It's odd, because she says nothing, merely standing between the chair and the radiator and waiting for Viktor, the Swiss, to get up and switch seats. Then, in very fast and whispered tones, she harangues Viktor's wife Hanni, who only contradicts her once. And even then it's only a mild objection. But it's met with a whole dumb pantomime of outrage on Marga's part, who stares at the rest of us silent onlookers, first imploringly and then furiously, before standing up and leaving the table, her napkin still clutched in her clueless hands.

'What was all that about?'

Hanni shakes her head. She hadn't understood much of Marga's diatribe; most of it had been dialect, and the rest ...

'I don't think we have to spell it out. She sees you as some kind of threat.'

We stroll out on deck. The clouds aren't sitting on the horizon line, but seem rather to be dipping below it. Then a dirty cloud-sponge wipes across the horizon, leaving behind streaks, while heaps of cumulus swell up and a rainbow makes a sudden appearance. The black banks of cloud, which have developed from what was just a narrow strip, form a striking backdrop to it until they too dissipate and the rainbow fades and vanishes. The remaining clouds take on new layers of colour before fraying and melting away. New, sharp-edged cloud banks now weigh on the horizon line and dim the light until the wind draws a pink feather boa over them as well. The ship is accompanied by a flight of seagulls in formation, which abruptly drop down en masse and land on the water.

All of a sudden, the captain's guttural Russian crackles out of the loudspeakers on deck; its brusque and imperious tone tells even the non-Russians on board that this is no routine announcement but the real thing, a shouted emergency order that is being urgently relayed from one post to the next.

The icebreaker shudders, and so abruptly are the engines slammed into reverse that the whole bow section shakes. The sea boils up dirtily at the stern, and chunks of ice that have already been broken up are sucked into the undertow of the propellers, while up ahead the bows heel drunkenly to port. The turning manoeuvre is hardly recognizable as such; the vessel has to take so wide a curve and execute its turn over such a wide expanse of sea that it almost seems like it's trying to take in the horizon, too. And indeed, eventually we really do catch sight of the changed course we've steered, a channel filled with smashed ice, far-off to port. But by this stage, nobody's paying any attention to the exertions of the ship anymore.

'Look, there's someone in the water!' someone shouts out, and someone else yells: 'Man overboard!' which is then passed on in several languages.

Groups of passengers, their faces and body language frozen in shock, gather at the railings on both sides of the ship. Their exaggerated slowness, their literal petrification, reveals how they've been seized, gripped by a shock wave that has its crystallization point out there at some unidentifiable spot on the ice.

Sailors rush down the gangways, asking questions in Russian and shoving the rubberneckers back into their cabins. When Victor Boyarski dashes past, asking 'Who? Who is it?' I call out that he should check in Marga's cabin first. He nods at this, sober and self-controlled.

A quarter of an hour later the rescue boat has been lowered. Standing in its bows, two sailors have endeavoured to catch hold of Marga's blouse with boathooks, and are now busy manoeuvring her body between the large ice floes towards the boat. She's dressed in the outfit she had on at dinner; her white jeans with a white blouse over them. As she's dragged aboard with a large boathook, her arms are spread out like a Christ figure. This is how her body is recovered. Right up to the last, her face has centred on a point just above the root of her nose.

So here we are, in the middle of the Arctic ice with a dead body on board. The authorities in Murmansk are notified. But we're only allowed to proceed on our way once the captain has testified that the dead woman's cabin door was locked from the inside, and therefore that nobody on board could have thrown her overboard into the ice.

The remaining travellers stand on deck and sweep together the shards of their shattered memories of Marga. With hindsight, all those things she said which sounded merely whimsical at the time, just like bees in her bonnet, are now clearly identifiable as a direct path toward her self-destruction. Marga's life can only be given some semblance of order from its endpoint, posthumously. All the little manifestations of incomprehensibility and distractedness were stations on a headlong trajectory of someone who was beyond help, and whose 'odd' propensity for standing by the railing and gazing down at the water people noticed repeatedly. Days are reconstructed on which not a soul saw anything of Marga, on which she must have been just sitting in her cabin … and doing what? Maybe working up the courage to end it all?

But what are we to make of her gentler, unguarded moments? There was that naked couple cast in silver on her ring, for instance. When she'd told me about Tel Aviv, where she claimed to have acquired it, the look in her eyes told me it was a gift, and as she was talking, she kept stroking the ring and smiling. Another time we were standing at the railing. She was trying and failing to capture the view on her little camera; eventually she put the camera aside and said:

'The ends of the earth really don't work in portrait format.'

I'd wanted to know whether she still found travelling as easy as she always had. Her answer surprised me: she claimed travelling had got more difficult for her because she now had real trouble deciding where she'd be welcome and who she should revisit. That was the first time any other people had featured in her reply and, even then, they were only mentioned in this questionable context.

The passengers tell one another how shaken up they are. A British woman can't stop sobbing, and incessantly keeps saying 'Not again ... not again ...' We ultimately learn that this is now the third time she's been on a ship where another passenger has died. Another woman is furious at Marga's selfishness for not considering how her suicide would affect her fellow passengers' holidays:

'Some people have saved up for years to come on this trip, and then this!'

Another traveller philosophises:

'Only this afternoon, we met two men who risked their lives at the Pole. They were so full of vigour, so adventurous and so life-affirming, and a few hours later one of us ends up dead under the ice.'

A fourth says, without emotion: 'People just don't do that.'

A fifth confesses:

'I know this is going to sound dreadful, but for me this is the first highlight of the trip.'

A sixth says it is now our duty as citizens not to let this incident ruin our trip, and tries to move seamlessly on to routine matters:

'Look, I can understand anyone being in shock right now. But, guys, whatever you do don't forget to apply sunscreen – that'd be another way of committing suicide.'

Two fellow travellers come up to me and silently console me.

A French woman takes a new tack, claiming that Marga had now found her salvation, her suffering was over, and we didn't need to mourn her any more.

'It's what she would have wanted', she says. But in truth, none of us really know what Marga would have wanted.

Before dinner, the captain gives a short speech:

'Good evening, everybody.'

He goes on to say that he's sorry to have to inform us that the crew could do nothing except recover the body of 'Margarethe'. The insurance company will decide where her final resting place should be. For the present, her body would be flown by helicopter to a storage facility on Franz Josef Land.

'Good evening.'

Later, a piano and violin duo play a selection of old classical, movie and swing favourites, and below decks an Austrian expert delivers a lecture on the topic: 'How Animals and Plants Survive Arctic Conditions.'

Our sense of unease lends all these proceedings an air of moral ambiguity, given that the yardsticks of piety have not yet been defined: Is it too soon to start laughing again? Then again, the common wisdom is that the show must go on.

Viktor Boyarski tells me that Marga tried to jump into the ice on the expedition three years ago. On that occasion, she was saved. He'd only recalled this incident when he welcomed her on board this time. What's more, in the interim, she'd clearly done her homework on the properties of Arctic ice, since the place she'd jumped in was precisely where the ice floes were packed sufficiently densely to make a successful rescue unlikely.

When we dock again in Murmansk, the authorities will want to question me and a couple of the other passengers, but particularly me, since according to witnesses I was Marga's friend. I'll be required to sit in the captain's cabin and provide answers to various subtle questions, which will find their laborious way via an interpreter into the official report and hours later will need to be signed off by me as an accurate account of events. The crew will be exonerated of any negligence in the matter, and the finding reached that Marga, acting of her own volition, could not reasonably have been prevented from taking her own life.

The morning after her death, it is still very early when I hear the approaching helicopter. The day is suitably grey, and the ship is entering a debris field of scattered ice sculptures, glassy formations in white, algal green and blue, but occasionally also yellow or brown from the guano of seabirds – the black-footed kittiwake, the northern fulmar, the thick-billed murre and also the skuas, whose speciality it is to harass other birds and force them to regurgitate their food so that they can then feed on it.

The wag from Berlin is standing alone at the railings. He greets me with the words: 'The early bird catches the worm!' but in the next instant his eye is caught by his Stuttgart drinking buddy from the evening before:

'Oho, there's a sight for sore eyes!'

The light today sometimes spreads out in brilliant sheets, and sometimes in frosted-glass reflections. On the still-unfrozen water, the wind leaves a succession of new textures, on which the crystalline chunks float, embedded in frozen frost-magma. This morning, I open my porthole, and an ice floe floats by, with a man's footprint clearly visible on it, the fragment of a sequence of steps that disappeared somewhere in time. We navigate the landscape in which the tracks of so many well-known and unknown people have vanished. How many famous deaths there have been here, but also how many trawlermen or deckhands from whalers have drifted away on ice floes? At best, their disappearance was only noted in a commercial shipping register.

'She clearly planned it all out in advance,' says Viktor, who wants to understand my relationship with Marga a bit better. 'Did you know she had a twin sister? Do you want to know the first thing she said when we told her what happened here? She said it didn't surprise her one bit.'

This is the sister who, months later, I'll walk up to on a station platform and be struck dumb by the sight of this revenant, this living-dead spitting image of Marga, who approaches me with her hands in her pockets and just says: 'So?'

It's one degree below zero and the wind is blowing harder now. But visibility is good, and there's a diffuse light over this lake region. A strip of pale yellow sun glows on the horizon like light shining through a crack under a door then is promptly extinguished. We pass monumental, tectonically layered plates of ice; black pools; whimsical formations of hard-packed snow, covered with grated ice splinters; panicles of ice spliced into fibrous bundles; miniature mountains; slumped table mountains; and in between whiles, these extensive black lake areas open up, over which the ship glides quietly and the gentlest of bow-waves lap against the distant snow coasts. These pools and basins are dotted about like the patches on a cow's hide; sometimes, as they're picked out by a flash of sunlight, they'll shimmer briefly and then fade once more.

Yesterday, two scrawny polar bears shambled past. Can there be any more isolated animals than these, who shy away mistrustfully from the ship and lumber off into a vast expanse covering several thousand kilometres? There are no birds in the sky and the seals' ice-holes are empty. The cracks that the ship's bow is making in the ice fan out far ahead on both sides of the vessel, taking an unpredictable course into the distance.

Sometimes, as we approach them, ice floes several metres thick tilt up vertically and plunge down into the black polar sea, while others, blue and weighty, slide under more recently formed plates or butt up against one another like huge pieces of a jigsaw puzzle. Then water gets pressed through the cracks; it's full of plankton and occasionally we glimpse a small cod dancing in the light or flapping, exposed, in the gap between the ice blocks.

At the ship's bar – a two-metre-long counter in one of the gangways – Julio Iglesias is singing 'La Paloma', or rather he's wallowing through his vibrato, as though he's having to decide, from line to line, whether he wouldn't actually prefer to expire.

The Berliner, the Blocker and the man from Stuttgart are working their way down a line of vodka glasses. I hear the Berliner say: 'Hmm, tastes like an old woman's armpit.' The Stuttgarter has a distracted air about him. His queen of hearts from Sylt suddenly appears.

'Where have you been hiding?'

'I've been reading.'

'A person without a head is a cripple his whole life,' drones the Berliner, but nobody joins in his laughter.

The friendly wife of a businessman from Dresden chips in: 'We all read Karl May as children, but to think that we now get to visit all the countries he described! And that we can afford to – it's just amazing!'

'I'm sorry, Ilse,' the Berliner snaps back. 'You may think you're smart but you really haven't got a clue. Karl May never actually visited the countries in his stories; all he ever did was stick his finger on a map. You've truly excelled yourself again!'

'How come?' replies Ilse, getting the wrong end of the stick again. 'This trip isn't costing us anything. It's just coming off the kids' inheritance.'

Everyone laughs. Just then, the joker in our party walks by, and thinks we're in the middle of telling gags.

'I've heard Vladimir Putin likes petunias,' he quickly chips in. 'That's why they're called putinias here now.'

'God, that one's a bit laboured, isn't it?' says the Berliner, casting an eye over the bar bill.

The party disperses.

The variations in the polar landscape continue to be novel and magnificent, but the differences grow more subtle and the formations more similar to one another. Now oval, teardrop-like formations predominate. Sometimes, an island of light glistens in the far distance, and sometimes a snowdrift rears up, with a dark shadow of algae on it, and the light incidence keeps opening up new perspectives on the landscape.

Around 150 kilometres from the North Pole, the ship slows once more and finally comes to a standstill. An hour later, an announcement informs us that there's been a technical problem, and that the crew are already trying to fix it. Now we're sitting there motionless, with no engine noise, no cracking of the ice floes to be heard, the silence couldn't be more complete. This is a time to really savour, where something unforeseen, a minor emergency has intervened, gracing and threatening us at the same time with stasis.

In these circumstances, our perspective shifts. While we were underway, we were conquerors, becalmed we're objects. Tiny and defenceless, we pause in a landscape that's trying to undercut us. The ice presses against the ship's sides, freezes hard and holds us fast. We are locked in place, and because we can no longer budge, we suddenly start noticing every movement, however slight, in the landscape, even if it's nothing more major than the moiré effect produced by the wind ruffling the water.

Then the first passengers start grumbling. This is 'typically Russian', with no information forthcoming and no attempts made to appease or reassure us.

'It doesn't matter whether it's Gorbachev, Yeltsin or Putin at the helm, they're all just czars.'

'Haven't you noticed? The rich Russians on board, they're all the children of either the *nomenklatura* or the Mafia. That's the long and short of it.'

'Same as in China.'

'Exactly.'

Now there are mutterings among the passengers that this is all costing us time – time which, because of the earlier death, we could ill afford anyhow. That had lost us several hours to start with. And now here we are lying idle. Brilliant. Another lecture, another couple of slideshows. Terrific. Maybe a captain's dinner, or a masked ball to try and placate us... If they'd only offer us something real, like a helicopter flight for instance ...'

'But that's out of the question in this wind.'

'So how come they've got two rescue helicopters on board if they can't be flown?'

Lines of mutineers start to assemble at the railings and especially on deck below at the bar. In this situation, Viktor Boyarski organises a trip onshore, and at last we really do find ourselves rolling down the gangway, setting our feet in the snow, which when seen close up isn't actually snow any more, at least not snow as we know it – it doesn't stick together, its crystals are large and glassy and if you try to form it into a Christmas bauble, it crumbles instantly. People take photos of the ship from a distance. We take a few steps to the right, and to the left, into the great expanse; thank you, and now what? What's it all about? It all looks the same.

Back on board, protest tactics are discussed. We're not going to let ourselves be fobbed off or taken for idiots. Considering all the things we're not experiencing, we have to assume the worst: the trip's about to be called off, we're going to be taken back, and then the whole messy business of demands for compensation will begin.

The expedition leaders ask us to please be patient.

There follows an attempt to restart the engine, which in the meantime has undergone running repairs, and to back the ship up a few metres. When that fails, we're asked to come to the conference room. We're told that the damage is worse than anticipated, and that our onward journey is now in doubt. Uproar ensues. A blind-drunk Taiwanese man starts yelling warnings, saying that this trip has been blighted by a curse right from the start; he is wrestled to the ground.

'You Asians with your stomach enzymes shouldn't drink so much,' someone taunts him. 'You can't handle your booze!'

The German men in the party want to know precisely what the fault is. They demand facts and technical data which, in the first instance, they can scoff at and, secondly, they won't have a clue how to interpret. Ultimately they'll offer their views on the ship's repairability.

'Look, if the gearing mechanism can run at 50 per cent capacity ...' the Stuttgarter begins.

'That's quite impossible!' screeches another man, his face white as a sheet 'They *can't* repair it!'

He is quite beside himself in a way that only children normally are; 'It *can't* be done!'

Someone calls out: 'I forgot to feel the snow when I was outside.'

The Berliner starts banging on about the 'typically Russian attitude towards information'. We're being told nothing. It's like it always is in Russia: everything gets swept under the carpet, so they can pretend nothing's happened.

'Just look at the *Kursk*, and at what happened in Chechnya!'

Others demand their 'money back' there and then. The quieter members of the party gradually begin to grow embarrassed by the company they're in. They sidle out of the room and go and stand at the railings; they're not going to have their wonder at the extreme nature of this landscape spoiled at any cost. Hanni and Viktor laugh. They spend hours on the upper deck, which, now that the ship is held fast, affords a quite different panoramic view, as though we were finally no longer active agents in this landscape but merely passive beings, here under sufferance.

Don't we at least want to lobby to get our money back, a thin-lipped man barks at us.

'Oh, listen,' Hanni says affably, 'the money for this trip was a bequest. We wanted to use it to realise our dream, and it really has been a dream come true!'

Her unquenchable enthusiasm sparks moral outrage among some fellow passengers.

'You'll put up with anything, won't you?'

Haven't we noticed the rust under the red paint, or taken a good look at the state of the ship's boat? The helicopter didn't work in any event, and doubtless we'd also failed to notice that Dr So-and-so had been confined to his cabin for two days with a stomach bug. Our laid-back attitude to external circumstances is held up as a character weakness, and if they only could, they'd really like to hold us jointly responsible for the mess we were all in. And yet our only crime is to be stuck in the ice and rather enjoying it.

Everyone has their own take on the ship's technological problems, too. That's all shit, one man reckons, he's known it right from the start, from the very word go. It'll never work properly, none of us will ever set eyes on the Pole, not in a million years.

But first and foremost, the hour of the 'Blocker' has now arrived.

'The key thing is that we all speak with one voice,' he announces, by which he means his own. Saying this, he casts a malevolent look around the room. He's trying to get the outraged passengers to form a united front against the expedition organisers. His adversaries are the Swiss couple and a group of enthusiasts, who are standing calmly at the rails, relishing the stationary ship and the magnificent panorama out into the great silence. They can't be torn away from there, they're wallowing so happily in the richness of monotony.

Accordingly, they are also the first to spot the polar bear mother and her two cubs, not far from the ship. The captain relays the sighting to the rest of us over the tannoy. Cameras are pointed like at a press conference, and some people who are videoing the scene whisper their commentaries into the mic as they're filming:

'Right now, a polar bear mother and her two cubs are approaching us from the port side. They're walking across the ice ...'

Whatever appears in the viewfinder has to be hyped up rhetorically. People have learned this technique from television, but ultimately all you end up doing is capturing a few objects on film that you've never actually seen with the naked eye.

The polar bear mother is nervous and starving, and her two young ones follow clumsily in her footsteps. They engage the interest of our party for half an hour. The passengers are almost unwilling to take this rare occurrence – rare north of the 88th Parallel at least – at face value, treating it like some cheesy bit of stage management by the ship's crew. Sure, lots of photos are taken, but people's looks say: Fair enough, but don't think we've forgotten that we've ground to a halt! People psych themselves up for a fresh round of indignation and new offensives of grim humour. Indeed, the guy from Stuttgart has just come into the bar and played his opening gambit: 'So, a seventy-year-old woman goes to the gynaecologist and says ...'

Sometime after midnight, I'm standing on the bridge in brilliant sunshine with Hanni and Viktor, marvelling at the brightness and the layer of mist lying over the ice plain, when suddenly and without any prior warning, the ship's engines kick into life and the vessel starts moving, crunching into the ice pack with its bow like before. We're not stuck, we're no longer lying idle, but instead making headway straight to the North Pole. So it sounds like he's being ironic when Viktor Boyarski starts his morning reveille the following day with the words:

'*Dobre Uta* and good morning. Once again, the most important virtue that people must have on polar expeditions has proved its worth: patience.'

We were stopped dead for a total of eleven hours, during which 'the group', which we never actually were, comprehensively fell apart, with different factions opposing one another, while others took sides, subordinated themselves or stood apart. Eleven hours in which we learned that all the preparations we'd made for the extremes of an expedition had done little to help us develop the character traits that were called for here.

We also learned that the sudden and violent stopping manoeuvre which had been executed to try and rescue Marga was the reason why the turbines had been damaged. Now we can't go full speed ahead any more, but at least we'll be able to reach the North Pole.

Over breakfast, those passengers who lost their rag are unwilling to reach a compromise with those who didn't. One man maintains:

'This whole Pole thing's a swindle anyhow. In photos it's always covered in snow, and now just look at the conditions out there: three degrees above zero and raining! And that's supposed to be the North Pole!'

This North Pole still lies ahead of us, but it's shrouded in gloom. The sky, which over the past few days has favoured us with fantastic visibility, has now clouded over completely. Even this morning, there was some light rain, and now the ship is manoeuvring slowly between the algae-smeared, dirty ice crags towards a point of indifference among the pools, the troughs and the fissures. Beneath the towering fragments of ice floes, two to three metres thick, is the inky black sea, down into which the bows push many a sheet of ice before the pack ice can close over it.

Surrounded on the bridge by amateur photographers who jostle to try and get a well-focussed shot of the needle's position on the master compass, the captain inches the *Yamal* forward.

When the compass reaches ninety degrees and remains stable at that position for a few seconds, it is greeted with a round of applause and congratulations. Then the unmoved Russian personnel hand round sweet sparkling wine and we all clink glasses, embrace each other and peer over the railings, beyond which the landscape looks exactly the same as it has done for days.

We're all groping for the right emotions to fit the moment. You call to mind famous polar explorers of the past, who reached the North Pole amid much cheering and crying, and you think of those who perished and whose bodies are still entombed in the ice, those who set out in vain to conquer the Pole, those who went hopelessly astray, and those who failed. All of us present now, it seems, are experiencing very small-scale emotions in comparison with our predecessors. The sublime mingles with the banal. We've reached a point of emptiness that is also an integral part of the North Pole: a sense that we're not equal to everything that's here, and that we're capable of being nothing but onlookers, arriving here but largely against our will, setting foot on this fabled place yet only fleetingly, with our faces already set on our return, our wretched return.

The captain delivers a brief speech, in which 'the old dream of reaching the North Pole' figures prominently.

'You've all now realised this dream,' he tells us.

We've realised nothing, is what we're all thinking. All we've done is board a ship and arrive at our destination.

Beyond the Pole, though, where the curvature of the earth begins again and the landscape disappears from view, where the ice lies unbroken in front of our hull and nature's death zone extends forbiddingly in a grand gesture of indifference, we spot a pristine and virgin patch of snow. We'll never get to walk on it, though. That New Year's morning in the Eifel comes to mind once more, and the ceiling of the hospital unfolds snow-white, and there's no sound save the echo of the frontier.